MIGRANTS AND STRANGERS
IN AN AFRICAN CITY

MIGRANTS AND STRANGERS IN AN AFRICAN CITY

EXILE, DIGNITY, BELONGING

BRUCE WHITEHOUSE

Indiana University Press
Bloomington and Indianapolis

This book is a publication of

Indiana University Press
601 North Morton Street
Bloomington, Indiana 47404-3797 USA

iupress.indiana.edu

Telephone orders 800-842-6796
Fax orders 812-855-7931

© 2012 by Bruce Whitehouse

All rights reserved

No part of this book may be reproduced or utilized in any form or by any means, electronic or mechanical, including photocopying and recording, or by any information storage and retrieval system, without permission in writing from the publisher. The Association of American University Presses' Resolution on Permissions constitutes the only exception to this prohibition.

∞ The paper used in this publication meets the minimum requirements of the American National Standard for Information Sciences—Permanence of Paper for Printed Library Materials, ANSI Z39.48-1992.

Manufactured in the United States of America

Library of Congress Cataloging-in-Publication Data

Whitehouse, Bruce, [date]
 Migrants and strangers in an African city / Bruce Whitehouse.
   p. cm.
 Includes bibliographical references and index.
 ISBN 978-0-253-00081-1 (cloth : alk. paper) — ISBN 978-0-253-00082-8 (pbk. : alk. paper) — ISBN 978-0-253-00075-0 (electronic book) 1. Congo (Brazzaville)—Emigration and immigration—History. 2. West Africans—Congo (Brazzaville)—Social conditions. 3. Congo (Brazzaville)—Commerce. 4. Congo (Brazzaville)—Religion. 5. Transnationalism—Social aspects. I. Title.
 JV9016.5.W84 2012
 305.896'606724—dc23
                                    2011040330

1 2 3 4 5 17 16 15 14 13 12

For three people who changed my life:

Cherif, who opened my eyes

Bakary, who put me on the path

Oumou, who accompanied me along the way

Contents

Acknowledgments · *ix*
Introduction: Exile Knows No Dignity · *1*

1. The Avenue of Sergeant Malamine · *25*
2. Enterprising Strangers · *58*
3. Among the Unbelievers · *92*
4. The Stranger's Code · *116*
5. Transnational Kinship · *149*
6. Children of Exile · *180*

Conclusion: The Anchoring of Identities · *203*
Epilogue: Displaced Dreams · *221*
Appendix 1. Notes on Methods · *225*
Appendix 2. Survey Results · *229*

Notes · *235*
Bibliography · *247*
Index · *269*

Acknowledgments

The cover of a book like this one often contains a fundamental falsehood: the notion that the author is single-handedly responsible for having dreamed up and expressed the ideas recounted within. I never appreciated the fallacy of this notion as much as upon the publication of *Migrants and Strangers in an African City*. This book is actually the product of many people, and as their names cannot appear on the cover I need to recognize their contributions here.

In Mali I have had the kindest of hosts, whose graciousness and guidance have been an essential aspect of my research over the years. The family of Mohammed Touré and Nana Keita Touré has welcomed me into their home and their lives, and has made my trips to Bamako both possible and pleasant. The extended family of the late Makansiré Dramé, of Missira, Bamako, has provided enlightenment and support both in the city and in their hometown. This project would never even have begun without them.

In the Republic of Congo I relied on a large network of individuals, both Congolese and foreign, who lent me their time, their words, and their wisdom. Because of the frequently sensitive nature of my research topic there, I cannot thank them by name. I am especially indebted to several faculty members of Marien Ngouabi University and the staff of the Consulate-General of Mali in Brazzaville. Moreover, I depended heavily on the willingness of the city's inhabitants to sit down with my wife or me and answer our questions. Every person who granted us an interview has shaped my outlook, and I hope that in giving them voice in these pages I have done justice to their views.

In the United States numerous people helped sharpen my understanding of transnationalism, globalization, and identity, from the West African migrants I once frequented in New York City to the faculty at Brown University where I completed my doctoral studies. At Brown's Department of Anthropology, David Kertzer, Dan Smith, and Nicholas Townsend read early chapter drafts and supplied invaluable feedback. I have been most fortunate to have Dan as my mentor. Matilde Andrade, Kathy Grimaldi, and Marjorie Sugrue always made sure I got what I needed. The Population Studies and Training Center (PSTC) at Brown provided me with numerous opportunities to discuss my findings and exchange ideas with fellow students and faculty members, especially during my postdoctoral year there working with Marida Hollos. I received vital assistance from the PSTC's Tom Alarie and Kelley Smith. Judy Lasker, chair of the Department of Sociology and Anthropology at Lehigh University, read a manuscript of this book and gave insightful comments. In 2009 I had the occasion to present my concluding chapter to a gathering of the African Seminar at Johns Hopkins University, where faculty members and students challenged me to rethink some of my basic assumptions. Lastly, two anonymous reviewers pointed out many mistakes and omissions in my earlier manuscript. All of their contributions have made this a better book.

In cyberspace, two virtual communities have constituted a wealth of information for my research. The "cyber-diaspora" emanating from Mali, especially as represented by the online forum Malilink, helped me follow events in that country from afar, sound out ideas, and check facts. The Congolese "cyber-diaspora," as embodied by user forums on Congopage.com and Mwinda.org, served a similar purpose.

While I am grateful for the input of all those mentioned above, in some cases (and not always for the right reasons) I have chosen to ignore it. There is therefore only one component of this text for which I can claim sole responsibility. The errors in these pages are mine alone, and not the fault of anyone whose collaboration or ideas have helped me conceive this book.

The fieldwork I conducted in Mali and Congo was funded by the Brown University PSTC, the Wenner-Gren Foundation for Anthropological Research (grant no. 7215), and the National Science Foundation (grant no. BCS-0413600).

I thank Dee Mortensen of Indiana University Press for her unfailing dedication to her editorial calling, through revisions and title changes that would have frustrated mere mortals. Her faith in this project helped me see it through to completion. Independent copy editor Rita Bernhard smoothed the rough edges of my prose with astounding thoroughness and skill.

Finally, my deepest appreciation and respect is for Oumou Coulibaly, who has been with me through every stage of this process from inception to fieldwork to publication. Her support has meant the world to me.

MIGRANTS AND STRANGERS
IN AN AFRICAN CITY

INTRODUCTION
EXILE KNOWS NO DIGNITY

In the heart of West Africa's arid Sahel region, on a dusty plain a few hours' drive north of the Niger River, lies a community of several thousand inhabitants. I call this community Togotala, although that is not its real name. It is a large village—more of a small town, really—set amid fields of rust-colored laterite earth dotted with scrub brush and thorny acacia trees.

Togotala, being in the Sahelian zone, receives almost no rain for nine months of the year, from October until June. What vegetation exists there is gradually consumed by local residents' livestock, until by April and May little is left growing at ground level; the only green visible is foliage above the reach of cattle and goats. Even after a good year, the animals grow thin and bony in this period. After a bad year they start dying in droves, endangering their owners' livelihoods and raising the specter of crop failure if the seasonal drought lasts too long. Usually between July and September rains finally fall, sometimes in torrents. During a big storm the water sluices through low-lying areas, eroding great gashes into the unpaved streets and occasionally collapsing the mud-brick homes many families build for themselves in this part of Africa. "We are threatened when the rain doesn't come," a resident once told me wryly during the rainy season, "and we are threatened when the rain comes."

But near the center of Togotala sturdy multistory houses made of concrete blocks and corrugated aluminum roofing weather any rainstorm. Their white- and green-painted facades stand out against the prevailing earth tones of the surrounding landscape. The homes overlook a public square where battered buses arrive twice daily to load and unload passengers and goods. These vehicles are Togotala's lifeline to the outside world: on them, one can easily take a ride south to Bamako, the capital of the Republic of Mali and the country's largest city, and from there to more distant destinations.

A brief exploration around town reveals other signs of Togotala's connections to the world beyond. There is a community health clinic with solar panels on the roof, necessary to run its refrigerator stocked with vaccines (like most rural communities in Mali, Togotala is off the national electrical grid). There is a landline telephone system. There is a water tower, also powered by solar panels, pumping ground water from a deep borehole to a system of taps in public spaces throughout town. There are blocks of classrooms for schoolchildren, grades 1 through 9. And there are several mosques of modern construction, with concrete walls and even their own electricity powering the Muslim call to prayer, five times daily, through loudspeakers.

Outsiders might presume that such economic improvements are the result of development initiatives by the Malian government, by foreign donor governments, by Islamic charities, or by some of the many nongovernmental organizations (NGOs) that dominate the business of international development in Africa. In fact, most of these projects were realized through the efforts of community members themselves. For many decades now, Togotalans have pooled their resources to fund their town's development, paying the national telecom company to bring in phone lines, building their own schools and paying their own teachers, and contributing money for the water tower installed by a Scandinavian development agency. Togotalans likewise paid for the clinic and mosques.

On the face of it, this community seems to embody hopes for progress in Africa, a spirit of cooperation and self-help. Togotalans are indeed proud of their collective achievements to better their town and are often dismissive of the role of national government in their community's development. "On n'a pas besoin de l'État," a Togotalan man told me flatly during an interview in 2006— "We don't need the state." In the era of neoliberalism, when market forces predominate and states are relegated to a backseat role in national economies, the people of Togotala might look like ideal neoliberal subjects.

Most Togotalans are of the Soninke ethnic group, a people renowned for their participation in regional trade networks. While agriculture has long been the foundation of their society, since medieval times the Soninke have also acted as merchants, profiting from their strategic location between the desert to the north and the forest to the south. They traded salt and acacia gum from desert caravans for kola nuts and cloth from coastal areas. Soninke people have maintained an active role in trade throughout the western Sahel, even after the onset of colonization by the French in the late nineteenth century (Manchuelle 1997). And they have taken part in another form of activity that has become vital to the survival of their communities: migration.

Migration researchers have identified several complementary forms of spatial mobility important to human livelihoods. People move to find work (labor migration); to attend school (educational migration); to work in cities when the rains cease and the harvests are in, and then come back to work on their families' farms when the rains return (seasonal migration); and after getting married or divorced (family migration). Of special relevance to West Africans generally, and Soninke people in particular, they move to take part in commerce (trade migration).

Elsewhere in Africa, people move to escape political violence (conflict migration). As in most of Mali, however, life in Togotala is peaceful, and the area has not been afflicted by warfare for generations. Economic factors are the main reasons people leave home. For this reason I do not consider migrants from Togotala and other parts of the western Sahel to be refugees or "forced migrants": despite their severe natural environment, these migrants do exercise choice in their decisions of whether, when, and where to go abroad.[1]

One last mobility classification which, for Togotalans, overlaps with those listed above is circular migration—the return to one's point of origin after migrating away from it for some length of time. Like others throughout the western Sahel, Togotalans stress the circularity of their migration trajectories. Loyalty to kin and home community is extremely important, irrespective of the migrant's destination: in their study of Soninke migrants from western Mali, Findley and Sow (1998:101) find that "there is no transfer of orientation from the village to the destination. . . . When they leave, it is always to come back home." Similarly, the departure of Soninke migrants from their home communities "is not a radical break but, to the contrary, indicates a strong tie to the community" (Quiminal 1991:27).

This somewhat unusual expression of loyalty, perhaps more than anything else, has enabled places like Togotala to survive. Given a harsh climate, regular droughts, and a near absence of state services, local forms of economic activity—mainly agricultural—are insufficient to meet families' immediate need for food, let alone fund community development. The town's community infrastructure projects were paid for not with local wealth but by emigrants living in

Malian cities, in neighboring countries like Senegal, Côte d'Ivoire, and Burkina Faso, in Central African states like Gabon and Congo, in southern Africa and beyond. A few dozen Togotalans are in the United States, France, Spain, and other wealthy Western countries, and others are in Asian commercial hubs including Dubai, Bangkok, Hong Kong, and Guangzhou. But the vast majority of the town's international migrants—most likely numbering in the thousands—have remained on the African continent. It is overwhelmingly these migrants' remittances that have paid for the construction of clinics and schools. Most of the town's lavish houses belong to migrants based not in Paris or New York but in Abidjan, Bouaké, Libreville, Brazzaville, and other African host cities. Their continued support of their kin and community enables Togotala to maintain its precarious existence on the Sahelian plain.

Communities throughout the Sahel are utterly dependent on the remittances of absent sons and daughters. "Migration is an apt response to the cyclical swings of poverty in this region," writes Findley (2004:1), and Mali has one of the highest net emigration rates on earth. World Bank data suggest that 1.2 million Malians—nearly 10 percent of the country's population—lived abroad in 2006. (Malian government estimates since the early 1990s have consistently put the number of Malian emigrants above 4 million, or more than a third of the country's official population.) The World Bank assesses Mali's 2008 remittances from abroad at $344 million, yet this figure overlooks significant flows passing through "informal" transfer mechanisms rather than banks and wire services. Mali's total remittances most likely rival the amount the country receives annually in foreign direct investment or official development assistance from its donors. And Mali is no exception in Africa: in fact, the country is not even among the continent's top ten remittance recipients (measured as a percentage of GDP), where it is outranked by nations such as Senegal, Kenya, Uganda, Ghana, Cape Verde, and Lesotho.[2]

While Sahelian labor migrants in France have received considerable scholarly attention, most migrants who depart the countries of the western Sahel are "intra-African" migrants, moving to other African countries. Mali's foreign ministry estimates that intra-African migrants comprise over 90 percent of Malian citizens abroad. Togotala's modern homes attest to the considerable economic clout of Malians living elsewhere in Africa. Mali's intra-African migrants make more than twice as many land purchases in the capital city of Bamako as migrants to France.[3]

Nor are Malians unique in undertaking and profiting from intra-African migration. The total number of intra-African migrants has been estimated at over 10 million, representing some two-thirds of the continent's migrants.

Southern Africa has a long history of extensive cross-border flows. International migration within Africa is part of a much larger phenomenon: levels of "South-South migration"—the flow of migrants between and among poor countries of the "global South"—are believed to equal or surpass levels of migration from poor southern countries to wealthy northern ones, and the absolute number of these migrants has risen steadily for decades.[4]

Yet South-South migration in general, and intra-African migration in particular, has been all but invisible to officials, policy makers, and researchers. These migrants are often unregistered, undocumented, and undetected by host-country governments. A great deal of social scientific research has focused on Africa's refugees and migrants to Europe or North America; Western news media, for their part, have been drawn to the gripping images of clandestine migrants setting out from the North African coast in rickety vessels for European shores, and disquieting headlines employing martial language, such as "EU's 'Fortress Europe' Buckles under Immigrant Siege" (Radio Free Europe–Radio Liberty 2009). Few scholars or journalists, however, have examined Africans' most widespread form of international migration: movement from one African country to another in search of economic opportunity. Thus a key aspect of life in the twenty-first century—the circulation of people among poor countries—has gone nearly unnoticed by the rest of the world. The goal of this book is to help correct this oversight.

In places like Togotala, migration is a central part of life. Virtually everyone living there (except for very young children) has been a migrant at some point, even if only to spend a dry season in Bamako; migration in its diverse forms is an expected part of adulthood for Togotalans, men and women alike. "A man who has not gone abroad is not complete," one head of household there told me. My aim as an anthropologist has been to study the effects of this generalized condition of mobility on individuals, families, and social groups. I initially went to Togotala in 2002 to understand why Togotalans leave home. Having completed service as a Peace Corps Volunteer just two years earlier in a more southern area of Mali, I believed I was prepared for this fieldwork. Arriving in the final month of a prolonged dry season, I found that I was not.

Shortly after arriving in Togotala, for the first time I witnessed a dust storm blacken the midday sky. I later watched children from my host family haul cattle, dead from starvation, from their corral into the bush for disposal. I experienced the unrelenting rhythms of farming during the short rainy season, as Togotalans did their best to scratch a living from depleted soil with hand tools. By the end of this research I was less interested in why Togotalans wanted to leave and more intrigued by another question: *Why did they come back?* In a setting where migration is universal, I failed to grasp why more Togotalans had not permanently resettled in a more hospitable environment. Many who remained abroad continued to play active roles in the political, economic, and social affairs of the town. Why make such sacrifices to sustain a community where human habitation seemed less and less sustainable? What forces bound Togotalans to this nearly barren patch of land at the edge of the encroaching desert?

The answers to these questions could not be found in Togotala alone. I needed to study Togotalans living abroad to learn more about this particular relationship between mobility and territory. As I discovered, the migration imperative prevails throughout the continent today, and responses to it offer insight into the ways people construct their identities in contemporary Africa.

Diasporas, Globalization, and Mobility

Migration, even on a massive scale, is not new to Africa, which has been the site of some of humankind's greatest migrations beginning with the spread of early humans from the continent more than one hundred thousand years ago and continuing with the dispersion of Bantu peoples from western to central and southern Africa five thousand years ago. Africa's more recent history has been marked by the trans-Saharan trade, the Indian Ocean trade, the transatlantic slave trade, and, since the colonial era, by multiple labor migration streams. African populations remain highly mobile today.

In the 1960s the concept of an "African Diaspora" emerged to encompass the experiences of populations of African origin, particularly formerly enslaved peoples living in the Americas. Over time the field of African diasporic studies expanded to include all "people of African descent who found (and find) themselves living either outside of the African continent or in parts of Africa that were territorially quite distant from their lands of birth" (Gomez 2005:1). The diaspora concept has long been applied to displaced peoples around the world, and scholars have proposed typologies of diaspora, including trade diasporas, victim diasporas, imperial diasporas, labor diasporas, and cultural diasporas (R. Cohen 1997). In the inaugural issue of the journal *African Diaspora*, Oliver Bakewell (2008:10) lists four key characteristics of diasporas:

1. Movement from an original homeland to more than one country, either through dispersal (forced) or expansion (voluntary) in search of improved livelihoods;

2. A collective myth of an ideal ancestral home;

3. A strong ethnic group consciousness sustained over a long time, based on a shared history, culture, and religion; and

4. A sustained network of social relationships with members of the group living in different countries of settlement.

These features allow us to differentiate between truly diasporic peoples maintaining distinctive connections (if only symbolic) to a perceived homeland and other dispersed groups whose members lack such a reference point. They also exclude migrants remaining within national boundaries: as we shall see, questions of citizenship and the modern nation-state have significant impact on the lives of Africa's international migrants and their descendants. (If people like the Togotalan man quoted earlier feel they might do without the state, nobody thinks he can ignore it.)

Although the concept of a singular "African Diaspora" once prevailed among scholars, today the emphasis is generally upon African *diasporas*. An emerging body of literature on "new African diasporas" highlights the experiences of various African migrant populations in Europe and North America, many of them only a generation or two old. The role such diasporas play in developing their home countries and communities has also generated interest. A problem remains, however: literature on these diasporas "is almost exclusively concerned with people living outside the continent" (Bakewell 2008:16). My focus is on Africans living in a diaspora *within* the African continent. Despite considerable research on transnational migration and diasporic groups since the 1990s, little attention has been devoted to Africa's internal diasporas—African migrants and their descendants living in African societies. The focus on Africa's "New World diaspora," and to a lesser extent its "Old World Diaspora," must not obscure from view those Africans displaced within the "African homeland."[5]

Particularly since the mid-twentieth century, migration has continued to expand and intensify throughout the continent. This dynamic of increasing spatial mobility may be understood as a component of "globalization"—another problematic term that carries the baggage of related concepts such as modernization and development. Many academics avoid "globalization" altogether, seeing it as a term that "embraces everything and means nothing," not least with respect to Africa (Cooper 2001:196). Let me specify here what I do and do not mean by globalization. I see it not as an entity, an agent, or a unified force either for good or ill. Despite frequent alternative uses, especially in the popular press, I do not take globalization to refer to something that acts upon the world, sweeping humanity toward some foreseeable end point. Rather, it refers to a set of discernible *consequences*. "Globalization cannot be separated from its effects," writes Burawoy (2001:156); "globalization is not a cause but an effect of processes in hierarchical chains that span the world." Those processes are multiplex, contested, and often contradictory.

Probably the most important theme running throughout scholars' discussions of globalization is that of connection on a worldwide scale. Inda and Rosaldo (2001:2), for example, define globalization as "the intensification of global interconnectedness, suggesting a world full of movement and mixture, contact and linkages, and persistent cultural interaction and exchange." For Hannerz (1996:17), it is "a matter of increasing long-distance interconnectedness," and Giddens (1990:64) describes it as "the intensification of world-wide social relations which link distant localities in such a way that local happenings are shaped by events occurring many miles away and vice-versa." Well before the widespread adoption of the word "globalization," Wolf (1982:3) argued that the whole of human history must be seen as a "totality of interconnected processes" rather than an agglomeration of analytically separate cultural units.

What is distinctive about current globalization processes is not the *existence* of global interconnectedness but rather its *scope* and the *pace* with which connections are made across great distances. New forms of information technology and capitalist organization surely contribute to the widening scope and accelerating pace of contemporary global interconnectedness. Trouillot (2003:48) identifies the most novel aspects of today's globalization as "changes in the spatialization of the world economy and in the volume and, especially, kinds of movements that occur across political boundaries." These are the same changes that Togotalans experience as migrants.

Globalization is often imagined as a set of processes operating from the top down, imposed by powerful bodies upon the powerless. Colonialism, imperialism, and the spread of the global economic "world-system" (Wallerstein 1974) certainly fit this mold, as do brands of corporate globalization and neoliberal governance whose most outspoken opponents are glossed in the U.S. news media as "anti-globalization activists." But globalization, when understood as a dynamic of interconnection, leaves space for actions by the less powerful. Many African migrants cannot be understood primarily, let alone solely, as proletarian pawns of global capital. Togotalans abroad work hard and exercise considerable agency, entrepreneurship, and creativity to bring the benefits of the global economy to their community. They and other members of Africa's internal diasporas participate in a kind of globalization from the ground up.

Globalization is characterized by contradictions. On the one hand, economies "open up" to world markets, and flows of capital and information increase across international boundaries; human beings and communities are displaced and inserted into long-distance streams of labor migration. On the other hand, people simultaneously confront multiple forms of exclusion from certain spaces: physical, through border controls; political, through discrimination; and economic, through marginalization and relegation to low-status forms of labor. Despite their cosmopolitan activities, moreover, many migrants continue to define themselves in highly "localist" terms according to their geographic place of origin and the people and ideas associated with it. Members of the Senegal-based Murid Islamic brotherhood, for example, preserve strong links with their Senegalese home villages and with their spiritual reference point, the sacred city of Touba. Even as they spend years overseas, as Riccio (2006:95) observes, they maintain

> an identity linked to village of origin, neighborhood, kinship, and the holy city. . . . They remain fundamentally attached to the relations and places meaningful for them, and it is this certainty that permits their organization to thrive in different arrival contexts, even in the least welcoming ones.

This sense of belonging to a particular homeland is a hallmark not only of Africa's internal diasporas but of many other populations engaged in transnationalism—that is, activities spanning two or more nation-states. Examples are as varied as Dominicans and Mexicans in the United States, Caribbeans in the United Kingdom, and Chinese in the countries of the Pacific Rim.[6] Studies of such groups have shown that human culture can be uncoupled from the specific locations with which it has long been associated; the "isomorphism of space, place and culture" (Gupta and Ferguson 1997:34), once taken for granted, has been unraveled. Yet human loyalties have not been deterritorialized to the same extent as our lives have. Indeed, groups constructing strong ideological, cultural, and religious connections to specific places may prove far better adapted to the practice of transnationalism than groups lacking such connections. To return to the case of the Murids, Riccio argues that

> It is not the diversity of references and multiple identifications that explains the success of the Murids' deterritorialization, but their continuous *reterritorialization*, their capacity to continually recompose their own points of

reference by linking them to a context to which they intend to return occasionally or definitively. (2006:104; emphasis added)

Despite the power of globalization to *dis*place populations and detach culture from territory, place still matters a great deal. In fact, especially for migrants in Africa, it seems to matter more than ever before. Being in Togotala opened my eyes to what is perhaps globalization's greatest paradox: mobility has never been more important for sustaining livelihoods, yet linkages to a particular territorially bounded community (a hometown, region, or nation-state) have also never been more vital for securing rights and political membership. In these pages I deconstruct the processes by which people, at the individual and group level, attach themselves to particular places (a process I describe in the conclusion to this book as "anchoring") and describe how these processes influence their notions of identity, citizenship, and belonging. Spatial mobility has led members of African internal diasporas to relate to places in inventive ways.

Lessons from these migrants' experiences may be applied beyond the fields of migration research or African studies. Studying migration, in Africa and the wider world, helps social scientists move toward a "reformulation of the concept of society" (Levitt and Glick Schiller 2004:1003) and, specifically, away from conventional notions of societies as place-bound units. By examining how people move, the social relationships they create and dissolve as they move, and how they anchor themselves to specific pieces of territory, we can begin to see how communities—from the locally grounded to the spatially discontinuous and multilocal—are evolving in the globalized world.

Strangers in a Strange Land

After completing my 2002 fieldwork in Togotala, I sought to trace the transnational networks in which Togotalan lives were embedded. Having studied the "sending community," I had to identify a suitable "receiving community" in which to study migrant life abroad. There were many to choose from; my Togotalan informants had relatives in the United States, France, Spain, Southeast Asia, and at least a dozen different African countries. I did not know where to continue my research.

Then I came across a news item with the memorable title "Brazzaville: World's Worst City" (BBC 2003). The article outlined the findings of a survey by a British human resources consulting firm whose investigators annually evaluated quality of life in more than four hundred world cities with respect to "political, social, economic and environmental factors, personal safety and health, education, transport and other public services." Brazzaville, capital of the Republic of Congo, ranked dead last in 2003, behind Bangui and even Baghdad.[7] Pointe-Noire, Congo's second city, was fourth from the bottom.

The survey in question clearly aimed to gauge quality of life for "expatriate staff"— employees of multinational corporations and wealthy governments— rather than the living conditions of ordinary residents. Still, the news piqued my curiosity. Not only had I interviewed several people in Togotala who had spent years working in Brazzaville, but I knew of many still living there. One informant had even conducted his own survey in 1995 (at the behest of a Togotalan community association) and counted eighty-one Togotalan men in Brazzaville that year, many of them accompanied by wives and children. The city certainly seemed an implausible destination: it had experienced repeated outbreaks of civil war in the 1990s and a long period of economic decline. If life there was really so bad, why did these people go? What attraction had been overlooked by the quality of life survey? These questions ultimately motivated my decision to conduct prolonged fieldwork in Brazzaville. When I first traveled there in 2003, I found the city home to a large population of immigrants from Mali (the Malian consulate estimated twenty to thirty thousand) and elsewhere in West Africa, a population with a very long history.

Returning to Brazzaville in early 2005, I settled in the Poto-Poto neighborhood with my wife and young daughter to begin a year of fieldwork. I was especially interested in learning how African migrants experienced their condition as outsiders in Congolese society, and I found the concept of the stranger to be extremely useful in this regard. This concept was first elaborated by sociologist Georg Simmel, who described the stranger as a paradoxical figure, integrally involved with a group but never attaining the status of true membership in it. Strangers are simultaneously part of and excluded from society; they are not acknowledged as members but are essential to its functioning. It is this "synthesis of nearness and distance which constitutes the formal position of the stranger" (Simmel 1950:404). Strangers' only place *within* the group is defined by their *opposition to* the group, by their differentiation from it. For Simmel, they are "organic members" of the host society who are nonetheless "inorganically appended" to it (1950:408). Strangers are often traders, and vice versa; European Jews form the classical example. The connection between diasporas and strangerhood is self-evident.

Strangers can spend years, sometimes their entire lives, living in a foreign culture without assimilating into it. This difficulty of assimilation has been observed by several scholars studying strangers in African societies. Meyer

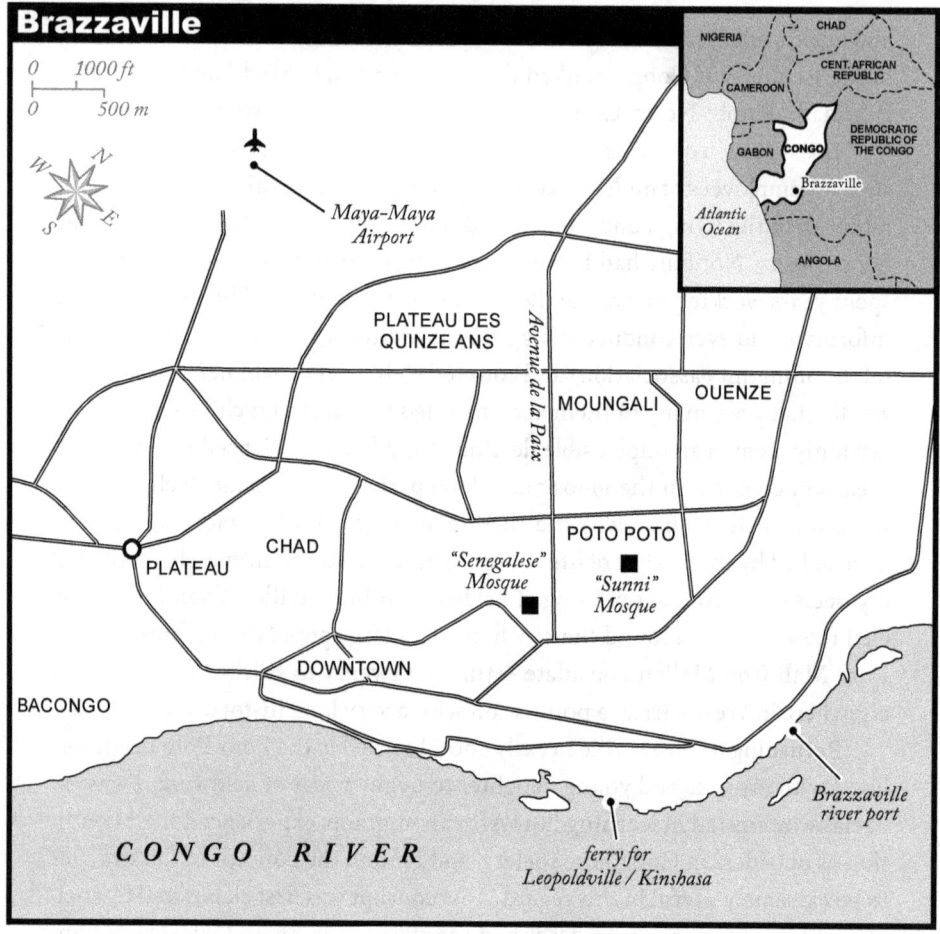

Map 1. Map of Brazzaville.

Fortes, for example, drawing from fieldwork in Tallensi and Asante communities in Ghana, describes strangers as the polar opposite of kin; their language, social organization, and often their religion differ from those of the host community. Outsiders, owing to their descent and their culture, they are often seen as "inassimilable aliens" (Fortes 1975:245). Many reside in enclave neighborhoods such as Sabo in Ibadan, Nigeria, Sabon Zongo of Accra, Ghana, or New Bell of Douala, Cameroon, where they are at least partially segregated from their hosts.[8]

Such ethnographic evidence shows that the concept of the stranger resonates deeply in numerous African cultures. In a city like Brazzaville, equivalents of the term "stranger" are in everyday use, though each, of course, has its own distinctive connotations. The French noun *étranger*, for example, means both stranger and foreigner; *mopaya* (Lingala) and *nzenza* (Kikongo) can designate anyone from outside one's village, whether from a nearby village or another country. Among the city's West African immigrants, the nouns *dunan* (Bamanan) and *mukke* (Soninke) denote stranger (i.e., an unknown person), foreigner (a person from somewhere else), and guest. All these words correspond to Simmel's sense of the stranger concept, because although they are usually translated as "foreigner," this category is not always ascribed based on nation-state citizenship. With their connotation of the inability to assimilate, these terms help brighten the boundaries between hosts and immigrants.

Perhaps even more significant than discourses of strangers in Africa are the discourses of those defining themselves *against* strangers: autochthons, natives, or "sons of the soil." In the current era of globalization, neoliberalism, and shrinking states, the question of autochthony—of who is considered to belong to a group and who is considered a stranger—is "among the most crucial and controversial in African politics" (Bøås 2009:20). This issue has become highly politicized since the early 1990s: to cite one prominent example, autochthony has been a divisive problem in Côte d'Ivoire since the early 1990s, and was at the core of the civil unrest leading to the outbreak of civil war in 2002 and disputed presidential elections in late 2010. If autochthony exists in infinite degrees, with each subgroup of insiders competing to prove itself more "local" than its rivals, strangerhood is a singular condition not specific to any particular place or culture. The concept of strangerhood is particularly relevant to Africa's internal diasporas today. Far from a residual category enfolding people who are "not autochthons," strangerhood is an actively generated condition. One of my primary goals in this book is to analyze this condition and its accompanying set of obligations and taboos.

In the chapters that follow I consider how strangerhood is constructed and reproduced in Brazzaville, and by whom. This is a sensitive, contested topic. Many migrants I spoke to in the city represented strangerhood as something imposed upon them by their Congolese hosts, a kind of second-class status they resented but were forced to accept. They felt compelled to abide by certain unspoken rules of strangerhood, surrendering many of their rights in return for being tolerated on foreign soil. West Africans attributed their minimal integration in the host society to the Congolese, who would not accept them for who they were, would not grant them a permanent place in their own society, and only grudgingly recognized their right to live there temporarily. Congolese viewed matters quite differently: they saw strangerhood as an organic feature of Brazzaville's West African community, an outgrowth of these migrants' insular character and their culturally derived unwillingness to open themselves to outside influences. West Africans' minimal integration into the host society, Congolese generally felt, was because of the West Africans themselves and their stubborn insistence on maintaining primordial attachments to their Sahelian communities of origin.

Although both logics contain some truth, I challenge them in these pages. Strangerhood is a phenomenon maintained jointly, if not always consciously, by hosts and migrants alike. Members of each group have stakes in reproducing and passing it on to their descendants. An array of historical, economic, and political dynamics has reinforced strangerhood as a discourse organizing migrants' lives, in Brazzaville and in many other parts of the African continent. As I will show, host-stranger relations cannot be reduced to the cultural characteristics of either of the populations concerned; rather, they are the products of long-term processes implicating multiple populations.

Identifying the Study Population

Early on, one of the most difficult conceptual aspects of my fieldwork in Brazzaville was defining the group of people I would study there. Limiting myself to migrants from Togotala would have provided too small a sample—no more than a few dozen. Before going to Congo, I had seen the study population through an "ethnic lens" (see Glick Schiller, Çağlar, and Guldbrandsen 2006): taking my cue from scholars depicting migration flows from a particular region of West Africa as "Soninke migration," I saw ethnicity as the way to decide who was "in" and who was "out" of my study, and I represented the practices my informants described to me as Soninke phenomena,[9] an easy task as Togotalans nearly all defined themselves as Soninke.

From my first visit to Brazzaville in 2003, however, I realized I would have to abandon the ethnic lens. The city was home to thousands of West African migrants who were not Soninke; nor were they fundamentally different from Soninke migrants in terms of their economic activities, social organization, and mobility patterns. Although the Soninke composed the largest single group, and appeared especially dominant among traders, I met migrants belonging to many different ethnic groups found in Mali and elsewhere in the western Sahel—most notably Bamanan, Maninka, and Halpulaaren, but also Khassonke, Wolof, Senufo, Sonrai, and Dogon.[10] Members of all these groups were in intimate contact with one another, often sharing the same residential compounds, working for the same businesses, belonging to the same associations, worshiping at the same mosques, and intermarrying. I did not feel I should exclude them merely because they were not Soninke.

Nor could I use a narrow geographic area of origin to decide who was "in." Though many migration studies in Africa are defined primarily by a specific sending zone, such as the Senegal River Valley, the migrants I found in Brazzaville came from all over Mali and several neighboring states. Migrants of the Soninke ethnic group and those from the Senegal River Valley undoubtedly played pioneering roles in opening up migration flows from West to Central Africa but were not alone in that process, nor do they have any exclusive claim to these flows today. It would have been similarly difficult to focus on a specific "stranger neighborhood" in the host city, as scholars have done elsewhere.[11] Poto-Poto is indeed home to many immigrants: nearly 90 percent of Malians who registered with their Brazzaville consulate in 2005, for example, lived there or in the adjoining neighborhood of Moungali. Yet most residents of Poto-Poto and Moungali are native Congolese; there is little residential segregation between Poto-Poto's hosts and strangers, and no neighborhood of Brazzaville has a majority stranger population.

My initial plan in Brazzaville was to limit the study population to Malians, who clearly composed the majority of West African immigrants there. Even if this plan excluded small numbers of people with other nationalities, I believed it would have the advantage of using an unambiguous criterion: either one had Malian citizenship, in the form of a passport or some other kind of official papers, or one did not. This plan quickly fell apart. I had anticipated that there would be many migrants from countries bordering Mali—Senegalese, Guineans, Ivoirians, and others—whose activities were little different from those of Malians, and who belonged to some of the same ethnic groups as Malians or who had intermarried with them. I had not anticipated, however, the number of people living in Brazzaville who considered themselves Malians but had *never* possessed Malian papers. Many were born to migrant parents in a third country (especially Côte d'Ivoire, home to millions of immigrants from throughout West Africa) and had never acquired Malian citizenship. Then there were the second- and third-generation Malian immigrants in Congo, most of whom had solely Congolese citizenship (see chapter 6). All these different groups formed a meaningful community in Brazzaville that was not bounded by citizenship in a single nation-state.

In the end, abandoning nationality as the main criterion for inclusion in this research was salutary for my project. It helped me avoid the pitfalls of "methodological nationalism," defined as "the naturalization of the nation-state by the social sciences" (Wimmer and Glick Schiller 2003:576). Too many researchers treat national identity as an empirical fact rather than a social construction; paradoxically, this has been true even of scholars studying transnational migration.[12] Perhaps because much of the pioneering research in this field focused on migrants from Caribbean islands with relatively homogeneous populations in terms of ethnicity and language, studies of transnationalism have often accentuated nationality above all other criteria of identity, and reified categories of national origin instead of deconstructing them. The very name "transnationalism" puts "nation" ahead of other geographic or cultural distinctions. It is no coincidence that in the literature on transnationalism one generally reads about migrants who are Mexican rather than Mixtec, Turkish rather than Kurdish, and Senegalese rather than Wolof.

One's analysis may transcend identities defined by ethnicity or nationality, but one must delimit one's study population somehow. After several weeks in Brazzaville, I knew I could not study *all* immigrants, as there were hundreds of thousands from neighboring Congo-Kinshasa, as well as other Central African states, who had little or nothing to do with West African immigrants. I could not target all Muslims, for that would bring in small numbers of Arabs, Chadians, and others who also seemed irrelevant to my purposes. Nor could I choose a "language community" defined by a West African tongue such as Bamanan, despite its role as the lingua franca for most people in central and southern Mali as well as for many immigrants in Brazzaville. In addition to Brazzaville-born individuals who often had not acquired their immigrant parents' language, many immigrants spoke Fulfulde or Soninke but not Bamanan. The immigrants I met in Brazzaville did not all share national, ethnic, or linguistic bonds, yet something made them cohere, regulated their interactions, and made them into a kind of community.

This cohesion stemmed from two factors. First, throughout Mali and its neighboring states, a system of joking relationships cuts across distinctions of social status and ethnicity. It establishes a pattern of ritualized informal ties between members of particular patronymic clans as well as between specific castes and ethnic groups. These ties are most commonly expressed through insults and what could best be described as trash-talking, which, though meant in jest, also constitute a vital form of social interaction. These jokes pervade social life in this part of West Africa, and for foreigners in that environment an adopted patronym can be a powerful tool for facilitating social interaction.[13] While they may seem like idiosyncrasies, they knit a diverse society together:

joking is "the idiom of amity" (Launay 1977:416), and I believe that ritual joking is indelibly associated with much of the social stability and harmony Mali has enjoyed throughout its history. Moreover, this system of joking relations connects Malians to peoples in neighboring countries (northern Guinea and Côte d'Ivoire, western Burkina Faso, southern Mauritania, and eastern Senegal), providing a common discourse of sociability as well as a sense of shared history. In Brazzaville these relationships enabled West Africans of various ethnicities and nationalities, with different native languages, and from different places of origin to relate to one another. They perceived themselves as a community partly because they were bound by the same network of joking relationships.

Second, as immigrants in Brazzaville, these immigrants from such diverse origins found themselves (probably for the first time) lumped into a single category by the Congolese around them. In Congo the term *Ouest Africain* generally denotes an immigrant who is Sahelian and Muslim.[14] Congolese rarely differentiate between the various nationalities or ethnicities of the West Africans in their midst, and tend to view what they call *la communauté ouest africaine* (the West African community) as a homogeneous entity. Seeing themselves reflected in their hosts' gaze, strangers who may have had little in common back home learn to think of themselves as bound together by defining aspects of their identity, especially Islam. Discrimination they encounter from members of the host population further enhances this solidarity dynamic.

I therefore chose to delimit my study population as one that coheres partially from within, through joking relations, and partially from without, through the experience of strangerhood in Brazzaville. Lacking a ready-made label for such a heterogeneous group, in these pages I simply call members of the population in question "West Africans," knowing that this label is imprecise and arbitrary. Although a few hundred immigrants from Benin, Nigeria, and other countries outside the western Sahel live in Brazzaville, they do not fit into the group I studied. In the end, all labels and delimitations of human beings are arbitrary; I have merely opted for a more inclusive arbitrary label. When I refer to West Africans in this book, I mean those united by a particular system of joking relationships, including all immigrants from Mali and its neighboring states, plus their descendants born in Congo or elsewhere. Likewise, when I refer to "West Africa" as a geographic space, I specifically mean the home regions of those people integrated into this system of joking cousinhood distributed across the western Sahel. There is no single "West African diaspora": Brazzaville's West Africans represent multiple internal diasporas defined by home villages, ethnicities, regions, and nation-states. This illustrates why it is productive to think about diasporas in the plural: the idea of a unified African Diaspora encompassing all these groups obscures too many important distinctions from view.

Transnational Ethnography in Africa

One afternoon about two months into my Brazzaville fieldwork, an elderly man I did not know called out to me as I walked past his tailor shop in the Poto-Poto market. He turned out to be a native of Sikasso, the southern Malian town where I had spent a year as a Peace Corps Volunteer. I never knew why Vieux Diallo invited me into his life that day, but he always made me feel welcome at his shop and we soon became friends. With a depth of experience in Brazzaville, an easygoing demeanor, and above all a mischievous sense of humor, he was a fixture of my days in Brazzaville.[15]

I spent hours with Vieux Diallo at his tiny rented tailor shop. We usually had plenty of time to chat, as few customers came in. Diallo was a font of forceful opinions and colorful but questionable information, a role he seemed to embellish for my benefit. He regaled me with stories about mythical creatures and beings he had encountered over the years. There were the *djinn*, spirits that could take the form of living people and that he claimed to have once encountered in a Parisian metro. There were the *bilisi*, nocturnal animals that emit a bright light and devour humans. There were also the *woklo*, dwarf-like creatures with magical powers and feet facing backward. One often hears that old men in Africa are like libraries—in the absence of many written records, they are the most important repositories of cultural knowledge and memory. Listening to Diallo's stories, I could recognize the truth in that saying, but I also knew that his particular library had an especially large fiction section.

Diallo claimed he was unsure how old he was, but I guessed about seventy-five because he had come of age in the twilight of French colonial rule in the 1950s. Following brief service in the colonial army, he left Mali immediately upon its independence from France in 1960 and traveled to Abidjan, Côte d'Ivoire, where he spent a decade. Around 1970 (the precise year varied according to the telling), he moved to Brazzaville where he had remained ever since. He had one wife, also from Sikasso, and thirteen living children; two other children had died. Diallo told me he first left home because of his opposition to the policies enacted by Mali's founding president, Modibo Keita:[16] Diallo saw Keita's socialist ideology as a threat to Malian cultural values, and he made exaggerated claims about its far-reaching scope. Once he tried to convince me that "Modibo" had even sought to suppress the institution of marriage in the country, allowing anyone to sleep with whomever they wished. I learned to take such accounts with a grain of salt.

A few weeks after our first meeting, Diallo brought me to the *zawiya*, or Sufi mosque, where he often prayed, and introduced me to some of the worshipers there. One asked what I was doing in Brazzaville. In his helpful manner, Diallo explained what he understood was my role and then added that people like me "used to be called *espions*." I was mortified: the old man had used the French word meaning "spies." Luckily another acquaintance whom I had interviewed a few days earlier intervened to offer a more benign explanation for my presence. Given the timing of my fieldwork—my first stay in Brazzaville began just four months after the U.S. invasion of Iraq in 2003—I could have expected to meet with considerable suspicion and even resistance by West Africans. In the prevailing climate of uncertainty over the Bush administration's "global war on terror," which many around the world perceived as a war on Islam, these Muslims would have been within their rights to regard any American among them as an interloper and potential threat. Some were aware of reports that the FBI was expanding its presence in Africa, and so, inevitably, Brazzaville's West Africans initially worried that I had been sent by the U.S. government.[17]

But generally I was welcomed warmly wherever I went in Brazzaville. In shops, private homes, and mosques, people responded to my presence with much more openness than mistrust, more curiosity than concern, and more friendliness than fear. It undoubtedly helped that I had previously lived in Mali, had learned Bamanan, was married to a Malian woman, practiced Islam, and knew the all-important idioms of joking relations. If anything, however, I experienced even greater conviviality among these immigrants in Congo than I ever knew in Mali or among Malians in the United States, perhaps because, for the first time, they and I now had something important in common: in Brazzaville we were all outsiders.

It is to my informants' credit, more than my own, that they opened up to me as much as they did. Sometimes I felt that the level of access these immigrants provided was wasted on such a neophyte ethnographer. Of course, I occasionally heard stories and accounts of which I was skeptical, and whenever I present these in the book I advise the reader of my misgivings. As anthropologists from Gluckman (1963) to Farmer (1993) have illustrated so well, however, even information that may be inaccurate or downright false—rumors, innuendo, and conspiracy theories—may nonetheless reveal how social relations and the exercise of power are popularly constructed. I have always tried to cross-check the information I received with as many different sources as possible, and, in the main, I am as confident as an ethnographer can be that the opinions and statements in these pages truly represent those of my informants. This is not to say that they are always "true."

From his experience doing ethnographic fieldwork in a Zambian Copperbelt town, anthropologist James Ferguson discusses the practical difficulties of doing research in an urban African context lacking social coherence or a sense of community. Learning any local language in a place where English was widely spoken was challenging, and the town's diverse population made for a particularly complex cultural landscape. Ferguson describes this urban environment as inherently puzzling, not just for a foreign ethnographer but for everyone living there. This complexity transformed the relationship between ethnographer and informant: "The question now becomes not who is the insider and who an outsider, who is local and who is not," Ferguson writes, "but rather which of the bits floating in the swirl of events does any given social actor 'get,' and which leave him more or less confused and mystified" (1999:208).

This passage provided reassurance during my Brazzaville fieldwork whenever the social "swirl" seemed indecipherable. On any given day, members of my research population heard and spoke at least four different languages—Bamanan, Soninke, Lingala, and French.[18] Alongside language, cultural heterogeneity made it hard to conceptualize Brazzaville's West African "community," with its many national and ethnic subdivisions, let alone the larger urban melting pot in which its members lived. How much mastery of such a variegated cultural landscape can even a gifted ethnographer expect to attain in one year? In five? Had I not already spent over three years in Mali and learned the Bamanan language, I might have found the task of studying this population insurmountable.

Although it is certainly true that in a place like Poto-Poto, as in the towns of the Copperbelt, "everyone is a little confused" (Ferguson 1999:208) with respect to the social setting, it is also true—as Ferguson admits—that some are more confused than others. In fact, many people do achieve a degree of mastery amid Poto-Poto's messy cultural jumble. Members of Africa's internal diasporas often display enviable linguistic talents; most Malians in Brazzaville had already learned two or three languages even before emigrating. I was constantly astounded at the ability of these immigrants—especially the women—to gain fluency in Lingala and interact with Congolese with what seemed like complete comfort and ease, often in less than a year. I never learned much Lingala and instead relied mainly on French (spoken by most Brazzaville residents) to communicate with Congolese, and Bamanan and French to communicate with West Africans.

Dignity and Strangerhood: A Preview of the Book's Chapters

A Bamanan proverb states *Tunga tè danbe dòn*—"Exile knows no dignity." When people go abroad, according to this notion, they lose dignity, which they derive from their ascribed status; they can only regain it when they return home. *Danbe*, or dignity, is a place-bound attribute, inextricably linked with local social hierarchies and family histories. Hence the saying also suggests that a person "has no value in foreign places" (Jonsson 2008:17): one's *danbe* is not transferable from the homeland, for it cannot be appreciated abroad. This proverb also exists in a longer form: "Exile knows no dignity, but it knows a good person" (*Tunga tè danbe dòn, nka a be den nyuman dòn*). Dignity may be place-bound, but one's achievements are recognizable anywhere. This fact offers strangers the chance to pursue opportunities unavailable to them at home. It also, as I will show, exposes strangers to exploitation and abuse from their hosts. The proverb "Exile knows no dignity" encapsulates several of this ethnography's central themes pertaining to belonging and strangerhood.

To understand West Africans' role in Brazzaville in the early twenty-first century we must consider how and why they came to the Congo Basin in the first place. It was European colonization that brought colonial personnel from France's West African colonies to the region. As soldiers, messengers, technicians, administrative workers, and laborers, these men were instrumental in establishing and maintaining colonial control from the early 1880s until well into the twentieth century throughout what was French Equatorial Africa and the neighboring Belgian Congo. Even as colonial penetration proceeded in the Congo Basin, West Africans developed their own commercial activities not directly related to their role as servants of European colonialism. The final decades of colonial rule and those following political independence in 1960 saw the consolidation of West Africans' commercial roles in Congolese cities and the emergence of important dynamics (most notably rapid urbanization) setting the stage for postcolonial social and economic transformations in the region. Urban growth, the development of the Central African diamond trade, and the expansion of the Congolese state bureaucracy had tremendous effects on relations between West African immigrants and their Congolese hosts during this period.

Historical precedent combines with economic opportunity to continue drawing West Africans to Brazzaville today. These immigrants constitute a trade diaspora in Congo with a particular and sometimes problematic structural relationship to the host society. This is one area where strangerhood confers distinct advantages and is actively maintained by the strangers themselves, who not only derive commercial profits from their outsider status but may perform certain types of labor that they could not perform in their home communities. In both cases, individuals capitalize on these advantages by using migration to adjust their level of embeddedness in social networks. This process represents the positive aspect of the proverb explained above: what matters in a foreign land is not one's ascribed status but one's accomplishments and one's ability to work hard.

Islam also figures prominently for members of Brazzaville's West African population. Religion is perhaps the most salient marker of difference between West Africans and Congolese, coming to the fore in West Africans' public life in Brazzaville in a way it seldom does at home. These immigrants use Muslim ritual practices and beliefs to construct their collective identity in the context of a non-Muslim host society, and Muslim ideologies and practices shape how they see themselves and their Congolese hosts. We therefore need to assess whether Islam hinders or even prevents these immigrants' integration into Congolese society.

Multiple areas of friction arise between immigrant and host populations in Brazzaville, with both groups interpreting these frictions through the lens of strangerhood. For West Africans and Congolese, strangerhood is a powerful idea that colors their understandings of one another and shapes their interactions; it is maintained by members of both populations. Constructions of strangerhood have a determining effect on concepts of citizenship and belonging, and constitute an unwritten code to which migrants must conform, influencing migrants' imaginings of their place in the host society and their relationship with their communities of origin. This fact reflects the negative side of "exile knows no dignity": in a foreign land, one's inherent worth as a human being and one's entitlements to basic rights are frequently not respected.

Given their precarious position in Congolese society, West African migrants maintain significant connections with the places they left behind. These transnational linkages exist at three levels: nation-states, hometowns, and households. Where the reproduction of group identity is concerned, the household level is key: migrant parents try to expose their Congo-born children to the cultural and social landscapes of their West African communities of origin, and their approaches condition the intergenerational durability of transnational identities. A full spectrum of transnational connections, both "narrow" (entailing regular physical movement) and "broad" (entailing only sporadic movement and including symbolic practices), is crucial to the long-term development of a transnational community in this setting, and enables some migrants to pass their transnational linkages on to their children.

These children, born and raised in Brazzaville, follow various paths to integration either into Congolese society or into the city's West African community. Belonging and citizenship are prickly topics for these second- and third-generation immigrants, as for many strangers in Africa. Considering the case of these native-born strangers allows us to develop a more nuanced understanding of the condition of strangerhood: some experience this condition as an external imposition, whereas others voluntarily embrace it. How can we account for these divergent outcomes? What variables influence individual choices about identity and belonging?

To complete its exploration of West African life in Brazzaville, the book returns to a paradox identified earlier in this introduction. Why is it that, even as lives are becoming increasingly mobile, the process of identity construction for many people has become increasingly circumscribed by territorial boundaries? If globalization is associated with deterritorialization, how do we explain concurrent processes of reterritorialization around the world? Answering these questions requires understanding how identities are generated and reproduced, and the role of historical, political, and economic forces in this process. The logic of strangerhood—which holds that people can only fully belong in places where they can demonstrate some ancestral affiliation—is not limited to West Africans in Brazzaville but fits into a web of ideas about place and belonging now common especially (but not exclusively) in postcolonial African societies. In reviewing the factors that reterritorialize or "anchor" identities in this context, we will illuminate some of the inherent tensions and contradictions of globalization processes, as well as the possibility of their resolution.

1
THE AVENUE OF SERGEANT MALAMINE

Quite little is known about the life of Malamine Camara. He was born in Senegal around the mid-nineteenth century, served as a soldier for France, and died young, probably in his thirties. His brief career in colonial service, however, made a tremendous mark on what became France's Congo colony. Like his white commanding officer who orchestrated France's claim to the region in the 1880s, Malamine Camara was present at the creation of the Congo colony and was instrumental in safeguarding it against encroachments by rival powers. And, like his commanding officer, he was esteemed by his fellow explorers, celebrated by the French press, and decorated by the French government. Unlike his commanding officer, however, within a few decades of his death he was virtually forgotten: all that bears his name in the Congolese capital today is a narrow, unpaved street running through the Poto-Poto market. During my Brazzaville fieldwork in 2005, no sign indicated its official designation known by a few of my informants: l'Avenue du Sergent Malamine. The story of this street's namesake reveals the extent to which, over more than seven decades of European colonial rule, the origins of France's Congo colony were intertwined with West African migration to the region.

West Africa and Its Laptots

For centuries prior to colonization Africa's Atlantic coastline had been an area of contact between Africans and Europeans. Portuguese ships arrived on the shores of what is now Senegal in the 1440s, and the transatlantic slave trade began shortly thereafter. The coastline between the port city of Saint-Louis, near the mouth of the Senegal River, and Gorée Island hosted a succession of Dutch, British, and French trading outposts until France gained exclusive rights in the early nineteenth century. By that time the French had recruited generations of men along the Senegalese coast to work alongside their traders, merchant sailors, and military personnel. These African workers, known as *laptots,* were "jacks-of-all-trades," doing everything from domestic chores to providing security for French trading posts and vessels on the Senegal River, where the trade in gum Arabic dominated interaction between locals and outsiders (Manchuelle 1987, 1997).

The term "laptot" is, according to Curtin (1975:114), "a Gallicized form of the Wolof term for sailor, and it originally had the same meaning in French. In time, however, it shifted to mean any African who worked with the Europeans, whether as a sailor, soldier, clerk, or administrator." Laptots were usually recruited in Saint-Louis to serve two-year contracts. Some were slaves whose Senegalese masters collected half their earnings. The French also bought slaves to serve in their army; these were often Bamanan from the interior, who as outsiders were less likely to fraternize with local populations. One of the greatest advantages to hiring Africans as troops and sailors was their resistance to the endemic diseases that wrought high mortality rates among Europeans in Africa until well into the twentieth century. Since it would have been too costly for European powers to send large numbers of their own troops to the continent, recruitment of indigenous men was the most expedient alternative. As early as 1827 these men served French colonial conquest when 200 Wolof troops were dispatched to Madagascar; 220 were sent to Guyana in 1831. The French army established an infantry unit of *tirailleurs sénégalais* (Senegalese riflemen) in 1857, which by the end of the century comprised more than 8,000 men. The terms tirailleur, laptot, and Sénégalais are used interchangeably in French literature from the period to designate West African personnel in colonial service.[1]

For years Wolof men from the coast dominated laptot work. After advancing to higher-status positions within the mercantile establishment, they were replaced by men from farther inland, particularly of Bamanan, Tukulor, or Soninke ethnicity who had migrated to the coast in search of wage labor. Soninke men were particularly numerous among the laptots and, by 1872, held most of these jobs. Laptots' wages, starting at 30 francs per month, were quite competitive—even compared to wages paid in France at the time—and generally attracted men of noble birth seeking to use their earnings to compete for status back home by investing in agriculture and purchasing slaves to work on their farms.[2] In fact, the French were frequently irritated by laptots' tendency to quit their service even before their contracts were complete to put their earnings to use. Thus Manchuelle (1997) concludes that, far from being coerced into migration by repressive policies such as head taxes and forced labor (which began much later in the West African colonial enterprise), these men should be considered "willing migrants"—a notion to which I will return.

Laptots serving aboard French naval and commercial vessels could sail to French forts at Grand-Bassam and Assinie in the future Côte d'Ivoire, to posts established along the Gabonese coast of Central Africa, and even as far as France. Some of these men learned local languages during their service and acted as interpreters for their French employers in parts of Africa quite distant from their native lands. Sergeant Camara was only one of many laptots who served in Central Africa before the official onset of France's colonial conquest of the region.

Claiming the Congo

In January 1880 a dozen laptots were recruited in Dakar for an expedition to Gabon. Camara was among them. They were to accompany a handful of Frenchmen led by a twenty-eight-year-old, Italian-born French naval officer named Pierre Savorgnan de Brazza. Brazza had already conducted one Central African expedition, during which he spent nearly three years trekking through equatorial forests with another mixed Franco-Senegalese contingent in hopes of finding a route up the Ogowé River to the continent's interior.[3] Although he never found such a route, merely surviving the ordeal gained him renown across Europe. Upon his return to France in early 1879 Brazza was feted by various European leaders including Belgium's King Leopold II, who was eager to establish a colony of his own in the Congo Basin.

The mission Camara had joined, Brazza's second, was funded in part by the French chapter of King Leopold's Association Internationale Africaine, ostensibly a humanitarian and scientific organization, and in part by the French naval ministry. The expedition arrived on the shores of Gabon in March 1880 and three months later established a French outpost on the upper Ogowé River. It then pressed on overland to the Congo.

It was during this trek that the party met an envoy of Makoko Iloo I, a king of the Téké people who soon signed a treaty granting Brazza possession of certain lands on the right bank of the wide section of the river known as the Pool.[4] The "Makoko treaty" became the foundation of French colonial rule in the Congo Basin. Brazza wrote the document (which neither the king nor

Figure 1.1. Sergeant Malamine Camara as sketched by Charles de Chavannes in Brazzaville, September 27, 1884.
IMAGE COURTESY OF THE SOCIÉTÉ DE GÉOGRAPHIE, PARIS

any of his aides was able to read) as a cession of territory, and three weeks after signing it he set up an outpost at M'Foa, on the Pool's right bank, flying a French tricolor to be visible to boats on the river. Before returning to the coast, Brazza instructed his men at M'Foa to show a copy of the treaty to any European who arrived.

The tiny detachment Brazza left behind was an unlikely group to represent the French Republic in its newest territorial acquisition. It consisted of a freed Gabonese slave and a Senegalese laptot under the command of Sergeant Malamine Camara. Malamine, as he became known, had already served with distinction during the voyage from the coast, learning local languages including Téké, which was widely spoken west of the Congo River. During the more than eighteen months that he commanded the M'Foa outpost, Malamine hunted buffalo, hippopotamus, and elephant, using a local musket when his Winchester rifle's cartridge supply ran low (Chavannes 1929). He distributed meat to his subordinates and to local political leaders as a goodwill gesture. His resourcefulness was noted by many observers, not least by local inhabitants who nicknamed him *Mayélé* (meaning a brilliant mind or resourceful character), as well as *Tara Nyama* ("meat father," for his gifts to their chiefs). Charles de Chavannes, Brazza's personal secretary and eventually a governor of colonial Congo, later described Malamine in the most glowing terms:

> The meager resources that his leader had left him were indeed small in comparison with those born of his ingenuity of spirit, his remarkable physical prowess, his hunting skill, and his initiative, which allowed him to handle all situations. It took only a few days for him to be profitably known by the whole region and to win the friendship of chiefs upon whom he bestowed the fruits of his hunts, venison and ivory. All the villages now kept the French tricolor hoisted; Malamine was at home everywhere. (Chavannes 1935:36; see also Guiral 1889:231)

He kept his hair braided in the fashion of the local Téké people, often wore local attire (donning his naval uniform only for exceptional circumstances), and adapted easily to the local milieu, even occasionally arbitrating disputes between local headmen.

Several months passed before Malamine was called to perform his primary duty of protecting French territorial claims to the area. In July 1881 the Welshborn American explorer Henry Morton Stanley, now seeking to secure Central Africa for Belgium's King Leopold, arrived at the Pool with a large expedition. Stanley had spent several months overseeing the laborious construction of a road through the forest from the mouth of the Congo. Malamine donned his uniform and, accompanied by his two subordinates, went immediately to notify him of the Makoko treaty. The following description of the encounter is based on Malamine's account to Chavannes two years later:

> Stanley, to impose upon [Malamine], had him surrounded with eight heavily armed Zanzibaris. Without losing his composure, Malamine planted his flag before Stanley's tent and, before saying anything to him, told [fellow laptot] Samba Thiam in his Tukulor language (incomprehensible to anyone else present), "I don't think anything serious will happen, but if it comes to gunfire, don't shoot at the blacks, shoot at the white man."

> Fortunately, nothing happened and Malamine, after informing Stanley of the treaty signed with Makoko, could offer some modest gifts of fresh food to Stanley, Braconnier, and the other Europeans before returning to his post. (Chavannes 1935:142)

Malamine's actions preempted the American's attempt to claim the Pool's right bank for King Leopold. Stanley, who normally had little regard for dark-skinned natives, described Malamine as

> a dashing looking Europeanized Negro (as I supposed him to be, though he had a superior type of face), in sailor costume, with the stripes of a non-commissioned officer on his arm. . . . [He] spoke French well, and his greeting was frank and manly. . . . A very short acquaintance with the sergeant proved to me that he was a superior man, even though he was a bronzed Senegalese. (1885:292–293)

Impressed by the sergeant's sense of duty, Stanley wrote that Malamine was "in his proper element among these Africans, who were of a lower grade than himself, and very tactfully and subtly he acted on his master's instructions" (ibid., 293).

In fact, Malamine exceeded those instructions to the point of becoming a thorn in Stanley's side. Besides following his orders from Brazza to the letter, the Senegalese sergeant conducted a disinformation campaign throughout the area to prevent Stanley from winning over local populations. Stanley later wrote,

> What fables Malameen [sic] uttered about our fondness for meat of tender children will never be published perhaps; but the effect of what he told [villagers] was known when the crier beat his tom-tom in the night, and shouted out along the river bank and amid the huts of the scattered village that [a local chief] had resolved that none of the people should speak with us, or sell us anything any more. (1885:299)

The mere existence of the Makoko treaty may not have dissuaded Stanley from trying to make inroads into French-claimed territory: he put little stock in the document, which was invalid under international law until it could be ratified. Malamine's operation to blacken his name, however, deterred Stanley for several months. It was not until New Year's Day 1882 that Stanley again crossed the Congo from his encampment aboard a newly assembled steamboat, the first of its kind in the area, with several Zanzibari mercenaries. He landed at M'Foa, perhaps hoping his show of force would convince Malamine's small contingent to abandon its post. One fanciful French account alleges that Stanley attempted to bribe the laptots into surrendering their station to him by offering a suitcase stuffed with British pound notes but was rebuffed at gunpoint. In any event, Malamine and his men stood their ground; most reports suggest that the sergeant gave Stanley a cordial greeting and reminded him of French sovereignty over the area and of the treaty. The explorer and his men soon crossed back to their camp on the left bank of the river.[5]

Weeks later Malamine received word via messenger that his post was to be relieved, that France would renounce its claims in the Congo Basin, and that he should return to Gabon forthwith. Malamine had doubts about the order, which was conveyed verbally; possibly fearing a trick by Stanley, he sent word back with the messenger that he would remain at M'Foa until relieved by a French officer. The lieutenant who eventually came was struck by Malamine's diplomatic victories there: "I could easily discern that he had the sympathy of all. I highly doubt that the Senegalese's successors in Stanley Pool would achieve such tasteful popularity" (Guiral 1889:234).

Malamine's fears of a ruse were not far-fetched: King Leopold had in fact used his influence over the association funding the Congo expedition to ensure that Brazza's bothersome outpost would be quietly abandoned. A letter from Mizon, Brazza's replacement, instructed Malamine to inform the local populace that France was giving up its ambitions in the area and to return to Gabon. Suspecting that something was amiss, and not wishing to disobey Brazza's original orders, he instead mounted a covert public relations operation unbeknownst to the lieutenant who had come bearing Mizon's orders. According to Chavannes (1935:40),

> [Malamine] never told the natives about the decision to pull up stakes. On the contrary, he swore to them and all the chiefs that his absence would be temporary, that he would come back with Major Brazza, and that until that day the French colors should continue to fly over their villages.

This task accomplished, the sergeant returned to Gabon, where he asked to be sent back to Senegal without delay, his contract having expired. His actions prior to departing M'Foa would have great significance for France's presence in the region.

The Mission de l'Ouest Africain

By the time these events transpired, Brazza was in France planning his third expedition. The French parliament ratified the Makoko treaty in November 1882, some six months after Malamine left the station at M'Foa, and in January 1883 the government approved full funding for another expedition. The following month a French army lieutenant arrived in Dakar to recruit the bulk of the mission's manpower. This time, instead of a mere dozen laptots, 139 were hired. The recruiter went to great lengths to track down Sergeant Malamine in Saint-Louis, as well as Samba Thiam, his former companion at M'Foa. Malamine also helped enlist other laptots, signing them to two-year contracts with 60 francs' pay per month, a very generous salary at the time. The expedition's personnel also included 25 Algerian riflemen, 25 noncommissioned military officers of whom Malamine was the only non-Frenchman, 21 auxiliary officers including Chavannes, and a general staff of 8. Many others picked by Brazza himself, including his younger brother Jacques (a naturalist), joined the roster, along with a motley assortment of unqualified men, nearly half of whom would be sent home within months. Finally, some 165 porters known as "kroomen" or "kroo-boys" were hired (perhaps more accurately press-ganged) in Liberia to perform the heavy hauling; they were given yearlong contracts, although Brazza hoped to replace most of them with local manpower in Gabon. Unlike Brazza's previous expeditions, the Mission de l'Ouest Africain was an enormous undertaking: between 400 and 500 men took part, only 87 of them European.[6]

Once this mass of men and equipment arrived on the Gabonese coast in late April 1883, it took months to acquire the necessary materiel, food, and canoes to set off. Eventually the mission divided its forces: while Brazza led some of its personnel down the coast to the mouth of the Congo, others penetrated the interior along the Ogowé and Niari valleys.

Albert Dolisie, the first member of l'Ouest Africain to arrive at the Pool in November 1883, did not receive the warm welcome he had hoped for. Residents of M'Foa remembered Malamine but apparently could not recall Brazza himself. Some accounts indicate that they had not flown the French tricolor during his absence, and there were even doubts over their loyalty to Makoko Iloo, whose sovereignty over the area was more ambiguous than Europeans realized.[7] Only in April 1884 did other members of the mission, including Chavannes and Jacques de Brazza, finally reach Makoko Iloo's royal court to present an official copy of the ratified treaty.

Malamine had accompanied Chavannes inland from Gabon and proved his worth wherever he went. In March 1884, wrote Chavannes (1935:142), upon recognizing the Senegalese sergeant, natives "were so happy to see him they danced with him"; "On the Congo," Chavannes would recall, "Malamine's presence was like a password" (1929:174). He was Brazza's interpreter on numerous official occasions, including negotiations and ritual ceremonies held to win and recognize local chiefs' loyalty.

Navigating down the Congo River, Chavannes's party found that Makoko Iloo remained faithful to his pact with Brazza: "The old chief had fully kept his word, resisting all attempts to weaken his fidelity. His immediate vassals had behaved the same way: Malamine's labor had paid off" (Chavannes 1929:175). After Makoko and his vassals ritually renewed their loyalty pledge to France, Chavannes described Malamine as "the linchpin of a long-term project of which this ceremony was the happy and formal consecration" (1929:179). Brazza and Chavannes spent several weeks in M'Foa, which was to become the new colony's administrative capital. The site, at that time just a small clearing dotted with a few thatched abodes, had already been dubbed "Brazzaville."[8]

On June 3, 1884, Brazza departed, leaving Chavannes in charge with Malamine as his trusted aide. Together Chavannes and the Senegalese sergeant chose sites for the construction of dwellings and administrative buildings along the riverbank; the first permanent structures were completed in September of that year. Malamine served as Chavannes's intermediary with the local populace and his most capable hunter, regularly bringing home antelope, buffalo, and hippopotamus he had killed outside the small settlement. Such was his importance in the emergent French possession that Belgian authorities across the river reportedly put a price on his head (Chavannes 1935). In February 1885, at Brazza's instructions, Chavannes, in a poignant ceremony, awarded the sergeant the *Médaille Militaire,* one of the rarest decorations given to noncitizens by the French military:

> The brave sergeant, who is usually moved by nothing, cannot manage to control his emotion, which is revealed by a barely perceptible trembling of his lips. For some time, he is suffering terribly from bladder problems and his features show clear signs of the pain he is in; he is thin, his hands are feverish, his gaze, still straight, has become less keen and his smile seems stiffened by a kind of worry as he is receiving his honors. I am doubtless the only one present who fully knows the man and I am gloomy. Rest is absolutely necessary for such a brave and devoted servant. (Chavannes 1935:248)

Chavannes was right: the post's doctor soon diagnosed Malamine's condition as probably fatal. A few months later the sergeant was sent home to Senegal and, in November, wrote to Chavannes and Brazza describing his dire situation.

Repatriated, beyond sick, to Senegal, able to collect in Gabon neither his pay nor the fairly significant reward justly granted him by a decision of the Government Commissioner for his exceptional services, he was dying in the Gorée hospital in the worst deprivation. His claims had still received no answer and he was calling upon the goodness of his former leader to help him out of this sorry state. This was expressed in terms full of respect and resignation. (Chavannes 1935:338)

Brazza, outraged that his Senegalese companion was so poorly treated by the country he had served so loyally, cabled French authorities urging them to remedy the situation. In January, however, he received news of Malamine's death; the sergeant had never been able to collect his pay.

At the conclusion of the Berlin Conference in February 1885, France and Belgium recognized each other's possessions in the Congo Basin and agreed on a border between them. France recalled Brazza the following month. With the end of the colonial land scramble, the French government ordered the personnel, resources, and stations of the Mission de l'Ouest Africain turned over to the navy. By July 1885 only about half the mission's original members remained in the new colony, and most of the African recruits left French service upon completing their two-year contracts (Coquery-Vidrovitch 1969b).

West Africans and the Extension of Colonial Rule in Central Africa

Now a formal colonial power in Equatorial Africa, France needed to gain effective administrative and military control over lands not yet fully explored and over populations resistant to its rule. Yet means were extremely limited: the French government was loath to invest funds in its new acquisition, and expected the colony to finance its own development. Brazza, who in 1886 became France's first colonial commissioner in Congo, no doubt encouraged the metropole's tightfistedness by wildly exaggerating the colony's mineral, agricultural, and human resources. By doing so, he unwittingly ensured that the colonial enterprise in Congo would remain chronically under-funded and under-manned.[9] Militarily speaking, at the onset of colonial occupation, the number of troops involved was minuscule: in 1885, writes Wagret (1963:25), "all the [French] possessions on the west coast of Africa, from Saint-Louis to Congo, were held by a company and a half of *tirailleurs sénégalais* [maximum 250 men] supported by a handful of artillerymen and a few engineers."

New contingents of West African laptots and *tirailleurs* arrived regularly on the Gabonese coast from 1886 on, however. These men formed both the backbone of the French colonial apparatus—serving as messengers, interpreters, and intermediaries—and the tip of its spear. Senegalese troops guarded French outposts, accompanied expeditions, and mounted punitive raids (led by white officers) on rebellious local communities. Though some European colonizers died during this period, mostly of disease, the laptots and *tirailleurs* bore far greater casualties. For the first few decades of colonial rule the ratio of West Africans to Europeans in most French posts was at least five to one, and often much higher. The numbers of West African soldiers grew steadily: by 1897 French military presence in Congo consisted of 630 *tirailleurs*, led by only 15 white officers. In contrast, there were just 100 French administrators in Equatorial Africa in 1905, fewer than half of them based outside Brazzaville.[10]

Across the Congo River, Belgian administrators of the so-called Congo Free State also depended on imported West African manpower. Faced with high costs of bringing Zanzibaris across the breadth of the continent, a shortage of personnel to occupy the lower rungs of its administration, and severe difficulties in recruiting manpower locally, Belgian authorities began looking for labor elsewhere in Africa. Between 1883 and 1901 they recruited 12,500 foreign troops for their Force Publique, primarily from Zanzibar, Sierra Leone, the Gold Coast (modern Ghana), and "Hausaland" in northern Nigeria. This recruitment was not limited to the militia: demand for workers was particularly strong for the construction of the Chemin de Fer Léopoldville-Matadi, the railway linking the Free State's capital Leopoldville with the coast. Recruitment took place in British posts from the Gambia to Lagos. Nearly 2,000 foreign Africans were recruited to work on this project between 1890 and 1898, when the railroad was inaugurated, while a mere 52 workers came from local populations. Mistreatment of British colonial subjects working in the Belgian colony, coupled with abuse of native populations, fueled a public outcry in Britain, eventually leading to a diplomatic row between the two European powers over trading rights and allegations of inhumane treatment.[11]

Belgian recruiters also traveled to Senegal to find skilled labor for their new railway, and in 1890 they began recruiting in Saint-Louis, where a railway had been completed eight years earlier. Although French authorities frowned upon these recruitments, King Leopold's agents nonetheless managed to hire significant numbers of West Africans in Senegal until 1894, when the French began intercepting vessels conveying these would-be emigrants from Senegalese harbors. Following the French crackdown, the Belgians moved their operations to the Gambia where they could tap the same workforce without French interference. Many of those recruited in the Gambia were probably relatives of those who had earlier gone to Congo from Senegal; most came from

Senegal and were of Soninke ethnicity. A large number of these recruits were eventually enrolled in the Belgian colonial army.[12]

As France extended its control into the African interior during the 1890s, its West African troops participated in some twenty exploratory missions through areas of what are today Congo, Cameroon, Chad, and the Central African Republic. French officers held their qualities in high esteem. "I have found in all the Senegalese I have brought with me a devotion which has not failed even in the most difficult circumstances," wrote Jean Dybowski (1893:78), after leading an expedition from the Gabonese coast into what is now Chad.

West African personnel were also used in routine punitive raids against rebellious local populations. These operations multiplied following the imposition of a colonial head tax in 1898. Administrative correspondence and memoirs report countless violent incidents resulting in the death or injury of Senegalese personnel. From 1897 until 1920, "more or less widespread uprisings were continual" in the colony (Coquery-Vidrovitch 1969a:172). Perhaps because of its inherent dangers, service in the Congo colony was so unpopular among West African recruits that in 1902 a French general in Senegal expressed concern that sending so many men to Congo would harm his country's overall recruiting efforts in West Africa.[13]

West African troops were hardly victims in these conflicts, however: as the instruments of French colonial power, they meted out far more violence than they received from Congolese populations. Nor did they always act within the disciplinary bounds set by their French commanders. Laptots were occasionally punished for looting supply caravans, shooting unarmed natives, and exacting tax payments. In theory, their role was merely to inform village chiefs of their duty to bring tax payments to the nearest French outpost (usually in the form of wild rubber, ivory, and occasionally grain to feed soldiers). In practice, troops sometimes demanded payment themselves and were often responsible for "abominable acts" against civilians:

> The most expeditious means were applied, outside the direct control of the administrator: the size of his district required him to entrust collection to a detachment of militia. Senegalese laptots put everything to fire and the sword and served themselves at villagers' expense; they left a terrified memory in the country. (Coquery-Vidrovitch 2001:127)

Perhaps foreseeing such difficulties, Brazza planned to employ West African troops to train a Congolese militia force, although these plans never came to fruition. In early 1891 two companies of *tirailleurs sénégalais* were dispatched from Congo to assist in the French invasion of Dahomey (today known as Benin), intensifying a shortage of troops in Central Africa. Administrators hoped to recruit an eight-hundred-man local militia, but budget constraints limited its size to only three hundred. Ultimately France turned to its new possessions to the north, Ubangi-Shari (now the Central African Republic) and Chad, to supply soldiers for Congo; compared to Congolese, outsiders like Chadians and Senegalese were "reported to be tougher and ran less risk of fraternizing with recalcitrant populations" (Gondola 1996:60–61). By 1903 Senegalese made up only 35 percent of France's troop presence in Congo (though they still constituted half or more in Gabon and Chad); eight years later there were twelve hundred *tirailleurs* in Congo, most of them from Chad and Ubangi-Shari. It was not until the end of the First World War that native Congolese troops formed a majority in the colony's security forces.[14]

In 1899, strapped for funds, French administrators parceled their Congo colony out to forty-one private "concessionary companies," granting each sole rights to exploit its concession of land. More than two-thirds of present-day Congolese territory was ceded to these companies. Brazza himself had lobbied for such an arrangement, which he felt would protect native populations from the excesses of unfettered competition between European businesses.[15] But the so-called concessionary regime in Congo turned into a humanitarian and economic disaster, stemming from "the same unholy alliance of state authority and private monopoly which had provoked such a catastrophic situation in the Congo Free State" (Manchuelle 1987:369). Companies resorted to the most abhorrent methods to extract raw materials (particularly wild rubber) and labor from local populations.[16] In May 1905 Brazza led an official inquiry into reports of widespread mistreatment of colonial subjects by concessionary companies and complicit colonial administrators. This was to be his final African mission: suffering from dysentery, he died during the return voyage but not before writing a report so damning of the concessionary regime that France's parliament voted to have it suppressed. Nonetheless, revelations that French rule in Central Africa was scarcely less rapacious than that of King Leopold in the Belgian Congo, which by then had generated considerable public scandal around the world (Hochschild 1998), belied France's pretensions of conducting a "civilizing mission" in Africa.

Like the colonial administration itself, concessionary companies relied on West African personnel for many of their operations. They often had Senegalese operate their trading posts, and "gladly hired former *tirailleurs* or militiamen to watch over and intimidate workers and villagers in their domain" (Coquery-Vidrovitch 2001:94). In 1904, a year before Brazza's inquest, the concessionary companies in Congo employed a total of 206 Senegalese, 291 Sierra Leoneans, and 200 "miscellaneous" Africans, compared to 210 Europeans.[17] Though some of its worst abuses were curbed in the wake of Brazza's mission, the concessionary regime remained in place for several more years before most of the participating companies went bankrupt.

Emerging West African Communities

In 1921 construction finally began on both ends of the 500-km route of the Chemin de Fer Congo-Océan (CFCO) in Brazzaville and the port city of Pointe-Noire. The railroad project employed local workers as well as laborers recruited from outside the colony, principally from Chad and Ubangi-Shari but, by 1929, even from Hong Kong and Vietnam. The colony remained dependent on West African and other foreign African workers to fill skilled jobs: according to a government report, quoted by Martin (1995:22), the administration made a priority of recruiting "mechanics, smiths, and carpenters from Senegal, woodworkers from Sierra Leone and Accra, smiths and laundrymen from Cabinda, and plantation overseers from São Tomé." Oral accounts gathered in Brazzaville indicate that skilled West African workers were also brought to Congo as railroad employees upon the CFCO's completion in 1934. Colonial preference for outside labor was a hallmark of European rule in Africa: administrators in each colony tended to cast local subjects as lazy and recalcitrant, and subjects from other colonies as dynamic and entrepreneurial.[18]

In Brazzaville from the 1890s a *village sénégalais* named "Dakar," adjacent to the French administrative center, was home to a sizable West African community with its own chief. In 1909 the French demarcated Poto-Poto[19] and Bacongo, two "indigenous quarters" (so-called to distinguish them from Brazzaville proper, reserved for whites); at the same time they relocated the Senegalese neighborhood, which had apparently grown too close to the administrative zone for comfort, to a spot adjoining Poto-Poto. A camp for the *tirailleurs* known as "Chad" also existed. By 1914 some four thousand Africans were living in Brazzaville, and the indigenous neighborhood of Poto-Poto had been subdivided into seven ethnically organized *quartiers,* including a Senegalese quarter. A Qur'anic school was established in Poto-Poto around the turn of the century, and Brazzaville's first mosque was built in the heart of this neighborhood in the 1920s on land donated by a Senegalese woman named Fatou Diagne; its construction was entirely financed by members of the local Muslim population, most of them West Africans. The neighborhood included unaccompanied West African workers and some families: until cost-cutting measures eliminated the practice in 1905, the colonial administration paid for foreign employees' wives to be brought to the colony. Many West African men sent for their own wives from home or went home for visits and returned with their families; others married Congolese women who converted to Islam.[20]

On the Pool's opposite bank, Leopoldville (which was subsequently renamed Kinshasa) had its own West African neighborhood by the early twentieth century: Manchuelle reports that

> Soninke migrants who left Senegal in the 1890s to go work on the Matadi-Kinshasa railway . . . were certainly well established by the turn of the century. In fact, oral tradition among the Soninke even mentions that the Soninke had a permanent establishment in the Belgian Congo even before the building of Kinshasa. (1987:444)

In the 1920s one of Leopoldville's first officially recognized voluntary associations was the Mutuelle Sénégalaise, which was soon joined by a corresponding association for immigrants from Togo and Dahomey. In the 1930s Leopoldville was home to hundreds of African Muslims, most of them Senegalese; they were described as well-dressed, organized, and cohesive, with their own *qadi* (Islamic judge) to settle internal disputes. By the 1940s their community boasted two mosques, one of them dating to 1910.[21]

West Africans in the Congo Basin as Private Entrepreneurs

Thus far in my narrative, West African presence in the Congo Basin has appeared entirely dependent on European colonization; this population constituted an "auxiliary diaspora," to use Robin Cohen's term (1997:84). It was the French and the Belgians, after all, who brought soldiers, messengers, porters, and other laborers from Senegal and elsewhere in the West African region. If Europeans helped introduce West Africans to Congo, however, once that introduction was made many West Africans began following their own agendas. Theirs is the least-documented and least-emphasized aspect of this history. The few times they are mentioned in the historical record are nonetheless telling.

Upon arriving on the Gabonese coast with Malamine and the rest of his second expedition in April 1880, Brazza noted in his journal that, since his previous visit, a *factorerie* (trading post) had been set up there by Woermann, a German firm. This was not unusual, as non-French traders had been allowed in Gabon since 1849, and large British firms like John Holt and Hatton & Cookson had come to dominate business in the territory. What made this new trading post noteworthy was its mostly Senegalese personnel, all of them ex-laptots who had remained in Gabon after the end of their contracts, *including two of the thirteen laptots from Brazza's first mission.* At that time six Senegalese and four Gabonese worked at the post under a Senegalese trader named Boubou N'Diaye. By the end of 1880 N'Diaye's staff had grown to fifteen Senegalese and more than twenty local Gabonese agents. They operated trading posts hundreds of miles inland, where they sold trade goods to local inhabitants and bought wild rubber in return.[22]

These traders complicated Brazza's work as an explorer and representative of France. At the outset he had great difficulty finding enough dugout canoes to equip his second and third expeditions, partly because, by the time Brazza's group arrived on the Ogowé River, N'Diaye's men had bought up most available canoes there for their own use. Their commercial activities also generated problems for the French. Brazza, fearing the damaging effects of unrestrained commercial competition, sought to bar the traders from doing business upriver of a certain falls on the Ogowé. Some of N'Diaye's Senegalese employees had already had violent encounters with local populations, and hence Brazza's deputy Mizon wrote in 1882 that it was "impossible ... to permit the traders to penetrate among the gentle and fearful populations of the upper river, given the actions committed by the Senegalese" (Brunschwig 1972:253).

West African traders eventually threatened French colonial authority in Equatorial Africa. At the end of his third mission in 1885, Brazza wrote that trading companies in the lower Ogowé had hired former laptots as agents, arming them with modern rifles and even cannons. The colonial administration banned the possession of modern rifles by private subjects but could not enforce this measure beyond the coastal areas (Coquery-Vidrovitch 1969b:280).

In the 1890s West African laborers and tradesmen bound for the Belgian Congo also profited from their mobility by taking part in commerce. When ships taking them from Dakar to the Congolese port of Matadi stopped off in Lagos, Nigeria, West Africans would buy Dutch wax-print cloth to sell to Congolese at their destination. "Thus many," writes Manchuelle (1987:445), "became cloth merchants, first in the localities along the Boma-Matadi-Kinshasa railway, then in Kinshasa, and then finally later on in all the regional towns of the Belgian Congo, and in Brazzaville."

Gradually entrepreneurial activity became a mainstay for West Africans in the Congo Basin. It may have been a sideline for many who practiced it in the early decades of colonization, but a number of commercial specialists did emerge in colonial Brazzaville's small-business sector. By 1899 three of the six retail businesses in Brazzaville belonged to Senegalese entrepreneurs, the remainder belonging to Portuguese and Spanish traders. Whether as agents of trading firms, employees of concessionary companies, or independent merchants, West Africans were clearly enthusiastic participants in the budding commercial activity of the Congo colonies. Oral histories collected in a Senegalese Soninke village show that the Congo Basin was a popular destination for that community's traders from the 1920s. Thus what began as an auxiliary diaspora soon morphed into a commercial diaspora.[23]

These traders had a great impact on Congolese life, particularly in urban areas. The textiles they imported and sold shaped the region's emerging fashion trends. Martin (1995:164) reports that the influx of imported fabrics was well established by the 1920s in Brazzaville, where

> [the] Poto-Poto and Bacongo markets were described as a "mass of cloths." Although a great deal of cloth was marketed by the Senegalese, Dahomeyan traders also established an important community in Brazzaville between the wars.... For women, wax and fancy prints sold by West Africans were most valued.

Imported clothing material and styles have been fixtures of Congolese society since the early twentieth century.[24] The emergence of these colonial-era clothing fashions was enabled in large part by West African commerce in the Congo Basin.

What were these migrants after? Whether through colonial service or independent commerce or some combination of the two, their main goal was acquiring wealth with which to compete for status in their home communities. I contend that migration from West Africa to the Congo Basin was a "strategy of extraversion," a means of mobilizing resources derived from the unequal relationship between colonized African societies and their external environment.[25] These migrants used French colonial service to gain access not only to salaries but also to other rewards on the African continent. Entrée to the Congo Basin, initially provided by the Europeans, soon became a means for individuals and families in the western Sahel to acquire wealth and prestige, and to expand their existing commercial networks into previously undeveloped markets. Far from simply occupying a void left by the colonizer, they had to carve out a commercial space within which to operate in Central Africa, one that at times interfered with colonial interests.

New Urban Dynamics in the Congo Basin

From the 1930s on, new Congolese identities were constructed in cities. In the French and Belgian colonies alike, modern identities emerged in urban communities during the period. Georges Balandier, whose research in Brazzaville's burgeoning African quarters (the "black Brazzavilles," as he called them) in the late 1940s and early 1950s was the first to analyze *urban* social dynamics in a French African colony, identified the city as "the site of a grand transformation, the front lines of a modernity advancing in fits and starts" (1985:vii). The city was the birthplace of new social norms and the site where Europeans definitively demarcated their African subjects' ethnic affiliations: as elsewhere in Africa, rather than reflecting primordial ties of culture and kinship, these affiliations were essentially colonial creations. The colonial capital city (characterized by a rigid segregation of African and European residents, and the saturation of all public space with manifestations of power) molded an enduring, highly centralized, and exclusivist political framework that has proven especially destructive in recent years.[26] Moreover, economic developments in these colonies during the postwar period transformed the ways in which Congolese related to the city and to West Africans.

Brazzaville had been the capital of French Equatorial Africa since 1910 but rose to greater prominence during the Second World War as the temporary capital of Free France. Charles de Gaulle established Radio-Brazzaville as the voice of Free France, and in October 1940 he made a triumphal visit to the city where he was greeted at the airport by thousands of cheering Congolese, including members of Brazzaville's West African community hoisting a banner proclaiming "We Want to Stay French" (West 1972:223). In 1944 de Gaulle presided over the "Brazzaville Conference" introducing important reforms in the colonies such as freedom of association and the end of forced labor.

The war's political consequences for Brazzaville were matched by equally momentous economic and social consequences extending to both banks of the Congo River. First, the war effort induced colonial administrators to increase production of raw materials, particularly minerals and rubber (large supplies of which had been cut off by the Japanese in the Pacific). From 1941 to 1942 port activity in the Belgian Congo rose nearly 40 percent. Next, in both French and Belgian colonies, as Europeans went off to fight, many Africans subsequently found themselves "raised to levels of responsibility previously reserved only for

Europeans" in government offices and private firms (Gondola 1996:128); some of these were indigenous Congolese, and others were West Africans brought in to fill the vacant positions. Finally, the colonizer's reliance on forced labor in the rural areas prior to 1944 constituted a powerful "push factor" impelling young men toward the city. The combined effect was explosive demographic growth: in Leopoldville the population swelled from about 47,000 to 96,000 between 1940 and 1946, and in Brazzaville it rose from 22,000 to 33,500 over the same period (Gondola 1996).

Brazzaville continued to grow despite diminished economic prospects after the war. Vennetier (1963:277–278) states that "migration to cities [was] less economic than psychological," stemming from unreasonable expectations nourished by the educational system. Formal schooling had also experienced a vigorous development in the colony beginning before the war. From 1935 to 1945 the number of students in public primary schools in Congo increased by 116 percent. By 1951 Congo had the highest rate of primary school enrollment in French Equatorial Africa with 51 percent of Congolese children attending school, nearly double the rates in neighboring Gabon and Cameroon.[27] Education, according to the French construction of the "evolved" African subject, was the most crucial requirement for becoming modern, and the demand for schooling in the colony reflected the desire of most Congolese to achieve that status for their children if not for themselves. By law, schooling could only be conducted in the French language, and so by the 1950s French fluency, though no longer limited to a small *évolué* class, remained the primary criterion of modern, "civilized" life for Africans in the colony.

Despite these advances in education, immigrants from outside Congo continued to dominate the colony's administrative apparatus and private sector even until the end of the colonial era. In the mid-1950s the colonial labor department found that "at least 80 percent of [salaried] jobs are held by natives [i.e., Africans] foreign to French Equatorial Africa—Dahomeyans, Cameroonians, Togolese, Senegalese" (Balandier 1985:68). This imbalance contributed to growing rivalry and resentment between West Africans and Congolese, as did the political privileges of some West Africans: natives of Senegal's "Four Communes" (Dakar, Gorée, Rufisque, and Saint-Louis) had held French citizenship rights since 1848 and could vote in French national elections. In France's Congo colony, however, colonial subjects had no voting rights until 1946, and then only in a separate African electoral college. Natives of the Belgian Congo, for their part, had no civil rights until independence in 1960. Throughout most of the colonial period, therefore, West African immigrants enjoyed freedoms that their Congolese hosts could scarcely dream of, a fact that fostered "feelings of frustration and envy among the [Congolese] population" (Manchuelle 1987:447).

Immigrants' own actions further stoked this resentment. West Africans living in French equatorial colonies tended to be very public in their support for the colonial administration, which they saw as their only source of protection in a foreign land. They were suspected of supplying informants to the French security services at a time when anti-colonial activism was taking root in the region. They often adopted disdainful attitudes toward Congolese, calling them *Congo zoba*—from the Lingala word *zoba* meaning "idiot" or "stupid"—as well as other insults.[28] Such condescension stemmed from the West Africans' superior economic and political status in the region, evident in the words of one of my interviewees, the Brazzaville-born son of a man who came from Mali in the 1940s. "In our fathers' time, after *tubabuw* [whites], West Africans. After West Africans, locals," he told me, describing prerogatives West Africans enjoyed that locals did not. "White people had been in West Africa for a long time and knew it well; they respected our fathers. Our fathers could take the *vedette* [speed boat] over to Leopoldville at midnight and go dancing then return at 5:00 AM. The boat was driven by white people."

Work and Entrepreneurship in Postwar Congo

When I asked West African traders in Brazzaville—from importers to shopkeepers to ambulant vendors—why they came to do business there, they often said something to the effect that "Congolese do not trade." Sometimes they explain this response in terms of an innate predisposition and sometimes in terms of a preference conditioned by the social environment in Congo. Congolese simply do not *like* to engage in commerce, I was told repeatedly by West Africans and sometimes by Congolese themselves. Congolese prefer to put on a coat and tie and work in a government office.

Historical data and statistics bear these claims out. The French expanded recruitment of Congolese clerks and administrative assistants in 1948, and the opportunity to earn a civil service salary thoroughly transformed Congo's social fabric. For the colony's first parliamentary elections in the 1950s, half the candidates were local civil servants. Congo's upper-level government workers formed what John Clark (2005:107) calls a "bureaucratic bourgeoisie," an urban political and economic elite that has supplied virtually every member of the Congolese ruling class since the end of the colonial era. Membership in this class was determined by access not to property but to government salaries and benefits; social and cultural assets, particularly education, were much more important than economic capital for gaining entrée to the upper strata of society. To this day, the Congolese elite remains highly dependent on the Congolese state.[29]

Most West Africans who came to Brazzaville in the decades following the Second World War had no such reliance on salaried employment. Instead, they came as entrepreneurs. As we have seen, from the onset of colonial penetration, West African personnel in the Congo Basin turned to commerce upon completing their contracts. By the mid-twentieth century West Africans came to the region for the express purpose of pursuing opportunities in trade. The testimonies I gathered from informants in Brazzaville, whether of their own or their parents' or grandparents' lives, suggest that by the 1940s the migration flow from the West African Sahel to the Congo Basin was dominated by independent migrants and no longer by colonial employees. Some came to Congo almost by accident, diverted from overland pilgrimages to Mecca or attempts to emigrate elsewhere. Others had heard of Brazzaville before leaving home (by then, many told me, the city already had a reputation as a good place to do business) and set out for Congo on ships from ports in Côte d'Ivoire or Senegal. Some who came by sea settled in Pointe-Noire, and others continued to Brazzaville by train.

Once in Congo, a new arrival had to find a *jatigi* or host.[30] The *jatigi* could be anyone who was willing to provide housing; this person was usually a senior male and preferably a relative of the new immigrant. The *jatigi* often owned a large residential compound with multiple rooms and dozens of lodgers. Lodgers were expected to pay a daily sum to the *jatigi* for room and board. Meals were prepared in common by the women who lived in the compound; informants told me that the ratio of men to women could be as high as ten to one in a West African compound during the 1950s. Domestic labor was also hired from outside the home to offset the shortage of women; young men, mostly from the Belgian Congo, did chores such as washing and ironing.[31]

People coming to Brazzaville in the postwar years found a rapidly expanding city, which by the early 1950s was home to one hundred thousand people. Most West African arrivals, like those before them, settled in Poto-Poto, the city's fastest-growing district. From 1945 to 1950 Poto-Poto welcomed between three thousand and five thousand new residents every year. By 1951 it was a densely populated neighborhood with nearly sixty thousand residents, the cosmopolitan heart of the city's African population (Balandier 1985).

Brazzaville's West African immigrants during this period were dominated by members of four ethnic groups: the Hausa, the Wolof, the Soninke, and the Halpulaaren. The Hausa came from northern Nigeria and had a small community in Poto-Poto composed of exclusively unaccompanied men, mainly merchants or laborers; this community shrank from the 1950s and has all but vanished today. The Wolof, who had been active in colonial service and as skilled tradesmen, had a larger and more visible presence: they controlled the *grande mosquée* or main mosque, which also became known as the *mosquée sénégalaise* or "Senegalese mosque," the imam of which was always Wolof. They were also well established in the jewelry trade, and Wolof families still own many shops in Poto-Poto's small jewelry district. The Wolof population declined steadily over the years, however, as many of the jobs Wolofs had occupied were taken over by Congolese. By the 1960s they formed a small minority of the city's West African population.

The Soninke and Halpulaaren, who came from Senegal and especially from Mali, were primarily involved in commerce. They ran the gamut from ambulant vendors to small shopkeepers to wholesale merchants. Many hailed from western Mali and from the zone bordering Mauritania to the north. Others, especially Bamanan and Maninka from central and southern Mali, were also present in Brazzaville's emerging commercial sector, which was never the domain of a single ethnic group or geographic area. From its inception, the West African population in Brazzaville was multiethnic, encompassing peoples from throughout the western Sahel. Nor did these migrants come only from higher social strata: some of the most successful were *nyamakala*, members of hereditary castes such as blacksmiths, griots, and leatherworkers, whose status in their society of origin was marginal at best.[32]

The case of Modi, the father of one of my informants, illustrates not only the diverse origins of Brazzaville's West African population but also the wide range of economic activities in which its members engaged during the third quarter of the twentieth century.

> Modi arrived in Brazzaville as a young man shortly after World War Two. He was a leatherworker of the *garanke* caste from a village in Mali's Segou region. After leaving home he spent some time in Abidjan, Côte d'Ivoire, where he met another leatherworker from south of Bamako, and the two of them worked together curing hides and making leather bags for sale. Hearing about Brazzaville from a friend's uncle who claimed that business there was better than in Abidjan, they decided to make the trip. Once in Brazzaville they looked up the head of the town's Malian association who became their *jatigi*. They continued to make and sell bags, now using croco-

dile, snake, and lizard skins instead of cattle hides. Many of their customers were Frenchmen, as well as Belgians who took the ferry across the river from Leopoldville for the day.

The two men established their own clienteles, accumulated savings, and set up their own households. Modi married a Congolese woman in 1949. In 1955 he made a return visit to Abidjan, where he bought a house for his mother to live in. Four years later, after learning that diamonds had been discovered near Bangui, he immediately traveled there and became the regular customer of a diamond seller in a remote village. Modi took his stones to a Malian friend in Bangui and sold them at a 150 percent profit; his friend would then resell them to European buyers. Modi was only in the diamond business for a year before being arrested by the French and deported to Mali. Subsequently he returned to Congo where he began trading in crocodile skins and ivory. He bought real estate in Brazzaville and established bakeries there and in a provincial town. Eventually Modi built a commercial empire, which his sons continued to manage after his death in 1989.

Modi's success demonstrates the potential rewards available to those willing to run risks in Central Africa during the mid-twentieth century. Many informants represented wealth as simply there for the taking during the late colonial and early postcolonial era. People entering an emerging market stood to make huge returns on their initial investments during this period. This was particularly true where precious gems were concerned: although few Sahelian migrants were ever directly involved in them, transnational diamond trading networks shaped migration patterns for many West Africans from the 1950s on.

The Development of the African Diamond Trade

West Africa's first "diamond rush" began in 1952, when tens of thousands of would-be diggers—many of them Malians—descended on newly opened diamond fields in Sierra Leone, Guinea, and western Côte d'Ivoire hoping to strike it rich. The actual diggers were usually local men; migrants were more likely to be buyers and intermediaries. The most successful were those who set themselves up as shopkeepers to supply the diggers and buyers with provisions, while others found ways to profit indirectly as griots or *marabouts* (Muslim clerics) working near the diamond fields.[33]

Migrants' activities were mostly clandestine: they often lacked official authorization to buy or sell stones. Hence their presence in the mining areas was not long tolerated by host governments, which preferred to expel the foreigners rather than let them siphon away a strategic resource. In November 1956 Sierra Leone initiated a wave of crackdowns in the region by arresting thousands of foreigners in the mining zones and deporting them; authorities in Guinea and Côte d'Ivoire soon followed suit. Such expulsions subsequently became a preferred tactic of governments of Africa's gem-exporting countries: Congo-Kinshasa, Burundi, Zambia, and Angola all carried out repeated deportations of clandestine foreign miners and traders, many of them West Africans, from the 1960s.

As West African governments clamped down on clandestine mining activity on their territory, a more exclusive migration flow, originating mostly in Senegal, Mali, and Guinea, developed in the direction of Central Africa. Now Ubangi-Shari and the Belgian Congo began to attract West African diamond traffickers, known as *diamantaires*, many of whom came directly from the closed-off diamond zones of Guinea, Sierra Leone, and Côte d'Ivoire. Though the French Congo colony produced virtually no diamonds of its own, Brazzaville became a central hub of the diamantaire networks. Because of its relative calm and stable currency pegged to the French franc, traders preferred to set up their headquarters there while maintaining "satellite offices" near the diamond fields in Congo-Kinshasa. This role was not new: diamond-buying offices, or *comptoirs*, had already been established in Brazzaville in the 1930s to trade in stones brought there from the colony's neighbors. The French colonial administration even found it necessary, in 1938, to ban the possession and sale of diamonds except by those granted explicit government authorization.[34]

Nonetheless, diamantaires found room to operate in the French colonies and throughout the Belgian Congo. They had a freer hand following independence in 1960. By 1961 there were seventeen comptoirs in Brazzaville belonging to traders of various nationalities, doing enough business to pose a threat to the monopoly held by the international diamond cartel de Beers. The quantities in question were significant: in the first three months of 1963 up to 3.1 million carats of rough diamonds were exported from Congo-Brazzaville, most of them having been smuggled from Congo-Kinshasa; by 1965 the number of stones exported from Brazzaville was equivalent to 42 percent of its neighbor's total annual production. Such a large volume of supposedly clandestine trafficking could only take place with the collusion of customs and police officials on both banks of the Congo. In 1963 de Beers urged the government of the newly independent Republic of Congo to shut down the independent Brazzaville comptoirs, but Congolese President Fulbert Youlou, who had an especially close relationship with at least one wealthy Malian diamantaire, refused to take action against them.[35]

Those diamantaires who did not sell their stones in Brazzaville did so in West African towns such as Monrovia, Bamako, or Abidjan. A circuit for the trade of precious gems developed during the 1960s linking these cities to Brazzaville and Kinshasa. The circuit also extended to the South African city of Johannesburg (Africa's diamond capital), the Zambian capital Lusaka (where emeralds were bought and sold), and eventually Bujumbura, Burundi, and Nairobi, Kenya. Cities in the interior of Congo-Kinshasa such as Lubumbashi, M'Buji-Mayi, and Kisangani were also home to small West African commercial communities. "Frontline" areas like M'Buji-Mayi, close to the diamond fields, attracted diamantaires whose families stayed behind in safer locations such as Brazzaville or Bujumbura. Thus the circuits within which diamantaires moved widened progressively through the 1960s, and as their locations branched out so did their economic interests. While living in many of these peripheral locations, they traded in other minerals including malachite, tanzanite, and gold. Some became involved in the parallel commerce in ivory, closely connected to transnational gem trading and dominated by Malian businessmen who controlled the entire commodity chain from the buying offices in Burundi and Zambia to the ivory comptoirs of Antwerp.[36]

Diamantaires transferred their operations between these locations according to local economic and political climates: when one country tightened its customs and export controls, business would shift elsewhere; a rise in political instability or the threat of expulsion in one place would similarly reorient traders' activities to lower-risk areas. (The most common displacement during the 1960s and 1970s took the form of moving to Brazzaville when things turned sour in Kinshasa and then returning to Kinshasa when the situation improved.) The lives of some of my Brazzaville informants reflect the expansion of these various networks across Africa: children of gem traders, they were born in Sierra Leone, Liberia, Congo-Kinshasa, the Central African Republic, Kenya, or Angola. Some spent several years growing up in these countries, and others were raised in Mali, Côte d'Ivoire, or elsewhere prior to undertaking their own migrations as young adults. Some remember bits and pieces of the English, Kiswahili, Portuguese, or other languages they acquired as children abroad, and a few retain the citizenship of those countries where they were born.

As in the days of the West African diamond rush, much of the profits from Central Africa's diamond trade were indirect. Men acting as *jatigi* hosts for gem traders created an especially important niche for themselves. The *jatigi* would take in a newly arrived diamantaire, provide him with temporary lodging, and arrange to find a buyer for his stones. (In doing so he put himself at risk: he could be arrested for complicity if his charge's contraband were discovered.) Having the trust of both parties, he acted as guarantor for the transaction. He might also provide money-changing or interpreting services, all for a percentage of the sale. It was the *jatigi*'s very rootedness, his familiarity with the local community, and especially the relationships he cultivated with local officials that permitted the highly mobile lifestyle of the diamantaire (see chapter 5). Some Brazzaville *jatigis* used their accumulated profits from this activity to establish themselves as merchants or acquire real estate holdings. A few obtained expensive government authorizations and became legitimate diamond traders in their own right.

Since the twilight of the colonial era, the figure of the diamantaire has been the stuff of legends in the West African Sahel. The image in the popular imagination has been of a supremely wealthy individual who holds multiple passports, owns palatial homes, and jets regularly between Africa and glamorous European destinations. But being a diamantaire was and remains an extremely risky profession: crime, civil unrest, and troubles with the authorities are all endemic to the business and pose an ever-present danger to one's assets; the threat of sudden arrest and deportation, resulting in the loss of all one's assets in the host country, is acute. For these reasons, the hardest thing for a diamantaire with money to do is to hold on to it. "Everything they earned, they weren't able to invest it," one elderly informant in Brazzaville told me of the diamantaires he knew. "Money came in and went out, came in and went out. Today, they've got problems."

The stereotype of the jet-setting diamantaire also obscures an important fact about the Central African diamond trade: as Modi's example in the previous section shows, not every immigrant who participated in the trade came to the region purposely to do so, nor did they remain in the business indefinitely. Many traded in diamonds for only a few years or even a few months. The most successful entrepreneurs over the long term were those who, like Modi, managed at an early stage to diversify their operations and invest their diamond profits in safer interests such as building construction, real estate, and retail commerce. The big players in Brazzaville's West African commercial community during my fieldwork, those who got their start there during the 1950s and 1960s, were often involved in diamonds before moving into other activities that permitted them to safeguard their fortunes. Most acquired Congolese citizenship in the 1970s, finding powerful patrons in the Congolese elite to protect their interests and discourage the predations of various authorities. Some took Congolese wives and used their marriage alliances to cement their ties to those in power; sometimes they registered their businesses in their wives' names to lower their visibility as foreigners and head off potential recriminations in the event of trouble. Such tactics were common to West African businessmen and diamantaires throughout Africa (Bredeloup 1994).

One must be careful not to overstate the diamantaires' significance, both in terms of their numbers and their economic impact. In Congo-Kinshasa, which was home to the largest concentration of diamantaires in the 1960s, very few members of the "Senegalese" community (most of whom were, in fact, Malian and Guinean) were actually involved in the trade of precious gems.

> Contrary to popular opinion, the diamond trade holds a very marginal place in Senegalese activities and, in the smuggling capital of M'Buji-Mayi, there are perhaps 100 to 150 "Senegalese" in the broad sense. Almost all of these merchants are in general commerce, sometimes in transportation. Certainly some large fortunes have been made there which are spoken of in émigré circles; but it doesn't appear that these were made in diamonds, but are rather for marabouts who undoubtedly found there a naïve clientele. (Amin 1969:164)

Throughout the Congo Basin, diamantaires have always constituted a tiny fraction of the West Africans in the region. Their activities, however, did help cement West African commercial domination in cities like Brazzaville and contributed to an aura of prosperity around the immigrant population there, which kindled hope among would-be migrants back home as well as resentment among many Congolese.

Independence and Its Aftermath in the Congo Basin

The Belgian Congo became the independent Democratic Republic of Congo on June 30, 1960, and on August 15 France's Congo colony became the independent Republic of Congo. Congo-Kinshasa quickly sank into political turmoil, beset by secessionist movements and Cold War intrigue, and West Africans living there faced new challenges. Kinshasa became a difficult place to do business: prices were in constant flux along with the national currency, and supplies of goods were erratic even in the best of times.

Across the Congo River, the Republic of Congo remained more stable and tranquil than its larger neighbor. It also remained firmly dependent upon France which, in addition to supporting its currency, kept a strong presence there. Unlike Congo-Kinshasa, Congo-Brazzaville had a tiny population (fewer than eight hundred thousand inhabitants in 1960, with one hundred thousand in Brazzaville) and a tiny economy. Its industrial and commercial sectors remained underdeveloped. Apart from the diamonds transiting its territory, it had few strategic minerals (offshore oil deposits, discovered in the 1950s, would not contribute significantly to national revenues until the early 1970s). Timber, logged in the country's northern forests, was the primary export. During this period Brazzaville became a kind of regional entrepôt, a distribution center profiting from its central location and its stable currency to provide a reliable market for buyers from neighboring countries. The city's merchants attracted a foreign wholesale clientele, especially from Kinshasa, buying products that were unavailable or prohibitively expensive in their city. This commerce drew growing numbers of West African immigrants to Brazzaville.

Young Congolese also flocked to the city from the countryside. Some sought to escape the oppressive domination of traditional lineage systems, while others wanted to continue their schooling (secondary schools were concentrated in urban areas) or access the social benefits of city life. Statistics from the period reveal a constantly shrinking workforce and aging population in rural areas, while urban populations grew ever younger. This "rural exodus" dealt a serious blow to agricultural activity in Congo: in 1964 three-quarters of the national labor force was involved in farming, but by 1983 that figure had fallen to just one-third. Domestic food production fell as urban demand grew, making the country increasingly dependent on imported food products, the value of which skyrocketed over 300 percent during the 1970s.[37]

The Congolese government only worsened this imbalance with policies marked by what development experts call "urban bias." It subsidized imported foods such as beef, rice, and flour, which were staples of the urban diet, but invested very little money in the agricultural sector. Inefficient state control of food marketing boards discouraged farmers from producing. Furthermore, the government tried to solve most of the country's economic problems by enlarging the state, and hiring more and more civil servants and contract laborers. This was especially true after oil exploitation off the Congolese coast expanded in the 1970s. Oil rents enabled the government to guarantee secondary school and university graduates full employment in the civil service and state-owned enterprises, and most of these jobs were in Brazzaville. The government workforce expanded dramatically, with public-sector workers increasing from about twenty-two thousand workers in 1971 to more than forty-four thousand by 1980. In the late 1980s—the Congolese public sector's high-water mark—Congo had eighty-five thousand government employees, and civil servants headed a third of all Brazzaville households.[38] By the beginning of the 1990s Congo was perhaps the most heavily urbanized country in Africa, with two out of three residents living in cities; it also enjoyed the dubious distinction of having "one of the largest bureaucracies on the continent, relative to its population" (Pourtier 1998:25).

It was this same "bureaucratic bourgeoisie" that continued to make Brazzaville an appealing destination for immigrants from other parts of Africa. With Congolese so strongly oriented toward public-sector employment, there was high demand for people to supply the goods and services those bureaucrats could buy with their salaries. Tradesmen, domestic servants, and laborers came from Kinshasa; shopkeepers came from Mali, Senegal, Guinea, Mauritania, and Chad. My informants recalled the 1980s with nostalgia: civil servants were numerous and usually were paid on time; their paychecks were more than enough to cover necessary expenses, so they did not hesitate to spend their income in the marketplace, buying imported European garments and wax-print cloth in West African shops. Oil was flowing, cash was plentiful, and life was good. Many Brazzaville residents consider the oil boom years of the late 1970s and early 1980s to have been the city's golden age.

Oil revenue made Congo a lower-middle-income country, with annual per-capita income approaching $1,000 in 1985. At that time the country enjoyed one of the highest levels of school enrollment in the developing world: primary schooling had been compulsory for two decades, and 75 percent of eligible youth attended secondary school. But the country's reliance on the state to manage the economy and employ much of its workforce proved untenable once oil prices fell in the mid-1980s. From that moment the Congolese economy entered a prolonged steep decline: real per-capital income in 2003 was only 70 percent of what it had been two decades before, and rates of school enrollment, immunization, and nutrition all fell correspondingly. In 1994 France devalued the CFA franc, doubling the price of imported goods overnight and cutting the buying power of ordinary Congolese in half. As the 1990s wore on, increasing poverty and unemployment undid the economic advances of the boom years. Young people in Brazzaville, 60 percent of whom had been born and raised in the city, clung resolutely to their urban identities; where they had once looked forward to secure jobs, they now faced a bleak future, and their "expectations of modernity" (cf. Ferguson 1999) had brought only tragic disappointment. Making matters worse, their leaders lacked the ability to address the gathering crisis.[39]

The 1990s and beyond: Armed Conflict and Its Aftermath

From the early 1990s a number of interconnected developments began to transform Congolese life and diminish Brazzaville's allure for West African migrants. Congo saw the end of single-party rule and the demise of state socialism as an official guiding principle, and President Denis Sassou-Nguesso, who had ruled since 1979, was voted out of office. These changes occurred as the national economy reeled from the drop in oil prices and runaway government debt, which ballooned from 98 percent of the gross national product in 1980 to 250 percent in 1993. By 2004 Congo owed more than $8 billion in external debt, including $2.8 billion to commercial banks, making it perhaps the most highly indebted country per capita in the world. Debt relief from the international community was slow in coming: only in 2006 did the Congolese government tentatively reestablish relations with international financial institutions such as the World Bank and the International Monetary Fund, after repeatedly reneging on agreements made during the 1980s and early 1990s. In the first decade of the twenty-first century, with oil prices at an all-time high, Congo continued to benefit very little from its oil revenues, the management of which was marked by opacity and fraud.[40]

In this context, political violence became widespread. Before the 1990s violence perpetrated by members of the ruling elite was usually contained within the *classe politique*. From 1993 to 2003, however, Congolese political leaders recruited their own militias and orchestrated multiple armed conflicts resulting in tens of thousands of civilian deaths and the displacement of hundreds of thousands of refugees. In 1997 Sassou used his "Cobra" militia fighters to reclaim the presidency by force, following fighting which enveloped nearly every neighborhood of Brazzaville and forced hundreds of thousands of the city's inhabitants to flee. The city's buildings were badly damaged and its businesses thoroughly pillaged by the militias. Two years later, after the United Nations organized a return of refugees from Kinshasa, hundreds of returnees were allegedly taken into custody and "disappeared" en masse by government security forces after disembarking at Brazzaville's "Beach" river port. The so-called Beach Affair became a serious legal and public relations problem for Sassou the following year, when victims' families filed suit in a French court accusing his government of orchestrating the disappearances; the Congolese government opened its own prosecution of the case in 2005 (see the discussion in chapter 4).[41]

When I carried out my fieldwork in Brazzaville, between 2003 and 2006, the city was still broken in many ways, as divided as ever by politics and ethnicity. Refugees had returned, businesses and offices were open, and goods were available. The thirty-story Nabemba Tower, a symbol of Congo's boom years financed by the French oil company Elf in the 1980s, had been fitted with new windows to replace those shattered by gunfire. Sassou remained comfortably in power as he had since 1997, and the city was mostly free of fighting, as a truce signed between the government and rebel forces in 2003 officially put an end to the conflict. But violence still broke out periodically, as it did in October 2005 when government troops and helicopter gunships attacked rebel fighters in Bacongo, sparking a day of chaos and looting in that neighborhood. Throughout Brazzaville the scars of war were still visible in the facades of buildings pocked by bullets and rocket craters, and in the roofs of houses collapsed by mortar shells. Most building owners apparently lacked either the means or the desire to patch up the damage. Soldiers were everywhere, walking through the markets and patrolling the streets in pickup trucks bristling with weapons.

Despite considerable turmoil since the early 1990s, however, Congo continued to attract migrants from West Africa and elsewhere. Most immigrants left during the 1997 civil war, taking refuge either across the river in Kinshasa or back in their home countries, but began trickling back shortly after the fighting subsided. In the months and years following the war, West Africans were instrumental in revitalizing Brazzaville's commercial sector and rebuilding damaged housing, and both the country and its capital have made progress toward recovery since the late 1990s. But life remained precarious for most of the city's residents, hosts and strangers alike.

Conclusion: Lessons from History

Several important points may be drawn from this review of West African participation in Congolese society from early colonial penetration on. First, although the West African experience in the Congo Basin was intricately interwoven with the experience of European colonization, it was not solely an aspect of that colonization. From the outset, even before Brazza claimed any territory for France, or Stanley for King Leopold, West Africans diverged from the path of colonial service to pursue goals not only distinct from colonial projects but sometimes quite at odds with them. Moreover, laptots and other West Africans recruited by the French to work in Congo during this early period were overwhelmingly volunteers, not draftees: France did not resort to military conscription in its African colonies until the First World War. Like Manchuelle (1997), I would describe this population as "willing migrants." The Africans who joined this migration stream from the late nineteenth century were, much like their descendants today, neither mere pawns of global capitalism nor victims of imperialism nor passive recipients of historical forces emanating from elsewhere. At the same time that they were subject to the coercive effects of colonial power, they profited from their relationship with the colonizers to make their own mark on the pages of Africa's modern history. The European colonial sphere provided space for independent action which these migrants learned to turn to their advantage; Gary-Tounkara (2008:192) even describes the spread of entrepreneurial migrants from the western Sahel into other parts of the continent as "a kind of colonization in reverse."

The second point is that tensions between Congolese hosts and West African "strangers" have been determined largely by political and economic factors that formed during more than a century of interaction. Malamine Camara, the first West African to live at the site of what is now Brazzaville, was welcomed by members of local populations and made efforts to adapt to their customs during his time there. As colonial commercial and political domination was extended, however, the relationship between Congolese and West Africans was transformed. West African soldiers, employees of concessionary companies, and merchants exploited local populations. Moreover, the preferential treatment West Africans in Congo received from the French, especially with respect to political rights, contributed to rising resentment among Congolese toward the African foreigners in their midst. This resentment was only heightened by perceptions that West African merchants were enriching themselves at the expense of the Congolese people. Such sentiments have carried over into the postcolonial period, with many Congolese suspecting West Africans of enjoying privileged and even conspiratorial relationships with Congolese political leaders (see chapter 4).

The third point to stress here is that the flow of migrants from West Africa to the Congo Basin in general, and to Brazzaville specifically, has been intimately associated with economic and demographic trends in the host society that created a niche for these migrants. West Africans recognized the potential for commerce in the Congo colony from the very beginning, but it was the development of a large and centralized government bureaucracy after independence that helped them find a lasting place in the Congolese economy. As the fortunes of the postcolonial Congolese state have risen and fallen, West Africans have continued to exploit commercial opportunities in urban Congolese markets.

Finally, although West African migration to Brazzaville has been conditioned by these economic and demographic trends, it has also evolved to become partially independent of them. Despite the recent period of instability and decline I have described, new arrivals continue to follow in Malamine's footsteps, often bringing their families from West Africa to join them. As I will show later in this book, Brazzaville has remained a key node in West African transnational networks long after its economic heyday has passed. Moreover, although commercial activity in the city may not be as profitable as it once was, West Africans continue to dominate it. In the following chapter I examine how this domination came about and why it persists.

ENTERPRISING STRANGERS

From the beginning of my Brazzaville research, I tried to understand why West Africans went there at such expense and often physical risk. What was the city's attraction to them? Answers were unsatisfying, and migrants' life histories rarely seemed to indicate a compelling reason for them to have come to that particular place. My elderly friend and informant, Vieux Diallo, for example, who had left Mali upon independence in 1960, never could or would explain to me precisely what had brought him to Brazzaville in the first place. If socialism was truly the reason why he left Mali, as he claimed, why come to Congo, which, at the time Diallo arrived there, was officially known as the People's Republic of Congo, with a government espousing a stricter approach to socialism than Mali had ever known? Why not stay in Abidjan? Why not go to Gabon?

To listen to Diallo and most other West African informants narrate their life histories, their presence in Brazzaville appeared to be the outcome of a series of random encounters, not carefully planned strategies. They knew little about the place before arriving there. Some knew of friends or relatives in the city with whom they might seek employment, but many others did not. Brazzaville was somewhere they had simply ended up, and their specific destination was less important than the fact of *l'aventure*—a term literally meaning "adventure" but used in French-speaking Africa for the experience of going abroad to seek one's fortune. For *aventuriers* (young men undertaking l'aventure) the crucial thing was to leave home; the destination was secondary. A term that regularly cropped up in their parlance was *yaala*, which, in Bamanan, roughly means "wandering about."[1] I once asked a Malian aventurier making a living pushing a handcart on Poto-Poto's rutted streets why he had not stayed in his home country to do that kind of work. "Yaala tè?" he replied with nonchalance. "Isn't it for wandering?"

In the previous chapter I outlined the introduction of West African colonial personnel to the Congo Basin by the French in the late 1800s, the emergence of a bureaucratic bourgeoisie in postcolonial Congo, and the creation of an oil rent economy, all of which fostered the flow of migration from West Africa to Brazzaville and maintained it at least into the 1980s. But these factors alone hardly account for the fact that migrants continued in the early twenty-first century to make the long, costly journey from the western Sahel to the banks of the Congo River. Nor do they fully explain why West African entrepreneurs—from large-scale importers to shopkeepers to tailors—came to be so dominant in Brazzaville's marketplaces to begin with.

It was clear from my initial visit to Congo that many West Africans who went there became traders. Walking through the marketplace in Poto-Poto, one of the principal markets in Brazzaville, the dominance of West African merchants in the city's retail commerce was apparent to me in a number of ways. It was visible in shop names reflecting West African hometowns and family names, and in the clothing the merchants wore—most often Muslim-style *boubous* of damask or wax-print cotton cloth, with skullcaps on their heads, in contrast to the Western clothing preferred by Congolese. I saw them sitting outside their shops fingering prayer beads, poring over worn copies of the Qur'an, or drinking glasses of strong gunpowder tea. The heavy concentration of West Africans in the Poto-Poto market would literally have been evident to a blind person: instead of the driving beats of Congolese *ndombolo* music heard elsewhere in Brazzaville, the loudspeakers outside these shops blasted West African sounds—the latest pop sensations from Mali or Guinea, African reggae by Ivoirian superstars Alpha Blondy and Tiken Jah Fakoly, and spoken-word epics (called *mana*) performed by griots over languid accompaniment from the *ngoni*, a four-stringed lute. Walking through this market, seeing these sights and hearing these sounds, I could almost trick myself into believing I was in Bamako or another West African town, rather than a few hundred meters from the Congo River.

Not all Brazzaville's entrepreneurs were foreigners, of course. Congolese were quite active in specific sectors including transportation, hotels, restaurants and bars, and selling cassava, the primary staple of the Congolese diet (almost exclusively controlled by women). Some Congolese were also entrepreneurs abroad, a point to which I return later. Yet these few areas only highlighted the under-representation of Congolese in other sectors of the economy, most notably retail and wholesale commerce, and their slim presence in many artisanal trades. Generations after Congolese took over their country's political and administrative affairs from the French, their conspicuous absence from areas of the country's private sector has remained a problem for social scientists to explain.[2] The ranks of Brazzaville's foreign entrepreneurs have swelled even more since the end of the civil wars of the 1990s, as a new contingent of foreign entrepreneurs has arrived on the scene. Lining Brazzaville's main boulevards, especially the Avenue de la Paix in Poto-Poto, are scores of shops owned and operated by Chinese merchants, selling low-cost goods manufactured in their home country.

The palpable supremacy of Brazzaville's foreign merchants, both in overall numbers and their ability to succeed, raises a question: What has enabled these merchants to flourish in business where native Congolese have not? Posed from the alternative perspective, what constrains native Congolese in Brazzaville from doing better in business? Can it be simply that, as some informants suggested, Congolese do not like commerce? This subject is the focus of occasional public discussion in the national media, in web forums for the Congolese diaspora, and in salons and bars throughout the country. Lively and often acrimonious debates attribute the success of foreign entrepreneurs in Brazzaville to factors of cultural difference, corruption, and political favoritism. As I indicated in the book's introduction, however, the mantle of strangerhood entails certain benefits for those who wear it. This point is key to understanding the elusive attraction of a place like Brazzaville to West African migrants.

Commerce is only part of the story, however, because not all West Africans in Brazzaville are entrepreneurs. In a sample of 1,000 Malians registered with their consulate in Brazzaville in 2005, 332 listed their profession as *commerçant* (merchant), meaning they owned a commercial business and were registered with the commerce ministry, and 487 listed their profession as "*employé commercial*," a category that comprised over 55 percent of males in the sample.[3] Consular staff told me that the designation "*employé commercial*" was something of a residual category for the people registering with them, and included people with various odd jobs as well as the unemployed. Many young immigrants in Brazzaville are unskilled laborers; they load and unload cargo trucks, haul goods in handcarts, and do various odd jobs to make ends meet. How can we account for their presence in the city? In the second part of this chapter, I try to explain why migrants may find certain forms of unskilled labor even in Brazzaville's marginal and occasionally hazardous setting preferable to similar work back home. In this respect, too, strangerhood has its privileges.

To begin exploring all these questions, in the following sections I describe the markets in which West Africans are active, review Brazzaville's business environment, and analyze the structural relationship between the city's West Africans and the larger host community. Using a case study of a successful West African entrepreneur, I discuss the experiences that prepare these migrants for their entrepreneurial role. I then engage with scholarly discussions about social relations and the ways that people are both helped and constrained by the networks in which they are embedded. Using the example of Brazzaville's immigrant entrepreneurs and laborers, I aim to expose some of the overlooked processes by which social relationships and dynamics of reciprocal obligation shape modern African societies. These processes constitute some of the strongest forces underlying migration and the construction of strangerhood on the African continent.

Brazzaville: A Marketplace Guide

In the course of meeting my family's material needs during a year in Poto-Poto, more often than not I found myself dealing with West African merchants and artisans. Sidibé, the shopkeeper from whom I bought bread every morning, came from Guinea; Fodé and Diallo, the tailors who sewed new clothing for my wife and me, were both Malian; Kanté, the blacksmith who welded a new steel door for our apartment, was Guinean; I bought many supplies from Gakou, a Malian who owned the nearest hardware store; most of the meat in our diet was sold by a Malian named Ali who owned a butcher shop down the street; and we bought fried fish and plantains from Mamou, a woman from Burkina Faso. The only items we regularly purchased from Congolese were fruits and vegetables grown outside the city, or occasionally dried fish caught in the river. Local produce is one of the few preserves of indigenous enterprise in Brazzaville today and has been for many years—even if much of the produce sold originates across the river in Congo-Kinshasa.[4]

When one needs nonperishable food items, one goes to an *alimentation*, a neighborhood dry goods store. There is one on most residential blocks in Brazzaville. Many are housed in cramped one-room shacks made of corrugated roofing sheets, but in commercial areas there are also well-appointed and air-conditioned alimentations with two or three aisles. Even the smallest have refrigerators stocked with drinking water and soft drinks. On the shelves you can find batteries, matches, candles, canned goods, and several varieties of the MSG-laden spice cubes that have become an almost universal ingredient of the modern African diet. Most everything is imported; only sugar, bread, and some of the cigarettes are of local origin (though the wheat flour, yeast, and tobacco used to make them are also imported). Goods are sold *en détail,* in the smallest possible quantity so as to be accessible to even the tightest budgets: cigarettes can be purchased one at a time from the carton, and necessities like cooking oil, rice, salt, powdered milk, and sugar are repackaged by alimentation employees into smaller affordable quantities. Pre-paid cards may also be purchased for cell phones: the most expensive card costs 10,000 CFA francs, about $20, but the cheapest sells for a mere 1,000 francs, about $2. Of course one pays more in the long run to purchase items in small amounts, but the market must respond to the needs of the perpetually cash-strapped consumer.

Running an alimentation is perhaps the most demanding work in the retail sector, at least in terms of the hours required. Alimentations in the neighborhoods typically open at 6:00 AM and stay open until 10:00 or 11:00 PM, seven days a week; the majority of these shops have only one employee, typically a relative of the owner or a member of his home community, who must stay in the shop for this entire period every day. Moreover, profits are minute: given the degree of competition in this area, margins and volumes are quite low, and, in any case, clients usually cannot afford to buy much to begin with. West Africans run a significant number of Brazzaville's alimentations. Upon first coming to Congo, many start out working at alimentations belonging to family members; after a few years, if they can put something aside, they move on to other forms of business offering more free time and greater revenues.

Other types of shops follow a less rigorous schedule, typically opening around 8:00 AM and closing around 5:30 PM daily, except on Friday and Sunday afternoons when they often close earlier. These businesses are located in the city's market areas and along its main thoroughfares, and specialize in manufactured goods. The most common categories include hardware, auto parts, fabrics, clothing, shoes, kitchen utensils, beauty products, and home electronics. The vast majority of these goods today, from plastic sandals to hair extensions, are imported from Asia. Many entrepreneurs have direct suppliers in industrial centers in China and elsewhere in the Pacific Rim, particularly Bangkok, Jakarta, and Hong Kong. There are even a few large-scale West African exporters in Hong Kong and Guangzhou who arrange shipments to clients throughout Africa.[5] Other merchants in Brazzaville buy their imported merchandise locally from wholesalers who have such connections. One importer I interviewed in Brazzaville estimated that West African traders bring in 95 percent of the manufactured goods in Congolese markets.

A number of different West African artisans also work in the marketplace. The largest category is tailors, who make garments to order for their clients. In addition to "general practice" tailors like my friend Diallo, some tailors specialize in women's apparel, menswear, or embroidery. Customers purchase a length of cloth and bring it to a tailor to make into a shirt, dress, or *complet* (matching two- or three-piece ensemble). Tailors also sew students' school uniforms and even soldiers' military fatigues. In general, however, their business has been on the decline for many years, as inexpensive ready-to-wear garments from Asia and used clothing from Western countries have flooded the market, rendering tailor-made clothing a luxury. In Brazzaville, tailoring has long been one of the few trades in which a significant number of native Congolese can also be found.

Jewelers constitute a second category of artisans in the marketplace, and they are almost exclusively of Senegalese and Malian origin. They work with gold and silver, as well as with copper, bronze, and other base metals. In much of the West African region, jewelers belong to a blacksmith caste, and their businesses tend to be passed on from father to son. The jewelry businesses I knew in Brazzaville were all family enterprises of this type, had existed for at least two generations, and had both Congolese and West African clientele.

All the business types I have discussed so far, housed in fixed locations (shops or market stalls), belong to the "formal" sector of the economy—that is, they are registered with the Congolese government and must pay various taxes.[6] Many other types of businesses fall outside this category. Most women selling cooked food on the street, for example, lack documentation for their businesses; ambulant vendors, shoe shiners, and other "micro-entrepreneurs" may also escape the formal regulatory control of the Congolese state (though *informal* regulation, in the form of exactions by authorities, remains a problem for them; see chapter 4). Some vendors prefer to work without any fixed base: one Malian friend who had lost his clothing shop in the 1997 civil war later began selling West African CDs and DVDs, primarily to other Malians he knew. He stored his merchandise, which was pirated in and imported from Togo, in his apartment and carried a case of samples with him around town, thereby avoiding the costs of having a shop and the many official permits required to operate one. Several West African women I knew in Brazzaville, whose husbands were traders in the "formal" economy, had micro-enterprises of their own, selling fabric (especially damask cloth, prized by West Africans but hard to find in Congo), prepared food, or other goods, usually out of their homes and to fellow West Africans. In fact, West African women's economic activities in Brazzaville were almost entirely within the informal economy.

Finally, a few rather exclusive categories of activity are dominated by small numbers of West African entrepreneurs. The diamond trade, discussed in the previous chapter, is among them. Another is known in French as *le transit* or "customs brokerage." *Transitaires,* as they are called, act as the intermediaries between importers and the Congolese customs office, expediting the arrival of merchandise for a percentage of the shipment's value. By law, all transitaires must be Congolese citizens, but many are naturalized Congolese of West African origin, and it is with these individuals that West African merchants prefer to deal. One very successful transitaire of Malian origin in Brazzaville has branched out into shipping, travel agencies, and many other areas, with offices in a number of cities in Mali as well as Congo. His business success was such that by 2002 he could single-handedly finance the construction of a three-story mosque next to his Brazzaville office—the only air-conditioned mosque in Congo.

A third special category is the import sector. We have seen that since the colonial era Congolese consumers have shown a strong preference for imported goods, including foodstuffs and clothing, and the quantity of such imports has only increased over time. Some traders have capitalized on this fact to concentrate on wholesale imported consumer goods, but such traders have always been few.[7] Only entrepreneurs with considerable economic capital can deal in the sorts of volumes in question here. I knew of a mere handful of such individuals in Brazzaville, all of them men of Malian origin who had acquired Congolese citizenship.

The fourth and final special category worth noting is manufacturing. In general, manufacturing composes a tiny portion of the Congolese economy. What little large-scale industry there is in Congo has been dominated by a few state-owned (or, nowadays, formerly state-owned) factories producing sugar, cigarettes, and other commodities, and by private breweries. Nonetheless, a few West African entrepreneurs have been able to succeed in small- and medium-scale manufacturing. One Malian businessman started a company in 2003 out of his home in Poto-Poto making dairy products—yogurt and sweetened *lait caillé,* or curdled milk—using processing equipment imported from China. He supplied his products to alimentations across Brazzaville, soon opened up a second small plant in Pointe-Noire, and within two years had a small fleet of delivery vehicles and a score of employees. (Since Congo has virtually no dairy production of its own, all the milk used in his plants was imported in powdered form.) Another Malian, having already established a plastics factory in Bamako, started up a sawmill outside Brazzaville and a lumberyard in Poto-Poto. Eventually he also created a plant in Pointe-Noire making corrugated aluminum roofing sheets; by 2007 his aluminum factory employed one hundred workers (*Dépêches de Brazzaville* 2007).

Brazzaville's Business Environment

Such success stories cannot hide the fact that Congo is a tough, risky place to run a business. Political violence and its consequences have placed a heavy burden on entrepreneurs, many of whose establishments were destroyed or looted during the civil wars of the 1990s (see Yengo 2006:326–327). One of my informants who owned a clothing boutique in 1997 could only watch from his home across the street while Cobra militiamen, over the course of several hours, used sledgehammers to knock a hole through his store's cinderblock wall and made off with its entire inventory; eight years later he had still not restocked and was using his shop to sell other traders' merchandise on commission. I knew many businessmen whose assets (vehicles, buildings, and merchandise, in a few cases worth millions of dollars) were similarly wiped out in the fighting. Few had insurance, and none was able to obtain compensation from the Congolese government. They simply had to start over from scratch once the fighting subsided.[8]

Episodes of widespread looting have unfortunately not been limited to periods of all-out warfare but are perpetrated regularly by security forces themselves (rather euphemistically known in official parlance as *les forces de l'ordre*, "the forces of order"). When army and police units mounted a three-day operation to purge Bacongo of rebel militia fighters in October 2005, troops profited from the flight of the area's residents to shake down refugees for cash and cell phones, and to ransack at least forty-five neighborhood homes and warehouses. One soldier even wounded himself while trying to shoot the padlock off a shop door. These incidents fit into a systemic pattern of pillage by the very people nominally responsible for assuring security in Congo. "It's really unfortunate that, each time there's a routine police operation, everything ends in looting," the leader of a merchants' association observed to a reporter a few days after the events in Bacongo (*La Semaine Africaine* 2005a). Even in the absence of large-scale security crackdowns, Brazzaville police and military patrols sometimes ransack shops in broad daylight.[9]

Macroeconomic conditions in recent years have also been grim. Hopes that oil exports would boost Congo's flagging economy have faded: despite the oil boom and the billions of dollars of annual oil revenue throughout the first decade of the twenty-first century, state agencies remained perpetually broke; civil service salaries, which form Brazzaville's economic bedrock, have been all but frozen since 1994, despite enormous rises in the cost of living, and often arrive late or not at all. Furthermore, the buying power of ordinary Congolese has declined so much over the years that a typical civil service income can no longer support a family. Although official economic figures show robust expansion, with Congo's non-oil GDP growing above 5 percent annually since 2001, evidence from Brazzaville's marketplaces suggested that for most people conditions were deteriorating.[10] My informants in marketplaces all over the city reported that retail sales were down in 2005, for the simple reason that many residents could no longer afford more than basic necessities, and some could not even afford those. Many Brazzaville families ate only one daily meal. International agencies including the UN and the IMF have estimated that 70 percent of Congolese live in absolute poverty—that is, getting by on a dollar per day or less.

Even during the best of times, however, when guns are silent and salaries paid on time, doing business in Congo involves many challenges that predate the conflicts and economic collapse of the 1990s and that constitute daily headaches for entrepreneurs. Infrastructure, or the lack of it, is a serious problem. Roads are few and in poor condition, and at the time of my fieldwork in 2005, the entire country had only one paved highway, leading from Brazzaville north to Sassou's hometown of Oyo. This made transporting goods to most of the country a very difficult proposition. Even Brazzaville faces chronic shortages of electricity, water, and gasoline (all of which are even more scarce outside the capital, the city of Pointe-Noire, and a few provincial towns). Along with the general population, entrepreneurs face constant blackouts: tailors and blacksmiths endure recurring, sometimes protracted periods of "unpaid leave" when they cannot work because of power cuts, and shopkeepers with freezers and refrigerators are always concerned about their goods spoiling during outages. In 2005 the longest blackout in our neighborhood, caused by a burned-out transformer, lasted thirty-five days; outages in other parts of town have gone on for months. Even owning a generator does not guarantee electricity, as fuel is often in short supply—a real paradox in a country with its own oil production and refining capacity.

The Congolese government has only exacerbated these problems. If the colonial regime was largely indifferent to the private sector, governments since independence have been downright hostile to it. The state's socialist orientation from 1963 to the early 1990s led administrators to disdain private businesses and, in many cases, to create state-owned enterprises to compete with them. The situation scarcely improved after Congo's official shift away from socialist rhetoric: three-quarters of entrepreneurs polled in Brazzaville in the 1990s expressed their dissatisfaction with government administration, complaining of high taxes and long delays in obtaining permits (Dzaka and Milandou 1995). In 2005 the government announced that it would be unable to pay many of its debts to local businesses. A Congolese editorialist summed up the issue: "in Congo-Brazzaville, successive regimes running the state have often made a policy of killing private enterprise" (*La Semaine Africaine* 2005b).

One way that the state complicates life for entrepreneurs is through unfavorable taxation and regulatory systems. Total official taxes amount to two-thirds of an enterprise's profits, and tariffs and import duties are unusually high (54 percent for most manufactured goods). The World Bank's annual "Doing Business" report evaluates each country's business climate according to such criteria as ease of starting a business, the burden of complying with government regulations and paperwork, the speed of the permitting processes, taxation, the ease of obtaining credit, and the ability to enforce contracts. The 2010 "Doing Business" report ranked Congo among the five worst countries on earth, 179 out of 183 countries; its neighbor, Congo-Kinshasa, came in 182nd (World Bank 2009).

The state requires business owners to pay a multitude of fees and acquire a corresponding array of permits, licenses, and authorizations. From interviews with merchants in the Poto-Poto market, I compiled a list of seven official fees and taxes that all businesses must pay, either weekly, monthly, or annually, each to a different set of authorities.[11] Even for a well-educated individual, let alone an illiterate or semi-literate one, it was challenging to keep track of whether one was up-to-date on payments and paperwork. Moreover, foreign business operators had to pay two hefty additional fees from which Congolese were exempt. These were the *Fond de Garantie pour le Commerce* (also known as a *cautionnement*), worth 1 million francs (about $2,000), and the *caution de rapatriement*, equivalent to the value of a one-way air ticket home for each foreign entrepreneur (about $500 for Malians), both payable to the Ministry of Commerce. These fees were officially deposits that entrepreneurs could collect upon leaving the country, though in practice few did so (see chapter 4). There was also the serious problem of exactions by government employees and officials, an issue I examine in detail later in this book.

Finally, the Congolese state has failed to ensure some of the most basic requirements of commercial transactions. In addition to the problem of insecurity, traders have no guarantee that contracts will be enforced. The Congolese court system is widely seen as corrupt, rendering favorable verdicts to the highest bidder. Moreover, the Congolese government has a record of confiscating private property, especially from foreign Africans, without paying compensation (see chapter 4).

One could argue that the climate for doing business in West African countries is equally as bad as in Congo. Many of my informants' home countries also ranked near the bottom of the 2010 "Doing Business" survey of 183 countries, including Mali (in 156th place) and Guinea (173rd), while poverty rates in those countries are comparable to or higher than Congo's. Nonetheless, in some respects, immigrant entrepreneurs saw the Brazzaville environment as far worse. A Malian trader establishing a business in Bamako, for example, would not have to pay exorbitant "deposits" to the Malian government merely to open a shop, nor face any significant risk of the business being looted by renegade troops or rebels. The supply of electricity and water would be more reliable. And urban poverty is generally lower in West African countries than in Congo, meaning that West African cities have more potential customers with money. Entrepreneur informants stressed that all these factors were unfavorable in Brazzaville. In policy and macroeconomic terms, it was impossible to identify any clear incentive these migrants had to do business there.

Still, West Africans were not the only immigrants establishing themselves in the city's commercial sector. Small numbers of Lebanese, Chinese, and other foreign entrepreneurs had also set up shop in Brazzaville, and clearly had their reasons for locating there. We can learn more about the basis of "immigrant enterprise" by comparing Brazzaville's West African entrepreneurs to similar entrepreneurial populations around the world.

A Model Middleman Minority?

The economic activities in which Brazzaville's West Africans engage fit into a larger pattern, related to the structural position of this stranger community within its host society. In other words, these immigrants' role in Brazzaville is analogous to that played by other immigrant groups in other times and places; examples of such groups include Jews in pre-Holocaust Europe, South Asians in East Africa, Chinese in the Pacific Rim, and Lebanese in West Africa.[12] Blalock (1967:79–84) coined the term "middleman minority" for such groups sharing certain characteristics, three of which deserve special mention here and reveal close parallels with Simmel's "stranger" concept.

First, members of a middleman minority are outsiders occupying an intermediate position between a society's ruling elite and the masses. There have been different historical variations of this intermediary role: in a feudal society, middleman minorities came between landowners and peasants; in a colonial society, between colonizers and colonized; and in postcolonial and industrial societies, between the national elite and local "autochthonous" populations. Scholars have advanced functional explanations for this intermediary position, hypothesizing that it reduces social instability. Blalock theorized that a triadic relationship of this type is inherently more stable than a dyadic one, because rulers can use the middleman minority as a pawn in their struggle for power with the subordinate classes. The middleman minority acts as a buffer between the elite and the masses, allowing the latter to vent their frustrations against the foreign intermediary without directly challenging the political status quo.[13]

Second, middleman minorities occupy specific niches within local economies. Their members are particularly drawn to commerce, money lending, brokerage, and other forms of small business. The homeward orientation of these groups accounts for this clustering in a few occupations: their members tend to see themselves as sojourners and have aspirations, however indefinite, to return to their homeland someday. They feel insecure in their present location, where they may face discrimination and even the threat of expulsion, and do not foresee settling there permanently. They therefore avoid activities that might tie up their assets in the host country, instead establishing businesses that can easily be liquidated if the need arises. These businesses are usually family owned and operated, and can prosper in difficult settings.

Finally, these middleman groups resist assimilation into host societies, remaining "perpetual minorities," according to Blalock (1967:79). Their status as sojourners and their homeward orientation are handed down, more or less intact, from one generation to the next, reminiscent of Fortes's description of strangers as "inassimilable aliens" (1975:245). Hostility from the host society strengthens their resistance to assimilation. The minority group's economic success makes it the target of resentment and suspicion by the members of the host population, who may come to see these foreigners in their midst as parasites. The minority responds by reinforcing its intra-community solidarity and isolating itself socially from the surrounding society, while still dependent on it for clients and customers. Increasing discrimination ultimately pushes the minority from voluntary to forced segregation.

Scholarly attention since the 1980s has shifted from middleman minorities to "ethnic economies" and transnational entrepreneurs, particularly those based in the United States and other Western countries. People in these categories do not always fit the middleman minority paradigm: some lack the "sojourner mentality" or have transformed their businesses from small family enterprises into multinational corporations. New concepts, from "global tribes" to "market-dominant minorities," have emerged to explain the success of particular national or ethnic groups in the contemporary global economy.[14]

In much of the developing world, however, and particularly for the strangers composing Africa's internal diasporas, the middleman minority concept remains useful. It applies especially well to West Africans in the Congo Basin who, ever since they came to the region, have occupied an intermediary position between rulers and ruled. As detailed in the previous chapter, their role of filling the "status gap" between French and Congolese during the colonial period was clear to hosts and strangers alike. West Africans provided many goods and services required by the French and, in return, received higher status than Congolese. Since independence, members of this minority have maintained a relatively privileged position, holding on to their economic advantages and maintaining their commercial dominance.

West African entrepreneurial success in Brazzaville proves how effective and resilient the business practices of immigrant minority groups can be, even—perhaps especially—amid widespread economic uncertainty. Although social scientists once predicted the demise of ethnic trading diasporas at the hands of multinational corporations, these "traditional" commercial networks have retained an enduring role in the global economy. Wherever economies are depressed, profit margins small, credit hard to obtain, and people distrustful of the state's ability to regulate trade or enforce contracts, minority traders can be better adapted to doing business than larger, more institutionalized, and better capitalized firms, and may actually thrive under these circumstances. Granovetter (1995:154) suggests that immigrant entrepreneurs "find their main advantage under difficult economic conditions." Businesses organized by kinship, ethnicity, or other ascriptive criteria, formerly dismissed as archaic, are, in fact, quite well adapted to chaotic postcolonial settings like Congo. At least for the foreseeable future, these middleman minority traders are unlikely to be superseded by more formalized, "rationally organized" entities.

Enterprise, Culture, and Migration

Whether one chooses to call them a middleman minority or transnational entrepreneurs, Brazzaville's West Africans plainly fit into a broad pattern of immigrant groups carving out distinct economic and cultural spaces in host societies. These minorities are frequently successful in business. But what accounts for this success? Some scholars, in the tradition of Max Weber's (2001) "Protestant ethic" concept, turn to culture. The "cultural values" thesis (Li 1993:220) holds that "immigrants remain attached to certain traditional values of their home country" that facilitate their success in the host country. This thesis ascribes to the culture of origin such qualities as self-reliance, industry, risk-taking, cooperation, and a preference for savings over consumption; it presumes that minority group members possess cultural assets lacking among members of the majority. This thesis has been rearticulated in recent years by a host of writers, mainly outside the social sciences, stressing the importance of values in fostering entrepreneurial success and economic development.[15] Kotkin (1993:9–10), for example, identifies core values among certain diasporic groups including "a strong ethnic identity, a belief in self-help, hard work, thrift, education and the family," stating that "the relationship between such values and group success is simply too self-evident to ignore." This argument reproduces earlier ones made in the 1960s and early 1970s.[16]

Many of my informants, both West African and Congolese, voiced similar culturalist explanations. Members of ethnic groups such as the Soninke with long and celebrated mercantile traditions liked to tell me that commerce was simply "in their blood," something inherited from their ancestors. "We Soninke, the first work we know is trade," a young man I interviewed in Togotala said. "Our fathers were engaged in it when we were born, as were their fathers before them. Trade is our primary activity; we know it better than any other." Many West Africans in Brazzaville likewise saw their cultural values as promoting an entrepreneurial spirit. Quite a few Congolese, for their part, told me that their people simply were not cut out to sit in shops all day, and 68 percent of Congolese university students participating in my survey agreed with the statement "Congolese, in general, are not good at commerce." Such notions ignore the centuries of Central African participation in the Atlantic trade (Vansina 1990), as well as the activities of Congolese traders abroad today. They also reinforce cultural fallacies while overlooking the historical and social foundations of immigrant entrepreneurial success.

It is true that entrepreneurship is valued very differently in Congo compared to West Africa. In Mali, where commerce carries a customary association with nobility, every young person knows of elders who, even without the benefit of schooling, acquired tremendous wealth and social status through trade at home or abroad. These elders became role models, channeling young people's aspirations down similar paths. In Congo, conversely, private enterprise was not a conduit to prestige but drew the least-educated members of society and those who dropped out of school. Commerce could even be described as a "dishonorable occupation" for Congolese, an activity of last resort for those excluded from public-sector employment.[17]

Such facts notwithstanding, I am among the many social scientists who find the cultural values thesis unsatisfactory, largely because it uncritically assumes culture to be a static entity rather than a dynamic system. Culture does not exist in a vacuum and is never simply "transmitted" unchanged from one generation to the next; it is constantly reshaped by social, political, and economic forces. Anthropologists and historians emphasize that cultural continuity is often more illusion than reality, and sociologists point to the lack of a clear causal link between cultural traits and entrepreneurial success. In the words of Portes and Zhou (1992:513):

> Culturalistic explanations have little predictive power since they are invoked only *after* a particular group has demonstrated its economic prowess. Such explanations are ultimately tautological: if a certain minority is successful, it must be because it originally had or later acquired the right values.

It may be true that West Africans prize business careers more highly than Congolese do, and it may be true that West Africans in Brazzaville (or Lebanese in Dakar or Indians in Nairobi or Koreans in south-central Los Angeles) place more emphasis on hard work, cooperation, and thrift than do members of the majority population. Such observations do not settle the question of why immigrants succeed but only raise more fundamental questions. How did those cultural values originate? How are they maintained? Why *aren't* they more widespread among members of the host society?

To begin unraveling these questions, let us consider the following case study of a successful West African migrant in Brazzaville. Barou was a Soninke man from the town of Baroueli in central Mali. He was thirty-nine years old when I interviewed him and had lived most of his life abroad.

Barou grew up with an uncle in Baroueli while his father worked in Bamako. As a boy he attended primary and Qur'anic schools, worked in his uncle's fields, and spent many school breaks in Bamako. In Baroueli migration was a virtual necessity, particularly for young men. As Barou told me, "80 percent of the young men leaving en aventure had been working in their families' fields, and had no resources, absolutely nothing. They went to work in the morning and came home in the evening. It's only on holidays that you can get together with others. Those who maybe had the luck to leave, when they returned the other youth could see that they were a bit clean and had certain things others didn't, maybe a motorcycle that others didn't have."

Many young men like Barou left Baroueli seasonally to find work in Bamako, spurred by the difficulty of agricultural production amid regular droughts. "You know, what is grown in our village has never been sufficient for a whole year," Barou said. "So given the working conditions and the fact that it doesn't bring anything to the kids, many go out and try to earn something, to fill the gap, the lack of earnings that the family has."

At the age of fifteen he decided to go to Bouaké, Côte d'Ivoire, even though he said he knew nobody there. "It was just a place to get away from my home village, in a way," he told me. Barou shined shoes and sold umbrellas and perfume as an ambulant vendor. From Bouaké he went to Abidjan, where he sold drinks and pushed handcarts. "That's the place from which—you know, it's often a matter of information, in such and such a country you can earn a little. So one tries to go someplace where one didn't intend to go in the beginning." In less than a year he had saved enough to buy a plane ticket to Congo.

Barou spent six years selling sandals at a table in the Moungali market, accumulating enough savings to establish a clothing store in Poto-Poto. He helped a younger brother come to Brazzaville to join his business. Barou began making trips to buy garments in Thailand to sell in their shop. By the mid-1990s, after three good years for their business, competition from Kinshasa-based vendors drove down profits in the clothing trade. Barou had noticed that Brazzaville had few auto parts vendors. He flew to Lagos, Nigeria, with $8,000 in cash and returned with enough parts to stock his new shop in the Bacongo market, where few West African traders operated. After two years he switched his main source of merchandise from Lagos to Dubai, flying there regularly to buy parts. Although his business was looted in 1997, by 2005 it was thriving. He employed two of his brothers and two Congolese workers.

Barou exemplifies many key aspects of these entrepreneurs' migration experience. He came from a rural background and had limited education. If West Africans succeed in business, it is usually despite their level of schooling rather than because of it, and they seldom see formal training as useful for one's commercial career. During an interview in 2002 with an elderly Malian in his home village, I asked whether he had instructed any of his migrant sons on how to succeed in business. "Julaya tè kalan dè," he scoffed in Bamanan—"Trade cannot be studied." There is only one universal rule for successful commerce which everyone already knows: buy low, sell high. Most everything else about doing business in Africa must be learned by doing.

Barou's decision to leave home was motivated in part by the insufficiency of local agricultural production to provide for his household's needs. Throughout the Sahel, extensive rain-fed agricultural production—growing cereal crops like millet, sorghum, and maize—forms the foundation of rural economies, yet for various reasons including drought, poor soil, and a shortage of arable land or labor, rural households in many areas of the Sahel grow half the amount of food they need each year. In the Senegal River Valley, for example, households buy, on average, 55 percent of their annual food consumption; in Togotala, household heads reported that they could grow only enough crops to last about six months of the year. In such conditions farming may be more valuable as a symbolic activity than as a form of economic production: laboring in the family's millet fields can serve to inculcate in young people an appreciation for labor, sacrifice, and even thrift.[18] Ultimately, however, young men must leave home to "fill the gap."

As with most of my informants, Barou's migration to Brazzaville took place in a series of steps rather than a single journey. He began by migrating internally to Mali's capital city, less than half a day's drive from his hometown, to spend school breaks with family there. Eventually his migration changed character, distancing him from kin and taking him abroad. It is crucial to state that the end point was never predetermined: each step of the process was shaped by the information, contacts, and resources Barou acquired along the way. At each step of his migratory career, he found a different means to make money.

This highlights a crucial quality evident in many migrants' success stories: flexibility. Over the course of a decade in Brazzaville, Barou traded in three different types of goods in three different locations, and found a way to increase his earnings with each successive change. Given dynamic market conditions, entrepreneurs like him must be prepared to transform their businesses dramatically if they are to stay afloat. West African merchants rarely specialize in a single type of product for very long but repeatedly switch between separate and unrelated fields, moving from clothing to auto parts, from bakeries to shoes, from alimentations to hardware.[19] They must constantly identify emerging market needs, recognize and exploit new opportunities, and find new suppliers.

Such versatility is hardly fostered by formal education in Mali or Congo, which in keeping with French pedagogical norms encourages early subject and vocational specialization from the start of secondary school, locking students into career paths from which they are reluctant to deviate. The West Africans I knew learned to embrace change well before arriving in Congo, while they were young, independent migrants—shoeshine boys, street hawkers, ambulant vendors, and manual laborers. It was primarily the *experience of migration*, with its inherent challenges and risks, that prepared them to become entrepreneurs.

The reasons for these migrants' success are complex. Cultural values do play a role in the formation of immigrant entrepreneurs, but such values are not always something the migrant possesses at the outset of the migration process. What if these values are, instead of "traditional" features of the home country, emergent qualities acquired in the course of young migrants' careers? In any case they are not, in my view, the primary foundation of immigrant entrepreneurial success. To grasp that foundation, we must consider the types of social relations in which those merchants are embedded. Two concepts are critical in this analysis: social networks and social capital.

Social Networks and Social Capital

Like people everywhere, West Africans belong to social networks composed of relatives, people from their hometowns, co-ethnics, and others. These networks are spatially dispersed: many people in Mali, for example, know and remain in contact with friends and kin in a host of other countries in Africa, Europe, North America, and increasingly the Far East. Families rely on remittances from abroad to make ends meet; as Barou's case demonstrates, even in rural areas households depend heavily on the contributions of members in distant locations.

Social networks are commonly associated with cooperation, reciprocity, and mutual assistance. In the context of transnational immigration, networks are also characterized by what Portes and Zhou (1992:514) call "bounded solidarity." As members of a distinct foreign minority, immigrants feel a heightened sense of shared identity, a common bond with their fellows much stronger than any bonds existing above the level of kinship in their communities of origin. In Brazzaville, bounded solidarity unifies immigrants from the western Sahel, who would have little in common back home but now find themselves strangers in a strange land. Various kinds of associations, organized at the level of kin, village, regional, religious, and national communities, reinforce this sense of solidarity and facilitate its mobilization by community members. Minority groups defined by ethnicity or immigrant status experience the strongest bounded solidarity owing partly to discrimination by members of the host society and partly to the members of the minority population's total dependence on one another for social and economic support (see Granovetter 1995). For them, the price of exclusion from their group would be too high.

In such settings, bounded solidarity also fosters what Portes and Sensenbrenner (1993:1332) call "enforceable trust." This mechanism discourages wrongdoing by network members, who as part of a tightly bounded group must rely on one another for their mutual security and livelihoods. In Congo, where the state justice system is seen as thoroughly corrupt (siding with the rich or powerful rather than the just), it is more promising for entrepreneurs to rely on the collective power of the social network to sanction malfeasance and reward good behavior. We saw that Barou entrusted his clothing shop to a younger brother while making trips to buy auto parts abroad. Many entrepreneurs similarly rely on siblings, cousins, children, or other relatives to "mind the store" for them, take charge of new ventures, purchase merchandise, or assist in other ways. Increasingly enforceable trust even permits local family businesses to operate transnationally: in 2005 the Malian owner of the Congolese metal sheeting plant mentioned above had one relative in charge of his Bamako plastics factory, another in charge of his Congolese sawmill, and another running an export office in China.

Enforceable trust can be effective in promoting intra-group bonds and minimizing risk. In an environment where the legal system is deficient, and where one may never even be investigated—let alone prosecuted and convicted—for theft or breach of contract, knowing whom to trust is among the entrepreneur's greatest challenges. Where the state fails to create a climate of enforceable trust, kinship, ethnicity, friendship, and other more informal varieties of association intervene to provide a solution.[20] This solution is certainly not foolproof, as I knew many business owners in Brazzaville who had been betrayed by someone close to them whom they had trusted. Such cautionary tales constitute the exceptions to the rule, however: friends and trusted relatives are less likely to risk such a deception for fear of the social sanctions they would face as a result.

The concepts of bounded solidarity and enforceable trust show the importance of social relationships for entrepreneurial success. By promoting in-group loyalty and reliability, these mechanisms help disseminate valuable information among trading partners and effectively lower their "transaction costs" (see Grabowski 1997). Yet it would be a mistake to portray social relationships and networks in this context as purely positive phenomena.

Social capital has been saddled with overlapping but frequently dissonant definitions.[21] Bourdieu (1986:249) originally defined social capital as "the aggregate of the actual or potential resources which are linked to possession of a durable network of more or less institutionalized relationships of mutual acquaintance and recognition." His definition was later adapted by Coleman (1988:98), who described social capital as a facilitating quality that "inheres in the structure of relationships between actors." For both Coleman and Bourdieu, social capital was conceptualized in instrumental terms, as a quality individuals may generate and exploit within societal norms of reciprocity.

The notion of social capital acquired clout in policy-making circles in the 1990s, when a report published by the World Bank identified social capital as the "missing link" in economic development; developmentalist discourse bundled social capital with related understandings of microenterprise and informal economies as mechanisms to promote economic growth while bypassing the state.[22] Such formulations have been controversial, however. As the concept's appeal has grown, scholars and policy makers have pushed it beyond its feasible limits. Its definition has become so diffuse that some claim the concept is "at risk of becoming the ether that fills the universe" (Robison, Schmid, and Siles 2002:1).

In light of these difficulties, many scholars, including distinguished economists and political scientists, have advocated that social capital be abandoned or replaced as a conceptual tool in the social sciences.[23] But the social capital genie is out of the bottle: the term, despite disagreements over its fundamental qualities, is deeply embedded in today's social science discourse, and the concept is a regular theme in leading social science journals. As with terms like "diaspora" and "globalization," its popularity could prove its undoing. I address this problem by defining the concept as narrowly as possible. Like Bourdieu and Coleman, I take "social capital" to be a property of individuals embedded in specific relationships, not a diffuse quality obtaining even among strangers.

I use the term here to designate a certain affinity—Robison and colleagues (2002:6) prefer the term "sympathy"—toward individuals or groups that carries the potential for instrumental benefits (such as information, employment, housing, and other forms of support). This definition, something of a lowest common denominator, reflects the concept's use in migration research as a capacity both manifested in and exercised through social networks.

In much social science literature, social capital and social networks are virtually coterminous. Giddens (2000:78), for example, describes social capital as "trust networks that individuals can draw on for social support, just as financial capital can be drawn upon to be used for investment." The World Bank (2007) defines social capital as "the norms and networks that enable collective action." Social scientists have a strong tendency to see social networks as a universal good; they help people solve problems, achieve their goals, and live better lives. Social scientists are particularly prone to seeing "good things emerging out of sociability" (Portes 1998:15). We recognize that certain relationships can be detrimental to society: the close ties between members of a mafia crime family or a street gang, for example, only permit the more efficient victimization of law-abiding citizens.[24] Nonetheless, scholars usually presume that social relationships are beneficial at least to the individuals embedded in them.

Social capital and social networks are indeed closely intertwined. In any setting, "networking" (cultivating social contacts for instrumental purposes) is a vital means of building up social capital, and the human relationships that the social capital concept indexes are perhaps the most important means through which people, not least entrepreneurs, achieve their ends. At the same time, however, social relationships can cut both ways, doing harm as well as good from the individual's point of view. In other words, social capital and social networks are *not* coterminous. This is especially evident in sub-Saharan African settings like Brazzaville, where bonds based on kinship, ethnicity, regional affiliation, and other commonalities are of utmost importance in daily affairs (Milandou 1997). Social scientists have not adequately explored the capacity of one's social connections to be detrimental to one's interests in such environments.

The Burden of Social Relations

A common theme in my discussions with people in Mali and Congo has been the weight of their obligations to kin. It is exceedingly difficult to refuse a request by a family member, particularly when that person is in serious need—as so many are. Strong kinship bonds, as well as patron-clientelism, encourage the fortunate to provide for the poorest and most vulnerable members of society. This system applies throughout Africa and in many other parts of the world. Analyses of social capital are prone to stress the positive effects of this communitarian ethic and the "social safety net" it establishes, but they often overlook its "dark side"—the penalization of personal success and the stifling of individual initiative.

Anthropologist Keith Hart (1975:16) has examined this dark side among urban entrepreneurs from northern Ghana; "those who manage to enrich themselves," he writes, are "a widespread target for the aspirations, hopes, fears, and antipathies of their less fortunate fellows." Tension is inevitable between any individual who accumulates wealth and members of that individual's group who do not. As Sandefur and Laumann (1998:493) put it, "visibly successful members of a solidary group may become targets of less successful members who may wish to 'free-ride' on their success, and are able to do so because of norms that require successful individuals to aid less fortunate members of the group." Entrepreneurial success requires exploiting kin and social relationships while also breaking free of those relationships that might hold one back. Thus arises what Hart (1975:28) calls the "entrepreneur's social dilemma": how to divide one's resources between, on the one hand, a "public social security fund of reciprocal exchanges" and, on the other, the private accumulation of personal wealth.

In Africa, contributing to the "public social security fund" of one's elders is vital. Most elderly Africans depend utterly on support from their offspring to survive in their old age, and one of the worst faults of which adults may be accused is failing to provide for their parents. Underlying West African Muslims' norms of filial piety and obedience is the concept of *danga*, a kind of curse a parent can invoke upon a wayward child. Sanneh (1996:172) defines *danga* as "ill-omen, sometimes incurred by the curse but more often from the ill-will of those unjustly wronged" which "haunts and tracks down its subjects." A *dangaden* (literally, "curse-child") is a common Bamanan term for someone "good-for-nothing, damned" (Bailleul 2000:88).[25] Anyone defying parental authority, such as migrants who neglect parents back home or disobey their families' wishes regarding marriage, is at risk of *danga*. As one elderly head of household in Togotala told me,

> If you leave here to go to America, and find work within two or three months, and start collecting your pay, you should come back to take a wife here. But if you stay, and marry a white woman, and you don't send anything to your father, your mother, or anybody, just looking out for yourself, well,

then you're a *dangaden. You can pray, you can fast, you can give alms and everything, but if you don't think of your mother and father, it's finished! You get no blessing, it's over. You're ruined.*

In the words of one Malian sociologist, there is a "very real fear that if you do not spread what you have around, people will curse you, and you will lose everything, perhaps go blind, or even die" (French 1997). *Danga,* moreover, negates the value of one's wealth. According to one Togotalan interviewee in his late teens, "even if [a *dangaden*] makes millions abroad, he'll lose all of it and he'll be stuck in a foreign land with empty pockets and all sorts of problems."

By some Islamic beliefs, incurring *danga* also means losing favor in the eyes of God and, with it, all hope of going to heaven. The importance of this sanction—blocked access to the afterlife—should not be underestimated in any analysis of these migrants' behavior. Muslims are encouraged to strive for paradise and avoid the torments of Hell in the afterlife. Selfish acts, particularly not sharing one's wealth with one's parents, can irreversibly bar the gateway to heaven. *Baraka,* or "blessing," represents the other side of the coin; it is *baraka* that the pious seek to amass through good deeds. Significantly, one may obtain it only from one's elders or superiors; *baraka* can be passed down a social hierarchy but never up (Sanneh 1996). These migrants seek to accumulate not only value (the rewards of which exist only in the short term) but also virtue (with rewards in the long term). For devout Muslims, there would be no point in building up short-term rewards if it meant forfeiting long-term ones—the blessings that accompany righteous acts.

Choosing whether to fulfill a parent's request for funds or material support therefore entails more than just economic consequences: one's very salvation may depend on it. For a potential or current entrepreneur, however, kin relations often constitute a burden that places the entrepreneur in a tough position. The "entrepreneurial ethic" requires one to accumulate savings and start-up capital. Doing so is difficult, however, as long as one must take care of one's relatives: the "dutiful kin ethic" requires that one provide for the needy, and hence any surplus generated is automatically claimed by and distributed to kin.

The problem of reconciling entrepreneurship with kin obligations is similar for Congolese. For them, instead of Islamic injunctions and the threat of a parent's *danga* hanging over one's head, it is *bunganga*—a powerful form of supernatural aggression—that enforces relatives' demands. Congolese widely adhere to a belief in the power to manipulate spiritual forces: 85 percent of Brazzaville university students surveyed said they believed in sorcery, and national politics is dominated by references to the occult. Within the lineage structures of Congolese society, *bunganga* is wielded by powerful elders to enforce their will upon junior members.[26] Like an evil twin of Muslims' *baraka*, *bunganga* moves only from senior to junior members of a hierarchy, but instead of blessings it carries ill fortune, sickness, and in extreme instances death. An elder can unleash this spiritual force through conscious or even unconscious expressions of discontent with a junior member of his or her lineage, usually a maternal nephew. The most common impetus for *bunganga* from these senior relatives is the junior relative's failure to satisfy their demands. Congolese entrepreneurs frequently interpret their elders' claims for money and goods as not just insatiable but malicious, intended to bring about their ruin. Fears of sorcery even keep some Congolese from keeping their money in banks, where their funds' fusion with those of anonymous depositors could expose them to supernatural aggression. For good reason, sorcery has been called "the dark side of kinship" (Geschiere 1997:11) and described in the Congolese context as an "instrument in the struggle against scarcity" (Dzaka and Milandou 1994:109) and even a "social recognition tax" (Tsika 1995:251).[27]

The intra-lineage power structure discourages attempts by junior members of a lineage to build up their own wealth. Under the logic of the lineage system, the entrepreneur's most essential characteristics—risk taking, innovation, organizational talent, and the drive to accumulate capital—pose a threat to the status quo unless they are embodied in a socially dominant figure. Lineages promote a particularly powerful communitarian ethic: historically, for groups such as the Kongo, "the right to individual enrichment was almost unknown" (Dzaka and Milandou 1994:116). Business success has been constructed not as the reward of individual talent but as the manifestation of an inherited family trait (*lusolo*), the fruits of which must be redistributed to kin (MacGaffey and Bazenguissa-Ganga 2000:126ff.).

The observation that their family and social obligations may hinder would-be entrepreneurs is nothing new, and anthropologists have studied the entrepreneur's social dilemma for decades.[28] Yet they have too often overlooked the most important responses to it.

Escaping the "Entrepreneur's Social Dilemma"

There are three main ways out of the conundrum confronting those seeking to accumulate wealth without alienating their kin networks, their greatest source of support. The first is to join a social group with different internal norms than one's home community. This strategy often takes the form of religious conversion: in Ghana, for example, Hart (1975:28) found that many entrepreneurs eased the burden of kin obligations by "joining a religious congregation which did not place the same degree of moral restriction on self-enrichment" as did their kin groups. Similar linkages between successful entrepreneurship and religious conversion have been observed in settings all over the world, from Ecuador to Nigeria to Congo; in Mali the rise of Islamic reformism since the 1950s was intimately associated with the country's merchants. Alternately, individuals can attempt to "disembed" themselves from communal obligations through membership in certain types of secular voluntary associations, such as social clubs or credit societies.[29]

A second "escape route" is to conceal one's sources of income and keep one's economic success under wraps. This approach is mainly for individuals who work for themselves and do not collect a salary. For example, Seydou Keita, a well-known Malian portrait photographer, toward the end of his life reportedly projected the image of "the exploited artist, left with nothing at the end of a brilliant career," despite earning generous royalties and owning homes all over Bamako (French 1997). In Côte d'Ivoire many urban youth prefer informal and even criminal forms of economic activity (known in Abidjan as "*le bizness*") to regular salaried work, since "having a real job is too high profile to save any money" (Newell 2006:185). This option is less feasible for entrepreneurs with capital assets such as shops and merchandise.

The third way out, and the most central to my analysis, is emigration. By physically distancing oneself from one's neediest family members (who are also the least likely to emigrate), one dramatically reduces the weight of obligations one must uphold. This is true for a number of reasons. Distance has the effect of filtering out all but the most urgent requests. Once one goes abroad, it becomes more difficult for kin to convey their demands: telecommunication remains very expensive in much of Africa, and scarce Internet access and low computer literacy restrict e-mail use. Just as important, when requests do manage to bridge the distance, migrants have more leeway to ignore them or postpone replying than they would back home. Although it is hard to say no to any family request, the more distant the origins of a request, the easier it becomes to practice artful deflection, deferral, and delay, all of which I noted repeatedly during participant observation in Brazzaville. Excuses that might not sway a demand in person (e.g., "my goods are stuck in customs," "nobody's buying," "tax collectors just cleaned me out," etc.) are much more effective when the person hearing them cannot verify whether they are actually true. As Cliggett (2005:152) finds in her study of rural-to-urban migrants in Zambia, "physical distance from relatives means that the most direct and effective form of pressure for support, a face-to-face request, is simply not an option." Of course, migrants still must be responsive to the needs of their kin back home, but they can respond at their discretion and on their own terms, without sacrificing capital for their enterprises. This theme recurred in my conversations with West African entrepreneurs in Brazzaville and is visible among West Africans elsewhere (Barten 2009).

It is especially difficult for entrepreneurs to do business in their home communities, where they face an unrelenting barrage of requests by kin, both close and distant, for goods on credit, discounts, employment, and short-term loans or grants outright to help pay for weddings, baptisms, and burials. During research on informal manufacturers in Nigeria, Meagher (2006:568) found that entrepreneurs were disinclined to trade with "townsmen," that is, people from their home communities:

> Suppliers of shoe parts claimed that townsmen were the most problematic customers, because they exercise moral pressure to get credit and then expect the trader to understand their problems when the time comes for repayment. Associative ties, especially through the church, were considered more reliable.

In Bamako I met a taxi driver who would not accept a fare to his home neighborhood, where he knew he would likely be spotted by some relative who would insist on being driven somewhere for free. It is always possible to turn down such requests—in fact most requests *are* turned down, but the necessity to do so creates relentless tension for the entrepreneur. It is far easier to manage one's affairs a little farther from home. During my research in Togotala, in 2002, I noticed that most shopkeepers there were not only outsiders to the village but came from a different region of Mali altogether, hundreds of miles away (cf. Jonsson 2008). At the national level some observers feel that Malians are underrepresented in their own country's private business sector. "To an unhealthy degree, entrepreneurship is still left to the Lebanese and other foreigners," writes Pringle (2006:37) of Mali's national commercial scene. These other foreigners include Libyans (whom some Malians describe as "infesting" the Bamako business sector) and increasingly Chinese, who have been gradually moving into retail commerce since the 1990s. In many parts of Africa, one finds that traders and small- and medium-sized business operators hail from someplace else. "The merchant," it has been said, "is always a stranger."[30]

Congolese entrepreneurs find themselves, to borrow an evocative phrase from Tsika (1995), "between the anvil of the state and the hammer of the family." Not only do they face a poor regulatory and tax environment, but they are too close to too many burdensome relations, and face grave dangers if they choose to ignore the claims placed upon them by members of their lineage. They would thus do well to put some distance between themselves and their kin. Congolese traders do better abroad, particularly in informal commercial activities, in France as well as in some of Congo's neighboring countries. But business success remains challenging on home soil. Some Congolese interest groups such as trade unions have responded to this situation by advocating government training and credit programs for would-be entrepreneurs, and by pressing for laws to bar foreigners from performing certain types of work in Congo. Indeed, a few such laws have been enacted pertaining to street vendors, truck drivers, and bakers, and the government experimented with even more draconian measures in the past. The evidence suggests that such measures will not bring about the desired effects. The roots of the problem lie less in government policy or official favoritism toward foreigners and more in the power of social relations in this context to favor collective welfare over individual ambitions vital to entrepreneurial success. Brazzaville's growing number of Pentecostal churches, which promote an ethic of individual initiative and encourage members to break from their lineages, may offer Congolese a more promising prescription for business success.[31]

To sum up my argument thus far, cultural factors are secondary to social factors in accounting for groups' differential levels of entrepreneurial success. As Granovetter (1995:143) puts it, "cultural understandings and practices do not emerge out of thin air; they are shaped by and in turn shape structures of social interaction." Members of immigrant entrepreneurial groups do not thrive primarily because they are Soninke, Igbo, Lebanese, Chinese, or Jewish; they thrive primarily *because they are strangers*. The mere fact of being abroad confers upon them a number of advantages that they would not enjoy at home. Those who compose Africa's internal diasporas, having been enticed or compelled by geographic and historical factors to leave their home communities behind and take part in long-distance forms of migration, are in many cases the same Africans renowned for their "entrepreneurial spirit."

What Happens in Brazzaville: The Labor/Dignity/Migration Nexus

Not all African immigrants in Brazzaville fit the same entrepreneurial profile as the merchants, shopkeepers, and other traders described above. A second category consists of *aventuriers*—young, single males without many assets. They are highly mobile. Some aspire to become entrepreneurs and business owners in a formal sense, but given their lack of capital they must find alternative sources of income. To meet their basic needs and, ideally, save up for their weddings, for their next business or migratory ventures, they must perform unskilled jobs. Some work as manual laborers, loading trucks and manhandling pushcarts loaded with merchandise through the rutted Brazzaville streets. Others wander the marketplaces and residential neighborhoods selling tea from Thermos bottles. They could find similar work back in Bamako, Conakry, or elsewhere in their home region. Why not stay home?

The answer to this question reflects particular constructions of labor, social status, and individual dignity. I explore these constructions through a case study from outside my target population, a young Cameroonian man I met in the Poto-Poto market.

> Vincent was twenty-two years old and hailed from the town of Buea in Cameroon's Southwest Province. After finishing secondary school in Bamenda, he decided to seek his fortune abroad. He traveled overland to Congo, which borders Cameroon to the south, and eventually to Brazzaville. There he bought some loaves of bread, some containers of margarine and corned beef, and became an ambulant food vendor, walking Poto-Poto's streets with his sandwich supplies.
>
> Vincent sold sandwiches for 100 francs (about $0.20) each. He estimated that he made 30 francs profit (about $0.06) per sandwich, and sold anywhere from 100 to 150 sandwiches every day. This brought in 3,000 to 3,500 francs. Sharing a dingy room in Poto-Poto with another immigrant and needing only about 500 francs ($1) for his daily living expenses, he could save 2,500 to 3,000 francs per day. By working seven days a week, Vincent hoped to build up enough savings to pay for additional education and, ultimately, emigration to America.
>
> Vincent was satisfied with his short-term prospects in Brazzaville but admitted that he would never have considered being a street vendor before going abroad. "If I did this work at home, people would feel sorry for me," Vincent said. "They would say, 'Oh, look at this son of a respectable father, reduced to selling bread in the streets.' People look at me and think I'm suffering."

In fact, Vincent was making a better living than most Congolese with "real jobs." In the wake of devaluation and government austerity measures, many civil servants earned less than $100 per month, whereas Vincent could *save* $150

Figure 2.1. West African laborers take a break in the Poto-Poto market.
PHOTO BY AUTHOR

or more per month. Yet despite his formidable business model, his social status was insignificant compared to even the lowest-paid salaried worker. Brazzaville natives consider jobs like street vending or pushing handcarts demeaning, fit only for immigrants.

"There are certain forms of work you can't do," said Mamedi, a fifty-five-year-old Togotalan trader who had lived and worked in five different African countries, during an interview in Mali in 2002. "But if you go abroad you can do it. For example, if I went to Côte d'Ivoire, I could work on a coffee or cocoa plantation. But here, even if you paid me a million francs per day to go farm for someone else, I wouldn't do it, because for us it's a humiliation."[32]

Modern constructions of dignified labor, indexed to hierarchies of social status, took shape during the colonial era, when European colonizers introduced new forms of work and compensation. Malian anthropologist Isaie

Dougnon (2007, 2009) shows how, over the course of the twentieth century, labor migrants from Mali's Dogon population adopted a dichotomized view of *le travail de Blanc* (white man's work) versus *le travail de Noir* (black man's work). *Le travail de Blanc* at first meant working for the colonizers, but the distinction survived into the era of independence. Although initially shunned and equated with hated practices of forced labor, today it is associated with modernity, high status, and the prospect of self-improvement. *Le travail de Noir*, by contrast, is associated with physical labor (especially agricultural work) and has become widely stigmatized. This division has been observed elsewhere in Africa. Researching in West Africa during the late colonial period, Rouch (1956:195) found that many forms of labor were considered "shameful for people not of servile caste; a free man does not work before the women of his country. The migrant, in emigrating, can thus work without shame." In Abidjan, Côte d'Ivoire, of the late 1990s, Newell (2006; in press: chap. 2) found that native Ivoirians prized office jobs and considered physical labor too degrading to perform, fit only for immigrants and strangers. Many Abidjan residents even saw driving a taxi as a low-status job, even though it paid far better than most "respectable" forms of employment. The problem, Newell notes, was neither the work per se nor its economic remuneration but rather the loss of face the worker would endure in the eyes of family and peers. To use Vincent's terminology, people commonly equate such work with "suffering."

Whereas these forms of labor are highly stigmatized at home, they are not off-limits to aventuriers like Vincent. In Cameroon he would have found working as an ambulant vendor demeaning; selling sandwiches in the street might offer better rewards than some higher-status forms of employment, but doing so appeared unworthy of a respectable father's son. After leaving home and becoming a stranger, however, Vincent could take up ambulant vending, as it did not make him lose face in the eyes of his own kin, friends, and home people. The same individuals who disdain certain jobs at home—such as sweeping streets, collecting trash, or driving a taxi—are often willing to do these jobs abroad, especially in countries perceived as more developed than their own. If anything, by emigrating to a faraway place aventuriers acquire a degree of recognition in their communities of origin and prove they have learned to take risks and struggle for their livelihoods. Parents back home might never find out what their migrant children do abroad, and those who are returned migrants themselves know better than to ask. They understand the sacrifices African migrants make when they go *en aventure*.

In Nigeria, the northern city of Kano has been a destination for migrants from the south of the country for generations. Southern Nigerians sometimes say "Kano hides a poor man" (see D. Smith 2008). This carries multiple meanings, one of which is that migrants in Kano can conceal their low employment status from their kin. As strangers, they can perform jobs that would have been unacceptable at home. Many Malian Dogon migrants in Cameroon, for example, manufacture metal cooking pots, thus breaking a Dogon cultural taboo against shaping metal—a ritually polluting task performed in their homeland only by members of the blacksmith caste (Cissé 2009). Soninke villagers in western Mali work as seasonal agricultural laborers in Senegal but consider the same type of work in their home communities to be humiliating (Jonsson 2008). Migrants' separation from home can protect their reputation even when they engage in degrading forms of labor. During my research in Congo, I came to think of this phenomenon as "What happens in Brazzaville stays in Brazzaville." It applied to ambulant vendors like Vincent and also to immigrants from Congo-Kinshasa who were the city's garbagemen, domestic helpers, and sex workers. It applied no less to West African aventuriers with their pushcarts and Thermos bottles.

Earlier in this book I introduced the Bamanan proverb "Tunga tè danbe dòn," or "Exile knows no dignity." The word *danbe* has been defined as dignity, honor, or reputation (Bailleul 2000). But *danbe*'s meaning is more nuanced: it is inextricably intertwined with one's homeland, or *faso* as it is called in Bamanan. By this notion, in one's *faso* (literally, "father's house") there is unique appreciation of one's intrinsic worth, particularly as it is associated with ascribed status—ancestry, family heritage, and renown.[33] This appreciation of one's *danbe* vanishes as soon as one leaves the *faso* and enters into *tunga* (a foreign land—the alien space of exile or *aventure*). There migrants become unknown quantities, and their illustrious ancestries, respected kin, and noble characters go unacknowledged.

West Africans often spoke of *danbe* as a cultural attribute unique to their home societies. In their minds the term encompassed a range of socially valued traits, from modesty and shame to respect for one's elders. "For us, *danbe* is in the center of everything," one Malian man in Brazzaville told me. "It's like water, people cannot live without it." Many of my unmarried male informants listed *danbe* as the most important quality to look for in a potential bride. "For me, if you take a wife, she must know *danbe*. The majority of people here [in Brazzaville] don't know *danbe*," said Alassan, the Congo-born son of a Togotalan immigrant. He linked the concept to his religious faith: "You can't know *danbe* if you don't know Islam. So that's it, whether the woman is Malian or Congolese." One informant likened *danbe* to a kind of patriotism, an affective relationship between the individual and the *faso* entailing its own set of rights and obligations: one must display certain positive qualities and, in return, be rewarded by one's family and home community with a good reputation. In an article on reputation and publicity in Mali, Schulz (1999:282) defines *danbe* as "the honor and prestige [one] gains from living up to the expectations" of one's people.

Recall the complete Bamanan proverb: "Exile knows no dignity, but it knows a good person." The proverb's latter phrase is embodied by West African aventuriers in Brazzaville who gain opportunity precisely because, as strangers, they are removed from place-bound constructions of dignity and respect. Where ascribed status is irrelevant, all that matters is one's individual accomplishments and successes. While abroad, strangers do not harm their reputations by stooping to degrading work. They can return home with their dignity intact.

Concern over status and reputation influences migrants' decisions about whether and when to return home, as well as which information concerning conditions in the place of destination to share with people back home. Migrants who have not succeeded, rather than lose face by returning home empty-handed, may remain abroad indefinitely and conceal their misfortune from their kin and peers in the place of origin. Aventuriers in Brazzaville were especially prone to this. Unlike the better-off traders, they had not yet accumulated much if any wealth, and were unable to send remittances home. Yet it was difficult for them to be open about their situations with people in their communities of origin: under pressure to prove themselves as future husbands and fathers, they were loath to appear incapable of making better lives than those who had stayed home. Instead, they remained abroad, hoping one day to reach the fabled diamond fields of Angola or perhaps find passage to a rich Western country. However desperate their situations became in Congo, return was almost out of the question.

When communicating with people back home, such migrants frequently misrepresent their circumstances, exaggerating successes and playing down hardships. In migrant-sending communities, this generates misinformation about migration and its prospects, creating a deceptive "demonstration effect" transmitting positive migration narratives but filtering out most negative information. This leads to a systemic bias in favor of migration even to destinations where real economic opportunities are scarce. Brazzaville has been such a destination for several years now, yet young migrants continue to arrive from West Africa without real knowledge of the economic and social difficulties awaiting them there.

Even when accurate information about hardship and lack of opportunity abroad *does* reach migrant-sending communities, its impact there is offset by widespread suspicions that migrants deliberately obscure their good fortunes abroad. Nonmigrants often believe (with some justification) that successful migrants conceal their good fortunes from those back home precisely in order to forestall the demands made by needy kin on their resources, as described above. Bad news from abroad, or even no news at all, comes to be interpreted as good news. Although some migrants do express a desire to tell those back home about the problems they encounter and the indignities they suffer abroad, as I have repeatedly found from my own experience in Africa, it is difficult for this kind of evidence to find a receptive audience among prospective migrants (a category including most males under the age of fifty in places like Mali, and increasing numbers of women). In their eyes, such warnings only suggest that many opportunities await them abroad, opportunities their selfish migrant kin would rather keep for themselves. Tensions between migrants and nonmigrants thus hinder the transmission of truthful reports about conditions at migration destinations, creating a "knowledge gap" that turns social networks into vehicles for disseminating false or deceptive information (see Barten 2009).

Conclusion: The Double-edged Sword

Migration, whether for labor or transnational trade, plainly stems from social as well as economic factors. The West African presence in Brazzaville demonstrates that people leave home for reasons that may have little to do with macroeconomic conditions. Governments, both African and European, have sought to keep Africa's potential migrants at home, or encourage existing migrants to return, with monetary incentives for starting businesses in their home communities. The Congolese government periodically announces new initiatives to encourage Congolese participation in private enterprise, and the French government has long advocated "co-development" policies geared to create enterprises in migrant-sending communities and provide alternatives to emigration. Despite meeting with little success, such programs keep cropping up. An accord between France and Congo budgeted 1.2 million euros to entice Congolese migrants in France to return home through small-business development between 2008 and 2010.[34] Such programs ignore the social dynamics of enterprise in African societies and particularly the difficulties of doing business "at home."

Studying strangers in Brazzaville reveals the importance of migration in contemporary African societies. More than a short-term response to conflict or economic crisis, migration offers possibilities of social and material advancement even to individuals from stable, peaceful communities. It has become vital to the livelihood strategies of millions of ordinary Africans, in part because of social pressures favoring entrepreneurial success abroad and discouraging certain forms of labor at home. These pressures may play only a secondary role in drawing migrants from poor African countries to wealthy countries in Europe and North America, with their higher wages and more auspicious business environments. They are a significant factor, however, behind existing migration *between* poor African countries, and particularly migration to impoverished, unstable, periodically violent countries like Congo. Strangerhood, in sum, confers economic advantages of which strangers are fully aware, inducing them to preserve their stranger status over the long term rather than integrate into their host community.

On a more theoretical level, West Africans' activities in Brazzaville provide insights into the nature of social relations, and specifically the often misunderstood relationship between social networks and social capital. Social scientists are likely to characterize the relationships making up social networks as unequivocally positive forces in people's lives, while overlooking their potential to undermine individuals' aspirations, threaten their interests, and penalize their successes. We can and should celebrate the ability of collectivities based on kinship, ethnicity, or other bonds to guard against hunger and destitution in poverty-stricken communities. But we must not forget the ability of these same collectivities to compel the successful few to share in the misfortunes of the majority—enacting what Portes calls "downward leveling norms." Embeddedness in social networks can drive people to distance themselves physically from those closest to them. Strong community bonds and embeddedness in social networks can even discourage individuals from being tested for the AIDS virus.[35] Like most anthropologists, I have long been inclined to see the virtues of sociability and group solidarity. This research, however, forces me to confront some of their ills as well and, in so doing, to recognize a key aspect of social dynamics in Africa: as these migrants' lives illustrate, social relations are a double-edged sword.

AMONG THE UNBELIEVERS

"Hold fast to prayer," Vieux Diallo counseled me as we walked back into the market from the nearby *zawiya*, the modest Sufi mosque, after the midday prayer. "All the other things, family, wealth, will abandon you at the grave," he said, "but the rewards from prayer, and fasting, and *zakat* [sacrifice] are the only things you can take with you after you die."

Diallo was more than devout in his Muslim faith. Not only did he perform all five daily prayers, but he did so in mosques near his work or home. Despite being in his seventies, he had recently made the decision to begin studying Arabic, the language of the holy Qur'an. Among West African men in Brazzaville, Diallo was by no means unusual in his devotion to Islam.

Mali's population is overwhelmingly Muslim, and signs of Islamic influence are omnipresent there: most Malians bear Muslim names, and many Bamanan nouns—from the names of the days of the week to the words for book, luck, obligation, and blessing—are derived from Arabic. I recognized all this during my initial years in Mali, and yet I was influenced by those who, following the lead of French colonial administrators, characterized West African societies as superficially Islamized. Islam, according to their logic, was only a veneer covering a more substantial African identity based on local "traditional beliefs." I held to the notion sometimes expressed by Western expatriates that "Mali is 90 percent Muslim and 100 percent animist."

Most Malians I knew seemed sincere in their Muslim faith, but they did not wear it on their sleeves. The Malian state is proudly secular, and though

I often heard recorded Islamic sermons in marketplaces and on public transport, few Malians ever talked to me about Islam, let alone tried to convert me. It did not appear to me that Islam had an especially privileged place in Malians' self-definitions. First and foremost they were Bamanan, Senufo, Soninke, or Halpulaaren; they were blacksmiths or griots, nobles or slaves, merchants or farmers. Islam seemed only a minor part of who they were, and an alien part at that. I was conditioned to believe that "true" Islam was elsewhere, particularly among the Arabs whose homeland was the cradle of the faith; the Islam practiced in West Africa had to be an adulterated, impure version.[1]

My first visit to Brazzaville forced me to rethink these perceptions. The most striking observation from my initial stay in the Congolese capital, abundantly clear from the morning of the first day, was the heightened importance of Islam for the West Africans living there. In the predawn hours, from my room on the southern edge of the Poto-Poto market, I heard at least four calls to predawn *fajr* prayers emanating from loudspeakers within half a mile. Many people I got to know in Brazzaville regularly attended prayers in any of the half-dozen neighborhood mosques. Back in Mali I had hardly known anyone who went to the mosque for all five required daily prayers, and those who did were almost exclusively elderly; in Brazzaville, it seemed, such men (for they were always men) were everywhere, and even for early morning prayers the neighborhood mosques were thronged with worshipers. Qur'anic study was a common activity for both males and females, young and old alike. And whereas in Mali males and females commonly wear Western clothes, the immigrants in Brazzaville tended to wear clothing more obviously Islamic in style—loose-fitting gowns (*boubous*) for men and Arab burnooses (*jelaba*) for women. In every respect these immigrants were more "visibly Muslim" than their peers back home.

Anthropologists have observed similar high levels of religiosity among Muslim strangers in other African communities. What accounts for it? Even during my initial visit to Brazzaville I suspected it was not entirely a matter of "selection bias" (a distinction based on the assumption that migrants are necessarily different from nonmigrants in certain respects): I spent most of my time with immigrants from the same town and even the same household where I had lived and conducted fieldwork in Mali the year before, and yet the contrast between their religiosity in Congo and in Mali was remarkable. Why were the immigrants I met in Brazzaville more likely than their kin back home to practice certain public expressions of their faith? I realized I could no longer assume Islam to be a marginal aspect of my informants' lives; moreover, I came to doubt that it was as marginal in Mali as I had assumed.

Throughout my Brazzaville fieldwork, I attended different mosques for daily prayers and evening classes to learn Arabic and to study Islamic scriptures. From this research, and from conversations with informants in Mali and Congo, I gradually acquired a very different view of the faith and its role. I learned that my informants saw Islam not only as an integral part of their identity but as something universal rather than inherently Arab and foreign. Though they venerated Islam's Middle Eastern holy sites, they did not necessarily see the Arabs' knowledge and practice of Islam as superior to their own. During an interview, a Malian imam in Brazzaville refuted the notion that one must study in the Arab world to be "properly trained": "Every kind of study which one needs in Islam, one can find in Mali," he said. If God chose to reveal the Qur'an in Arabic, another Malian once told me, it was because God knew that only the Arabs would be incapable of learning to read anyone else's language. A Soninke proverb likens Islam to a branding iron, which Arabs wield by the cool end while the red-hot end leaves its mark on Africans.[2]

One question that recurred during my fieldwork, particularly during conversations with Congolese, pertained to Islam's impact on West Africans' integration, or, more accurately, lack of integration, into Congolese society. Many hosts felt that these immigrants' Muslim faith set them apart and prevented them from fitting in with the Congolese mainstream. How accurate were these perceptions? Was religious difference really the reason for friction between these immigrants and their hosts? In the wake of the terrorist attacks of September 11, 2001, the Bush administration's "global war on terror," and subsequent attacks by Islamist terrorists in Madrid and London, this last question obviously had great resonance in my own country, as well as in many others where Muslim immigrants have become more visible in recent decades.

This chapter explores the ways that West Africans in Brazzaville use Islamic discourses and practices to condition their interactions with the host society and with one another. After briefly sketching the historical processes through which Islam came to dominate societies of the western Sahel, I describe its practice in Brazzaville and examine the tension between Islam as a universal faith and as an exclusive identity in this setting. I consider the role of religious devotion in fostering a shared sense of identity and solidarity among West Africans. Finally, I consider what part, if any, Islam plays in maintaining West Africans' "strangerhood" and even preventing them from blending into Congolese society.

Islam's Evolution in West Africa

Islam has deep roots in the Sahel. Although it remained a marginal religion there for centuries, it was introduced into West Africa by Arab traders as early as the tenth century CE (Common Era, equivalent to "AD"), and by the eleventh century some Sahelian towns were host to Muslim minorities living apart from the non-Muslim population. Muslim clerics and merchants forged close ties with local non-Muslim rulers, who sometimes embraced the faith and commanded their subjects to do likewise. Thus the inhabitants of the empire of Ghana (the ancestors of the Soninke people) converted to Islam en masse in the year 1076. From the thirteenth century, rulers of the Empire of Mali were at least nominally Muslim, and some went to great lengths to prove their religious fervor. Mansa Moussa, who ruled over Mali in the fourteenth century, made a legendary pilgrimage to Mecca with his royal entourage, giving away so much gold along the way that the precious metal's price remained depressed in the Cairo marketplace for years afterward.[3]

As in any region, Islamic belief and practice in West Africa vary from one specific locale to another. Yet a shared interpretation of Islam eventually formed in the western Sahel, encompassing parts of present-day Senegal, Mauritania, Guinea, Mali, Burkina Faso, and Côte d'Ivoire (the same zone from which Brazzaville's West African population originates). Studying Islamic scholars from the region and their educational pedigrees, historian Ivor Wilks has traced a shared set of teachings of the *hadith* (traditions of the Prophet Muhammad) to the writings of one al-Hajj Salim Suwari, a prominent West African Islamic teacher who probably lived in the fifteenth century CE. Wilks credits Suwari with originating many defining features of Islam in the region, and indeed other scholars have subsequently referred to a "Suwarian tradition" in this region.[4] This pedagogical tradition was itself influenced by the teachings of Jalal al-Din al-Suyuti, a Cairo-based Islamic scholar under whom Suwari may have studied. Al-Suyuti is generally described as a liberal, preaching tolerance toward non-Muslims and endorsing a strict separation between Islam and government; these views were central to Suwari's own teachings. He saw unbelief (*kufr*) as the result of ignorance rather than evil and believed that it was God's plan for some peoples of the world to remain unbelievers—a notion that renders militant *jihad* unacceptable. He furthermore taught that it was permissible for Muslims to submit to non-Muslim political authority when necessary, that is, when Muslims were in the minority—which until fairly recently was the case in most of West Africa, where Muslims long dominated trade but tended to stay out of politics. "Al-Hajj Salim Suwari thus formulated a praxis of coexistence," writes Wilks (2000:98), enabling Muslim merchants "to operate within lands of unbelief without prejudice to their distinctive Muslim identity, allowing them access to the material resources of this world without foregoing salvation in the next."

The Suwarian tradition's tolerance set the tone for the development of Islam in much of West Africa into the twentieth century. It was also because of this tradition that Islam remained largely associated with specific identities. Islamic scholars (*mori*), for example, issued from hereditary clans integrated into the upper levels of the social hierarchy. They maintained a strict segregation between the realms of religion and political power, viewing the latter domain as tarnished by tyranny and injustice. Yet they also supported the rule of non-Muslim aristocratic/warrior clans, providing spiritual "consulting services" and sometimes even their daughters' hands in marriage to the political elite. Among the Dyula of northern Côte d'Ivoire, only members of *mori* clans were expected to uphold high standards of piety, including regular prayer and abstention from alcohol, whereas other nominally Muslim Dyula lived much like their non-Muslim neighbors, expressing their Islamic identity mainly through participation in Muslim life-course rituals and holidays.[5]

Islam also marked the boundaries of the merchant community, most members of which came from *mori* clans; for generations West Africa's Muslim trading diaspora was like "Islamic islands in an animist sea" (Warms 1992:485). The strong association of Islam with commerce meant that Muslims dominated trade and held considerable economic power. Muslims would only take other Muslims as their trading partners, and propagating their faith would broaden the population of potential partners and rivals, thus undermining their special standing. For this reason, "merchants did not necessarily have any interest in converting their neighbors.... Islam was, at least in some regions, the mark of a hereditary trade monopoly" (Launay and Soares 1999:500). It was also ethnically marked: a few groups (notably Soninke and Halpulaaren) were overwhelmingly Muslim, whereas others remained mostly non-Muslim for centuries.

The influence of the Suwarian tradition, coupled with the continuing importance of trade for the region's Muslims, contributed to the development of a relatively liberal, politically passive version of Islam in West Africa. The Islam that French colonizers encountered in much of West Africa from the 1800s on was heavily conditioned by al-Hajj Suwari's legacy, especially with respect to the relationships Muslims maintained with unbelievers and with non-Muslim political authority.[6] During the colonial era, this legacy provided the framework onto which Muslims made subsequent additions, such as the practices of certain Sufi brotherhoods. It was this framework, complete with adaptations and innovations, that became the focus of many more challenges after the onset of European rule in the region.

Islam in the western Sahel gained more followers during seventy years of colonialism than during the previous nine centuries. Yet France did its best *not* to promote Islam in its colonial territories. French officials were extremely wary of the religion, perceiving it as a potential threat to their political authority and republican ideals; wherever they could they sought to contain, if not roll back, Islamic influence, particularly stemming from Arabia.[7] Nonetheless, the effects of European colonization—especially monetization of the economy, pacification of local conflicts, and the abolition of slavery—led to unintended consequences that contributed to Islam's growth and transformation in West Africa.

One of these was the reorganization of the region's commercial activity. As the French promoted the flow of raw materials (such as peanuts, palm oil, cotton, rubber, cocoa, and coffee) for export, expanded internal markets also benefited the domestic trade in cattle, kola nuts, and dried fish. Muslim trade monopolies in these commodities were disrupted and Muslim traders' longtime rapport with local political elites was destabilized. A new commercial sector formed in which individuals could compete irrespective of their membership in mercantile clans, and Islamic identity shifted from a matter of group affiliation to one of individual choice. Subsequently both commerce and Islam became accessible to those who had previously not had entry, and though the link between clan, commerce, and faith remained strong, new converts eagerly participated in trade. As a result, the "Muslim commercial sector no longer hinged on collective hereditary identities" (Launay and Soares 1999:506).

Another consequence of colonial rule was a dramatic increase in West African migration, both within the region and beyond. The new cash economy and colonial head taxes made seasonal labor migration a key strategy for many households and individuals (particularly unmarried men) to obtain needed cash. The suppression of slavery within the region also freed up a significant portion of the population to participate in the emerging labor market, even as the imposition of French military control quelled multiple small-scale wars in the region, facilitating long-distance travel. As a result, unprecedented numbers of people circulated throughout West Africa, migrating to coastal areas during inland dry seasons, working on plantations or in rapidly growing colonial towns. Southern Côte d'Ivoire, in particular, saw large migrant influxes from the mostly Muslim lands to the north beginning in the early twentieth century. People settled in new urban centers, mixing with populations from other regions. Moreover, small numbers of migrants began traveling to other French colonies, including in Central Africa, and even to the metropole itself. The *hajj*, or pilgrimage, to Mecca, which had previously been an almost impossible dream for ordinary West African Muslims, became feasible for increasing numbers of people.[8]

A natural result of this expanded human mobility was a flood of new ideas pertaining to the interpretation and practice of Islam, originating from all over the Muslim world and particularly the Arabian Peninsula. The ensuing tension between competing versions of Islam brought about what Eickelman and Piscatori (1996:38) call "objectification," "the process by which basic questions come to the fore in the consciousness of large numbers of believers." In cosmopolitan settings, Muslims gave fresh scrutiny to religious customs once taken for granted. Islam was no longer a direct correlate, for example, of a given ethnicity or of merchant status; as the category of "being Muslim" came to be seen as something one attained less by birth than by practice, Islam was gradually uncoupled from the particular identities with which it had been associated. From the 1940s, reformist movements influenced by customs and doctrines emanating from the Arab world took root in West African cities, bringing new interpretations of the faith from Egypt and Saudi Arabia.[9] These movements contributed to the construction of Islam as a universal faith demanding a strict set of behaviors from its adherents.

In the postcolonial context, the universal aspects of Islam have assumed ever-greater prominence. Some scholars identify a process of standardization at work, as a unified "Islamic sphere" emerges to supplant the manifold local Islamic versions that existed previously. This sphere rests on an objectified and text-based understanding of Islam entailing a common standard of Islamic practice. Throughout West Africa "a more generally shared (though hardly uniform) sense of being Muslim and a commitment to Islam as a religion . . . has developed in the postcolonial period, which allows Muslims to imagine themselves as part of the global Islamic community" (Soares 1999:229). Some refer to this as an "Arabized" interpretation of Islam, not least because it places strong emphasis on Arabic literacy enabling individual access to sacred texts. The stress on a more standardized, universal interpretation of the faith reflects similar trends throughout the wider Muslim world during the modern era.[10]

Before turning my attention to Islamic identity and practice in Congo, I should add two caveats about the formation of this universalized Islam in West Africa. First of all, "traditional Islam" there was hardly isolated from the rest of the global community of Muslims (the *umma*) until Europeans appeared on the scene: from medieval times, scholars and texts originating in other parts of the Muslim world profoundly influenced the ways in which Islam was understood in West Africa. We can say, however, that once the changes in the region's political economy induced by colonialism took full effect, the *degree* of interaction between Muslims in West Africa and Muslims elsewhere increased considerably; these interactions multiplied further with the advent of telecommunications and transportation technology (changes commonly associated with globalization) facilitating flows of ideas among geographically distant believers. Second, Islam in West Africa remains a diverse faith today, and the standardization dynamic outlined above has by no means brought about the homogenization of Islamic practice in this region. Major conflicts continue to divide Muslims there with respect to religious authority, Sufi mysticism, reformist doctrine, scriptural interpretation, state politics, and a host of other issues. Nor is it the case that religious beliefs and practices associated with particular (as opposed to universal) places and identities have been eliminated. Most noteworthy here is the entity against which Muslims define such local beliefs and practices: a shared, expanding, and cosmopolitan brand of Islam featuring a novel set of reference points and perspectives on the relationship between the individual believer and sacred texts. It is this understanding of Islam in West Africa, dubbed the "postcolonial tradition" by Soares (2005b:10), that also pervades the Muslim community in Brazzaville.

Dynamics and Divisions of an Immigrant Faith

Since the middle of the colonial era most people in Congo have adhered to various forms of Christianity, especially Catholicism, often in tandem with local spiritualist beliefs and practices, and today at least 90 percent of its population is believed to be Christian.[11] Congo sits far outside the area of Africa penetrated by Islam prior to European rule. The first Muslims to settle in Congo were West Africans arriving during the nineteenth century (see chapter 1); *wara*, the most common name used by Congolese to refer to West Africans in Brazzaville, is virtually synonymous with Muslim in local parlance. Of course the city is home to some non-Muslim West African immigrants—from Nigeria, Benin, and elsewhere—but the Sahelians (Malians, Senegalese, Mauritanians, Guineans, and a few others) who compose the vast majority of this immigrant population are *all* Muslims. It is interesting to note that although there are Christian and "animist" minorities throughout the western Sahel, I never met or even heard of any non-Muslims from this region residing in Brazzaville. Selection bias may be at work in this case, with non-Muslim Sahelians opting to stay home or migrating to alternative destinations.

If we can consider all Brazzaville's Sahelian West Africans to be Muslims, not all Brazzaville's Muslims are Sahelian West Africans. In addition to several hundred Muslims from Chad, the Central African Republic, Morocco, Lebanon, Egypt, and elsewhere, there is a small but growing population of Congolese Muslim converts and their descendants. I examine this group and its relations with West African Muslims later in this chapter. For now it suffices to say that West Africans dominate Muslim life in Brazzaville: it was they who introduced Islam to Congo during the onset of colonial rule, they who constitute the overwhelming majority of the city's Muslim population today, they who funded the construction of most of the city's mosques and Muslim schools, and they who supply most of the imams and teachers for these institutions. So close is the association in Congo between West Africans and Islam that the chairman of the Islamic Council of Congo, a Congolese with no West African ancestry, is frequently mistaken for a West African whenever he wears Muslim-style garb; despite his fluency in a number of Congolese languages, he sometimes meets compatriots who refuse to believe he is a Congolese like them. "Here in Congo, once you hear the word 'Muslim,' you think 'immigrant,'" another member of the Islamic Council, himself a native-born Congolese, told me.

Although Islam has won local converts and figures among the seven religious traditions officially recognized by the Congolese state since 1978 (see Gruénais, Mouanda Mbambi, and Tonda 1995), many non-Muslim Congolese regard both the faith and its adherents with suspicion. When I surveyed Congolese university students in Brazzaville about their views of West Africans and their religion, I asked them to respond to the statement "Islam is concordant with Congolese society and mores." More than twice as many respondents disagreed than agreed. Nearly one-third of all respondents felt that Islam should not be recognized by the state. Such views are an outward sign of latent tensions between Muslims and non-Muslims in Congo.

In many cities around the world where Muslim immigrants reside, the so-called Muslim community is a heterogeneous collection of people with divergent geographic and ethnic origins and often very different ideas about

Figure 3.1. Poto-Poto's Malikiyya mosque under construction in 2005, with new minarets going up. PHOTO BY AUTHOR

Islam. In mosques throughout Europe and North America, notably, Arabs share space with South Asians and Africans as well as with local converts. Interpretations of the faith may vary substantially between these subgroups, leading Muslims to reevaluate or adapt their religious practices to new circumstances. In Brazzaville, however, Islam remains a predominantly West African concern, despite the presence of various other Muslim groups noted above.

Divisions within the city's Muslim community therefore correspond to similar divisions among Muslims in West Africa. Although almost all Brazzaville's Muslims consider themselves Sunni (as opposed to Shi'a), their ranks are nonetheless split into two main camps. Members of the first, formerly dominant camp follow what Soares (2005b:9) calls the "Sufi tradition." They are associated with various Sufi orders. They venerate *wali* or Muslim saints and their descendants, in whom they invest great religious and political authority. Members of the second camp, today comprising the majority of Brazzaville's Muslims, could be described as following the "reformist tradition" (Soares 2005b:10), often somewhat misleadingly glossed as "Wahhabism" or even "fundamentalism."[12] Members of this group stress a version of "correct Muslim practice" patterned after Islamic interpretations originating in Saudi Arabia. They look down upon saint worship and other practices associated with Sufism, which they see as committing two types of grave error, *shirk* (associating something else with God) and *bid'a* (introducing innovations to the faith).

The divide between Sufi and reformist West Africans dates back many decades. While Sufism, in the form of the Tijaniyya order, was the dominant form of practice among West African Muslims for most of the twentieth century, challenges to the Sufi tradition began to gather strength in the 1940s and 1950s. With travel from sub-Saharan Africa to the Middle East becoming faster, easier, and cheaper, an increasing number of West African Muslims began going to Egypt and Saudi Arabia to study or perform the *hajj*. Upon returning to West Africa, they formed the nucleus of a growing reformist movement. This movement also took root in Central Africa, particularly among second-generation West Africans. In the late 1960s the generational conflict between established Sufis and young reformists in Kinshasa provoked a leadership crisis in the city's Muslim community. In 1969 long-simmering tensions between worshipers in Brazzaville's *grande mosquée* boiled over when reformists voiced their opposition to Sufi rituals, which they described as un-Islamic. This conflict led to the intervention of Congolese authorities and to the dissident group splitting off from the Sufi congregation. A few years later reformists built a separate mosque in Poto-Poto where they could worship behind one of their own imams; known as the "Sunni mosque,"[13] it became only the third mosque in Brazzaville where Friday prayers were conducted. A number of other mosques were subsequently built in neighborhoods around the city, and today there are at least six in which Friday prayers are held, four of which are regarded as reformist mosques. Immigrant Muslim communities in Brazzaville and Kinshasa appear to have played an important role in helping to diffuse reformist ideals within West Africa: returned migrants from the Congo Basin were among the first reformist Muslims in the upper Senegal River Valley.[14]

Many partisans on each side still distrust or even demonize those on the other. Vieux Diallo, for example, considered himself a devout follower of the Tijaniyya Sufi brotherhood and represented reformists as, at best, deeply misguided and, at worst, heretics and false believers. He warned me against associating with them: "They engage in fornication, corruption, and theft," he once said in hushed tones, looking around dramatically for eavesdroppers, "then get together at the mosque to brag about it." In his thirty-five years in Brazzaville, Diallo told me, he had never set foot inside a reformist mosque. Meanwhile, my neighbor Modibo was a reformist who prayed at home only in cases of severe illness or driving rain, and otherwise went to mosques for each of the five required daily prayers (I know because I often accompanied him, especially for the predawn *fajr* prayers). Modibo told me he had never, since coming to Brazzaville twenty-five years earlier, set foot in any of the city's Sufi mosques.

Despite such examples, however, relations between supporters of Sufi and reformist traditions in Brazzaville have reached a kind of entente in recent years. There seemed to be a consensus among imams and many of their followers that open disagreement was unproductive. In Brazzaville, as in West Africa, a practical rapprochement that Kaba (2000:203) describes as a "new ethic of disagreement" holds that "the enemy resides within oneself, and the Muslims must act on the basis of their unity rather than differences." Moreover, many elements of the "Suwarian tradition" remain intact in the Congo Basin, where Islam's presence recalls its role in nineteenth-century West Africa. In both settings Muslims were "islands in a non-Muslim sea," to adapt the expression cited earlier, and Islam was strongly associated with commerce. In both contexts Muslims had similar relationships with non-Muslim political authority, often cooperating with animist or Christian rulers. And in both contexts Muslims maintained a firm boundary between themselves and members of the non-Muslim host population, as well as a corresponding degree of internal solidarity.

Prayer and *Communitas*

One of the most remarkable features of Muslim life in Brazzaville, as I mentioned at the beginning of this chapter, is the high degree of public religious expression. The heightened sense of religious identity and the upsurge of religious expression I observed there are common among immigrants who have moved from Muslim-majority to Muslim-minority communities. For Muslims who migrate to Western countries, newfound religiosity is commonly attributed to their troubled relationship with the host society: estranged from the dominant non-Muslim culture, they embrace their faith in a manner they never had at home. Not all immigrants who adopt a more rigorous version of their faith, however, do so because they are disaffected or alone. My informants in Brazzaville generally developed the impulse toward greater religiosity not as isolated individuals but within the wider context of the West African immigrant community. Furthermore, their new approach to their faith was not simply a difference of degree; it entailed a qualitative shift in their beliefs and behavior. Immigrants' understanding of what it means to "be Muslim" tends to change over time from a matter of inherited status to a matter of personal practice. They come to view their religious faith as a set of rules governing their daily activities, which they may or may not have closely followed in their place of origin. This process has been studied in a variety of cultural and geographic settings, including among Sahelian migrants in colonial Ghana, second-generation North Africans in France, Turkish guest workers in Germany, and Sierra Leonean Muslims in the United States.[15] Many immigrants come to see respecting the "rules" of their faith as the primary means of preserving cultural as well as spiritual purity.

Many Muslims learn to calculate the reward earned by respecting Islam's commandments as derived from the Qur'an and the traditions of the Prophet. This reward is known in Bamanan as *baraji* (equivalent to the Arabic *al jiza*). One receives ten measures of *baraji*, for example, for each letter in a Qur'anic verse one recites. One accumulates *baraji* with each step one takes on the way to prayer at a mosque. Prayer during the holy month of Ramadan is said to bring more *baraji* than prayer at other times of the year. For almost any praiseworthy act one could perform, scriptures define a degree of reward to be held in one's favor on the Day of Judgment. The desire to build up this reward is a strong motivating factor in the everyday activities of pious Muslims, and this is especially true among West Africans in Brazzaville for whom the calculus of reward earned from praiseworthy acts has served to formalize a code of conduct in daily life.

This code sets out which actions are taboo and which are commendable. The prohibition on the consumption of alcohol, enjoined by God in the Qur'an, is well known, and it is not surprising given the popularity of alcoholic beverages in Congolese social life that Muslims in Brazzaville should give this taboo considerable emphasis. A few of my West African informants did not let this rule prevent them from socializing with Congolese; for them it was perfectly acceptable to go to *ngandas* (off-license beer joints), bars, or nightclubs with Congolese friends and have soft drinks instead of beer. Most Muslims I knew, however, considered that merely stepping into a bar was akin to actually drinking alcohol; they discouraged any of their fellows from partaking in Brazzaville's famous nightlife. Entering a bar, *nganda,* or club entails subtracting oneself from the gaze of the Muslim community, an act many of my informants perceive as a betrayal of one's Muslim religion and identity.

Together with the taboos, the prevailing Islamic code of conduct among West Africans in Brazzaville encourages the observation of certain religious duties, including fasting during the holy month of Ramadan and giving alms to the poor. Proper dress is another crucial area: as I have mentioned, in Brazzaville one is more likely than in Bamako to see West Africans, male and female alike, wearing garb that is clearly identified as Islamic. Many of my informants, particularly women, expressed a sense that in Brazzaville they were expected to conform to a higher religious standard of dress, and that they put more emphasis on proper Islamic conduct in general than they had back home.

The Islamic practice that receives the most prominent emphasis is collective prayer (in Arabic, *salāt al-jama'a*; in Bamanan, *jama seli*). It is well known that prayer is one of Islam's "five pillars," a central duty for all Muslims; according to many of my informants, it is *the* central duty.[16] The Qur'an instructs the faithful to pray five times daily at prescribed moments and in a prescribed fashion. One can pray individually or alongside others, but various traditions of the Prophet state that collective prayer brings a much greater reward than individual prayer to the person praying. Clerics and ordinary Muslims to whom I spoke agreed that *salāt al-jama'a*, even if it involves only two people praying together, carries far more *baraji* than praying alone (twenty-five or twenty-seven times as much, in fact, depending on the source of one's information). Muslims therefore have a strong incentive to perform their daily prayers collectively whenever possible.

And yet Muslims in the Malian communities where I have lived often pray individually. Many Muslim men in Mali perform *salāt al-jama'a* only once a week, at the mosque during Friday worship (in Arabic, *salāt al-juma*; in Bamanan, *juma seli*).[17] Even where a group of people gathers together, one often sees them praying consecutively, one after the other, rather than simultaneously.

In Brazzaville the situation is markedly different: West Africans there are likely to address God not individually but as a community. Not only do many Muslim males pray collectively several times every day, but they do so in mosques. This is the case even though *salāt al-jama'a* carries the same reward regardless of where it is conducted, and it can be performed wherever there is sufficient space and prayer mats for everyone. Many men, both young and old, go to a mosque three, four, or five times a day for *salāt al-jama'a*. Even for the predawn *fajr* prayer, when Muslims could be reasonably expected to pray at home, mosques around Brazzaville welcome hundreds of worshipers, whereas in Mali one is likely to see only a small number of elderly and particularly pious Muslims in mosques for *fajr*.

Informants downplayed any inconsistency between how they prayed in their homeland versus abroad, ascribing difference to the specific conditions of their life in Brazzaville. Haruna, a Malian shopkeeper in his late forties who sold schoolbags and sandals in one of the capital's main markets, was typical in this regard.

> In Mali I didn't go to mosque often, only on Fridays. But I was young then, and also because of my work I didn't have time to go to mosque. You're in the fields all day, and when you come home it's already late. . . . When I took up commerce, trading in the bush, I didn't have time to go to the mosque then either. When I came [to Brazzaville], I didn't have anything. . . . Day and night I was in this shop, an alimentation, *and I prayed there*. When I had a little bit saved up I left the alimentation to come to the marketplace. Here, when prayer is called you have the time to go. You don't work in the evenings, from sundown to sunrise. When I left the alimentation to come to the market I found I had much more time to go pray at the mosque.

The age and professional activities of these men condition their ability to attend mosque prayers regularly, and it is true that frequent mosque-goers in Brazzaville are more likely to be in their forties and fifties than in their twenties. While shop owners are in the mosque for the two afternoon prayers, their younger assistants must stay behind to mind the store. Yet such factors still cannot account for why these more established men feel compelled to carry out their collective prayers in the mosque rather than somewhere more convenient, such as their shops or homes, with nearby colleagues, friends, or family members.

Mosques, for these immigrants, serve a purpose over and above their function as sites for prayer. They are the spatial focal points of Brazzaville's West African community, and play a number of roles distinct from their mission as places of worship. Perhaps most important, they constitute the primary space in which West Africans physically come together. During prayer the community—or, more accurately, a good portion of its male half—literally stands shoulder to shoulder, publicly affirming its unity in a demonstration of Victor Turner's (1969) concept of *communitas*, a state of equality induced by shared liminality. Whereas individual prayer is often performed quickly, in mosques (particularly reformist ones) *salāt al-jama'a* can take anywhere from twelve to twenty minutes to complete, not including the time for ablutions beforehand, and many worshipers remain in the mosque once the required prayers are complete to perform supplementary prayers or recite sacred incantations. After prayer in the mosque Muslims can see one another, exchange greetings, and engage in conversation that their responsibilities and schedules might prevent them from conducting elsewhere. The community of believers polices itself: regular worshipers who miss a prayer for any reason will be gently called to account by their fellow mosque-goers and reminded of their religious responsibilities. In the evening, between *salāt al-maghreb* (the prayer at sunset) and *salāt al-isha'a* (the final prayer conducted about an hour later), a mosque might host dozens or hundreds of men and boys studying Arabic, learning the Qur'an and other Islamic texts. (Like prayer, religious study for women in this population is conducted at home.)

It is true that many West Africans in Brazzaville do not attend mosque prayers every day; women mainly avoid the mosque altogether, and male workers and young people generally are less likely to go than their more established elders. Nonetheless, the mosque's amplified importance in the life of this community is undeniable, and points to the manner in which migrants employ Islam, and the physical spaces associated with it, to reinforce their relationships with one another.

The importance of communal prayer spaces in this community is suggested not only by the frequency of Muslims' trips to the mosque but by the number of new mosques erected over the years by West African traders. In 2003, during a visit to the Congolese port city of Pointe-Noire, I accompanied a Malian friend to Nzassy, a nearby village on the border with the Angolan enclave of Cabinda. Nzassy is a transit point for goods moving between Angola and Congo, and consequently a number of West African merchants do business there. The occasion of our visit was the inauguration of a site for the construction of the village's first mosque. I asked my host how many Muslims lived in Nzassy. None, he replied; the mosque would only be used by traders from Pointe-Noire doing business there during the day. I was surprised that even in a location with no resident Muslims, where Muslims would likely be present for just two or three of the daily prayers, improvised spaces for *salāt al-jama'a*—commonplace in West Africa—were unacceptable and an official mosque was deemed necessary. Some might see the proliferation of mosques in Brazzaville (where there are currently about two dozen in all), as well as other Congolese towns, as part of a concerted campaign by West Africans to "mark their territory," inscribing their presence and culture onto the host society's urban landscape. Indeed, Congolese frequently volunteered such judgments to me, describing mosques as an invasive presence in their neighborhoods. The creation of these mosques, however, is less about claiming space than protecting a particular form of community, and providing a physical environment in which it can be fostered.

Building upon its chief purpose as a space for prayer and the physical enactment of community, the mosque is also a privileged site for the dissemination of information. When the Malian consulate in Brazzaville calls a general meeting, for example, it is through the sound systems of the *grande mosquée*, the "Sunni mosque," and other such buildings following prayer times that the announcements are made (although meetings themselves are held at the consulate). Visiting politicians from Mali sometimes make special visits to Brazzaville's mosques to reach out to potential supporters. When illness or death strikes a member of the community, the imam breaks the news after prayers and asks Muslims to recite *du'a* (specific petitionary prayers) for the persons and families concerned. On several occasions I heard appeals for financial assistance for elderly immigrants wanting to return to West Africa but lacking the means to do so. The births, weddings, and deaths of West Africans in faraway places, particularly Bamako and Abidjan, are also often announced at the mosque, as are the homeward departures of many migrants, who ask their fellow Muslims to forgive any outstanding disputes they may have with them and pray for their safe journey. These factors make the mosque a key site in this transnational space, a locus of what Giddens (1990:14) calls "time-space distanciation" connecting present and absent members of the community.

The elevated importance of public prayer in Brazzaville's mosques seems to apply regardless of one's particular Islamic tradition or one's ethnic or national origin. Yet despite the power of such public rituals of shared identity and purpose, complete solidarity among Brazzaville's Muslims remains an elusive quality—especially concerning the distinction between West Africans and native Congolese adherents of Islam.

Converts and Novices

Congolese Muslims, though relatively few in number, pose a problem to the neat binary opposition that West Africans often draw between themselves as Muslims and Congolese as *kafiri*, unbelievers. In their discourse about the host society, West Africans emphasize its un-Islamic or even anti-Islamic features, particularly the consumption of alcoholic beverages and what West Africans often described as wanton sexuality. Their discourse often reduces Congolese culture to a collection of stereotypes revolving around sinful behaviors such as drinking, dishonesty, fornication, and disrespect for elders. Such a discourse allows for little common ground between members of these populations.

Although the total number of Muslims of Congolese origin is probably still quite small (several thousand, out of a population of more than three million), this community has undergone steady growth since the early twentieth century. Congolese Muslim students have won scholarships from Arab governments and Islamic religious organizations for religious studies in centers of Islamic learning, including Cairo's Al-Azhar University and the Islamic University of Medina in Saudi Arabia. Moreover, since the early 1990s Brazzaville has seen a proliferation of Muslim nongovernmental organizations (NGOs) and micro-credit associations, almost entirely at the initiative of Congolese Muslims. The leadership of the national Muslim organization, the Islamic Council of Congo, as well as its predecessors dating back to the 1940s, has always been held by Congolese. With no long-standing indigenous Islamic tradition to conform to, these Muslims have adopted a highly standardized, universalist, and "Arabized" approach to their faith, along the lines of West Africa's reformist tradition.

Publicly many West Africans, particularly clerics, affirm their support for their Congolese "brothers and sisters" in Islam. One Malian imam I interviewed praised Congolese Muslims for the depth of their learning and their genuine devotion to their religion, and stressed the religious bond that West Africans and Congolese shared. "We're all the same; I can't say that we're better than they, no," he told me. This was a veiled rejoinder to West Africans who were more dubious of Congolese Muslims' sincerity. According to these opinions, Congolese converted to Islam for selfish reasons or because of simplistic notions about the faith. Some of my informants opined that when young Congolese men see wealthy West African traders praying in the mosque, they develop a syllogistic understanding of the relationship between being Islam and wealth: "Muslims pray at the mosque; Muslims are wealthy; therefore, if I pray at the mosque, I too will become wealthy." Such converts were only looking for handouts, I was told, and I was warned not to trust them if ever they approached me.

West Africans' suspicions and sometimes condescending attitudes regarding Congolese Muslims are nothing new. They have existed in Brazzaville at least as long as the tensions between partisans of the Sufi and reformist traditions in the city. In March 1954 a dispute erupted between West African and Congolese Muslims in Poto-Poto's *grande mosquée*. According to an account of the incident reported by Kane (n.d.:54),

> [West Africans] treated Congolese as beginners [*débutants*] because it was [the West Africans] who had brought them "Islamic knowledge" and who therefore remained "masters of the subject." In the course of this misunderstanding, a Halpulaar Muslim slapped a Congolese. Given this anti-Islamic behavior, Al Hajj Ibrahim Paraiso [a prominent local Muslim of Dahomeyan descent] left the *grande mosquée* and decided henceforth to pray at home. The indigenous [Congolese] Muslim community also reacted and instituted Friday prayers in the Ouenzé neighborhood mosque.

This was the first significant schism within Brazzaville's Muslim community, the first instance of a group of Muslims in the city deciding to hold Friday prayers somewhere other than the *grande mosquée*. To this day the mosque in Ouenzé remains the focal point of the Congolese Muslim community, and prayers there have been led exclusively by Congolese imams since the 1960s, whereas the primary imams of each of Brazzaville's other principal mosques, as well as most of their assistants, are either West African–born or the sons of West African immigrants.

The construction and leadership of mosques has been an issue of crucial importance to Brazzaville's Muslims. West Africans pride themselves on having financed and built a number of large, expensive mosques in Brazzaville without assistance from governments or organizations in the Arab world. Most are located inside or close to market areas. Poto-Poto's "Sunni mosque," with a capacity of nearly two thousand worshipers (twice that of the *grande mosquée*), is an especially impressive structure. It is three stories high with two minarets towering over the neighborhood; its walls are tiled and its floors carpeted, and scores of ceiling fans whir overhead to keep worshipers cool. During blackouts, a powerful generator assures that the mosque remains lit at night. Its construction occurred in stages over several years funded by contributions from worshipers and merchants, and West African reformists see it as very much "their" mosque, just as West African Sufis see the more modest *grande mosquée* as their own. Any Muslim may worship in these mosques, and Friday sermons are translated from Arabic into Bamanan and Lingala, as well as Soninke, Fulfulde, or French depending on the venue. There is a tacit understanding, however, that only West Africans may have leadership positions in these mosques, and the religious study classes held there are conducted almost entirely in West African languages (Soninke and Bamanan); a Congolese student of Islam would not feel especially welcome.

The Ouenzé mosque, by contrast, is a single-story structure with painted concrete walls and holds only about four hundred worshipers; it is officially known as the "King Faisal mosque," because the Saudi government donated funds for its refurbishment and expansion in 1976. There Congolese languages predominate, and, although some West Africans from the nearby market attend prayers inside, the mosque has the reputation of being "for Congolese."

The 1954 conflict at the *grande mosquée* also speaks to a problem that still rankles Congolese Muslims: no matter how much Islamic knowledge they acquire, too often West Africans treat them like novices in matters of faith. Many of my West African informants believed they had "seniority" in Islamic affairs over Congolese Muslims, supposing that many centuries of tradition give them greater religious legitimacy. Many were reluctant to recognize that a Congolese could attain a high degree of Islamic knowledge. One clear example of this bias became visible to me during the early part of my fieldwork in Brazzaville after I began Qur'anic study in the "Sunni mosque." My instructor, Hassan, was the only one of the mosque's half-dozen instructors who was not obviously West African. His classical Arabic was exquisite and he had thorough knowledge of the Qur'an, but unlike the other instructors, who taught their classes in Soninke or Bamanan, Hassan spoke French with his students (who, apart from me, were all West Africans)—an educated, metropolitan style of French, complete with the guttural "r" sound most Malians I know are either unable or unwilling to make since they associate it with *tubabuw*, white people. I was curious about Hassan and his origins. Some West African friends told me that Hassan hailed from the northeastern region of Congo-Kinshasa, an area to which Islam had been introduced by Arab traders and slave merchants (see Bibeau 1975) and which, they told me, produced that country's most learned Islamic specialists. Eventually Hassan told me that he was a Brazzaville native, born and bred, and had acquired all of his Islamic training there. My informants' misperception of his identity signaled their unwillingness to recognize that a local Congolese could equal or exceed West Africans in Islamic learning.

As mentioned above, members of the indigenous Congolese segment of Brazzaville's Muslim community tend to have a "universal" and extraverted outlook on what it means to be Muslim. Issues of *IQRA*, the Islamic Council of Congo's newsletter published between 2001 and 2004, provide a glimpse of this global perspective on Islamic identity. Their pages contained editorials on the Israeli-Palestinian conflict, the invasion of Iraq, and the "war on terror," alongside articles on Islamic conduct dealing with subjects from women's dress to fasting to the permissibility of photography and videography. Within Congolese society, Islam's official public face is represented by Congolese rather than West African Muslims. The delegation that visited President Sassou-Nguesso in the wake of 9/11 to express the Muslim community's solidarity with the government in the "struggle against terrorism toward the triumph of the values of peace" was led by Al Hajj Abubakar Nguelouoli, an employee of the Congolese foreign ministry who had studied in Saudi Arabia (*IQRA* 2001). On national television the chairman of the Islamic Council (a Congolese with no West African ancestry) hosts a weekly broadcast explaining the tenets of the religion to viewers. In general, proselytizing to non-Muslims in Congo is the domain of Congolese Muslims, sometimes working alongside visiting delegations of Middle Eastern Muslims.

By comparison, Brazzaville's West African Muslim community is much more introverted. While West Africans are active in hometown associations and other organizations oriented toward their countries of origin (see chapter 5), few participate in religious voluntary associations in Brazzaville, with the exception of the administrative committees of the mosques they dominate. Friday lessons in these "West African" mosques dwell primarily on aspects of correct Muslim practice, particularly prayer, its proper execution, motivations, and potential rewards. Compared to private religious duties like prayer and theological topics such as the oneness of God (*tawhid*), which receive great attention in imams' weekly sermons, one hears less about domestic matters like marital relations or child rearing, very little regarding public conduct in interpersonal or business affairs, and nothing at all that could be remotely construed as political, whether in a local, national, or international sense. This version of Islam is inwardly oriented, directed primarily at helping Muslims better themselves as individuals and creations of God. As we have seen, Islamic leaders in the western Sahel, influenced by the Suwarian tradition, have long steered clear of politics, and this largely remains the case in Mali and elsewhere in the region today.[18] The separation between Islam and politics is even greater in Congo, where as strangers West Africans have a tacit pact with their hosts to avoid any political involvement. Hence there is no discourse among Brazzaville's West African Muslims about, for example, *jihad*, either in public or in private, nor do they devote much effort to proselytizing, even though many Muslims around the world see it as every Muslim's responsibility to propagate the faith. For these West Africans, always mindful of their outsider status, seeking converts would be overstepping their bounds, a violation of the unofficial rules strangers must obey (see chapter 4).

Near the midpoint of my fieldwork in Brazzaville, a dozen proselytizers belonging to the transnational Islamic movement Tablīghī Jamāʿat came to town and spent a few weeks preaching in local mosques.[19] Most were Saudis, despite the fact that the movement is banned in Saudi Arabia. When they came to Poto-Poto's "Sunni mosque" and spoke after evening prayers, a crowd of perhaps two hundred Muslims, mostly West Africans, gathered to listen. While one of the Tablighis preached to the group in Arabic and a West African translated into Bamanan and Soninke for the audience, I sat off to the side and chatted with the only member of the group who spoke a little English. (None of them seemed to speak French, let alone any African languages; I was reminded of the remark I had heard in Mali about Arabs being unable to learn anyone else's tongue.) This young man said he and his fellow missionaries spent four months each year on international *daʿwa* (Islamic proselytism) tours, and he had already been on *daʿwa* missions to Jordan, Malawi, and South Africa. Group members lived in spartan conditions while on these missions, sleeping in mosques, cooking their own meals, and preaching God's word primarily to Muslim audiences whom they exhorted to adopt a more rigorous observation of the tenets of their faith.

The night after the Tablighis' first appearance, they returned and drew another large audience. This time, however, after giving the evening's lesson, the group leader asked for volunteers to join their proselytizing mission as it continued to other countries. There was a pause after the interpreter translated the leader's request and low murmurs as audience members looked around to see whether anyone would come forward. Eventually two men raised their hands and the meeting broke up. Walking home I asked my host Modibo and his friend Hamidu what they thought of the Tablighis' invitation. Both men were extremely devout, and I knew that they only missed prayers at the mosque in the event of heavy rain or illness. Yet both thought it unreasonable for anyone to expect them to abandon their families and businesses to join a group of Arabs on a *daʿwa* tour. Hamidu told me he did not recognize the two men who had volunteered; he expected they were Congolese converts, he added dismissively, who were not serious about spreading the message of Islam and were only looking for a way to get out of the country.

In hindsight, this episode encapsulates much of what I learned about West Africans' approach to Islam and their relations with Congolese Muslims. West Africans were more than eager to come listen to the missionaries' message; in fact the crowd at the "Sunni mosque" was about ten times the size of the (primarily Congolese) group that gathered to hear the same Tablighi group at the Ouenzé mosque a few weeks later. But my West African friends saw the actual activity of spreading the faith as none of their business, and they had no reservations about tending to their shops and families rather than participating in missionary activity. Moreover, they believed that the few who did respond to the Tablighis' invitation were not only Congolese but insincere in their motivations. Rather than viewing the volunteers as men partaking in an honorable enterprise, my friends saw them as foolish and possibly fraudulent.

Conclusion: Immigrants, Strangers, and Islam

To what extent can religious difference explain the social divide between West African immigrants and their Congolese hosts, and the enduring role of strangerhood among these immigrants? Does Islam prevent them from integrating into Congolese society? On the face of things, one could certainly conclude that it does: a good number of Congolese apparently see Islam as inconsistent with their society's values, and many West Africans portray the culture of the host society as fundamentally incompatible with their religious faith.

When we dig deeper, however, we find little support for this notion. If sharing the same religion was sufficient reason for people to get along with one another, relations between West African and Congolese Muslims would not have been marked by the mutual suspicion and animosity that have plagued them for more than half a century. Congolese and West African Muslims would attend the same mosques, partake in the same proselytizing activities, and intermarry without regard for distinctions of national origin. But this has emphatically *not* been the case. Social fault lines between Muslim strangers and their non-Muslim hosts do not automatically vanish when the hosts convert to Islam, as demonstrated by Abner Cohen's classic study (1969) of ethnicity, religion, and politics in a Nigerian town. The old fault lines merely reassert themselves in new ways, perhaps as a means for immigrant Muslims to preserve the advantages they derive from their stranger status (see chapter 2).

In light of this evidence I conclude that although people on both sides of Congo's host-immigrant divide use religion as a *justification* for separation, religion is not a primary *cause* of that separation. As I will show in chapter 5, West Africans in Brazzaville go to great lengths to preserve their distinct cultural and religious identities. Yet Islam, with its rules governing behavior and its promotion of group solidarity, is best seen as a tool they employ toward that end, rather than the reason they desire that end to begin with.

Sociologists have long noted religion's capacity to foster immigrants' social incorporation in the United States. Immigrants in many contexts embrace their faith as a means of social integration; in France, for example, many Muslim immigrants and their children turn to Islam in order to find a place *within* the host society.[20] Through affiliation with a universal faith such as Islam, outsiders can find meaning and belonging denied to them in other arenas of life. They cast off what they see as the vestigial cultural components of their religious practice and adopt a more standardized and less place-specific version. But they usually do so only when they realize that returning to their country of origin is no longer possible and that they and their children have settled in the host society for good. In the French context, the desire of Muslim immigrants to reconcile their religion with their existence in the host country has been a necessary aspect of sedentarization, as they abandon practices of circular migration and opt for definitive settlement. "Islam is the recourse which gives meaning and finality to the existence of those who find themselves caught, in France, in a problematic sedentarization process which they cannot really master," writes Kepel (1987:44).

If West African Muslims in Brazzaville have been content to set themselves apart from Congolese society, rather than seeking to find a place for themselves within it, I believe this is because most have not initiated that sedentarization process. As we shall see, the expectation of return remains very strong among members of this population, if not for the immigrants themselves then at least for their offspring: extensive transnational connections continue to link them with their places of origin. Only a tiny fraction of my West African informants in Brazzaville, all of them elderly, entertained the prospect of staying in Congo for the rest of their lives. For the vast majority, Congo is a place of sojourn rather than settlement. Their homeward orientation means that they have little incentive to adapt to the realities of the host country.

I do not dismiss the potential of religious difference to complicate immigrants' incorporation into a host society. From Australia to Western Europe to North America, religion is a divisive issue with respect to immigration's impact on host countries. Rather, my aim here has been to show that religion may not be the "independent variable" or ultimate cause of these conflicts. Ruling out religion as the cause of the problem in Brazzaville means we must find other factors to explain West Africans' lack of integration in Congolese society. To do so, we need to examine the problems they experience as immigrants and strangers in Congo.

THE STRANGER'S CODE

On the morning of Christmas eve, in 2005, I was conversing with a friend in his shop when three Congolese men in civilian clothes suddenly entered. One rapped loudly on the counter and bellowed, "Séjours et recensements, s'il vous plaît." They were apparently policemen who had come to conduct a *contrôle*, a spot-check of individuals' official documents, in this case residence permits (*permis de séjour*) and *recensements de police*, forms showing that the bearer had registered with the local police station. There was no formal requirement in Congo to have a *recensement*, but many of my West African friends had had to pay modest fees to obtain the document after policemen had discovered them without one. As always, I was carrying my passport with a valid one-year Congolese visa, but I had never gotten a *recensement*, and though the men had taken no notice of me up to that point, given their brusque entry and aggressive demeanor I thought they might choose to make an issue of this. In any case my friend behind the counter, a Malian in his forties named Balla, quickly launched into a verbal counteroffensive at maximum volume, matching bluster with bluster. Balla's cousin, who also worked in the shop and had good relations with the local police chief, hurriedly came in from the street upon hearing the commotion. He took one of the three visitors aside and began speaking to him in a low voice. Concerned that my presence might be attracting unwanted attention for Balla and his business, I sneaked out the door and went home while Balla and one of the Congolese continued talking loudly past each other.

On Christmas day I returned to Balla's shop. Seeing me arrive, he immediately asked why I had left in such a hurry the day before. I told him of my concern about the police and the papers they were asking for. "Oh, never mind them," Balla huffed, adding, "We've never paid ten francs to those fraudsters." "But don't agents of the state have a right to ask for papers?" I asked. "Those people are just thieves out looking for money," he replied. I had heard that such visits tended to increase at Christmas, as civil servants sought to generate extra cash for the holidays.

Although my migrant friends often projected a casual air about such matters, the question of contrôles and the collection of taxes and fees have long troubled relations between Brazzaville's West Africans and their Congolese hosts. Many Congolese are convinced that foreign business operators in general, and West Africans in particular, flout the country's laws and avoid paying their fair share of taxes to the Congolese state. They think immigrants get a "free ride" from the government and exploit Congo's hospitality to make huge profits which they then send back to their home countries. Congolese often perceive the activities of West African entrepreneurs as a drain on the national economy, even a threat to the rule of law in the country.

West African business operators in Brazzaville have a diametrically opposite point of view. They see their enterprises as the engines that keep the Congolese economy running, the providers of vital goods and services (not to mention some jobs) to Congolese. Far from getting a free ride, they are convinced that they carry excessively *more* than their rightful share of the country's tax burden. They believe that they are unfairly targeted by agents of the Congolese state, forced to pay bribes and bogus fees just to do their lawful business, merely because they are outsiders. The problem, they claim, is that there is no rule of law in Congo, a situation allowing corrupt state employees to demand payments from anyone with a little money, especially foreigners.

Debates about civic responsibility, legality, and corruption lie at the heart of how Congolese and West Africans view themselves and each other. My task in this chapter is to review some of the areas of friction between these populations, examine each group's representations of the other, and analyze the pattern underlying interactions between natives and immigrants in Congo. In particular, I describe an unwritten set of rules governing the behavior of immigrants in Congo, which I call the "stranger's code." This code determines the boundaries of acceptable conduct for immigrants and even their descendants, and defines certain areas of host-society life as off-limits to them.

Hospitality, Hostility, and Irreconcilable Difference

In Congo there are two prevailing but opposing discourses regarding relations between strangers—by which I mean foreign Africans—and hosts. One is the discourse of African hospitality, whereby Africans treat one another and outsiders as their own brothers and sisters; strangers are welcomed warmly and live in harmony with the host population. One tends to hear this discourse, often tinged with Pan-Africanist overtones, expressed in official circles by Congolese political leaders and representatives of stranger communities; it may be expressed for the benefit of non-Africans.

In recent years, however, the discourse of Pan-Africanist hospitality has been dismissed as a failed elite project.[1] Another discourse, marked by mutual suspicion and hostility, posits irreconcilable differences between host and stranger. It was this discourse that I was most likely to hear from ordinary people in Brazzaville, whether Congolese or foreign; it reinforced the bright boundaries between Congolese and immigrants. In extreme manifestations, one could describe this discourse as xenophobic. The discourse of irreconcilable difference applies even to peoples with great cultural similarities to the Congolese themselves, most notably to immigrants from Congo-Kinshasa who overwhelmingly speak the same languages (Kikongo and Lingala), practice the same forms of charismatic Christianity, and even identify with some of the same ethnic groups as people in and around Brazzaville. Migrants from the other Congo are almost universally labeled *Zaïrois* by residents of Brazzaville, where the term has become synonymous with "domestic helper"; immigrants from Congo-Kinshasa are usually the ones hired to wash clothes, clean floors, and do other household chores. The label *Zaïrois* in this context is more than a simple anachronism (Zaire having officially been renamed the Democratic Republic of Congo in 1997): for Brazzaville residents, *Zaïrois* is a pejorative term invoking the dismal reign of Mobutu Seke Seko, the notoriously corrupt president who changed his country's name to Zaire in 1971. Immigrants from Congo-Kinshasa are often blamed for Brazzaville's social ills, including AIDS and prostitution, petty crime, and general lawlessness, or *"anarchie,"* in city life.[2] Many Congolese perceive *Zaïrois* as inherently dishonest. Despite the fact that the peoples of the two Congos have only been "separated" from each other by a few generations of colonial and postcolonial history, commonalities between the twin Congolese populations are dramatically muted in Brazzaville, and differences are overstated.

The discourse of difference is even more striking for West African immigrants. With their alien religion, languages, and customs, West Africans embody the Other more than Central African foreigners do. West Africans' history, their stance vis-à-vis Western schooling and modernity, even their bodily practices and the way they express their emotions all set them apart from Congolese, who widely regard them as poorly educated, unable to speak proper French, illiterate, even uncivilized. Many Congolese find them too emotionally reserved, a trait they may interpret as hostility. Congolese have applied a number of labels to West Africans over the years, including the metonymical *Sénégalais*, the abbreviated *west-af*, and, most recently, *wara*. There appears to be nothing derogatory about its etymology,[3] but the word chafes at many West African immigrants who hear it. "It's not well received," a Guinean informant in his fifties replied when I asked him how West Africans living in Brazzaville felt about the term. He continued,

> For me personally, it hurts every time I hear it. . . . It's a word that really bothers me. They say it with an ironic tone. . . . There's a Malian who was killed here in 1999. Later they caught the criminals, thieves who'd broken into his house and murdered him. When one of them was arrested, his mother started to cry and said in Lingala, "Bastangi mwana na ngai pona wara pamba." "My son was arrested for a simple, common *wara*." She said this in front of people, I saw it right here on Baya Street near the mosque. "For a common *wara*." For her, the life of the one who died was insignificant and her son shouldn't have been arrested for it. You see this mentality?

West Africans, for their part, are also likely to portray Congolese as utterly alien from themselves. As Muslims, many express disdain for what they see as a permissive Congolese culture marked by alcohol consumption, informal sexual liaisons, and childbearing out of wedlock. They fault Congolese for slavishly following French customs, and abandoning their own traditions; many see the Congolese as victims of an inferiority complex with respect to the French in particular and white people in general. West Africans criticize the perceived prevalence of sorcery in Congolese society, which they interpret not as superstition but as a manifestation of pure evil, a sign of profound disharmony within Congolese families and their society as a whole.

How and why have these differences come to be seen as irreconcilable? How does the apparent inability of these strangers to assimilate translate into their lived experience? How does strangerhood fit with modern discourses

Figure 4.1. West African women at a child's naming ceremony in Poto-Poto. PHOTO BY AUTHOR

about rights and citizenship? To answer these questions, I describe some of the ways that West Africans encounter their strangerhood in Brazzaville.

Harassment

Verbal abuse is a problem suffered particularly by West African women, who are more easily identified as foreigners by their dress. For female informants, harassment in public places was a daily affliction, often culminating in being told to go back where they came from. "Congolese people bother immigrants a lot! They insult us on the street, and even if we don't say anything back we can't escape them," said Nafi, a twenty-two-year-old Malian woman. "Wherever we go, they insult us and call us *wara,* foreigners. They really bother us." A few interviewees went so far as to state that Congolese disliked people in general; Mami, a thirty-one-year-old woman from Côte d'Ivoire who ran an informal street-side restaurant in Poto-Poto, had particularly strong words:

> *Living here! If you can put up with things, you can live here. If not, you can't, because Congolese don't like people. They don't like people. You put up with it, and if someone says something to you, you just ignore it. Because you came to make a living. . . . Even in my workplace I get their disrespect. Somebody will order, and then tell me he's a policeman and threaten me, a lot of things like that.*

Subtler forms of verbal harassment rankle West African men as well. Barou, the successful thirty-nine-year-old auto parts dealer described in chapter 2, spoke at length about this issue during an interview.

> *Every day when you leave your house, you feel like an* étranger *[stranger or foreigner]. Even the house that you rent, they call you a foreigner there. The [Congolese] child you see growing up, when he reaches a certain level, maybe he'll join the police or the gendarmes, and he'll call you a foreigner. If the Congolese learned to integrate foreigners, [the foreigners] would forget they're not at home. . . . It's not we who don't want integration. But it's practically a mentality, a child who is born today, when they introduce him to his neighbor they'll introduce the neighbor as a foreigner. Instead of saying "That's your uncle Barou," no, they say "Ça c'est wara [That's a wara]." Now when he grows up, he'll say* wara *too, not Uncle Barou. He won't give you the same respect your own children or a West African or another foreigner would give.*

Barou believed that Congolese socialized their children to discriminate against foreigners, to see them as aliens rather than as fellow human beings. He articulated a widely held West African belief that Congolese keep them at arm's length, constantly casting them as outsiders because of a local notion of strangerhood, leaving them no room in the host society.

The harassment of individuals who stand out from the majority because of foreign origins or ancestry reveals not only antagonism in host-stranger dynamics but also a desire among hosts to brighten the boundaries separating them from strangers. This verbal manifestation is relatively benign; other types of encounters entail penalties for strangers ranging from the economic to the criminal to the physical. These typically involve Congolese civil servants, government officials, and members of the security forces.

Exactions and Violence

During my Brazzaville fieldwork, I spent countless hours in the Poto-Poto marketplace with West African friends in the cramped, tiny shops they owned or worked in. No matter the location, season, or time of day, I was sure to see people whom the West Africans called *famaw* (a composite of the Bamanan words *fanga maa*, "power people," i.e., authorities). These were Congolese men and occasionally women, usually middle-aged, neatly dressed in uniforms or civilian clothes, carrying notebooks or clipboards and traveling in groups of two or three. They would enter a shop and greet the person behind the counter. They might then show an *ordre de mission*, a printed document indicating that they were carrying out an official duty from a government agency such as the commerce ministry or the tax office; they might instead show their badges from the local police, gendarmerie, or some other unit. The official purpose of their visit was to perform some kind of contrôle. The contrôle, whether carried out by members of the security forces at roadside checkpoints or by roaming police and other officials in town, is a feature of daily life in Brazzaville, one of the most banal areas of interaction between people and the state.

Once the visitors arrived to perform their contrôle, what happened next depended on the particular setting and the individuals involved. Only rarely did I witness disputes like the one between Balla and the policemen described above. Sometimes the visitors would ask to see documents for the shop and its owner—any of the many licenses, permits, authorizations, attestations, receipts, and other forms required by various branches of government in Congo (see chapter 2). This request could set in motion a flurry of activity as the owner or his assistants would produce stacks of papers, bound registers, and dossiers for the visitors to inspect. More often, however, the owner would preempt any such request and begin negotiating directly with the visitors. In the end the owner might hand over 500 or 1000 francs—worth a dollar or two—whereupon the *famaw* would move on to the next shop. Before long the process would repeat itself as a different group of *famaw* appeared in the doorway. They came from the commerce ministry, the finance ministry, the police, the gendarmerie, local city hall, even the environment ministry. During the slow times—which was most of 2005—I often saw more *famaw* than shoppers coming into the stores.

Contrary to popular perceptions among Congolese, most entrepreneurs I knew tried to acquit themselves of their financial responsibilities to the Congolese state. They collectively paid millions of dollars every year for the myriad fees and taxes they and their businesses officially owed to government bodies at the local and national level. The problem was that taxation was too often arbitrary, and only the whim of the official overseeing the dossier determined the amount a given entrepreneur had to pay. Merchants alleged that their tax collector issued receipts for far less than they had actually paid and embezzled the difference. The woman heading the tax division responsible for the Poto-Poto market in 2005 pressured several local business owners into negotiating higher payments than they were legally obliged to make. By refusing to process their tax dossiers, she put these owners at her mercy: the police could close down any business lacking an official document showing that its taxes had been paid. A Guinean man I knew who was negotiating with this woman on behalf of shop owners complained that she was violating every agreement they had previously reached with her, but ultimately he advised his peers to pay the extra sums. "What else can we do?" he asked.

Moreover, my shopkeeper informants stressed that having the required papers was never enough—the daily contrôles were only a pretext for the *famaw* to come calling, and what they really wanted was cash. Even if you could supply every document they asked to see, eventually they would either ask for a fictitious one or just demand money outright. They gave no receipts for these payments but sometimes would jot things down in their notebooks, presumably so they could remember which businesses they had covered (or, in their professional jargon, "scratched") that day. I saw officials ask business owners for "voluntary" contributions to paint the local police precinct and patch holes in the street. Occasionally the shopkeepers and the visitors appeared to know each other well, exchanging friendly greetings; more often the two parties were businesslike.

My informants deployed a number of strategies to deal with the problem of rent-seeking visitors. The most common was simply accommodating the officials with a small cash payment. Some merchants practiced evasion: a shopkeeper might see the *famaw* coming and duck out of his shop for a few minutes, which would only delay the encounter as the group would inevitably come back later. Other merchants would actually send the visitors away empty-handed after making some excuse. (Vieux Diallo did this masterfully, using the respect accorded him as an elder to his full advantage.) A few became the regular clients of Congolese officials to help get the regulators off their backs. These were often casual arrangements but could be quite formalized: one Malian I knew who owned three butcher shops in Brazzaville paid a monthly retainer to a Congolese woman at the Chamber of Commerce to help him obtain permits and other necessary documents, and to protect him from the predations of other Congolese officials visiting his shops. "If they don't go, I call her up and she asks them where they work. They tell her. She says to them, 'Leave this guy alone.' I give them money to buy soft drinks and they leave," he told me.

Congolese see such arrangements as examples of foreign entrepreneurs' corrupting influence on Congolese officials, of the foreigners' unwillingness to "play by the rules." The entrepreneurs, however, feel they cannot avoid such strategies because respecting the rules offers no protection against predations and exactions. "Sariya tè yan," they would repeat to me—"There is no law here." Actually, one might say that by forming alliances with high-ranking individuals within the local power structure and using these alliances to ward off bogus contrôles from other rent-seeking civil servants, these entrepreneurs *are* playing by the rules, which, although unwritten and largely unspoken, are recognized by all players.[4] Personal connections and patron-client relations often trump official regulations: "In Brazzaville," writes Milandou (1997:124–125), "laws and regulations are only for the anonymous; here everything, or almost everything, is a matter of relationships."

Some exactions involved real or threatened violence. Amadu was one of many of my informants who had been arbitrarily detained by the police. He was arrested one morning in 2004 along with seven Malian friends after they had hailed a taxi to attend a burial. A truckload of police stopped to fine the taxi for improper parking. The police said they had to take Amadu and his friends downtown. Amadu believes that he and his companions stood out as foreigners because of their West African garb. "Congolese and foreigners can't be mistaken for each other," he said, stating a pervasive opinion in Brazzaville. "If [the police] see a foreigner, they'll get money from him. But if they see a Congolese, that rarely happens. If you're a citizen and I'm a citizen, I won't allow you to threaten me, ever. But if I'm a foreigner, and you threaten me and hit me, I'll give you some money to make you leave me alone." Amadu and his friends did not protest at first. He told me,

> We didn't make a fuss. They had their rifles, kelekelekele, we said, "No, don't do that, c'est pas la guerre." They said, "You're under arrest." We told them, "We haven't stolen anything, we haven't killed anyone, we haven't done anything. Our friend died and we were leaving for his burial at the cemetery when you stopped us. If the taxi wasn't properly parked that

isn't our problem, it doesn't belong to us. Arrest the driver, not us. But if you arrest us, okay, let's go." We got into the taxi and they accompanied us to the station. We got there and they told us we each had to pay 12,500 francs [about $25]. We said, "Why should we? We're not criminals. We won't pay." One of them came with a stick and rapped us each on the hands, twice. A big stick like this. They said we would pay or we'd be locked up. One of us knew French well, they called him over to talk. They said we'd each have to pay 7,500 francs. . . . We decided we couldn't pay because we hadn't done anything wrong. They started hitting us, knocking us around. One of us had a phone and he called up the Malian consul. The consul came to the station and said, "Eight of my countrymen were arrested by your men this morning. I want you to let them go." They hid us and told him we weren't there. The consul said yes, we were there and in custody. We called out to him, "We're here!" Then the consul spoke to the chief, asking why we'd been detained. He was told there was a problem over a taxi and that we had started a fight. The consul told them we were on our way to the cemetery. He said the police had arrested a Malian tea vendor earlier and beaten him up. He told the chief, "Many of my people have been brought here even if they didn't do anything." He asked, "Which colonel ordered your men to go out and arrest foreigners?" The chief couldn't answer him. They agreed to release us to the consul.

They retrieved most of the belongings confiscated from them in detention, but Amadu did not get 2,000 francs of his own money. He described such shakedowns as routine for West Africans in Brazzaville.

When I asked the Malian consul about such incidents, he made light of the issue, saying it was a matter of a few bad apples in the security forces and not a question of systematic discrimination. Nonetheless, unlawful detention and other abuse of foreigners by the security forces is a problem that the Malian consulate has lobbied the Congolese government to address for years. The consul cultivates close relationships with the various chiefs of police and military officials responsible for the state security apparatus, and goes to them whenever there is a problem involving his compatriots. The common belief among West Africans in Brazzaville is that Congolese police, gendarmes, and soldiers engage in abusive activity without the knowledge of their superiors; they see the main problem as a lack of discipline coupled with the generalized idea among rank-and-file troops that strangers constitute a preferred, even legitimate target for their exactions.

Legal Rights and Discrimination

A stranger can never get justice: this was a common sentiment among West Africans I spoke to in Brazzaville. Regardless of the rights they legally possessed as foreign residents, a parallel register of justice and governance independent of courts and legal statutes governed their lives. In the course of a year in Brazzaville I heard about at least three incidents in which young West African men riding motorcycles had gotten into accidents with Congolese. The motorcyclists were held responsible in every case and were required to pay compensation, even though the West Africans felt that the accidents were not their fault. In one case the motorcycle rider struck a pedestrian and fled the scene, believing that angry mobs would lynch him once they identified him as a *wara* (an easy step to make, since motorcycles were mainly a West African mode of transportation in Brazzaville). His fears may not have been farfetched: during my fieldwork, an Italian Catholic priest was hacked to death with machetes after his car struck a girl near a village in northern Congo.[5] If even a *mondélé* (white person), a priest no less, could be murdered after such an accident, the motorcyclist had good reason to believe that he would meet a similar fate. West Africans had no faith in the Congolese justice system to protect their rights or to apportion guilt properly.

Many West Africans did have Congolese residence permits, but this seldom prevented agents of the state from preying on them. The same formula sometimes expressed by rent-seeking market regulators—"On ne mange pas le papier," "We don't eat paper"—was used by policemen stopping them on the street. The expense of an official Congolese residence permit (about $200 per person per year) seemed like a poor investment to immigrants when they would face authorities' exactions whether or not they obtained one.[6] This was especially true for young aventuriers who traveled overland from Guinea to Congo without using their passports (see chapter 5). Among the most mobile and vulnerable of strangers, aventuriers expected to pay to get out of every run-in with immigration officials, policemen, and border guards. For them, the idea of paying for a visa or residence permit was like paying cash up front for something and going without one was like paying on an installment plan, shelling out a small amount with each subsequent contrôle.

The problem of papers and contrôles in Brazzaville was a much lighter burden for *mindélé*, white people. I spent hours every day in the marketplace or traveling around the city, and stood right next to West Africans as they had to show their IDs or other papers to roving officials, and yet, curiously, these officials almost always acted as though I were not even there—even though, by appearance, I was more obviously foreign than anyone around. Only once, from the moment I walked out of the Brazzaville airport the day I arrived until the moment I walked back in to catch my departing flight, did agents of the state subject me to a contrôle. I was sitting outside a friend's shop in the marketplace when a trio of plainclothes police approached, two men and a woman. The man who asked me for my papers had nothing to identify him as a policeman, nor did his male colleague, but the woman with them produced a police ID card upon my request. I took out my passport and handed it to her; she looked through it, found my one-year visa—still valid for several months—and returned the passport to me. As the trio continued up the street, stopping for contrôles at other shops, one young Malian laborer sitting next to me expressed surprise that I actually had a Congolese visa. Hearing this, a nearby shopkeeper replied, "What did you expect? He's not an African like you."

The Stranger Penalty

West Africans may be justified in seeing themselves as victims of systematic discrimination owing to their foreign origins. Their encounters with the parallel register of justice described above often begin as soon as they leave their home countries: border guards, immigration officials, and customs agents are more likely to extort money from an arriving foreigner, especially an African one, than from one of their fellow citizens. They are also more likely to impose other exactions on the foreigner, including confiscation of money, documents, and property, and arbitrary arrest and detention. The first sign I saw of this "stranger penalty" was on the day I arrived in Brazzaville with my family. As we emerged from the airport terminal, my wife, Oumou, a few steps behind me, was stopped by a Congolese policeman just outside the door who asked to see her papers. (He never asked for mine, probably assuming we were not traveling together.) She handed him her Malian passport, containing a valid Congolese entry visa and stamp. He looked at it, put it down on a small table in front of him, and then simply stared at her without speaking; he did not budge when Oumou asked him to return her passport to her. After a tense moment, a Malian friend who had come to meet us intervened and retrieved the passport with a few words of Lingala and a handful of pocket change.

"Undocumented" migrants in Africa can face more severe penalties, sometimes as an unofficial means of discouraging them from future attempts to enter a given country. Among Senegalese migrants in Cameroon studied by Ba (1995:34), for example, there is a unanimous view that "crossing Nigeria without being stripped of your possessions or tortured [by the police] is something extraordinary." Shakedowns by border officials are ordinary occurrences for African travelers. In Morocco, during 2005, members of the government security forces routinely attacked camps of African migrants in transit to Europe; they beat men, raped women, and confiscated migrants' cash, cell phones, and other belongings. Sometimes they would arrest and deport the migrants or abandon them on the desert border with Algeria; sometimes they would merely leave them in place to await the next victimization. Such penalties are a part of life for many strangers in Africa.[7]

Many Congolese see the stranger penalty as a figment of the foreigners' imagination. The pattern I have described of rent-seeking, abuse, and violence practiced by Congolese civil servants and members of the security forces applies just as much to Congolese, they argue, as to foreigners (and, as I will show, some believe that it applies *more* to Congolese than to foreigners). They see exactions as motivated more by economics than hostility: "regulators" in the marketplace only follow the money when conducting their contrôles in private businesses, and it just so happens that most of the business owners are *wara*. One need only read the Congolese press (such as *La Semaine Africaine* or Mwinda.org) for evidence that Congo's courts and government agencies are corrupt, and that members of the security forces act like beggars with guns, intimidating natives and foreigners alike. Brazzaville's West Africans are caught up in the same system of bad governance and exploitation as native Congolese.

Most West Africans nevertheless remain convinced that they are specifically targeted as strangers by government officials for exactions and arbitrary taxation, and by corrupt policemen who go out of their way to bully and extort bribes. Were they not asked to pay special fees (including the *cautionnement* and the *caution de rapatriement*—see chapter 2) that Congolese did not have to pay? My West African informants interpreted the steady stream of exactions levied upon them in the context of the daily verbal harassment and the occasional violence they endured. For them, all these events added up to a pattern of discrimination directed specifically against foreigners, intended and experienced as a penalty on outsiders, on *wara*.

Was the stranger penalty myth or reality? Several West Africans I knew seemed to suffer from a persecution complex: whenever anything bad happened to them in Brazzaville, as far as they were concerned, it happened only because they were foreigners. What if the real problem, I wondered, was simply the lack of the rule of law—a situation lending itself to generalized abuses and affecting almost everyone? Ultimately, however, I concluded that my West African informants were indeed the victims of systematic discrimination based on their foreign origins—at least *some* of the time. Accounts by Congolese-born West Africans in particular convinced me that the stranger penalty is a genuine phenomenon, and that people are in fact singled out for such abuses by virtue of their apparent foreignness much of the time—even if they do not consider themselves foreigners. The degree of harassment and exactions does appear to vary according to how visibly one stands out as a West African (see chapter 6). This is not to say that Congolese are spared similar indignities. It simply means that people with positions of authority often seek out foreigners, especially foreign Africans, as targets for their exactions *because* they are foreigners, and not merely because they just happen to own a shop or because they are more likely to have money than Congolese (although the two motives undoubtedly may work in concert). West Africans are sometimes targeted, in short, because they are strangers.

Le Rapatriement

To support their view that Congolese authorities marked them for discrimination, exactions, and abuse, my West African informants cited one incident in particular. This event, although it occurred nearly three decades before my fieldwork, held a prominent place in West Africans' collective memory and discourse. It began in the predawn hours of Saturday, 3 September 1977, when residents in residential neighborhoods around Brazzaville were awakened by the sounds of truck engines, footsteps, and men barking orders. The army was in the streets. At first many people assumed another coup d'état was under way: the city had been living under a curfew and a state of emergency since the assassination of President Marien Ngouabi less than six months earlier, and the country's political situation remained tense.

It soon became clear, however, that the military action in progress was different from recent ones, which had been directed at the president's enemies and select members of Congo's *classe politique*. This time troops targeted West Africans exclusively and concentrated in the areas where they lived, particularly Poto-Poto and the adjoining neighborhood of Moungali. In the course of a few hours, soldiers took thousands of West Africans—men, women, and children alike—from their homes and brought them to makeshift detention centers set up in school compounds around the city. Soon indications trickled in from the provinces that the operation was national in scope: from the Atlantic coast to the rain forests of the interior, West Africans were detained and brought to Brazzaville. It was a massive undertaking, carried out in a single stroke, and it had come completely without warning.

Those arrested could only take what few items they could carry to the detention centers. Many still wore their pajamas. Immigrants whose children were born in Congo (thus having Congolese citizenship) and those married to Congolese citizens were separated from their families. In the detention centers, they had to turn over passports, identity documents, and residence permits to the authorities, ostensibly for verification. They endured harsh conditions for several days, receiving little or no food. Informants told me there was no consideration for the pregnant or sick; everyone was held together.

Detainees initially had no indication as to the official reasons for the roundup, and the Congolese government in Brazzaville issued no public statements on the matter for weeks. West Africans were told that they were being held because they were in violation of Congolese immigration laws. From the detainees' perspective, however, documentation mattered little. Those with valid Congolese visas, residence permits, and commercial authorizations were treated no differently than those who lacked them. The aim of the operation was to gather up as many West Africans as quickly as possible and ready them for expulsion or, as it was euphemistically glossed, le rapatriement—repatriation. "The essential thing was just to get the foreigners out, it didn't matter if you had your papers or not," one Malian who had been detained that September told me. "It wasn't about papers. It was about kicking out the foreigners. Even those who had their papers had to leave." The first expulsions began only five days after the detentions started, with hundreds of people sent on chartered airliners to Senegal, Nigeria, and Mali during the second week of September. Repatriation flights continued for two weeks. West Africans remaining in Congo after that time were those who had been able to obtain their release from the detention camps or had avoided arrest altogether, often by exploiting connections with high-ranking Congolese officials.

The arrival of the first deportees caused consternation in West African capitals. Senegal recalled its ambassador to Congo and vowed to lodge a complaint with the Organization for African Unity. Official delegations from Benin, Mali, Mauritania, and Senegal traveled to Brazzaville demanding an explanation for the expulsion of their countries' citizens. By that time, however, it was too late to halt the process. According to statistics gathered by the Malian state newspaper *L'Essor,* nearly sixty-four hundred West Africans had already been deported.[8]

On September 22, three weeks after the operation began, the Congolese foreign minister, Théophile Obenga, specified that these measures were part of a *contrôle générale* (general verification) of the restructuring of production, aiming to "curb the anarchical entry of foreigners in Congo" (*Marchés Tropicaux et Méditerranéens* 1977). Such assertions only generated more West African resentment, particularly in Mali, which was home to the largest number of deportees. According to a Malian official sent to Brazzaville in October to investigate, instead of trying to verify the detainees' true legal status, Congolese authorities simply collected and destroyed their documents. "It is therefore the authorities themselves who created *irréguliers* [undocumented immigrants] there, foreigners living on the margins of the immigration laws and thus unable to justify their presence and activities in Congo," claimed *L'Essor* (1977). West African governments complained of inhumane detention conditions and demanded compensation. The majority of deportees left with only the clothes they wore; all their property including homes, shops, and merchandise was confiscated by the Congolese state. Ownership of their homes was transferred to the state and then to Congolese citizens. Shops and other enterprises were officially taken over by the government, which delegated their management to private citizens who were supposed to turn their revenues over to the state. Responding to these complaints, the government of Congolese President Joachim Yhomby-Opango eventually acknowledged making mistakes and promised to compensate anyone who could prove they had lost homes, goods, or other possessions. The problem was that many West Africans had never had documents proving their ownership of property, and most of those who did were unable to bring them when they were detained. Restitution was therefore out of the question.

It would be difficult to verify the allegations that Congolese authorities knowingly destroyed residence permits and other documents that would have demonstrated the legal status of the people they deported as well as their ownership of houses and other belongings. But West African interviewees who had been in Congo at the time were unanimous in their contention that the operation had nothing to do with legality or papers. In their eyes, it was motivated by the simple desire among those in power to appropriate foreigners' property. The justification that Congolese officials wanted stricter adherence to the country's legal codes held no sway with them. Wherever official laws are ignored as a matter of routine, people have good reason to suspect a hidden rationale lurking behind any selective attempt at enforcement. As far as West Africans were concerned, the Congolese state's expropriation of their homes and belongings was an act of theft by the ruling elite.

There is reason for such skepticism of official claims. The operation's narrow focus—targeting only West Africans—belied the notion that the expulsion aimed "to ensure strict respect for the laws and regulations in effect on Congolese soil," as claimed in the Congolese state newspaper *Mweti* (1977). According to census data from the period, the largest communities of foreigners in Congo came from Zaire and from the Central African Republic (Recensement Général de la Population et l'Habitat [RGPH] 1974). These groups dwarfed the West African population, and yet Congolese authorities took no action to round up Zaireans or immigrants from other Central African states and verify their legal status. If they singled out the much smaller West African population for arrest and deportation, it was probably for reasons other than ensuring respect for the law.

Moreover, the regime's justification of its actions to the Congolese public was inconsistent with its justification of them abroad. Whereas the message to other African countries was that the Congolese government was getting serious about compliance with its immigration laws, the dominant message within Congo linked the expulsion to economic imperatives. In the wake of le rapatriement, the ruling military committee decreed that retail commerce would henceforth be off-limits for foreigners, explaining this ban to a local newspaper as an effort to prevent the transfer of funds abroad, which had "provoked a hemorrhage of currency that Congo needed to develop its economy" (*La Semaine Africaine* 1977). The expulsion was also presented to the public as part of a campaign to favor Congolese over foreign entrepreneurs. When the Congolese commerce ministry organized a workshop in Brazzaville to give four hundred new managers of confiscated shops a crash course in the retail business, an official quoted by the state information agency stated that the "philosophy which allowed the creation of these shops" was situated "within the framework of our party's policies, namely to encourage and train the national private sector" (Agence Congolaise d'Information [ACI] 1977).

Thus it is quite plausible that West Africans were targeted for expulsion mainly because they had something that the Congolese officials wanted. Expelling them provided an easy means to acquire economic assets for distribution by high-ranking members of the regime as patronage to their supporters. It could be justified at home in terms of creating opportunities for Congolese where few had existed before (encouraging the "national," as opposed to foreign, private sector).[9] The cost, politically, was negligible, as it provoked conflicts neither with any of Congo's neighbors nor with its powerful donors outside Africa, although it tainted bilateral relations with West African countries for several years.

The economic consequences of le rapatriement, however, were disastrous for Congo. Consumer prices almost doubled within a few months (Sanders 1983). By early 1978 the nationalized shops were virtually empty, and some were converted into bars. There were shortages of basic goods; one of my friends in Brazzaville remembered having to walk from Moungali to downtown, a distance of a few miles, just to find a box of matches. A Malian trader who remained after the expulsions explained the reason for the problem:

> *When my neighbor, for example, the landowner, takes over the shop that I had filled with merchandise, he doesn't know who my suppliers were. He doesn't know where I got my stock.... Sure, for a short time he can sell the merchandise that's there. But does he know where I got my supplies, in Congo or in France or in China or in South Africa? No. He can sell it, but that's all he can do.*

A Congolese informant recalled that few of his compatriots had predicted the difficulty of running the shops, and soon people began to appreciate the value of the foreign shopkeepers.

> *The shops had to be stocked. Those people [who took over the shops] confused revenue with profit. So the people of the neighborhood who benefited from the presence of the little West African couldn't benefit anymore. The profits [from the shop] aren't free, you have to pay for them. But at least if you have a little money in your pocket, you can have your tin of powdered milk and your butter, your children are happy. You're the first person to lose out with the West African gone. The second person to lose out is the guy who wanted to take over the shop and is now the object of resentment by the whole neighborhood because the shop is empty. No more bread, no oil, no kerosene, the little daily necessities are all gone. In less than a month the place is shuttered.*

The government's efforts to train the new shopkeepers were clearly inadequate, and there was little or no planning and organization of the supply chains necessary to make the nationalization of retail commerce succeed. Moreover, the project did not address the social hurdles to entrepreneurship in Congo (discussed in chapter 2). The takeover's rapid failure only reinforced the perception among Brazzaville residents, both Congolese and foreign, that Congolese people were simply "not meant to be merchants."

The economic crisis dissipated gradually, and within a few months of the expulsion limited numbers of West Africans began trickling back to Congo—even though President Yhomby remained in power and the laws against foreign traders were still on the books. Many West African immigrants acquired "borrowed nationalities" of various Central African countries, which enabled them to obtain the permits they needed to get back to business. (This extralegal tactic, which usually required only a modest payment at the Brazzaville consulate of the country in question, had also enabled some to avoid deportation in the first place.) Once Denis Sassou-Nguesso toppled Yhomby from power in February 1979 and became president, West Africans started coming back to Congo in larger numbers. They had many incentives to return despite what had happened: some had left their families behind there, others hoped to recuperate their confiscated property (though most deportees had to restart from scratch), and a few had found that after living for so many years abroad they no longer felt at home in their native countries. They generally interpreted the 1977 expulsion as the misguided action of an individual who was no longer in power and they held no grudges against the Congolese people, who for the most part were happy to see their commercial sector functioning smoothly again.

Outside Congo's West African community, few remember the mass expulsion today. It is at most a minor incident in the collective memory of a country where far worse things have happened. Le rapatriement remains indelibly etched, however, in the minds of Congo's West African residents, both those who lived through it and those who came later. Some believe that this type of trouble is unlikely to arise again because Congo's rulers learned their lesson from the affair. As one West African merchant with over four decades of experience in Congo told me, "It's a stain on a country's credibility to make a mistake like that. We're all Africans. Congo isn't ready to repeat the same mistake." Others, however, saw the expulsion as a cautionary tale of what can befall members of Africa's internal diasporas; it was just another type of stranger penalty. "For a Congolese, anyone who comes to his country can be made to leave at any time," an elderly Malian living in Brazzaville told me. "You need to expect to be sent packing at any time. Those who have come recently don't understand this, but I lived through the events of 1977 and I understand it."

Congolese Attitudes toward West Africans

Several weeks into my research in Brazzaville I met with Michel, a Congolese official with the government's scientific research bureau. I had been hearing complaints from West Africans about discrimination and hostility toward them, and I took the opportunity to ask Michel how he thought Congolese looked upon the West Africans in their midst. He replied, "Avec bienveillance. Nous les Congolais nous sommes un peuple hospitalier" ("With benevolence. We Congolese are a hospitable people"). The only problems occur when an immigrant doesn't respect the law, Michel told me. After I described how West Africans tended to retain their culture and values within the host society, Michel voiced his personal disapproval. They should integrate, he said, by accepting the dominant host culture.

At first I found Michel's attitude surprising, and wondered how he could overlook the evidence of bias against foreigners in his own society and even describe his compatriots' stance toward immigrants as "benevolent." How could he blame West Africans for their lack of integration when the problem of discrimination seemed so acute? Yet many Congolese shared Michel's views. Toward the end of my stay in Brazzaville, I conducted a survey of students enrolled at the Université Marien Ngouabi, a state-run institution that remains Congo's lone university. Not only did survey respondents strongly echo Michel's ideas, they harbored opinions of West Africans and their place in Congolese society that were polar opposites of the opinions my West African informants harbored of themselves (see Appendix II).

Overall, students saw immigrants from West Africa in an unflattering light. Twice as many respondents disagreed with the statement "West Africans are respectful of the law" as agreed with it, and respondents broadly perceived West Africans as dishonest, corrupt, and not paying their fair share of taxes and other fiscal obligations to the state. Also, by a two-to-one margin, students described the activities of West Africans in Congo as hindering national economic development.

Among the most astonishing findings, from my perspective, was respondents' pervasive opinion that, far from being burdened with a stranger penalty, West Africans in Congo are actually *favored* over the local population by Congolese officials, particularly in the realms of business and the courts. More than four times as many students agreed than disagreed with the statement "West Africans are favored by the Congolese government in judicial matters compared to natives"; for the statement "West Africans are favored in business compared to natives," the ratio of supporters to dissenters was ten to one. In open-ended questions and a focus group, some students expressed the opinion that their government grants credit to foreign businessmen, whereas Congolese businessmen have no access to loans. From these responses, a picture emerged of West Africans buying off Congolese public officials to establish commercial monopolies and fleece the Congolese public, then sending their profits out of the country through their remittances home. This perception feeds into a belief that Congolese are marginalized in their own homeland, that "Congo has become the sole country on earth where foreigners have rights and natives only have responsibilities" (Mampouya 2009).

I was also troubled by the fact that nearly ten times as many Congolese disagreed with the statement "West Africans are clean and hygienic" as agreed. When respondents listed stereotypes that Congolese commonly held about West Africans, the largest category by far pertained to dirtiness, with 110 cases.[10] This stereotype may stem from Muslim men's frequently public practice of performing ablutions before prayer: to become ritually pure, they must rinse their hands, mouth, nose, face and scalp, ears, forearms, feet, and ankles with water. (Muslim women do the same ablutions but usually in private.) Some Congolese believe that this is the only way West Africans ever wash themselves. Others see West Africans as unclean because they use water instead of toilet paper after defecating; toilet paper is a staple for most Brazzaville households, and many Congolese see using it as cleaner, more hygienic, and more civilized than using water.

Despite the negative opinions and stereotypes expressed in the survey, respondents overwhelmingly agreed (by a seven-to-one margin) with the statement "Congolese are benevolent toward foreigners living in Congo." Like my friend Michel, they perceived little prejudice against outsiders in their society.

I added one item to the survey after a respondent on a pretest version wrote about the shortage of coins in the Congolese money supply. Throughout 2005 obtaining small change in Brazzaville was inevitably a nuisance: vendors in the marketplace often lacked enough coins to break even a small bill of the local currency. Responding to an open-ended question about West Africans' impact on Congo, one student wrote in a pretest questionnaire that West Africans were responsible for this coin shortage because they used coins to "make their medallions." I had never heard about this and asked some Congolese acquaintances about it. There turned out to be a rumor around town that West Africans were hoarding small change and doing frivolous things with it; the rumor was even reported (albeit skeptically) by a local newspaper. I decided to add the statement "West Africans' manufacture of medallions is responsible for the shortage of coins in Congo" to the final version of the survey to see the sort of traction the story would get with a larger group; 176 respondents agreed with this statement (all but 7 of them strongly), 35 disagreed, and another 53 did not know or had no opinion.

Although I am not sure what caused the lack of coins in Brazzaville's money supply in 2005, one should consider the purpose this myth might serve. The very absurdity of this account speaks to the ways that hosts demonize and blame strangers for even the most unlikely problems. Throughout the survey responses a process of psychological displacement was at work: by characterizing West Africans as disorderly, criminal, corrupt, violent, aggressive, and ethnocentric, respondents projected the ills of their own society onto the strangers in their midst.

My own interpretation of the rumors about vanishing coins is that they embody inchoate fears among Congolese that foreigners are making off with their country's wealth. These fears are actually quite justified, but the true culprits are not West Africans. They are the executives and owners of French and American oil conglomerates, Swiss banks, offshore investment firms in the Caymans and the Channel Islands, Ukrainian arms dealers, Chinese and European timber companies, and the many other multinational businesses, some shady and others supposedly respectable, with which the Congolese regime does billions of dollars worth of business every year. Since it is dangerous to express such fears openly in Congo, West Africans provide an expedient proxy. Unlike the real foreign perpetrators and their partners in the Congolese elite plundering the country's riches, West Africans are both near and visible to Congolese in their everyday lives, and they are in no position to defend themselves against whatever falsehoods others might perpetuate about them. As noted in chapter 2, middleman minorities offer a convenient buffer between ruling elites and impoverished masses. Their activities in Congo provide an ideal distraction from the fact that President Sassou and his family are estimated to control half the Congolese economy.[11]

The Stranger's Code

In 2002 I interviewed a man in Togotala who had lived and worked in eight different African countries (not including Mali) over a twenty-year period. He spoke of the difference between life at home in the fatherland (*faso*) and abroad (*tunga*): "This is your *faso*, you are known here. If you go abroad, even if you find wealth, they'll tell you you're a stranger. Even a child can disrespect you, and you can say nothing. That's what being a stranger is." His words articulated three common notions among my informants in Mali and Congo about the condition of being a stranger and occupying a foreign space (*tunga*): it is equivalent to being socially unknown; it entails losing the most basic entitlements, such as the expectation of respect from one's juniors; and it cannot be effaced by economic success. These notions recall the Bamanan saying "Tunga tè danbe dòn," "Exile knows no dignity."

Shared ideas about strangerhood, coupled with the hostility expressed by Congolese toward West Africans, have generated over many years a set of unwritten rules governing the conduct of strangers, which I call the stranger's code. This code is understood and enforced by hosts and strangers alike, and consists of three main rules.

1. Do not get involved in host-country politics.

For strangers, politics is the proverbial "third rail." The political sphere in this case encompasses multiple areas: party politics and elections, to be sure, but also the state bureaucracy and the related informal networks overseeing the distribution of resources and patronage. This is politics in the sense of "who gets what, when and how" (Lasswell 1965:3). This rule applies not only to immigrants but also to their descendants, who have not succeeded in throwing off the mantle of strangerhood (see chapter 6). Bonacich (1973:586) observes in all middleman minorities "a tendency to avoid involvement in local politics except in affairs that directly affect their group."

There is a strong taboo against strangers merely appearing to be involved in the politics of their host community or country. This holds true for domestic migrants and their descendants as well as for cross-border migrants, and, in fact, the taboo has become more powerful since the spread of electoral politics in the early 1990s (cf. Geschiere 2009). Strangers should avoid even expressing opinions on politically sensitive topics. In 2005 fifteen Congolese officials went on trial in Brazzaville over their alleged involvement in the 1999 "Beach affair," the disappearance of hundreds of young men. This trial, which lasted for weeks, was broadcast live in its entirety on Congolese television; viewers were riveted by the sight of some of the highest-ranking figures in the state security apparatus (including the head of the national police, the interior minister, and the inspector-general of the armed forces), normally secretive men, being publicly questioned over the matter. Almost everyone I knew in Brazzaville spent hours tuning into the trial. Banzoumana, a Malian friend of mine who worked at an electronics store, had to change the channels of his display TV sets to Kinshasa stations during the trial, otherwise the spectacle of the trial coverage would clog the doors with onlookers and keep paying customers from entering.

Banzoumana told me that during the Beach trial several Congolese approached him at work wanting to know why he was not showing the trial; he said they often tried to sound out his opinions on the case. He made a point, however, not to comment on the trial, at least when speaking with Congolese. He thought some of his interlocutors might be plainclothes officials wanting to lure him into a political debate, thus causing him to transgress the bounds his strangerhood imposed on him. A rumor was circulating at the time that some West Africans had recently been arrested in the Moungali market: according to this story, a plainclothes policeman had overheard them discussing the Beach trial and returned with a squad of soldiers to round them up. The immigrants were supposedly hauled off to detention, where an officer told them the Beach affair was Congolese business, not for foreigners to talk about. The detainees had to come up with a large sum of money to be released. Although I doubt this story is true, it exposes an important reality: strangers clearly perceive a bright line separating everyday life in the host country from sensitive political topics, and merely by talking about the latter they risk stepping over that line.[12] The morning before the presiding panel of judges in the Beach trial were to hand down their verdicts, West African merchants shuttered their shops, afraid that members of the security forces would go on a looting spree targeting their businesses if any of the accused was found guilty. In the end there was no cause for alarm, as the court acquitted all fifteen defendants.

Despite West Africans' efforts to avoid the appearance of involvement in host-country politics, many Congolese remained wary of these strangers' political influence in their society. Given the statement "West Africans are overly involved in Congolese internal politics," 108 survey respondents agreed, 98 disagreed, and 66 had no opinion. Considering their central role in the nation's economy, West Africans face an especially difficult task in convincing their hosts that they are living up to their obligation as strangers not to overstep their bounds.

2. Do not flaunt your wealth.

West Africans and other African foreigners in Brazzaville must not engage in conspicuous consumption or appear to raise themselves too high above their Congolese hosts. One Brazzaville-born West African man linked Congolese verbal harassment of strangers to conspicuous consumption. "If [Congolese] see you well dressed or riding in a car, *wara* it's a way to insult you. Even if you have something, a nice house or car, people from here will see that with a bad eye," he told me. Strangers must keep a low profile to avoid arousing the resentment of the host population. They must not appear to engage in ostentatious behaviors that might arouse the resentment of the majority.[13]

West Africans in the Congo Basin have learned this lesson the hard way. In Kinshasa, during the 1960s, their community encountered rising levels of intolerance and allegations of criminal activity, especially diamond smuggling. It seems that a small number of immigrants involved in illicit activities spoiled the atmosphere for the rest of the community, a fact many West Africans who had lived in Kinshasa at the time remained bitter about decades later. A few of my informants reproached their juniors, claiming that they had not learned to be discreet with the wealth they were earning and thereby broke the tacit rule against drawing undue attention to their group. Tensions were such that in 1962 Mali had to relocate its Kinshasa embassy—its only diplomatic mission in the region at the time—to Brazzaville. "If you're rich, and you have some money, you have cars, can the [Congolese] people accept you? Can they be in good faith with you? No, they'll be unpleasant.... *Les jeunes se montraient trop* [the young people were displaying themselves too much]," declared a man who had worked for the embassy at the time. Between 1964 and 1971 the government of Congo-Kinshasa organized no fewer than five waves of expulsions, each targeting West Africans (sometimes with other foreign populations) and each more sweeping than the last.[14]

The stranger's taboo against flamboyance may be linked to the fact that public displays of wealth have been defined since Congo's independence as a privilege of the country's ruling elite. The first Congolese president, Fulbert Youlou, helped solidify a political culture during the early 1960s in which "practices of ostentation expressing the abuse of power" became a defining characteristic of Congolese leaders (Bazenguissa-Ganga 1997:67).[15] Political patrons are expected to indulge in conspicuous consumption and to flaunt their privilege as a means of setting themselves above the masses. Doing so demonstrates their capacity to perform their roles well by commanding vast amounts of wealth for redistribution within their patronage networks. Strangers must not appear to compete with their hosts in this regard. For a stranger to show off his economic advantages in such a context, therefore, not only upsets the host society's precarious social balance but also contravenes the first rule of the stranger's code—the command to keep out of host-country politics.

Some African migrants manage to escape the stricture against flaunting wealth, at least temporarily. Among Congolese in Paris, for example, Mac-

Gaffey and Bazenguissa-Ganga (2000:27) find ostentatious expenditure to be a primary means of affirming social status; "being visible was an important element in their lifestyle." This visibility, however, extends only within their own community. Even these migrants can never allow their displays to attract unwanted scrutiny from their hosts.

3. Do not protest violations of your rights.

Jakaliya was a Malian trader in his seventies who had lived abroad since 1956, mostly in Central African countries. He had worked as an ambulant vendor and clandestine gem buyer in Congo-Kinshasa and Zambia, but left that business after one of his companions was shot and killed in the bush by a Zambian army patrol hunting for smugglers. He came to Brazzaville and sold shoes in the market. He and his wife had nine children, all of them grown by the time I met him in 2003. Jakaliya told me that he wanted to return to Mali but lacked the financial means to do so; most of his sons had emigrated and could not help him, and he had been unable to get back the money he had deposited as a *cautionnement* and *caution de rapatriement* (see chapter 2) from the Congolese government. In Mali a man his age would be an established patriarch and would rule over a large household with an army of grandchildren at his disposal; in Brazzaville he was just another marginal figure in a dingy rented room, scraping to make ends meet. I wondered if I could do anything to help him.

One day in 2005 an opportunity seemed to present itself. A radio program on the BBC World Service called "Outlook" asked listeners to report problems they were having in their communities and the Outlook team would send someone to find a solution. A journalist from "Outlook" helped a listener in Phnom Penh address grievances involving police corruption. I thought some unwanted media publicity might shame Congolese officials into returning Jakaliya's deposits to him. The next morning I went to a cybercafé and sent an e-mail to the "Outlook" team describing Jakaliya's situation and asking for their assistance. Less than thirty minutes later my cell phone rang, and an "Outlook" producer in London told me they would like to send somebody to investigate. She asked, however, that I first get Jakaliya to send them a request personally.

When I brought the news to Jakaliya, his reaction was guarded. He did not look eager to enlist outsiders' aid in this matter but said he would consider the offer. A few days later Jakaliya told me that he had decided not to get the BBC involved. He clearly believed that such an intervention would not help and might even have negative consequences. After some prodding, the old man admitted that he had never actually gone to the commerce ministry to ask for his cautionnement back; he had simply been told by other West Africans that he would not get it if he tried.

I was disappointed but not surprised by Jakaliya's unwillingness to defend his own interests. West African immigrants seldom protested violations of their rights. Their tolerance of abuse did have its limits, as I will show in chapter 6, but these limits were high: routine violations such as exactions, unlawful arrest, imposition of arbitrary fees and bribes, and the withholding of deposits were considered unavoidable or at least not worth making a fuss over. They were just the price one paid for being a stranger. The rhetorical question posed by an informant earlier in this chapter summarized the prevailing attitude: "What else can we do?"

Some people believed immigrants' reluctance to protest stemmed from their lack of education. Illiterate people do not know their rights, according to this argument, and are therefore unable to assert and defend them. A Malian consular official articulated this notion in an interview:

> *These are illiterate people, they don't know how to read or write, they don't know their responsibilities or rights as citizens. And they're afraid, because they find themselves on foreign soil and they are very wary, very afraid. So they aren't people who will struggle [for their rights]. Very often in cases like that, they prefer to give a little money so that they'll be left alone, that's their mentality! That's how it is. These aren't citizens who know their rights; they're illiterates who come directly from the village. It's not part of their culture.*

Such condescension is typical of educated African officials toward their uneducated compatriots. I doubt, however, that illiteracy is the primary issue here. Jakaliya, despite being uneducated, knew that the Congolese government was officially supposed to refund his deposits, and yet he had not even tried to seek their return. For him, the very fact of being on foreign soil meant that any attempt to exercise his rights would be futile at best and, at worst, could bring negative repercussions upon him and his community. This notion was widely shared by West Africans in Brazzaville, both literate and illiterate.

Jakaliya was in good company by forfeiting his deposits with the government. A commerce ministry employee in Brazzaville told me the deposit known as the cautionnement, now worth one million francs (about $2000), is meant to prevent entrepreneurs from running up debts and leaving the country. This is why it is only levied on foreign business owners and not Congolese, who are already assumed to have substantial ties to their homeland. Officially the cautionnement is refundable to entrepreneurs once they close their business and prove they have no outstanding debts or unpaid taxes. But when I asked the employee how many people came to reclaim their deposit, he replied, with a chuckle, "They are not very, very numerous. In fact, they are insignificant."

There are clearly bureaucratic obstacles for foreign entrepreneurs who might wish to reclaim their deposits, and the tenuous rule of law in commercial affairs means that many business owners would have difficulty obtaining the documents to show that their debts and taxes were paid up. Based on Jakaliya's story and those of other traders I knew, I suspect that most West Africans gave up their deposits without a struggle. Not only was there no mobilization to press for the refund of this money to those eligible for it, but apparently few had even asked to get theirs back. Consequently a policy not likely *intended* as a means of extracting rents from foreign merchants eventually came to be practiced and understood by all parties involved as precisely that. The same is true of the caution de rapatriement, the repatriation deposit, meant to ensure that foreign entrepreneurs like Jakaliya are not stranded in the country; my West African informants universally saw this deposit as a stranger penalty, and none expected to collect theirs when the time came to pack their bags and return home.

Under the stranger's code immigrants and their descendants give up their rights, believing they can never expect the same rights that they would enjoy back home. Since justice is unattainable, they feel that the only resolution to a conflict with their hosts comes through paying a stranger penalty. No matter what documents they acquire, they remain subject to the predations of rent-seeking officials and multiple other forms of exactions as long they continue to think that their only option is to tolerate these abuses. Rather than exercising the "politics of recognition" (Taylor 1994), which has become commonplace in African societies since the 1990s (Englund and Nyamnjoh 2004), they opt for a "politics of invisibility," keeping a low profile and hoping for the best. Most believe they have no choice.

If they defended their interests en masse—by collectively refusing to pay bribes, refusing to be cheated out of their due, and refusing to put up with abuse—these migrants could guarantee greater respect for their rights. Taking such a stand, however, would be unseemly, a breach of their tacit agreement as strangers not to "rock the boat" in the host country. The stranger's code compels them to refrain from any activity that might unsettle the tenuous balance between hosts and immigrants. This includes not only political engagement and conspicuous consumption but also anything that might draw unwanted scrutiny to the strangers' presence and their ostensibly subordinate role in the host society; one could add the taboo against religious proselytizing by strangers (see chapter 3), for example, to the three rules discussed above. In exchange for permission to stay in a land constructed as "belonging" to someone else, strangers feel obliged to keep their heads down and stay quiet. I believe the notion among my informants that honor and dignity are to a great extent place-bound, that the value of an individual cannot be appreciated on foreign soil—in short, that exile knows no dignity (see chapter 2)—only adds to their willingness to suffer indignities while living abroad.

Xenophobia and Integration

The specter of xenophobia lurked throughout my time in Brazzaville. Many of the West Africans I knew felt strongly that xenophobia was a major problem in Congo. They experienced their strangerhood every day as an imposition upon them by the host society, a refusal to accept them or make them feel at home. They would tell me time and again that Congolese simply "do not like foreigners" or even that they disliked people in general. The notion that Congolese were prone to anti-immigrant sentiments was a powerful means of explaining their ill-treatment, something they contrasted with their own society, which they saw as warm and hospitable to outsiders. I also had ample reason to be on the lookout for anti-foreign bias: xenophobia seems to crop up frequently in tandem with processes of globalization. Some political movements have embraced xenophobic discourse more or less openly: a placard popular among southern pro-government youths (the so-called Young Patriots) after the start of civil war in Côte d'Ivoire read "JE SUIS XENOPHOBE, ET APRES?" which translates as "I'M A XENOPHOBE, SO WHAT?" (see Geschiere 2009).

The problem with casting xenophobia as a trait particular to a given culture or society is that the same society that appears tolerant and welcoming to one person may seem hostile to another. For the final leg of my African fieldwork, I returned with my family to Bamako in early 2006 to do follow-up research and pursue contacts I had made in Congo. One of these leads was a woman named Jamila, the Cameroonian wife of a Brazzaville-based Malian entrepreneur I had gotten to know. She originally came to Bamako to study at the university there, and then met and married her husband and had children; she was now living with his family in Bamako. After sitting down to talk with her, I was astounded at how closely her views of Malians mirrored my Malian informants' views of their Congolese hosts. Jamila described Malians as unwelcoming, intolerant, and ignorant of the outside world; despite learning to speak Bamanan at an intermediate level, she found Malian people unwilling to accept her or take her seriously in social interactions because she lacked fluency. They kept her at arm's length, she felt, and constantly made her feel that she did not belong. Jamila introduced me to some Congolese friends who had also married Malian merchants, and there was a consensus among them that Malians did not like foreigners—unlike people back home, of course, who welcomed them with open arms and did everything to accommodate them.

Despite rising anti-foreign public rhetoric around the globe since the 1990s, few people see themselves as xenophobic. Whether in Brazzaville, Bamako, or elsewhere, locals tend to believe that they are welcoming and benevolent toward foreigners. They also judge outsiders by the standards of their own culture: they impose conditions, sometimes unconsciously, on the way foreigners must behave if they are to merit continued benevolence. To be accepted, immigrants must give up something of their old ways and habits; they must make an effort to "fit in." Africans with this expectation are no different from citizens of wealthy, immigrant-receiving countries in North America and Europe. They merely operate under the same assimilationist paradigm that continues to dominate political and sociological discourse about immigration in Western countries (Castles 2007).

Problems only arise when hosts require sacrifices that immigrants are unwilling to make. Immigrants then decide that the price of "fitting in" is too great. They feel they should not be expected to give up important aspects of their identity—their language, their rituals, their faith—that make them who they are.[16] My Congolese informants and survey respondents felt strongly that certain Islamic practices were antithetical to Congolese social norms, and they cast immigrants who clung to these practices as willfully isolating themselves from the society around them. My West African informants, for their part, balked at having to let go of any aspect of their religion; what human concerns, they wondered, could possibly contravene divine prescriptions for daily life? They felt they should be able to practice their religion freely and retain their West African customs. These opposing discourses do not encourage members of either population to search for common ground.

When Congolese cast West African immigrants as parasites, or when West Africans cast Congolese as lazy and corrupt, they are not necessarily motivated by irrational prejudice. However biased and harmful such stereotypes may be, we cannot assume that the diffusion of more positive images—in the manner of a "diversity awareness" campaign—would suffice to smooth over the rift between these groups. Underlying this rift is the structural relationship between the host society and its "middleman minority" population. Some scholars have described the interests and goals of the minority group as fundamentally incompatible with those of the host society, such that resentment and hostility become inevitable.[17] This structural tension makes it easy for Congolese to overlook the positive role foreigners play in their country. Even when immigrants attempt to contribute to the host society—such as funding the reconstruction of the Poto-Poto marketplace after the civil war and paying for the resurfacing of streets—Congolese dismiss these efforts as exceptions to the rule. They ignore the millions of francs West African businesses pay annually in taxes and various fees (both legitimate and bogus), believing instead that foreigners are getting a "free ride" in their country. They even use this conviction to justify harassment of, and informal exactions on, immigrants. Foreigners respond to this treatment by hunkering down even more within their own community and isolating themselves from Congolese society, convinced that their hosts are ungrateful bigots who only wish to exploit them. In this manner, the discourse of irreconcilable difference becomes overpowering, and members of the stranger population become ever more inassimilable.

Stereotypes of the "dirty West African" revealed by the survey fit into what Geschiere and Nyamnjoh (2000:441) call "metaphors of cleanliness and defilement." Host societies around the world persistently cast foreign newcomers as impure and posing the danger of contagion. Strangers defy dreams of purity and expectations of order; it should be no surprise that "locals" associate them with dirt or even call for their elimination as a hygienic measure.[18]

This is not to suggest that intolerant, even abusive behavior toward immigrants is somehow more acceptable when spurred by something other than mere irrationality or primordial hatred. My argument is that intolerance and hostility directed at strangers or outsiders often stem from larger social processes, and cannot be explained away by the presence of mutual misperceptions or supposedly endemic cultural traits like xenophobia. Disseminating accurate information regarding, for example, West Africans' economic contributions both to the Congolese state and to local communities would surely lessen some of the tensions I have described in this chapter and improve host-stranger relations. Yet no amount of accurate information could dispel these tensions altogether.

Conclusion: The Lessons of Strangerhood

The stranger's code discourages West Africans in Brazzaville from defending themselves when their interests are threatened, whether by local elites or routine bureaucratic indifference. Immigrants understand, under the terms of the stranger's code, that they do not and can never belong in the host country. They live perpetually on edge, uneasy in the knowledge that they could someday be "sent packing" merely by virtue of their strangerhood. Having host-country citizenship or possessing legal title to land there cannot guarantee that they will remain unmolested in a land where they are regarded as inassimilable aliens. Something utterly beyond the strangers' control—a war, a change of government, an economic crisis, a political leader's manipulation of public anti-foreigner sentiments, even something as seemingly trivial as a soccer game[19]—could trigger a chain of events leading to their arbitrary arrest, the loss of their livelihoods, or their expulsion. As long as they remain on foreign soil, these people live in a state of existential insecurity.

By dwelling only on areas of conflict between Congolese hosts and West African strangers in this chapter, I have presented a somewhat skewed picture of affairs between these groups, obscuring the many areas of harmonious relations from view. Most of the time Congolese and West Africans "get along"; there are many business partnerships, friendships, and even marriages cutting across the boundary between their communities. Moreover, Brazzaville has seldom witnessed large-scale xenophobic violence of the sort that has played out in other cities of the world. These facts, however, do not diminish the weight of evidence suggesting that relations between Congolese and immigrants are and have long been laden with underlying structural tensions which have created resentment and suffering over the years for people on both sides of the host-stranger divide. By calling attention to them here, I hope to persuade readers to look beyond both the public "hospitality discourse" and allegations of savage xenophobia confronting members of Africa's internal diasporas.

The types of discrimination these migrants face are seldom embodied in official government policies and legal texts. Congo's constitution guarantees the rights of everyone, both citizens and noncitizens, residing on national territory. As for the state, although it has not been effective in protecting foreigners from abuse, given proper stimulus it *can* intervene and discipline those guilty of victimizing them. The problem does not lie in the realm of government capacity and policy but rather in popular imaginaries pertaining to strangers and their relationship to the host societies of which they are a part (albeit, to use

Simmel's terminology, an "inorganic" one). The stranger's code explains why hosts and immigrants alike in Brazzaville seldom pressure their leaders to ensure respect for immigrants' rights.

Simplistic ideas about prejudice and cultural clashes do nothing to illuminate host-stranger dynamics in places like Brazzaville. One must look instead to the multiple social and economic factors generating friction between immigrants and natives. Immigrants' occupation of particular economic niches simultaneously enables interaction with and breeds hostility from local populations. Conflict is a likely product of such social arrangements. Hosts and migrants may share certain notions about strangerhood, belonging, and rights that can lead to the indefinite disenfranchisement of immigrants and even their descendents. Foreigners and those with foreign ancestry may choose not to defend their rights simply because they are not on "their own soil" (however that soil may be defined), and hosts will seldom fail to exploit this weakness. Finally, prevailing constructions of citizenship and strangerhood in some postcolonial African countries may be very much at odds with modern Western constructions of rights, nationality, and state responsibility. If the case of West Africans in Congo is any guide, local informal constructions of these concepts continue to carry a great deal more social and political weight than formal legal constructions. Their precarious place in the host society conditions the way that these immigrants organize their lives and activities across borders.

TRANSNATIONAL KINSHIP

"Any West African who marries a Congolese is not one of us," Vieux Diallo declared to me bluntly one day during a conversation at his tailor shop. Congolese women, he went on to say, were interested only in money and would abandon their foreign husbands and their children without warning. You could not trust them.

The supposed shortcomings of Congolese constituted a recurring theme in the old man's statements to me, and the question of intermarriage was a particularly sensitive subject. His wife Hawa was Malian and hailed from the same town as he did. One of their sons, however, had married a Congolese woman. Without knowing many details, I could clearly see that Diallo's relations with his son were troubled, and he did not care for his daughter-in-law. Diallo's children were mostly in their teens and twenties by then, and he was concerned about their future. They had never been to Mali, and the best way for them to maintain some connection to their ancestral homeland was through marriage to Malians who had some exposure to it. At least two of his daughters had married Malians, but that his son had chosen differently was a source of concern for the old man.

Diallo's desire to keep the "old country" alive for his children reflected a much larger preoccupation among West African immigrants in the region. Through their everyday discourse and actions, they sought to insulate themselves from the cultural influences of the host society. In previous chapters I have shown how West Africans in Congo have, over decades and generations, formed a densely knit, introverted community set apart from Congolese society but inextricably intertwined with it. This process of introversion has been the outcome of a combination of historical contingencies and economic necessity. Religion is only one means through which they maintain their population's distinctive features. Another is their enduring connection with the places and people left behind in West Africa. These connections qualify as transnational: while they are "anchored in and span two or more nation-states" (Faist 2000:192), they also transcend, or in some cases bypass, national institutions and boundaries (cf. Levitt and Waters 2002).

Members of transnational populations preserve a variety of links to their communities and places of origin. Some shuttle regularly between "home" and "abroad." For others the homeland is a source of cultural influence, an important reference point but not necessarily a key physical space in the conduct of their affairs. Immigrants' descendants in the second and subsequent generations may make only sporadic trips to their country of origin, and may have little communication with people living there. The homeland might be more meaningful to them as a symbol for ordering social relations and constructing communal and personal identity than as a source of personal memory. Itzigsohn et al. (1999) dub such loosely held ties across national boundaries "broad transnationality" in contrast to "narrow transnationality," which entails regular physical movement between countries of destination and origin.[1]

The concept of transnationalism in the social sciences has suffered from ambiguous, competing, and sometimes contradictory definitions since it came into prominence in the mid-1990s. The pioneering scholars of the field have seldom included the broad or symbolic types of connections described above in their definitions. Portes, Guarnizo, and Landolt (1999:219), for example, define transnationalism rather exclusively as "occupations and activities that require regular and sustained social contacts over time across national borders for their implementation." Transnationalism is also frequently blurred with transnational migration, "the process by which immigrants forge and sustain simultaneous multi-stranded social relations that link together their societies of origin and settlement" (Glick Schiller, Basch, and Szanton Blanc 1995:48). These attempts to flesh out the meaning of transnationalism have concentrated on its "narrower" aspects—those involving migration or regular and sustained communication across borders. It is vital, however, to consider broad forms of transnationalism alongside narrow ones, and to consider the variety of ways that people identify with or "belong to" places where they do not reside and may never even have set foot in. The quality of "being from" somewhere is, as we shall see, socially constructed: people can "be from" a given place in many different ways. They may have been born there or raised there, or born and raised elsewhere but their parents or earlier ancestors came from there, or their connection to the place may be even more diffuse. How people demarcate their affiliation with a geographically situated place and community has a deep impact on their lived social realities. Considerable research suggests, moreover, that nonmigrants as well as migrants can practice transnationalism. In other words, people can be transnational in significant respects without going anywhere.[2]

Some of the most important questions about transnationalism today concern its durability and accessibility: To what extent can transnational activities be passed from migrants to their children and grandchildren, and who can take part in them? There is no consensus on these questions, in part because transnationalism is too recent in many settings to be studied intergenerationally. Another problem, however, is that different scholars define transnationalism differently. Narrowly associating the concept with regular physical movement across borders, Alejandro Portes has stated that transnationalism in the United States remains limited to a small, rather privileged minority of first-generation immigrants. By contrast, those who conceptualize transnationalism in broader terms, incorporating symbolic and cultural dimensions, leave open the possibility of a more diverse range of participants including members of the second and subsequent generations.[3]

I believe we can learn a great deal about the potential durability of transnationalism by examining it in alternative contexts, specifically, in developing countries that impose fewer barriers to immigration than do wealthy northern states. In a legal and logistical sense, it is not difficult for a West African to get to Brazzaville. Obtaining the necessary papers is relatively simple: Congolese entry visas—unlike those for Western countries which, at least in Africa, are offered only to a tiny fraction of applicants (see Piot 2010:chap. 3)—are readily available from the Republic of Congo's consulates in various African capitals to anyone willing to pay the application fee. At the consulate in Bamako this fee is set at 53,000 CFA francs or about $100, which, though not cheap, is also not prohibitively expensive for most would-be travelers. Proof of yellow fever vaccination is required for entry to Congo, as in most African countries. Although Congolese residence permits can be expensive—at least $200 per person per year—enforcement is lax, and most foreigners can stay in Congo without obtaining one. Moving from West Africa to Congo and back carries relatively few legal constraints.

This fact, coupled with the deep historical roots of Brazzaville's West African community reaching back to the late nineteenth century, means that this population can be an instructive example of the resilience and transmissibility of transnational linkages. My goal in this chapter is to map out the various types of connections linking Sahelians in Brazzaville with their places of origin, and to describe the conditions under which these connections are passed on from one generation to the next. Transnational connections in this population offer glimpses into the evolving relationship between people and place in the contemporary world.

A Transnational Social Field and Its Inhabitants

As we have seen, Brazzaville is only one of many cities throughout Africa and beyond to which West Africans migrate; the flow of migrants from Mali, Guinea, Senegal, and other countries of the western Sahel goes in many directions. Brazzaville does constitute an important node of the networks within which these migrants operate, however. Sahelians come and go between Brazzaville, Bamako, Dakar, Abidjan, Kinshasa, Luanda, Cotonou, Lagos, and a host of other African cities, not to mention commercial hubs in Western Europe (Paris, Brussels) and Asia (Dubai, Bangkok, Hong Kong), as well as the Muslim holy sites of Saudi Arabia. Many of my informants had previously lived outside their country of birth, particularly in Côte d'Ivoire, prior to migrating to Congo, and a few had highly cosmopolitan lives and families. Consider the example of Yacouba, a trader in his forties from Togotala.

> *Yacouba came to Congo from Mali in the 1980s after a few years working in Libya. He established a business specializing in imported foodstuffs; by the onset of the 1997 civil war he was worth millions of dollars, with vast stocks of merchandise, a warehouse, and a fleet of trucks. (Much of his property was looted during the war, but he managed to continue his operations, albeit on a reduced scale.) Yacouba lives in Pointe-Noire with his wife and four children but comes to Brazzaville, where his company has a branch office and he owns an apartment, at least monthly on business. In Brazzaville he cultivates contacts within the Congolese government and political elite that are essential for his business affairs. He holds both Congolese and Malian citizenship and has visited the United States on several occasions as well as China and a host of European countries. He has performed the hajj to Mecca seven times and paid for his parents to go as well. Capitalizing on*

his professional mobility, Yacouba made a conscious effort to "diversify" his children's nationalities, twice sending his wife abroad to give birth. Their youngest daughter was born in New York and has both U.S. and Malian citizenship; their youngest son was born in Paris and has both French and Malian citizenship; and their two older children, born in Congo, have both Malian and Congolese citizenship. He and his family visit Mali regularly (his wife and children annually, and he more often), where they stay in a house he built on the outskirts of Bamako.

In Brazzaville one occasionally meets West African entrepreneurs like Yacouba who are members of the global business class: they hold multiple passports, own multiple homes in Congo, West Africa, and elsewhere, and regularly travel to other continents in conducting their affairs. For him and others like him, Brazzaville and other cities of the Congo Basin have been a common destination for decades.

More often, however, one meets West African migrants who are young, male, and often single—so-called aventuriers—at or near the beginning of their migratory careers. For these individuals, Brazzaville is more a transit point than a destination (see chapter 2). Following the demise of single-party rule in 1991, repeated outbreaks of political violence and a stagnating commercial sector have relegated Congo to a fallback position in the international migration circuit. Aventuriers, usually Malians and Guineans in their twenties with little education, pass through Brazzaville to seek their fortunes in the diamond fields of Angola and Congo-Kinshasa; many of my younger male informants had, in fact, been on their way to Angola overland when difficulties forced them to settle in Brazzaville to earn some money and regroup for another attempt. These men often exhibit a dogged determination to reach their destination and overcome numerous obstacles, most of them imposed by representatives of the African states whose territory they enter. Consider the voyage of one such aventurier:

> Mamadou set out for Angola from his home in Guinea in January 2003 at the age of twenty-three carrying all his savings, worth about $600 in cash, and traveled across Mali, Burkina Faso, and Nigeria. He crossed borders clandestinely whenever possible to avoid having to bribe unscrupulous border guards. (He used his Guinean identity card when asked to present papers but kept his passport hidden: travel within West Africa had led him to conclude that ID cards brought fewer complications than passports.) Upon

reaching Cameroonian territory he was nearly out of money and spent five months doing odd jobs—from shining shoes to washing cars—to replenish his travel funds. He saved up nearly $300 but, after crossing into Congo, spent most of it just to pay off officials on both sides of the border and to acquire various "official" documents and stamps. These payments included $45 for a Cameroonian laissez-passer (a paper intended to make up for his lack of entry visa), $5 to get a stamp showing that he had been vaccinated (no vaccine was given), $10 to have his name recorded on the registry at a border guard's station, and a $20 "fine" for his lack of a passport. Near the northern Congolese town of Ouesso, immigration police arrested him and demanded $40 to let him go. He spent several weeks shining shoes in Ouesso before scraping together enough funds to continue on to Brazzaville, where he arrived seven months after leaving Guinea. He was subsequently arrested again after trying to enter Congo-Kinshasa clandestinely: after confiscating his money, immigration officials there sent him back to Brazzaville, where he was stripped of the passport he had secretly carried throughout his travels and was released after a night in jail. When I met him some eighteen months later, Mamadou was selling Chinese-made clothing at a rented stall in the Moungali market and had all but abandoned his dreams of striking it rich in Angola's diamond fields; sales were so poor, and his profit margins so low, that he could not save up enough money for another try.

Mamadou is typical of the many West African *aventuriers* I knew in Brazzaville. Motivated by the wealth displayed by successful returned migrants, and seeing no possibility beyond poverty at home, they set out with little idea of what awaits them abroad. Many make the trip overland, supposing that such travel will cost them less than going by air.[4] I met several young West Africans in Brazzaville who had been turned back or deported from Angola and Congo-Kinshasa, and a few who had come to Congo only after unsuccessful efforts to reach Europe via North Africa. Yacouba and others of his generation benefited from good timing: they started out in Congo during its economic heyday when opportunities were abundant. Today, its boom years a faded memory, Congo is a poor substitute for other, more enticing destinations.

The study of transnational populations, by necessity, entails the study of people in motion. Some migrants, like Yacouba, are wealthy cosmopolitans with the rights of citizenship in more than one state. Others, like Mamadou, are "undocumented"[5] clandestine migrants whose rights as human beings are routinely violated while they live and travel abroad. My analysis of transnational linkages cannot overlook Mamadou and his fellow aventuriers, who lack the resources for regular visits home and for whom life in the host country is more precarious than for well-off, well-connected traders such as Yacouba. One should also be wary of concentrating only on the most mobile members of this population. Studies of transnationalism tend to privilege circulation over settlement, obscuring important aspects of migrant communities from view. Rather than restrict our investigations only to mobile elements of a population or even to a single type of mobility, we should consider the "full house" of variation in patterns of movement and settlement.[6] In keeping with more expansive formulations of the concept, the object of the study of transnationalism is not mobility per se but rather how people stay connected with communities they do not live in and from which they are separated by national boundaries.

A concept I find useful in thinking about this population in all its diversity is that of the transnational social field. Itzigsohn et al. (1999:317) describe it as "a field of social interactions and exchanges that transcend political and geographical boundaries of one nation." Within the transnational social field linking Brazzaville's Sahelian migrants with their home communities, individuals, goods, and ideas flow from one location to another via telecommunications, air travel, and overland transport. The transnational social field concept encompasses all types of connection, not merely those entailing physical movement.

Whereas much research on transnationalism concentrates on the highly organized upper stratum of hometown associations, political parties, and the like, my work here fits into the growing literature on transnational families and connections operating through households and kin groups. These ties play a vital but underappreciated role in preserving the transnational social field.

In the following sections I map out some of the workings of the transnational social field my informants create and inhabit. By examining how migrants in Brazzaville relate to their Sahelian communities of origin, I consider the kinds of connections they maintain and the effects of these connections on their communities. I begin by studying national governments at the "macro level," focusing specifically on the government of Mali and its role in fostering transnational ties among its citizens abroad. Next I consider the "meso level" of hometowns and hometown associations. These two approaches allow us to flesh out the institutional framework of the transnational social field linking the Congo Basin with the western Sahel. In the third and most extensive section I examine the "micro level" of households and kin groups, characterized by informality rather than institutionalization, and analyze their vital role in facilitating social reproduction within the transnational social field.

Levels of Transnational Engagement

The Macro Level: The Role of Nation-states and Governments

The policies of national governments can have a decisive impact on migrants' ability to maintain transnational ties (Faist 2000). This holds true for both sending and receiving countries: in the case of Congo, for example, the relative ease with which noncitizens can come and go, coupled with the government's willingness to recognize dual citizenship, creates a legal and logistical environment that fosters transnational connections. My concern in this section, however, is the influence of migrant-*sending* countries on the development of transnationalism. Many such states have adopted policies to cultivate a sense of national belonging among their citizens abroad. Perhaps the most basic of these is offering consular services in host countries to ensure that their citizens can obtain government documents for themselves and their family members (e.g., passports, national identity cards, and certificates of birth, marriage, and death). Some governments extend political rights to emigrants pertaining to holding dual citizenship, voting, or even running for elected office in their country of origin. A growing number of governments have established ministries of migrant affairs to coordinate government services to their migrant populations in other countries. Capitalizing on the economic potential of their emigrants, governments also encourage migrants to invest at home. Others, such as the Mexican federal government, promote a sense of symbolic belonging, organizing sports clubs or literacy and history classes for Mexicans living in host countries so that members of the second generation there can feel connected to the country that they or their parents left behind.[7]

To consider the role of national governments in the life of Brazzaville's West African population, I focus on Mali, homeland of the largest portion of these migrants. The Malian government has created various bureaucratic structures to serve its citizens abroad. There is the General Delegation for Malians Abroad (Délégation Générale des Maliens de l'Extérieur [DGME]), part of the Ministry of Malians Abroad and African Integration (Ministère des Maliens de l'Extérieur et de l'Intégration Africaine); according to the DGME's website, its mission is

- to assure that the interests of Malian expatriates living temporarily or permanently abroad are protected;
- to conduct, coordinate, and monitor various actions helping Malians abroad return home;

- to assure the creation of conditions allowing Malians abroad to participate in the processes of economic and social development of the country;
- to initiate and coordinate Mali's consular action; [and]
- to assure the application of accords and treaties relating to the settlement and circulation of people and goods.[8]

The DGME conducts its mission through two primary channels. The first is Mali's diplomatic missions: the Malian Foreign Affairs Ministry operates embassies in twenty-nine countries on four continents, as well as consulates in another twenty-six countries. Mali's consulate in Brazzaville is headed by a consul general and staffed by about half a dozen other men and women. The consulate's mission does not pertain solely to services for Malians abroad: consular staff have other duties, such as promoting friendly relations between Mali and Congo and issuing Malian entry visas to foreign applicants. Most of their time, however, is spent serving the tens of thousands of Malian citizens living in Congo.

One Sunday afternoon in February 2005 I attended an annual "town meeting"-style gathering hosted by the Malian consulate. About two hundred Malians, all of them men, crowded into the building's courtyard. In the course of this meeting, the consul described his team's activities from the previous year. These included visiting Congolese provincial towns to issue consular ID cards to Malian nationals living outside the capital, collecting tens of thousands of dollars in private donations responding to famine in Mali, and helping an impoverished Malian immigrant in his nineties obtain airfare to return home. The consul also spoke of multiple delegations he had personally led to various Congolese cabinet ministries, municipal government offices, and police stations to promote goodwill toward Malian immigrants in Congo and to encourage Congolese officials to respect Malians' rights (a perennial problem for Malians and other African foreigners in Congo, as described in the previous chapter). The consul is the most visible official presence in Brazzaville's Malian community, frequently present at weddings, funerals, meetings, and other gatherings of the city's Malian population.

The second channel through which the DGME operates is the organizations formed in host countries to represent Malian immigrants. Officially these groups are separate from the Malian state: they are associations of private citizens, components of "civil society." The High Council of Malians Abroad (Haut Conseil des Maliens de l'Extérieur [HCME]) is a kind of international umbrella group of these associations. It has a headquarters and a small staff in Bamako, and receives no funds from the Malian government; an HCME official in Bamako told me that the group is entirely financed through member dues. In practice, however, the HCME and its worldwide host-country chapters (of which there are at least twenty-five as of this writing) work closely with the Malian government, and the lines between the activities of the DGME and the HCME are blurry. It would be inaccurate to characterize the HCME or any of its chapters as grassroots organizations, as their organization and leadership structures seem to have issued more from political directives in Bamako than from immigrant-led initiatives; from the 1990s the creation of the HCME and its chapters abroad has mostly been a top-down process.

In Congo the HCME chapter is known as the Malian Community of Congo (Communauté Malienne du Congo [COMACO]). It cooperates closely with the Malian consulate in Brazzaville and shares in many of its tasks in aiding Malian immigrants in distress—detained or imprisoned, sick, or facing some other emergency. COMACO's membership is subdivided into associations grouping together immigrants from six of Mali's administrative regions; each regional association sends a fixed number of delegates to sit on COMACO's governing council, in proportion to the number of immigrants from that region present in Congo. The role of these regional associations, which meet and collect dues monthly, is similar to that of rotating credit associations: they mainly provide a measure of social security to migrants in the host country. Dues are pooled to pay for association members' medical treatment, emergency trips home, and other contingencies. Working through these regional associations, COMACO's leaders may carry out tasks ordinarily done by state officials, including helping conduct a census of eligible Malian voters in Congo for the elections office of Mali's Interior Ministry.

COMACO officials also collaborate with representatives of the Banque d'Habitat du Mali (BHM), a Bamako-based bank mostly owned by the Malian state. The BHM finances the construction of affordable housing (*logements sociaux*), principally in Bamako. It offers savings accounts and mortgages to encourage Malian citizens to invest in housing, and its marketing campaigns focus on Malians living abroad whose buying power is usually greater than that of Malians at home. The working relationship between COMACO and the BHM is so close that the two institutions share the same Brazzaville office, and several members of COMACO's executive committee are also official representatives of the BHM in Congo. The coziness of the arrangement between

Figure 5.1. Members of Brazzaville's Malian community await the arrival of Mali's first lady outside the Maya-Maya airport, 2005. PHOTO BY AUTHOR

COMACO and the parastatal bank is emblematic of the larger relationship between the Malian state and "civil society," particularly with regard to Brazzaville's immigrant community; it is difficult to distinguish between ostensibly public and private representatives of "the community" or to know where one group's work ends and the other's begins.[9]

Apart from providing consular services and helping secure access to housing, the Malian state has little official role in the lives of Malians in Brazzaville. During my year in Brazzaville the consulate, in conjunction with COMACO leaders, did organize a handful of events geared at fostering a sense of national identity among Malian immigrants. The most elaborate of these was a reception at the airport—featuring hundreds of flag-waving Malians accompanied by drummers, praise singers, and a public address system—for the Malian first lady (who unfortunately had to cancel her visit at the last minute). A somewhat lower-key affair was also organized for the visit of a prominent Malian opposition party leader; in the past, Malian presidential candidates have campaigned for votes in Brazzaville's Malian community. In general, however, the Malian state's emigrant-oriented apparatus (DGME, HCME, and diplomatic missions) concerns itself with addressing emigrants' practical needs rather than strengthening their attachments to their country of origin. The HCME has considerable potential to perform this latter function, but its effectiveness has been undermined by bitter and very public leadership quarrels.[10]

For Malians abroad, such structures are not the sole sites of engagement with their national community. Malian state television and radio broadcasts, through the Office de Radio et Télédiffusion du Mali (ORTM), provide a vital link between Malian expatriates and their homeland. Brazzaville listeners can tune in to radio programs broadcast from Bamako via shortwave, though with some difficulty; on TV, anyone owning either a satellite dish or a special antenna for picking up satellite signals from a neighbor's dish can watch the same shows as those watched by viewers in Mali. Most Malians I knew in Brazzaville had at least indirect access to these broadcasts daily. By watching the ORTM evening news, its prime-time melodrama *Walaha*, and especially its popular music shows such as *Top Etoiles*, they could feel they were a part of the Malian public. Similarly listeners to ORTM's radio call-in shows hear fellow Malian listeners phoning in from around the world and come to understand their position within a transnational social field. Consumption of videodiscs and audio CDs featuring Malian musicians is another favorite form of participation in a transnational public. But the most important arena in which feelings of national belonging are encouraged and reinforced, at least with regard to male members of the community, is sporting events: by watching televised games of Mali's national soccer team and cheering on the players, Malians anywhere can experience and perform their sense of membership in the Malian nation. Such media connections have possibly done more to promote national identity among Malians abroad than any government initiative.

The Meso Level: The Role of Villages and Hometown Associations

One feature all but absent from macro-level transnational engagement in Brazzaville is the sending of remittances or the pooling of migrants' funds for community needs back home. Other than the collection taken up by the consulate for famine aid in 2004—an effort apparently targeted at a small number of wealthy donors—and the role of the BHM in stimulating private housing investment, the Malian government played no part in channeling migrant money from Congo. That process takes place at lower levels and concerns hometown associations and individual households. Let us now consider the associations' significance in strengthening transnational connections.

African villages often appear in social science literature as models of face-to-face community. Throughout the continent, however, villages and towns are becoming, to borrow Benedict Anderson's (1983) term, "imagined communities." The prevalence of migration, both within and between African countries, has led local communities to increasingly reach out to their sons and daughters living elsewhere; indeed, migrants often play the most active roles in promoting community development and financing the construction of schools, mosques, health clinics, water and sanitation projects, and even paved roads. This type of relationship between hometowns and emigrants in West Africa is nothing new: researchers have observed it in rural-to-urban migrants for decades.[11] In Togotala, where remittances have paid for a wide range of infrastructure and community development projects, migrants' primary importance in community affairs dates back at least to the 1950s.

The principal vehicle for the collection and disbursement of these funds is the hometown or home association, a multi-local organization with branches wherever significant numbers of a community's emigrants live. Togotala actually has two home associations—the product of long-standing political rivalries within the town—and both are represented not just in Togotala and Bamako but also in Brazzaville, Abidjan, New York, and many other cities. Association branches typically meet monthly. They may be highly institutionalized, with written charters and elaborate committee structures. In France, more than three hundred West African home association branches are registered with the government as nonprofit organizations; some have sister-city arrangements with French towns; a few with Internet-savvy members have even set up their own websites.[12]

The home associations I studied in Brazzaville were not so technologically advanced, but some displayed an impressive degree of organization. On another Sunday afternoon (association meetings are always held on Sunday afternoons, when shops in Brazzaville are closed), I attended a meeting of migrants from the western Malian town of Koniakary. Several dozen men, mostly in their twenties, were crowded into the living room of one of the members' homes. Business was conducted in Fulfulde, Koniakary's dominant language. Each member present paid 1,000 CFA francs (about $2) in monthly dues, and many brought the dues of friends unable to attend the meeting. In this association attendance is mandatory; latecomers to a meeting must pay a fine of 2,000 francs, and members who fail to attend or send in their dues are fined 3,000 francs. This disciplinary system raises the question of whether these associations are truly "voluntary" organizations: given the financial penalty and the social stigma migrants would face in opting out of the association, they have little choice but to participate. "Whether to remain involved in the rural community is no longer simply a matter of individual affection and calculus," writes Gugler (2002:24). Such mechanisms allow enforceable trust (see chapter 2) to extend beyond the immediate kin group.

The Koniakary association's funds are devoted entirely to development projects. "We've noticed," one of its leaders told me, "that the government of Mali can't do much to help our village, so we've decided to take our destiny into our own hands." So far, according to association officials as well as media reports, the association has provided finances for expanding a primary school, constructing a maternity clinic and training its staff, building a community health center with its own pharmacy, improving the main road into town, and developing a marketplace, a child-care center, a slaughterhouse, and a community radio station. Community residents provide construction labor. With the help of a German NGO, which funded the erection of a million-dollar water tower, the village now has forty-five water taps at which households purchase barrels of water for 100 francs, or about 20 cents each (down from 700–800 francs before the advent of tap water). The funds collected defray maintenance costs. Brazzaville is hardly this community's only source of migrant money: Koniakary's home association has chapters in Pointe-Noire, Gabon, South Africa, Zambia, Mozambique, China, France, New York, and Philadelphia. Koniakary has also recently established a partnership with the French town of Villetaneuse. All the town's chapters abroad coordinate their activities with the "home office" in Bamako.[13]

Koniakary's home association is probably an extreme example of what highly formalized migrant organizations can accomplish. Most hometown associations I encountered are much less strict, and many are downright disorganized. By the time I began my fieldwork the Brazzaville chapter of one of Togotala's two home associations had been inactive for two years because of disagreements over leadership. Togotalans still met unofficially to collect funds in response to hometown requests, including calls for relief after heavy rains destroyed several houses in Togotala, and they still pooled funds for future needs, though they were unable to spend any association money until a formal meeting could be held. This case suggests that a high degree of institutionalization is unnecessary to carry out the home association's mission, and that even in the absence of formal sanctions such as those the Koniakary association applied, migrants continue to play active roles in the affairs of their communities of origin. As Mercer, Page, and Evans (2009:156) point out, analyses of migrant associations have "tended to privilege the agency of relatively visible, formalized and familiar forms of associations," but "associational life can be 'transnational' outside the formalized structures and Eurocentric development hierarchies created by international NGOs and development institutions." Moreover, the most significant and perhaps surprising forms of transnational engagement in Brazzaville's West African population are visible at the level not of the hometown but of the household.

The Micro Level: The Role of Households and Kin Groups

During my 2002 fieldwork in Togotala I interviewed a middle-aged woman named Kadi, whose father had emigrated to Brazzaville in the 1940s. Kadi was born there a few years later but at around age three was sent to Togotala, her father's village, where she was raised by paternal relatives. She spent the rest of her childhood there and not once during that time did she see her biological parents, who remained in Brazzaville. At age nineteen Kadi married a Togotalan man who subsequently migrated to Brazzaville and brought Kadi there to join him. Only then was she reunited with her mother and father. Kadi spent thirteen years as a wife and mother in Brazzaville, during which time she sent all her own children to Mali before they turned four to protect them from Congolese cultural influences. She only saw these children again when she returned to Mali in her mid-thirties.

Kadi's case is remarkable in that it challenges received notions of motherhood and family. Kadi and her husband chose to remove their children from the social environment of Brazzaville explicitly to safeguard their cultural identities, just as her own parents had done with her. By having relatives in Mali foster their offspring, they could ensure that their children would grow up speaking their people's Soninke language, practicing their Muslim faith, and experiencing their home community as both a territorial and a social entity. In a sense, parents such as Kadi and her husband gave up their right to raise their own children in favor of the social reproduction of their home community. Kadi and many other returned migrants assured me that this practice was common, even the norm for Togotalans living abroad. When I began my fieldwork in Brazzaville a few years later, one of my main objectives was to discern just how widespread this pattern of transnational parenting was among West African migrants there. Inevitably, perhaps, fieldwork in Togotala highlighted the practice of sending children born abroad to be brought up "at home," whereas fieldwork in Brazzaville revealed a wide variety of child-rearing and enculturation practices among Sahelian families, as well as a complex relationship between them. In the remainder of this chapter I describe some of these practices, discuss how they map onto particular social factors, and consider their implications for the study of transnational communities and transnational families in other settings.

Brazzaville's West African population comprises people of all stages of life, living in several different kinds of households. The most visible component of this population, as seen in chapter 2, is the merchants, who are male and mostly middle-aged, and their employees, males usually in their twenties and thirties. In addition, hundreds of young Sahelian men work as ambulant vendors, maneuvering handcarts full of merchandise between depots and traders' shops, or doing odd jobs. Many are single, and they often share rented houses but take their meals with more established West African households where several women cook in rotation. Most traders are married, as are some of the shop assistants and laborers. Those who marry in West Africa become established in Brazzaville before bringing their wives to join them; if they have children before emigrating, these usually remain behind in West Africa. Many other migrant men only get married after going to Brazzaville, receiving brides sent from home or finding wives within the migrant West African population (ideally the daughters of established traders). A few marry Congolese women. Finally, some men who marry prior to emigrating choose to leave their wives behind in West Africa, but this arrangement is unpopular: many informants told me that spousal separation tempts husbands to engage in illicit sexual liaisons with local women, thus committing the grave sin of *jeneya* or fornication. (There is much less public discussion, however, of the situations of wives left behind.) The ideal, then, is for husbands and wives to cohabit in the migration destination, especially while the wives are of childbearing age.

Women in this population are portrayed as dependent migrants: almost exclusively, unmarried women move at the discretion of their fathers, and married women at the discretion of their husbands. Since women in Sahelian countries are supposed to be economically supported by their male kin, autonomous female mobility for economic purposes is shunned, even equated with prostitution. Some women nonetheless migrate by what amounts to choice: for example, an unmarried woman might arrange to visit her sister abroad and, during her visit, marry a migrant and thus prolong her stay indefinitely. Such cases are rare, however, and women almost never ascribe their moves to their own agency.[14] Many carry out informal trade, selling cloth or cooked food, often out of their home, or embroidering sheets for sale. Just once did I see a Sahelian trader's wife helping him out in his shop, when their eldest son had gone to Dubai to buy merchandise. In Brazzaville, West African–owned shops are a male space, at least behind the counter.

Polygamy is widespread in the Sahel: past surveys of Soninke villages in western Mali, for example, found that from 40 to 80 percent of men above the age of forty-five have multiple wives.[15] Various domestic arrangements are possible for a polygamous husband who emigrates. Most commonly one wife joins him abroad, and the other (or others) remains at home; after a time—at least one year, sometimes much longer—the wives change position. This arrangement is described as "taking turns" or "rotation," much as the women of an extended family take turns with household cooking responsibilities, and stems in part from Islamic requirements that a husband treat his wives equally.

Alternately, a husband may live with multiple wives in the migration destination. This is a more expensive arrangement for West Africans in Brazzaville, where the cost of living is higher than in West Africa, and therefore tends to be limited to the wealthiest merchants. These merchants are among the most well-established members of the immigrant community: some are or have been involved in the diamond trade; they may have interests in real estate, customs brokerage, import-export, and other economic areas. While amassing their wealth, such men may follow a pattern of polygamy suiting their business interests. The first marriages of West African men are often arranged marriages with young women from their home villages, especially their paternal parallel cousins (a type of union known in Bamanan as *balemafuru*, "kin marriage"). Once married, men have more latitude to choose their subsequent brides. In migrant destinations, wealthy West African businessmen may take wives from among the host population, provided they never exceed the maximum of four wives permitted under Islamic law. Such exogamous unions can cement ties with local elites, enable the husband to gain host-country citizenship, or secure his assets under his wife's name against expropriation by the host government.[16]

The lives of the West African wives, meanwhile, are oriented largely toward bearing children. According to Bredeloup, a migrant trader's wife returns home permanently after she bears six children or reaches menopause, while her husband continues his career abroad; "in a certain sense, the wife's conjugal life ends at the same time as her ability to procreate" (2002:161). In fact, although this pattern is quite common for the wives of the wealthiest migrants, especially the diamond traders' wives (who constitute a tiny fraction of the immigrant community) studied by Bredeloup, women's life trajectories among the wider West African community are much more varied. These trajectories intertwine closely with the lives of children born in migrant destinations.

In discussing this population's transnational child-rearing practices, I need to be clear about the language I use and—just as important—do not use. For instance, I do not refer to these practices as "strategies," as they are not always strictly intentional but are mediated by a household's available means; many Sahelian parents in Brazzaville might wish to send their children home but lack the economic or social capital to realize that goal. Nor do I use the term "types," which would suggest a series of discrete behaviors rather than the full spectrum (or "full house") described above. The spectrum, in this case, stands for the wide range of exposure to their home community and country that children born abroad experience; by "modes" I mean common child-rearing approaches clustered around particular points along that spectrum. These modes do not represent an exhaustive list of potential approaches to transnational child rearing but designate some of the most popular practices my informants and their parents employed.

Maximal Mode: Maximum Exposure to the Home Community

The life of Kadi, whose example I cited above, shows one approach to transnational child rearing: when their offspring are still in early childhood, preferably younger than five or six years of age, parents buy them a one-way airline ticket and send them off on a plane with a relative or family friend to their parents' home country, where they remain until entering adulthood and possibly much longer. This approach, which I call the "maximal mode," represents the maximum degree of exposure to the homeland. Both in West Africa and Congo, informants present the maximal mode as the preferred one, and it was practiced by thirty-nine of ninety-eight Sahelian parents interviewed in Brazzaville; another twenty-six stated a firm intention to adopt this mode when their children (infants and toddlers) were old enough. These parents are motivated by a powerful belief that children cannot grow up "properly" outside their ancestral homeland, and that West African children who do grow up abroad will turn out badly, no matter what pains their parents take regarding their upbringing and education. This notion constructs Congolese society as a corrupting influence that inevitably prevents West African children who are exposed to it from assuming their "true" cultural and religious identities. "Congolese ways are different from our ways," immigrants told me repeatedly during my research in Brazzaville.

West Africans there tend to see Congolese values as not only different from but actually hostile to their own. As we saw in chapter 3, they often equate Congolese lifeways with such illicit activities as the consumption of alcohol, fornication, and theft. "If you let your child stay in Congo and grow up there," Kadi told me in Togotala, "he'll become Congolese. If he doesn't become a beer drinker, he'll become a drug user. That's why, when our children are a few years old, we send them to grow up here." Most migrant parents I interviewed in Brazzaville employed similar language to describe the importance of sending their children home. Two terms they used frequently to describe the condition they most wished to avoid for their children were *bandit* and *vagabond*; both these French words roughly correspond to their English-language homonyms, but in this context they denote more a state of immorality and rebellion against parental authority than any specific criminal behavior.

Parents usually say that they want their children to enjoy the same kind of upbringing they themselves had. This means learning the same language (or languages) and religious tradition, and getting to know the same place (the homeland, or *faso*) and its people. Adults I interviewed who had been fostered to their parents' home villages as children tended to emphasize their exposure to their extended families, which helped them discover where they had come from and who "their people" were. As one migrant father in Brazzaville told me,

> We always like our children to grow up in the place where their parents come from, to know their culture.... The place where their grandfathers come from, we call that faso. So that, for us, is very important. Any child we [raise] like that is going to come, living their life they have no problems. We teach them what is right and what is good, what is not good.

Children's interests alone do not guide parents' concerns over their children's enculturation: the parents' own future welfare will depend in part on the degree to which their children acquire the "right" values, especially those pertaining to filial piety. Sahelians suspect that a child who "becomes Congolese" will be less likely to honor religious and cultural obligations to provide for parents in their old age. "Here, if you bring up a child, it won't benefit you, that's why we send them off," said a Malian mother in Brazzaville, whose two children were both living with their grandparents in Mali. After I asked how parents could recognize the signs of a child becoming a *bandit*, a father named Draman described the distinction between rebellious and dutiful children:

> *Okay, we see him smoking cannabis. Or taking pills. Or getting drunk. Or there are children who steal. Right away we send them off, because the upbringings aren't the same. Here, Congolese children, they depend on their parents for food, right up to twenty-five years of age, they can even hit [their parents]. But for us, already from the age of ten or so, a child says, "I must feed my father and my mother." There's the big difference. West African children work for their parents. Children here [in Congo] work for themselves. Not only do they work for themselves, but if they don't have anything it's their parents who must provide for them, even at the age of forty.*

Many migrants see maximal-mode child rearing as the most effective way to ensure that their children grow up to be part of their parents' communities, defined not only in terms of territory but also kinship, ethnicity, and religion, and thereby to build up social security for themselves later in life. Sending children back to spend their childhoods in the *faso* essentially prevents them from becoming "second-generation" immigrants in the host society and from assimilating even partially into it. The maximal-mode approach, of course, entails long periods when parents and children are separated. Kadi, who did not see her biological mother or father for nineteen years, is an extreme example; today, given cheaper transportation and telecommunications, migrant parents can more easily make return visits to West Africa and be in regular contact with their children. The distance remains great, nonetheless, and parents who adopt the maximal-mode approach must give up the kind of personal relationship with their children that they would otherwise expect.

Maximal-mode transnational parenting appears to have been the normative approach among West Africans in Brazzaville for generations. In the 1950s, writes Manchuelle (1987:452), West African elders "had long reacted against what they saw as the 'immoral' atmosphere of the Congolese cities by sending their children back 'home' to their villages to be educated in the traditional ways, and in the proper Islamic upbringing." Today such responses are common among Soninke immigrants in France, who send their children (especially daughters) to Africa at a young age to avoid the corrupting influence of Western secular education. Jacques Barou (2001:18) describes a mounting sentiment among Sahelians in France that it is "impossible to bring up children respectful of African values" there, and that children can only acquire these values by being sent home.[17] These "African values" would be more accurately described as specific to the parents' local, ethnic, and religious communities. They have come to dominate discourse in the transnational social field linking communities throughout the Sahel with their migrants in Africa, Europe, and beyond.

One could argue that parents who favor the maximal-mode approach deploy alternative constructions of parenthood, redefining their parental roles from caregivers to economic providers, as do transnational mothers elsewhere. But perhaps the reality is more complicated, given how common child fostering is in West Africa. Many children there are raised for long periods by their uncles, aunts, grandparents, or more distant kin; hence the home-fostered children of transnational West African migrants do not necessarily experience the same sense of dislocation, lack of intimacy, and loss attributed to children separated from their parents in other transnational contexts, such as Chinese "parachute kids" and "satellite kids" sent abroad for their education, or the children of Filipino migrant workers. I asked Kadi what it was like to be apart from her parents for so long. "It wasn't hard, because I was with my family," she told me. "Plus I wasn't alone; many kids came from Brazzaville. Whoever was born over there came back [to Togotala] to grow up." As in transnational families from the Caribbean, strong extended families have blunted the impact of parental separation for these Sahelian children; this distinguishes these populations from many others where family nucleation is or has become the norm.[18]

There is nothing unusual about children being sent "home" across national boundaries. Migrant parents in many settings send their children away to shield them from the cultural influences of the host society. In the United States, for example, this practice has been observed among migrants from Belize, Yemen and Korea, Guatemala, and Mexico.[19] For most of these parents, however, sending a child back is a form of "transnational disciplining" (Orellana et al. 2001:588)—a last resort responding to negative outcomes such as the child's involvement in criminal activity or social rebellion. Many migrant parents invoke the possibility of transnational disciplining to deter children's misbehavior. What seems distinctive about transnational parenting among West Africans in Brazzaville is that these parents send children home at an early age, before they can even be influenced by the host society. Although some West

Africans (such as Draman, the father quoted above) use home fostering as a corrective measure, most use it preemptively.

Intermediate Mode: Some Exposure to the Home Community

An alternative approach to transnational child rearing, which I call "intermediate mode," is for parents to keep children based in the place of destination but send (or sometimes accompany) them on occasional visits to the *faso*. These visits vary widely in frequency and duration. One common approach entails visits lasting from one to three months, timed to coincide with Congolese school vacations. Intermediate-mode parenting has the obvious advantage of enabling mothers and fathers to have more control over their children's upbringing and to spend more time with their children.

Intermediate-mode parenting also has the disadvantage, however, of stigmatizing the children in the eyes of many West Africans, particularly nonmigrants in the home communities. These people may see such individuals growing up outside their parent's home community as culturally impure, a status pejoratively called *tabushi*. I discuss this phenomenon in depth in the following chapter. Here I only need to point out that *tabushi* status does not automatically befall children born to West African migrants abroad. Children sent home at a sufficiently early age are not seen to be any different than their West Africa–born peers; through their parents' sacrifice, they benefit from the same socialization process as other children in their *faso*. Thus maximal-mode parenting guarantees that children do not acquire *tabushi* status, whereas intermediate-mode parenting does not: children who go to West Africa for relatively short and infrequent visits are only likely to call unwanted attention to their alien upbringing through their unfamiliarity with local landscapes, their ignorance of local customs, and their imperfect command of the local language.

It takes great effort and skill for a *tabushi* in such circumstances to "perform" a West African identity successfully. Madou, the twenty-three-year-old son of a wealthy Malian trader in Brazzaville, went to Mali for the first time at age thirteen and remained there for eight years. (His personal trajectory therefore falls somewhere between maximal and intermediate modes.) "I went to learn things, to know this is my *faso*, this is my father's younger sibling, this is my father's older brother, this is my aunt," he told me. "Now I can know my family, and even when I go away, I know that I come from Mali *ka koro* [literally, "of old," i.e., originally]." When Madou first arrived in Mali, he could understand Bamanan but could not speak it; within one year, he says, he had fully mastered the language.

> When I was in Mali, if I didn't tell you that I was a *tabushi,* you couldn't tell. Not from the way I spoke, the way I talked to my parents, even true Malians [*hali malien yèrè*] wouldn't be able to tell. . . . I was born abroad, but the kind of person I am, when people see me they don't know that. If I didn't tell you, you couldn't know. Look at me, I read Bamanan books. I can speak Bamanan that true Malians can't understand. I spent a year in Segou, where true Bamanan is spoken, where my mother comes from, she comes from a village nearby, I spent some time there and in the city. True Bamanan is spoken from Segou to Bamako.

Speaking "Bamanan that true Malians can't understand" meant that Madou took pains to learn a pure form of the language. He also acquired a Malian national ID card and attended school for seven of the eight years he spent in Mali, returning to Brazzaville to find work at the age of twenty-one.

Some informants who employed intermediate-mode parenting stressed direct parental involvement, not the environment outside the home, as the most important factor in their children's upbringing. "For me a child's education depends on the parents. The child will adopt my own behavior," said Barou, a thirty-nine-year-old Malian father of four (also the auto parts dealer mentioned in chapter 2). He was the only one of my interviewees to speak mostly French at home with his children. He had sent each of them (except the youngest, still an infant) for visits to Mali, and he saw these visits as a necessary complement to the upbringing he gave them in Brazzaville. He was building a house in his hometown that he envisioned as a kind of country home he and his family could use after they relocated to Bamako. Financially successful parents such as Barou wanted their children to have a quality education (in private schools) which would be unavailable in their rural West African communities of origin; for them, this factor outweighed their children's exposure to different cultural influences and the potential that they would be labeled *tabushis* during return trips. Barou and other intermediate-mode parents remained wary of allowing their offspring to "become Congolese," but they sought to reduce that risk by setting a proper example in the home rather than by fostering their children to their *faso* for a lengthy period. The high cost of home visits made this mode off-limits for most: only three of the ninety-eight parents in my interview sample, all of them quite wealthy, used this approach with all their children.

Minimal Mode:
Minimal or No Exposure to the Home Community

Unlike parents who adopted the intermediate mode of parenting, parents who had not sent their children to their *faso* at all were often near the bottom of the economic scale. These included fourteen of the ninety-eight parents interviewed. The fathers were generally commercial employees, laborers, or itinerant traders. Most, like Vieux Diallo, reported that they lacked either the financial means or the social relationships necessary to send their children back. A few were relatively well established and could have afforded to send their children to West Africa, but they did not have relatives there in a position to look after them. Nearly all parents in this category admitted that it was best to send children home but added that they simply had not been able to do so themselves. Many with younger children expressed hope that they would be able to send them to West Africa at some future date.

Maryam, a thirty-nine-year-old mother of two from Togotala, was in this latter category. She lived with her husband (a commercial employee) and eight-year-old son in a modest Poto-Poto apartment. She and her husband could not afford to send their son to Mali, and their son was already unable to speak either Bamanan or his parents' Soninke language (which they spoke at home). Still, Maryam couched their parenting approach in terms of preference rather than necessity.

> Now people understand there's no reason to send them too young. [It's best] to have your child with you, so you develop affection for each other. But if you send your child away young, when they grow up you've spent all those years apart, and you can't relate to each other. People have come to understand it's not good to send them away too young. So we can leave them even until age 10, once they start school they can take care of themselves. Now we understand that this is better than sending them off very young. ... To raise children here, if you send a young child to somebody you're giving them a burden. He can't wash himself, go to the bathroom and clean up after himself. What happens when the child gets sick in the bush? The other person [raising the child in the village] has a problem, and you yourself are here [in Congo]. That's why, in my opinion, it's better to leave the child here a few years until he can take care of himself, then send him away. All he will have to do is say when he's hungry, and then the guardian will give him something to eat.

Maryam's son was by then in his third year of school and was able to take care of himself in many ways, yet Maryam described him as still too young and dependent. Like many of the poorest migrant parents, Maryam and her husband had to make do while waiting for their fortunes to change. Although their son attended a Congolese public primary school, they also sent him in the afternoons to the neighborhood *madrasa*, a private Islamic school where young people (mostly the children of West African immigrants) learned the Qur'an and the fundamentals of their Muslim faith. They also sent him to spend school breaks with a prosperous uncle (Yacouba, profiled at the beginning of this chapter) in Pointe-Noire, whose own children made visits to Mali once every year or two.

Brazzaville's *madrasa* plays a significant role in the education and socialization of children in the West African community. It provides an Islamic-oriented learning environment similar to that of *madrasas* in West Africa, where they have become a widespread alternative (and complement) to secular schooling over the last few decades.[20] *Madrasa* proponents represent the institution as a bulwark against hostile cultural influences from the host society. For them, *madrasa* training helps form young minds while they are still pliant. "It's like clay, if you take it when it's wet, and squeeze it, you can form it the way you want to," a Brazzaville *madrasa* instructor told me. "But if you try to squeeze it when it's already dry, it will crumble. Children are like that, too." He added, however, that *madrasa* education was only effective in conditioning children's behavior when coupled with proper supervision at home. "[Children's] upbringing depends on those who are looking after them. The Prophet, peace and blessings be upon him, said that children are like a mirror. They will reflect whatever's in front of them. They can't reflect something they're never shown."

This last qualification echoes a common belief among West African parents in Brazzaville that even the best *madrasa* abroad is no substitute for a traditional upbringing in the *faso*. Another *madrasa* instructor, Salim, confided in me that most of his students came from families that were unable to send them home to West Africa. His own three children (the oldest was aged ten) were in the same position, and though he did everything he could to keep them on the "straight path," he felt that their fate was out of his hands as long as they remained in Brazzaville. They spoke only Lingala, the dominant Congolese language of the neighborhood, and spent most of their time with Congolese children. Like most West African fathers in Brazzaville, Salim lacked the time to monitor his children's activities adequately: in addition to teaching at the *ma-*

drasa, he worked in a relative's shop and taught in a local mosque in the evenings. Salim worried about his children's future but saw little alternative to keeping them in Brazzaville, where he felt he could at least provide for them better than he could back home.

Not all West African children raised entirely in Brazzaville face alienation, however; a few are able to integrate successfully into Brazzaville's West African community despite their lack of exposure to the homeland. These are the children, and sometimes the grandchildren, of successful West African entrepreneurs. One such parent and grandparent was Makan, a patriarch in his eighties who had spent six decades in Congo after migrating from Mali as a young man. He was a *jatigi*, a combination of host, landlord, and intermediary (see chapter 1), who used his connections in Brazzaville to help newly arrived West African immigrants as well as transnational traders, particularly diamond merchants. Makan told me that he had resorted to minimal-mode parenting because he lacked relatives in Mali who could take his children in; he had just one sibling, an older sister, who was already overburdened. His children had only Congolese citizenship. Nonetheless, every sign indicated that Makan's children, eighteen in all, had remained practicing Muslims; they had married Malians (mostly from his home region in western Mali). "My children haven't gone to Mali, but they came out fine, their father brought them up well," one of Makan's two wives told me in an interview. "They speak Bamanan, Soninke, French, same thing. God willing, if my children go back to their homeland, they won't be ashamed because they were brought up right." Many of Makan's children had gone to Mali after becoming adults, and some resided elsewhere in the transnational social field, including France and the United States. Even Makan's adult grandchildren who had never left Congo seemed to belong fully to Brazzaville's West African community, and spoke Soninke and Bamanan in addition to Lingala and French. "I've never been to Mali," said Fanta, Makan's twenty-one-year-old granddaughter, "but the way they do things, even Malian languages, I've been able to learn them little by little. It's as though I was born and raised there." Fanta was engaged to marry a fellow Congo-born Malian whose father had come from the same Malian region as Fanta's grandfather.

I asked Makan how, given the ease with which West African children in Brazzaville can grow apart from their parents' religious and cultural identity, he had managed to raise children who identified so strongly with their Malian ancestry without having lived there. He answered with evident pride: "You can congratulate me! They didn't change. Many here do change." They attended *madrasa* as well as public school, and he had paid for their private home tutoring by Muslim scholars. But these factors also applied to many other children, who were nowhere near as integrated into the West African community. Other less visible factors were shaping "successful" social reproduction in this immigrant population.

Determinants of "Success" in Transnational Child Rearing

As we have seen, two overarching discourses are evident among West African parents with regard to child rearing. The dominant discourse holds that identity is closely linked to territory, to soil, and that it can only be successfully reproduced in the *faso*, the parents' (or at least the father's) ancestral homeland. The other discourse holds that identity is in the blood, and reproducible anywhere provided parents give sufficient attention to their children's education and upbringing. This is the thinking adopted by those who deliberately choose intermediate or minimal-mode parenting practices. These two competing discourses, soil and blood, have very different implications for the transnational social field in which West Africans (both migrants and nonmigrants) reside. What I wish to analyze here, however, is the way that socioeconomic factors condition these approaches to child rearing.

We have also seen that migrant parents who adopt the intermediate mode of parenting are likely to be better off financially. The costs of this approach are high (a round-trip ticket from Brazzaville to Bamako currently costs about $700), and only the wealthy can afford to pay for their children's regular visits. These fathers tend to own multiple businesses. Fathers who adopt the maximal mode, which requires only a single one-way ticket, are more likely to be small-scale merchants and better-off commercial employees, whereas those who adopt the minimal mode are usually the poorest members of the community.

It may be, however, that the determinants of "successful" child-rearing outcomes for these migrant parents lie less in the specific mode of parenting adopted and more in the parents' socioeconomic status and position. Wealthy transnational entrepreneurs, who have employees to manage their commercial operations, can afford to spend more time at home; their wives can also spend more time with their children, as there may be one or more domestic servants in their households (either paid Congolese workers or young female relatives brought from West Africa). They are therefore able to play a greater role in their children's upbringing. By contrast, most ordinary shopkeepers, commercial employees, and laborers spend the vast majority of their time outside the home. Their wives are busy with their cooking rotations and leave their children to their own devices much of the time.

Moreover, the father's social and economic role within the transnational social field is another decisive factor in his children's enculturation. Established businessmen like Makan, the *jatigi* described above whose children were raised entirely in Brazzaville, form the epicenter of Brazzaville's West African community. Because of their stability and knowledge of the host society, they constantly receive new West African visitors and lodge paying West African guests and tenants, including circular migrants and aventuriers. As vital nodes in migrant social networks, they draw in other community members. Their spacious homes provide crucial sites of interaction between West African merchants and religious and community leaders (Makan himself had been a fund-raiser and organizer behind the construction of Poto-Poto's "Sunni mosque"). They are the loci of the migrant population, islands of permanence in a sea of flux. It is the very fixedness of these *jatigi* and their households that permits the itinerant and transnational activities of many members of this migrant population. "The mobility of some is made possible by the sedentariness of others," writes Agier (1983:159) in his study of *jatigi* in Togo. These men's importance means that the rest of the community comes to them. Their children grow up amid constant activity and intercourse in the languages of the West African population, which they easily master; they are exposed to constant discussion of their parents' homeland, thus enabling them to accumulate what Chamberlain and Leydesdorff (2004:235) call "vicarious memory" of a place they have never seen. Thanks to their fathers' wealth, they benefit from private religious instruction at home. The daughters become highly sought after as brides by other West Africans, virtually assuring them secure lifelong membership in the West African community.

The picture looks quite different for poorer migrants with less to offer their fellow West Africans. Their homes, cramped one- or two-room apartments, are literally on the margins of the community and receive few visitors. Their children seldom hear anyone else speak their parents' language and spend most of their time with their Congolese peers. They are consequently more comfortable speaking Lingala than any West African language. For these children, the ancestral homeland, its culture, and traditions are alien, and their parents' memories of home mean little to them. They are more likely to be belittled by other migrants as *tabushis* than seen as desirable marriage partners. Their existence is liminal and their future within the West African population uncertain. Though transnationalism is hardly the purview of only a wealthy segment of this population, as Portes (2003) has argued for Latin American migrants in the United States, social and economic assets clearly condition the types of transnationalism in which one engages, particularly concerning child-rearing practices.

The three parenting modes described in this chapter sometimes coexist within a single household: the final sixteen members of my interview sample were parents who adopted a mixture of child-rearing modes. Upon meeting one of Kadi's younger brothers in Brazzaville, I learned that he was one of five siblings who had never been sent to West Africa as a child (he went on his own for the first time at age twenty-three, an experience he described as "returning to the source"). Apparently Kadi's father employed all three parenting modes at various times, drifting away from the maximal mode as he grew older. Like Makan, he was also a *jatigi* and probably decided as he became more established that he no longer needed to foster his children to West Africa to ensure a proper upbringing. He and Makan were among a select number of household heads who could afford to raise their children entirely in Brazzaville without appearing to endanger their cultural identity. For the majority of migrant parents who lacked such social standing, the only way to raise children as "good West Africans" was to send them to West Africa, whether for regular visits or an indefinite stay.

It is noteworthy that even maximal-mode parenting cannot guarantee "success" in every context. In Ghana, for example, Dougnon (2007) finds that Dogon mothers from Mali have all but stopped sending their children home to grow up in their villages. "The women believe, more and more," he writes, "that sending a child to the village with the hope of giving him a good upbringing is an illusion" (219). Many children sent home are able to leave their villages on their own and return to Ghana, which is a relatively short journey from Dogon country involving only two border crossings. Once back in Ghana, these children are believed to become even more unruly than those who never left. Thus geographic distance is influential regarding transnational parenting approaches.

Conclusion: Explaining Cultural Distinction

Brazzaville's West African population offers important insights into the study of migration and transnationalism. Examining the "full house" of domestic variation among migrants helps us understand not only the diverse approaches to household organization and child rearing but also the complex relationships between these different approaches by members of a transnational population. A crucial complementary relationship exists between short-term sojourners—usually single migrants with few assets, such as the aventuriers described above—and settled heads of households with strong ties to the host community. The settled individuals provide the sojourners with material support, knowledge, and advice; newcomers and sojourners enable those who are settled to renew their links with their homeland and help provide their children with indirect exposure to their home country. This complementary relationship also exists between migrant parents who adopt different child-rearing modes. Recall the case of Maryam: unable to send her son to Mali, she and her husband arranged for him to spend school breaks with his uncle and cousins who visited Mali regularly. For these "minimal-mode" parents, a kin relationship with an "intermediate-mode family" offered their son the possibility of indirectly acquiring some of the cultural and social capital he could not obtain in Brazzaville.

Studies of transnational social fields and the people who occupy them must be sensitive to the variety of transnational family organization that exists. There is no uniform or unidirectional development whereby members of a transnational population move through the same steps of an evolutionary process, progressing from sojourners to settlers or from cultural cosmopolitans to assimilated immigrants; nor do transnational lives somehow eclipse processes of cultural assimilation in immigrant communities. Instead, given the "full house" of available transnational practices, we must pay attention to the dynamics connecting these different modes of living in a transnational social field.

With respect to the durability of transnational linkages, the case of Brazzaville's West Africans suggests that they *can* be passed on from one generation to the next—but only through a great deal of effort and sacrifice by parents and children alike. To reiterate a point from the introduction to this book, place still matters a great deal in processes of identity construction, even for inhabitants of a transnational social field. Transnational child rearing requires extremely flexible domestic arrangements, and it remains to be seen how technologies facilitating communication between parents and far-flung children will affect the practice of maximal-mode child rearing in the long term. But the example of Makan's children and grandchildren shows how, given the right circumstances (notably high social and economic status), second- and third-generation immigrants can also be socialized to consider themselves as belonging primarily to their ancestors' country and culture of origin, despite occasional jibes and doubts from people born and raised there. With the right combination of economic resources and social networks, it is possible to raise "good Malians" outside Mali, or "good Senegalese" outside Senegal. Such instances of broad transnationalism may always remain exceptions to the rule among migrants and their descendents, but they show how transnational communities can endure over the long term despite loose attachments to their geographical point of reference.

Strangerhood cannot merely be transmitted from one generation to the next; it must be actively reproduced. Transnational child-rearing practices are a vital means by which Brazzaville's West Africans maintain their cultural distinctiveness and separate identity. In short, transnational fostering allows West Africans to perpetuate their strangerhood. West African children born in Brazzaville who are *not* fostered out, however, often occupy a far more ambiguous position in the host society, one that carries the full burden of strangerhood while also distancing these children from their West African–born peers. It is to their case that I now turn.

CHILDREN OF EXILE

Although some of the circumstances surrounding the incident are uncertain, this much is clear: on a Sunday afternoon in mid-December 2005 Papa Doucouré was shot. He was driving a friend's car in a northern district of Brazzaville and allegedly failed to stop at an intersection when a policeman signaled him to do so. A pickup truck full of heavily armed paramilitary police sped after him and made him pull over a few hundred meters down the road. After he had stopped, sitting behind the wheel of the motionless car, he was hit by three bullets from a policeman's Kalashnikov rifle—once in the arm, once in the leg, and once in the stomach. The police put him into the bed of their truck and brought him to the Centre Hospitalier Universitaire, the city's largest public hospital. That is where Papa Doucouré, lying on a hospital gurney, was pronounced dead a short time later. He was one day short of his nineteenth birthday.

This young man's killing symbolized different things to different people in Brazzaville. To most ordinary Congolese, if they knew of the incident at all, it was yet another tragic display of heavy-handed police tactics, further proof of their government's failure to respect basic human rights, and evidence that the *forces de l'ordre* (the security forces) were in fact the greatest local threat to public safety. "Recurring incidents of blunders and holdups [*braquages*] by elements of the security forces are becoming more and more troubling," one online magazine commented a few weeks later, "yet it is they who ought to be assuring the safety of people and their property" (*Afriqu'Echos* 2005).

To members of the city's immigrant West African community, who called Doucouré one of their own, however, his killing was only the latest and most tangible sign of the hostility and discrimination they faced from Congolese people in general, and from agents of the Congolese state in particular. Many West Africans in Brazzaville were convinced that Doucouré had been targeted because he was a foreigner. The police, they believed, had identified him from his dress or facial features as a *wara* and made him pay the ultimate stranger penalty.

The Doucouré killing galvanized Brazzaville's immigrant West African population as no previous episode of discrimination, police harassment, or abuse had done. The next day West African–owned shops and businesses throughout the city closed in protest. This commercial strike came just as the holiday shopping season was getting under way, and so it was more than a symbolic gesture. Other immigrant entrepreneurs, such as Lebanese and Chadians, closed down in solidarity with their West African colleagues. Even the regular street hawkers, many of whom were not West African, were nowhere in sight. The day after Doucouré's death, as I walked down one of Poto-Poto's main avenues, I saw not one establishment open for business. My year of fieldwork in Brazzaville was nearing its end, and for most of the previous eleven months I had listened to my informants complain about their poor treatment without seeing them offer any resistance. That December morning, passing row upon row of shuttered shops, I could plainly see that Brazzaville's West Africans were a true community capable of standing up for its own interests.

Only two days earlier armed robbers had shot a trader from Guinea, Abdoulaye Barry, in the thigh after forcing their way into his Moungali home. According to a friend who accompanied him to the hospital, medical staff watched Barry bleed to death while waiting for his West African companions to provide surgical gloves, gauze, bandages, and other items, which, they said, the hospital had run out of.[1] As news of the Doucouré killing rapidly spread by word of mouth, the shock and indignation generated by reports of Barry's death turned to outrage. Brazzaville's West Africans tolerated incessant marketplace sweeps by various government officials demanding papers, permits, and bribes from shopkeepers. Under the unspoken tenets of the stranger's code, they ignored verbal abuse and even arbitrary arrests. They would not, however, stand for the unprovoked use of lethal force against one of their own.

The following afternoon hundreds of West African men went to the Poto-Poto home of Doucouré's family to pay their condolences. Rumors circulated that Mali's President Touré phoned Congo's President Sassou to discuss the matter, and the Congolese government had clearly taken notice of the situation. Among the visitors at the Doucouré home that afternoon were two Congolese officials, the local district mayor and the police commissioner, who promised the assembled mourners that they would get to the bottom of the affair. When Muslim funeral rites were conducted for Doucouré on December 13 at Poto-Poto's reformist "Sunni mosque," the building—which holds nearly two thousand people—was filled to capacity, with hundreds more worshipers outside in the street. Even Vieux Diallo, who disagreed vehemently with the reformists over just about everything, who had accused them of leading a conspiracy to destroy Islam, and who had sworn to me more than once that he would never set foot in their mosque, was one of the many praying inside it that afternoon.

The strike went on for three days. By the fourth day a policeman implicated in the shooting was put in prison, and West Africans felt that they had gotten their message across. Resentment lingered and emotions remained raw, but shops reopened and Christmas shopping resumed.

Although we had some friends in common, I never met Papa Doucouré, and it is not for personal reasons that I open this chapter with his tragic death. I use it not to illustrate the general climate of fear in which Brazzaville's West Africans lived nor to show the anger Doucouré's death sparked within the West African community, nor even to reveal the public discourse it elicited among Congolese and immigrants about the urban society they uneasily shared. These elements are important insofar as they reveal the social and political background against which this drama took place. My aim, however, in describing this killing is to stress precisely what was *not* said or written about it: at no point did the fact that Papa Doucouré was a Congolese citizen, born in Brazzaville, enter into discussions about his death and what that signified for the city's inhabitants. In conversations and press reports, he was invariably described as a Malian or a West African, never as Congolese.[2] Although Doucouré also held a Malian passport and had spent several years living in Mali, it is telling that his Congolese nationality was considered irrelevant in the affair and its aftermath.

Why did it apparently not matter to observers, Congolese and immigrant alike, that the victim had possessed Congolese citizenship? What does the silence around this fact suggest about the lives of "second-generation" immigrants in Brazzaville? And what do such questions signal about contemporary notions of nationhood and belonging in Congo? I explore these questions in this chapter to uncover some of the problematic aspects of belonging, rights, and citizenship for Congolese-born members of Brazzaville's West African population.

Tabushis: Betwixt and Between

As discussed in the previous chapter, *tabushi* is a label frequently attached to children born abroad to West African migrants. The origins of this word, variations of which exist in a number of languages including Bamanan, Dyula, Soninke, and Songhai, are uncertain, and its exact meaning is subject to revealing disagreement. One Soninke dictionary defines it as children of mixed ethnicity, and a Bamanan lexicon defines it as "Mande people abroad" or "children of Mande immigrants."[3] The definition of *tabushi* that I use here comes from West African informants, of many different ethnicities, who use it to designate West African children born and especially raised abroad. The term is most closely associated with children born to Malian parents in Côte d'Ivoire, which for several generations has attracted more immigrants from the western Sahel, especially Malians, than any other country.

The question of *tabushi* status is sensitive, because the word has mostly pejorative connotations. In fact, though I often heard first-generation migrants in Brazzaville use it, I almost never heard anyone apply it to him- or herself. To be a *tabushi* is to carry a certain stigma. In this respect the above definition connoting mixed ethnicity may be illuminating: many of my informants "born and bred" in Mali or Guinea considered *tabushis* to be akin to half-breeds, but their alleged impurity had nothing to do with their parentage; instead, it was their *cultural* identity, and the quality of their upbringing, that was suspect. First-generation migrants widely denigrate *tabushis* as poor Muslims, inherently disrespectful of authority, and prone to illicit behaviors such as alcohol consumption or fornication.[4] Lack of respect, particularly toward parents and elders, is viewed as perhaps the quintessential *tabushi* trait, as suggested by the following excerpt from my field notes.

> *While I'm at Diallo's shop the old man hails a passing woman and tells her about some behavior by one of her daughters the previous day that he found unacceptable. Apparently the girl had gotten an item of clothing from a nearby Senegalese merchant on credit, and when he asked her later for payment she was disrespectful to him: he'd called her "my child," to which she replied, "Can you give birth to me?" Diallo overheard this, and now he's sharing the news with her mom. He calls the Senegalese vendor over to recount the whole incident. The mother is very apologetic, while saying repeatedly that she can't control everything her daughter does—I get the impression she finds her daughter's wayward behavior just as objectionable*

as the elder males do, but feels herself powerless to do anything to rectify it. Diallo tells me the girl in question is 14 or 15, born and raised here.

The notion that West African parents cannot raise their children properly in Congo, and cannot instill the right behavior and values in them there, obviously fuels the practice of "maximal-mode" parenting discussed in the previous chapter. Sending children to be raised by relatives in West Africa at an early age, and allowing maximum exposure to their ancestral homeland, ensures their "proper" cultural, religious, and personal development and prevents them from becoming *tabushis* to begin with.

West Africans are not the only ones to use derisive labels for children raised outside their purported homeland. *Tabushi* could be seen as equivalent to *pocho*, a derisive Mexican word for an immigrant in the United States "who speaks both English and Spanish badly and who is disempowered in both societies" (R. Smith 1999:199). It is also analogous to ABCD, an abbreviation sometimes applied to the children of South Asian immigrants raised in the United States and conflicted about their identity; it stands for "American-born confused *desi*," where *desi* designates a member of the South Asian diaspora (see Shankar 2008:5). People in many societies with histories of emigration view such offspring as "confused" about their true nature.

Making matters worse, *tabushis* may be equally shunned by members of the host society. As one of my informants, the thirty-four-year-old Brazzaville-born daughter of a Malian immigrant, described it, *tabushis* like her are in a double bind:

> *It's very difficult because one never integrates. One is always a West African to them [Congolese], even if one was born here. For our West African relatives who come settle here, we're foreigners too, we're Congolese to them. So it's very difficult, we're not accepted by either side, we're caught in the middle. Especially the Congolese, they still consider us outsiders even though we were born here. The problem is that in our [ancestral] country, they see us as Congolese, while [in Congo] we're not even accepted. That's our problem.*

Tabushis' degree of incorporation into the host and immigrant communities varies a great deal from one individual to another. To illustrate this variability as well as some of the similarities in the lives of members of the second and subsequent generations, I present four case studies of *tabushis*, two women and two men, whom I met during the course of my fieldwork in Brazzaville. All are the products of "minimal-mode" upbringing (described in chapter 5), having spent their entire childhood in Congo. All four bear the full weight of *tabushi* status, but each in his or her own way.

Aisha

Aisha was born in Kinshasa and grew up in Brazzaville. Her parents, both Soninke of Malian origin, divorced when she was young, and she lived with her mother in her maternal grandfather's compound. Her grandfather, Makan, was a wealthy businessman and key figure in Brazzaville's West African community (see chapter 5). Aisha attended Brazzaville public schools and graduated from secondary school in 2004, at which time she married the son of another wealthy Malian immigrant. Their first child was born the following year. Although she was living with her husband in an apartment on Poto-Poto's Avenue de la Paix, she continued to spend time in her grandfather's large, busy residential compound a few blocks away, which was where my wife often visited her and where her interview took place. She was then in her early twenties.

Aisha had never been to Mali but considered it her home nonetheless. From her parents and grandparents, as well as from first-generation immigrants, she had absorbed information about Malian society and, in particular, about her ancestral hometown in the western Kayes region. She regularly talked with relatives in Mali by phone. Although she spoke Lingala with her mother and siblings at home and preferred to conduct her interview in French, she also mastered her parents' Soninke language and spoke good Bamanan. Insisting that she did not in any way feel split between Congolese and Malian cultures, Aisha instead described herself as "100 percent Malian." She represented her family's presence in Congo as temporary: "I wish that we should all return *au pays*, all of us, one day. It's good for us, it's advantageous. No, it's our country. Here we're foreigners. . . . Sooner or later, we'll always return [*on va toujours rentrer*]." She recalled being harassed in the schoolyard as a young girl by children, who would say, "You West Africans, this isn't your home," but she claimed she never let these incidents bother her.

Aisha enjoyed listening to both Congolese and West African popular music, and wore a blend of West African and European-style clothing while taking care not to transgress her family's Islamic-inspired dress code. Trousers and tight clothing were off-limits, but she often chose full-length skirts and long-sleeve blouses made of imported fabric and cut in European styles, along with dark-colored headscarves tied tightly over her hair. Aisha also dreamed of going to a university—she passed her *baccalauréat* exam shortly before getting married—and pursuing a law degree, a rare accomplishment for women (especially Soninke women) in Mali. At the time of our interview, however, she was occupied with her young son and her husband. She lived with them in the heart of the Poto-Poto district, and like most West African women in Brazzaville, she did not work outside the home.

Oumar

Oumar was born in Brazzaville. His late father, a jeweler, came to Congo from Mali in the 1960s along with his wife and brother, with whom he established a successful business. Oumar lived in Brazzaville until the 1997 civil war forced him and his family to flee the city; his parents then sent him off to complete his secondary schooling in Bamako. From there he earned admission to a university in the United States, where he received a degree in finance in 2004. When I first met Oumar in a Poto-Poto restaurant, he was home on summer vacation from his American MBA program. He was twenty-five years old.

Oumar felt very much at home in Congo, Mali, and the United States, but his greatest affection was for Brazzaville, the city where he grew up. To him Brazzaville was home. He generally traveled with his Congolese passport, using his Malian passport only for travel to Mali. Most of the time, he told me, he moved around Brazzaville without papers. When I asked about the legal requirement that everyone carry identity documents—something most foreigners in Congo, myself included, took very seriously—he replied, confidently, "It's my country," implying that he didn't need to prove his identity to anyone.

More than papers, Oumar relied on cultural competence whenever the need arose to assert his claim to belong in Congo. He spoke Lingala, French, and Bamanan fluently and with careful attention to the nuances of local linguistic convention. When speaking French with Congolese, he represented himself as "one of them" by consciously adopting Congolese verbal mannerisms distinguishing him from Malian immigrants (who tend to speak French, if at all, with an accent that Congolese perceive as "rustic"). When speaking French with Malians, he toned down these Congolese mannerisms (particularly pronunciations that Malians perceive as pretentious). Nothing about Oumar's appearance marked him as either Malian or Congolese. With his stylish eyeglasses and clean-cut Western clothes, he had a cosmopolitan air and would not have looked out of place in New York or Paris. Oumar described himself as Muslim, but he did not observe ritual practices such as praying regularly. "We don't have to pray to be Muslim," he told me; for him, Islam was more about belief than practice. It was part of his identity, and he did not feel compelled to dress or act a certain way to express belonging in the Muslim community.

For all his personal and sentimental attachments to Brazzaville, Oumar did not foresee settling there in the future. He hoped to get a job with an international corporation or organization and perhaps work in Mali one day. As for his personal life, he was delaying marriage until his studies were complete. The rule in his family, he said, was that he and his siblings could only marry Malians, either those born and raised in Mali or *tabushis* born in Brazzaville whose parents are both Malians.

Mata

Mata was born in Brazzaville. Her father, a Halpulaar from the Senegalese region of Matam, came to Congo in the early 1950s and took three Congolese wives, each of whom converted to Islam. Mata made her only visit to Senegal at the age of five, spending just a few months there. Otherwise, she and her siblings were raised entirely in Brazzaville. She never became acquainted with any relatives living in Senegal. Her father died when she was twelve; after that, Mata's upbringing was the responsibility of her Congolese mother and her co-wives, under the supervision of paternal uncles who arranged marriages for their late brother's children. She and her siblings all became practicing Muslims, but none of them learned to speak Pulaar or any other West African languages very well. Mata's arranged marriage with a West African Muslim did not last very long. When I interviewed her, Mata was living on a quiet residential street in the neighborhood of Ouenzé, far from Poto-Poto where most West Africans reside. She was in her mid-forties.

After finishing secondary school in Brazzaville, Mata earned a government scholarship to attend a university in the Soviet Union, where she spent four years. Upon returning to Congo in 1984, she took a position in the government tax office, where she continued to work at the time of our interview two decades later. In the course of her duties, she often dealt with West African businessmen who sought her out because of her West African name. She felt a special obligation to help these individuals. Mata liked her job but felt that her foreign ancestry had slowed her professional advancement.

> When you're a foreigner [*sic*] working in an administration, there's always a difference, you see? You're there, you need . . . to enter into an administration, you really need a support. You can have your diploma, but you

need contacts too, especially if you have a West African name. You might deserve a management position, but the first thing they'll see is that you're a foreigner. Even if you have Congolese nationality, the name that you have ... Someone who has a Congolese name will have a better chance than you.

Mata thought it was still possible for people in her situation to rise through the ranks, as long as they displayed hard work and skill, but they remained at a disadvantage compared to other employees who could call on local ethnic and kin-based networks to muster support within the bureaucracy.

As an educated woman, Mata wanted to assert a modern identity with respect to her appearance, but, like Aisha, she alternated between West African and European-style apparel. Her regular wardrobe included trousers, which most other West African women in Brazzaville do not wear. "Me personally, I've traveled, sometimes I dress like my colleagues, and sometimes I dress like *chez nous* [our home], like a Muslim. I wear a mix," she said. She recalled being hassled by schoolmates as a girl when she wore West African–style *boubous* to school or when she ate rice for lunch (since cassava, not rice, is the staple of the Congolese diet).

Moussa

Born in the 1930s in a small town southwest of Brazzaville to a Malian father and Congolese mother, Moussa lived his entire life in Congo. His father, a Soninke from Mali, came to Congo working for the French colonial telegraph service. Moussa was divorced after being married to a woman of native Congolese origin. I interviewed him in his home, a modest but well-appointed structure in a spacious compound overgrown with weeds, not far from Poto-Poto's *grande mosquée*. He was about seventy years old.

Moussa grew up attending both public school and Qur'anic school. By the time of our interview he had retired from a long career working for the Congolese public health service and had served as a high-level administrator in locations around the country. In addition to French, Moussa spoke Lingala, Lari (his mother's language), and Kituba but no West African language. Moussa described himself as Congolese, adding that he had *"un double appartenance,"* a double belonging. His mother's Lari people trace descent and inheritance through the maternal line, and his father's Soninke people trace them through the paternal line, but for Moussa these two systems meshed smoothly. His maternal relatives were non-Muslims but respected the Islamic traditions that Moussa and his siblings observed. Moussa dismissed the allegation, so widely articulated by West Africans in Brazzaville, that integration into Congolese society is problematic for immigrants and their descendants. "Today I'm the head of the family and chief of my mother's village," he said. "If all these problems existed, you wouldn't see me there."

Moussa experienced various forms of discrimination in his daily life, mostly from Congolese police and officials, but he attributed these incidents to the poor character of the individuals involved. "Each time I'm wearing a *boubou* I have all kinds of problems," he told me. "But that's only because the policemen there are of bad faith. In Maya-Maya [Brazzaville's airport], if I'm wearing a *boubou*, before I can show my ID card they tell me 'stand over there,' with the foreigners. To avoid problems I go stand with the foreigners." Even in his own neighborhood, he had noticed that policemen treated him differently according to his apparel: "Every evening they're there, from 10:00 or 11:00. As soon as you go out in a *boubou* it's over, they stop you. When I feel like having some fun, I go out in a *boubou*, and that's when they stop me; then I come back and change into trousers and go back out, and they don't stop me." Unlike first-generation West Africans in Brazzaville, Moussa categorically refused to pay any form of "stranger penalty" and recounted one particular case when he had returned by boat (the so-called *vedette*) from Kinshasa to the Brazzaville river port:

> I was with other Congolese, friends and relatives. I was the only one wearing a boubou. In the boat there was a military man, a colonel and younger relative of mine, who was there. And nobody asked anything from anybody except for me, they wanted me to pay a tax I'd already paid—when you come in the vedette there's a whole bunch of taxes to pay. You pay on the way over. But the officer followed me, "There's a tax to pay." He persisted. My best friend was next to me, and the colonel ahead of us. "Papa, there's a tax to pay." I said, "Look, the guy leaving over there is a colonel—he's exonerated from the tax. And him, he's my cousin, he's exonerated too. You didn't ask them, so why are you asking me? I'm not paying the tax. If they pay I'll pay too."

Moussa had one brother who went to live in Mali prior to independence in 1960, and Moussa visited him there three times as an adult. Otherwise, he had no real tie to his father's homeland. His main connection to Brazzaville's West African community was through the *grande mosquée* near his house, where he attended prayers regularly and served on administrative committees.

Accounting for Inclusion and Exclusion

The above case studies show how widely experiences can differ for *tabushis* growing up in Congo. Aisha, born into a well-off and high-status family, appeared secure in her identity as a Malian, and despite her obvious attachments to Brazzaville (such as speaking Lingala as her first language), she looked forward to the day when she would finally "return" to what she considered her true home in West Africa. She married very well within Brazzaville's Malian community, and her membership in that community was beyond question. Oumar also enjoyed the benefits of a relatively wealthy immigrant family in Brazzaville, but he made a clear distinction between *tabushis* like himself and Malians born in Mali; he chose a more cosmopolitan stance toward belonging, only loosely linked to territory. In this respect, Oumar could be considered a "cosmopolitan patriot," in that he was "attached to a home of [his] own, with its own cultural particularities, but [took] pleasure from the presence of other, different places that are home to other, different people" (Appiah 1997:618).[5]

Mata, by contrast, sought to build a life in Congo after studying abroad, and managed to obtain a coveted civil service post. Yet she also felt that her West African ancestry put her at a disadvantage in the politics of promotion and professional development. Compared to Aisha, Mata had little or no "vicarious memory" of her ancestral homeland but nonetheless found meaning in her identity as a Muslim. And Moussa, of these four individuals, had staked out a place for himself closest to the mainstream Congolese society, anchored by a distinguished civil service career. Integrated into Congolese life through kin, personal, and professional ties, he represented himself as Congolese and vigorously defended his claim to belong in Congo against any skeptics.

Taken together, these examples defy easy identification of a universal pattern of inclusion or exclusion. Several important differentiating factors shape these individuals' experiences. The most obvious is gender: Oumar and Moussa had rather more latitude than Aisha or Mata in cultivating hybrid identities. Oumar especially could pursue opportunities within a globalized economy, pursuing an advanced degree in the United States and contemplating an international career path; cosmopolitanism was a viable choice for him. As a male, he also had greater latitude to define his religious identity in a manner he saw fit, stressing belief and downplaying practice. Women like Aisha and Mata were more tightly bound to norms of proper Islamic comportment and faced more serious social sanctions if they departed from these norms. Although both women were well educated, their horizons were more limited than those of the men, as they were expected to become wives and eventually mothers, a status that would determine their primary responsibilities.

One's generation can also have tremendous impact on one's prospects for integration. Moussa came of age before Congo's independence in 1960 and began his career as a French colonial subject. Mata grew up in the two decades following independence, a period of nation building throughout Africa when public discourse in newly decolonized countries stressed national unity and when distinctions of ethnicity, although salient in many areas of everyday life, were officially downplayed (see Geschiere 2009). Aisha and Oumar, both born after 1980, grew up in a different world. Members of their generation, with Congo's violent ethno-regional politics of the 1990s forever seared into their memories, view national unity as a failed or failing project, and national identity as a highly unstable platform on which to engage in self-fashioning.

Another influential factor is the nature and extent of one's social and kin networks. Both Aisha and Oumar were born into large, prosperous Malian immigrant families, affording them plentiful opportunities to meet other Malians in Brazzaville and absorb their cultural knowledge, especially their language. Mata and Moussa, in contrast, were born into mixed families with fewer ties to the immigrant community. Mata's father was part of a Senegalese population of a few hundred people (compared to several thousand Malians), and his early death further isolated the surviving members of Mata's household from this population. Mata and her siblings had little chance to develop strong ties to other West Africans and, for this reason, were never able to master any West African language. The marginal status of individuals such as Mata among West Africans is reflected by the fact that Oumar's parents forbade him and his siblings from marrying *tabushis* of mixed parentage (born to a Malian father and Congolese mother, for example).

Such variations notwithstanding, the experiences of these *tabushis* also reveal strong parallels. From an early age, *tabushis* who engaged in practices constructed as alien to Congolese society encountered discrimination and hostility. Eating rice instead of cassava, wearing a *boubou* instead of a European-style shirt and trousers, or speaking French with the "wrong" accent could mark even a lifelong resident as an outsider. (Recall that in chapter 3 the native Congolese head of the Islamic Council of Congo reported being mistaken for a West African when he wore Muslim-style attire.) Standing out as Muslims or West Africans earned them unwanted attention. They could respond by demonstrating local cultural knowledge and attire: Oumar, for example, relied on Western clothing and linguistic nuance more than official documents in his bid to claim membership, and Moussa could claim kinship connections to escape an official's attempt to collect a "stranger penalty" ("And him, he's my cousin, he's exonerated too"). Yet such deployments of cultural knowledge were mainly effective as a response to short-term social situations—passing encounters with government officials, for example. They were less helpful in making a claim to membership over the long term. As long as one's name and ancestry are perceived as alien, one faces real limits to one's ability to blend in.

The enduring power of a family name to confer stranger status upon natives in this context became clear to me during an interview with Ladji Seck, a teacher in his mid-forties, born in Congo to a Senegalese father and Congolese mother. He considered himself Congolese, was married to a Congolese woman, had never lived in West Africa, and spoke no West African languages. He was nonetheless distressed over the abuse his children received because of their obvious foreign name.

> *At the time when I had children, if I had known, I would have added their mother's name to theirs [i.e., their Senegalese patronym], so that people will know that this is the child of a Congolese woman and an immigrant [sic].... I have a daughter named Khadija. Well, she has problems! They're always calling her "wara girl, wara girl, wara, wara, wara" at school.... That taught me a lesson. If I had also given her the name of her mother, Yoka Khadija Seck, that would have worked. She would have had fewer problems. And I thought, "Maybe I should have done that." Maybe one day people in this country will understand that immigration is a completely normal thing—because in Congo people haven't yet understood that. No, for changing the names, I should have done it, because it doesn't benefit the children like this.*

Individuals such as Moussa, Mata, and Ladji had "become Congolese" and were only marginally members of Brazzaville's West African community. None had learned to speak Bamanan, Soninke, or any other language of the immigrant population. For them, mainly because of this linguistic issue, becoming full-fledged members of their parents' community was problematic. Yet they also faced diminished prospects in Congolese society. To gain access to schools, jobs, promotions, or other kinds of opportunity, it helps to have highly placed sponsors or patrons to advocate on one's behalf. As Mata put it,

> Today when there's one patois [i.e., an ethnolinguistic group] in power, his brothers will succeed. If you're lucky it's still possible, even if you don't have connections, to be integrated.... But getting ahead is a little difficult, you need support, an "umbrella" to help you out.

By "umbrella" she meant a "protector." Congolese parlance has many similar terms for highly placed individuals who can lend support and patronage within an institutional framework, including *parrain* (godfather) and *poteau* (post or pole). A relationship with a patron typically derives from kinship ties, common ethnicity, and shared region of origin. Under patronage systems like those dominating social, educational, and professional life in Congo, patrons are under pressure to deliver favors (in the form of entrance to a university, contracts, promotions, etc.) to kin and to those from the same community or region of the country. People like Mata who bear foreign names have little ground on which to claim those patrons' support; by the logic of the patronage system, any Congolese would take priority in the competition for favors.

Within Brazzaville's West African population, individual lives have tremendous power to set normative examples. Young second- or third-generation West Africans growing up in the city today have few role models of successful integration into Congolese society. Although one could point to cases of children of West African immigrants rising to prominent positions in the Congolese government—such as Moussa's tenure as a regional director of health services or another son born to a Malian father and Congolese mother who became an ambassador—many West Africans construed these cases as the exceptions that proved the rule. They wondered why these individuals, whom they considered well qualified, never received cabinet appointments. They felt that such persons were at a permanent disadvantage compared to "true Congolese," believing that the "stranger's code" prevents anyone of West African descent from reaching their full potential in Congolese society. They reinterpreted even moderately successful cases as cautionary tales.

Perhaps the best-known cautionary tale is that of Ange Diawara, who enjoyed a short but high-profile career in Congolese politics in the late 1960s and early 1970s. Diawara was originally named Farimakan after his Malian paternal grandfather, but he chose to adopt the French name Ange instead, perhaps because his Congolese mother was Christian. As a young man he studied economics in France, where he became attracted to philosophy and left-wing ideals; following Congo's 1963 revolutionary turn he was chosen to head the new ruling party's youth militia. Diawara was a charismatic figure who soon developed a stature worthy of his hero, Che Guevara. He was reported to be gifted in karate, and his reputation for intellect and integrity helped garner him a wide following. He helped found the Parti Congolais du Travail (which has ruled Congo for all but five years since 1969) and anchored its left wing, holding at least two cabinet portfolios and associating with Pan-Africanist radicals including a visiting delegation of the Black Panther Party in 1971. But his ideals led him into conflict with President Marien Ngouabi, whom he saw as bourgeois and corrupt, and with other powerful figures such as future president Denis Sassou-Nguesso, whom he allegedly slapped in public for having seduced the wife of Diawara's uncle.[6] On February 22, 1972, Diawara launched a coup attempt and succeeded in taking over state radio, but failed to rally popular support and eventually fled with his companions into the bush where he led a guerilla insurgency against the government. The following year he was caught and executed, and his corpse was displayed in a Brazzaville sports stadium.

There is no obvious connection between Ange Diawara's West African ancestry and his political career and violent demise. The foreign origins of his paternal grandfather and family name seemed to figure little in the story of his life. For West Africans in Congo, however, the most significant aspect of his example is that, despite his immense talent and intelligence, his Christianized name, his cultural integration, and his extensive kin connections to Congolese society, he nonetheless failed in his bid for power and died a horrific death. No Congolese of West African descent has subsequently had such a high profile in Congolese politics. For *tabushis,* successful role models are those who adhere to the stranger's code, keeping out of politics and seeking inconspicuous fortunes in the private sector.

Thus *tabushis* in Congo today face limited options as they seek to construct their identities and fashion their lives. Though for a time they could aspire to a place in Congolese society, their foreign names hamper their efforts to fit in and climb the social ladder. They are, as one of my immigrant informants put it, "lost twice over." Many West Africans in Brazzaville saw *tabushis* like Mata or Moussa as lost sheep, without the cultural capital necessary to belong to the immigrant community but unable to claim full membership in the host society. Young Congolese of West African descent increasingly envision their lives beyond Congo's borders. Aisha saw no future for herself in the country, and used her strong kinship ties and cultural competence (especially her language skills) to claim full membership in the city's immigrant population. Oumar charted an alternative course to transcend the problem of belonging but still faced expectations of group endogamy; moreover, despite his sentimental attachments to his hometown, like Aisha he could not imagine himself living there definitively.

Purity and Hybridity

A Togotalan informant once told me a story about a fellow immigrant he knew in Brazzaville who took a liking to *kwanga*, glutinous sticks of pounded cassava flour that are a mainstay of the Congolese diet. Sahelians do not generally eat *kwanga*, which is not available in their homeland, but my informant told me that his friend persisted in enjoying it whenever he could. Eventually, however, he began experiencing severe abdominal pains and consulted a doctor. When asked about his diet, the West African replied that he had been eating *kwanga*. Well, that's the problem, the doctor told him: You can only digest *kwanga* properly if you drink beer, too. Since, as a Muslim, he did not want to start drinking beer, the patient gave up *kwanga* and never suffered the pains again.

I do not know if this story is true or if eating *kwanga* without drinking beer really does cause digestive problems. (For my part, I have eaten *kwanga* without beer and have experienced no ill effects.) However apocryphal its origins, the story's lessons are clear enough: Congolese food is for Congolese, and West Africans should "stick to their own kind."

Inevitably, in the course of generations of migration from West Africa to Congo and back, cultural influences have traveled between these two societies. In the western Sahel, for example, Congolese *soukouss* music and the spicy green-leaf *saka-saka* sauce have been popular for years. And, in Brazzaville, Congolese occasionally wear the loose West African–style *boubou* (which they sometimes call a *complet wara*), and the practice of surrounding one's home with a compound wall—initially an alien feature limited to West African households in the city—has spread in recent decades to Congolese as well. With the exception of a few cultural crossovers such as these, however, the relative absence of hybridization between Congolese and West Africans, especially given the duration and intensity of contact between these populations over the last century, has been striking.

The boundary separating Congolese and West African cultures remains unmistakably bright: it is so apparent that people have no doubt about which side a particular cultural practice falls on.[7] It is not sufficiently blurred for individuals to project a culturally ambiguous or hybrid identity. People must choose which side of the boundary to be on, for there is no grey area in between, and the notion of a "hyphenated identity" has yet to make significant inroads in popular discourse, either in Congo or West Africa. One therefore represents oneself as either Congolese or West African—and, if the latter, one had better steer clear of *kwanga*. Roth (2002:140) dubs such strategic, systematic exaggeration of differences, accompanied by a parallel downplaying of commonalities and shared interests, "oppositional florescence."

West Africans born and raised in Congo, who straddle the cultural divide, must negotiate the artificially bright boundary that this oppositional florescence creates. They have to identify as either Congolese or West African, not as "a little of both." I asked two young Brazzaville-born West Africans who had lived abroad about their own responses to this problem. In addition to Oumar, whose case is outlined above, I spoke to a young man named Ousmane, who had visited Mali only briefly when he was very young but otherwise lived entirely in Brazzaville before attending a university in France. What do you say, I asked each of them, when people abroad want to know where you are from? For Oumar the answer depended on the company he kept: in the United States, if he was with Malians he would say he was from Mali, and would sometimes add that he grew up in Congo; otherwise, he would say he was from Congo. Ousmane, for his part, said that in France he represented himself as Congolese, sometimes specifying "*d'origine malienne*" (of Malian origin). He also told me that his own understanding of the category he belonged to changed continually according to his circumstances. Each man could occasionally feel out of place in Mali and in Congo, as well as in France or the United States.

These stories illustrate the degree to which cultural and national identity, far from being inherited qualities, are in fact highly performative and situational, fluctuating from one moment and setting to the next. They also indicate a degree of cultural bifocality, a dual frame of reference accommodating sometimes conflicting identities.[8] The difficulty for these *tabushis*, as the *kwanga* story above suggests, is that they are seldom permitted to express that bifocality. Even in the United States, Oumar was careful not to highlight his Congolese affiliation when Malians were present, perhaps fearing their disapproval. He was reluctant to project a dual or ambiguous cultural identity.

Nonetheless *tabushis* do sometimes find ways to blur the otherwise bright line (see Alba 2005) between Congolese and West African cultures. During the time my wife and I spent visiting Makan, the elderly *jatigi*, we noticed that his granddaughter Aisha and her sisters had developed their own distinct form of dress. When going out with friends, they wore full-length skirts and long-sleeve blouses made of imported fabric and cut in European styles, along with dark-colored headscarves tied tightly over their hair but not over their ears and necks. This apparel had the advantage of fulfilling prevailing Islamic standards of female modesty in the West African community (their arms, legs, and hair were covered), while at the same time not making them appear obviously foreign. But they also tended not to wear clothing favored by the city's West African women, such as wax-print or damask cloth, or loose-flowing robes and colorful head ties. So although they did not exactly dress like young Congolese women (whose heads are usually uncovered), neither did they stand out on the streets of Poto-Poto as West African, or even especially Islamic. They had created a style unique to themselves. Makan's granddaughters favored being inconspicuous over standing out—if their attire adhered to Islamic tenets, it did not exactly designate the wearers as "Muslim and proud." In keeping with the stranger's code, they still had to maintain a low public profile.

There appears, then, to be some limited room for hybridity, at least concerning these second- and third-generation immigrants. My point is that this hybridity is the exception rather than the rule; it is resisted and discouraged by Congolese and West Africans alike, as it threatens to blur the bright boundary between these groups. In this context, and for reasons I discuss in the concluding chapter, people mistrust blurred boundaries and the ambiguity they create.

Hollow State, Hollow Citizens

Under the law, anyone born on Congolese soil qualifies automatically for Congolese citizenship. Yet this does not entitle them to citizenship in the fullest sense; contemporary constructions of de facto citizenship in Congo tend to exclude not only immigrants but even their Brazzaville-born descendants from membership in the host society. As we have seen, though they may enjoy de jure citizenship in Congo, the children and grandchildren of immigrants there, during encounters with agents of the Congolese state, are often treated like strangers.

A range of political and economic forces has contributed to an effective hollowing out of the Congolese state. These forces have struck the institutions of government bureaucracy and the people who constitute it especially hard. Even in the best of times, during years of peace and oil-boom prosperity, the Congolese state and the political process have never really been, to use Max

Weber's term, "emancipated" from narrow social interests, particularly those of the small clique of politicians and military officers who controlled it.[9] Economic hardship since the 1980s has only intensified this situation. Salaries in the civil service—the backbone of Brazzaville's formal labor force—have been frozen and sometimes gone unpaid for months. The 50 percent devaluation of the CFA franc in January 1994 slashed buying power by half, a crushing blow to a population so dependent on imported goods. Although many young Congolese still aspire to become civil servants, few Congolese government employees can survive on their official salaries today. This has encouraged numerous survival strategies among civil servants, including corrupt practices, from unwarranted payment for public services to commission for illicit services.[10] Moreover, the widespread destruction and looting that beset Brazzaville throughout the 1990s wiped out many government records and archives. These combined factors had a profoundly damaging effect on what is known in French bureaucratic language as *l'état civil,* the body of public administrative documents establishing individuals as citizens or legal residents.

By 2005 a common perception in Brazzaville was that anyone, even strangers, could obtain birth certificates, criminal background checks, residence permits, licenses, passports, and other official government documents for which they were ineligible. One simply had to pay a small commission to the appropriate bureaucrat. Indeed, I knew several West Africans in Brazzaville who had obtained official Congolese documents through dubious channels. One young auto-parts vendor had recruited a high-ranking civil servant (one of his regular customers) to vouch for him before a judge that he had lost his Congolese identity card during the war and needed a replacement; this was sufficient for him to acquire a valid, official Congolese ID. Others born in West Africa obtained birth certificates from city hall attesting to their birth in Congo. For instance, Vieux Diallo, though born in Mali, had papers claiming that he was born in Brazzaville. Technically such papers are not fakes, as they are issued in the same offices, by the same civil servants, and using the same procedures as "legitimate" papers. Their illegitimacy—for having been obtained under false pretense—is impossible for authorities to detect. Political manipulation has also contributed to the problem: in the run-up to the presidential elections in mid-2009, allegations arose that immigrants from Congo-Kinshasa were being granted national ID cards in Brazzaville in order to help stuff ballot boxes for the incumbent.[11]

The truth of such accounts is less important than the assumptions underlying them. Amid reports of widespread fraud, even genuine official documents confer little legitimacy, particularly when their bearer has a foreign name or foreign mannerisms. Congolese-born West Africans reported frequent problems with authorities who suspected that their papers were fraudulent. "My younger brother was born here," a fifty-year-old Malian man told me. "He had Congolese papers, but once when he was leaving from the airport here they confiscated them. They said his passport was fake. . . . Even today he hasn't gotten his passport back." Such stories contribute to a generalized atmosphere of uncertainty, in which immigrants and their children believe that no paper can fully validate their presence in Congo. Many, expecting continued exactions and harassment regardless of the documents in their possession, see no utility in "regularizing" their stay. One forty-two-year-old interviewee born in Côte d'Ivoire stated firmly that she would never seek documents from Congolese authorities "because if they give you papers, one day they'll come take them away from you. Some might give you false papers. You can't do anything with them." No one in Brazzaville can ever be sure that an identity document means what it appears to mean.

Any legal claims West Africans may have to live and work in Congo, either as legal immigrants or natural-born citizens, are undermined by the fundamental illegitimacy of the state bureaucracy and the papers it produces. "Even if you were born in Congo, you grew up here, you have Congolese citizenship, you need to try and get Malian citizenship," said Madou, the twenty-two-year-old, Brazzaville-born son of Malian parents (see chapter 5). "Otherwise, when you get older, Congolese don't consider you to be a person. Even if you went to school all the way, forget it, they won't hire you to work for them. . . . [They'll say] that you got a fake birth certificate, that you committed fraud to get the papers. That's how it goes."

Meaningful citizenship in Congo is effectively based on the informal criteria of kinship and ethnicity rather than on bureaucratically generated credentials. The perceived illegitimacy of the state and its documents has blurred, even erased, the distinction between legal and illegal immigrants, making it difficult for Brazzaville-born West Africans to assert their claims to belonging in the country. As Chabal (2009:99) writes, "the less secure and effective national institutions are, the weaker citizenship effectively becomes." Hence these individuals' place in Congo is always open to question, as they can never definitively establish their right to live there but must perpetually press their claims of belonging through daily encounters with state agents. The enforcement of laws pertaining to immigration and citizenship is conducted informally. In this context, notions of "ethnic nationalism" based on qualities such as language, religion, and perceived common descent displace notions of "civic nationalism" based on residency, common history, and allegiance to common ideals (cf. Gellner 1983). If West Africans in an "irregular situation" (i.e., lacking the necessary residence permits) are rarely deported from Congo, legal immigrants and even full citizens of foreign ancestry are by no means immune to everyday scrutiny and harassment. One Congolese politician has advocated changing the country's citizenship laws with the express purpose of barring West Africans born in Congo from obtaining Congolese nationality. "These are people who, in their mentality, in their soul, are not Congolese," he told a journalist (*La Semaine Africaine* 2010d).

Conclusion: An Exclusionary Trend

After his death in December 2005 Papa Doucouré was mourned as a foreigner by foreigners—not as a Congolese by Congolese. No Congolese civil society groups or human rights organizations protested his killing, and the incident received little coverage in the local media. If not for the marketplace shutdown orchestrated by West African merchants, Doucouré's murder would likely have gone unpunished and unnoticed by ordinary Congolese. The unprovoked shooting in Brazzaville of a resident of West African origin, even one who possessed Congolese citizenship, was not an affair concerning "true Congolese." Even though Doucouré was Congolese by official criteria, these were not the criteria that mattered in the end. It was immigrants alone who rallied to express their outrage, immigrants who demanded redress, and immigrants who buried him.

By all accounts Papa Doucouré was not a *tabushi*. He had spent enough of his childhood "back home" in Mali to avoid that status. Would his fate have been any different if he had been raised in Brazzaville? If he had been more knowledgeable of Congolese culture? If he had had Congolese kin? If he had been, in short, a true *tabushi*? Perhaps so, yet what became clear to me after interviewing many *tabushis*, particularly those in their twenties and thirties, was the extent to which they had internalized their own alien status. They referred to themselves, in casual conversation and without irony, as "immigrants" and "foreigners," not as "natives" and "citizens"; even those who had never visited their ancestors' West African country of origin still referred to it as *chez nous*, "our home." These descendants of immigrants had already absorbed the lesson I learned in the wake of Doucouré's death: in postcolonial Congo official citizenship and "civic nationality" count for little.

Ample research in African countries has shown how the politicization of ethnic identities can lead to the exclusion of strangers from local communities.[12] The lives of Doucouré and other second-generation Congolese West Africans suggest a similar exclusionary trend operating at the national level: having foreign ancestry or a foreign-sounding name is enough to cast even native-born Congolese as aliens. Never mind that West Africans have been present in Brazzaville since its establishment more than a century ago; the mere fact of having origins outside Congolese territory makes it difficult, if not impossible, for them to claim their own place in the city and the country.

If legal citizenship has become a hollow concept in Congo, this is not primarily the fault of a weak state or some ancient, intractable animosity to the Other. Nor does it stem from any inherent African tendency to resist processes of modernization and bureaucratic rationalization with informalization, a stubborn refusal to "play by the rules" of Western modernity, as some have claimed (e.g., Chabal 2009; Chabal and Daloz 1999). Rather, the devaluation of Congolese citizenship has been the outcome of changing configurations of identity and belonging, a powerful dynamic not only in Congo but in many parts of sub-Saharan Africa that makes the position of the African stranger tenuous today. This dynamic is the subject of the book's concluding chapter.

CONCLUSION
THE ANCHORING OF IDENTITIES

Of Logs and Crocodiles

There is an expression in the Bamanan language: "Yirikurun mèn o mèn ji la, a tè kè bama ye," which translates as "However long a log may float in the water, it will never become a crocodile." This adage is part of everyday discourse in Mali and even inspired the title of a book about that country (Belloncle 1981). Like all popular expressions, it applies to a broad range of contexts. One could interpret it generally to mean "the leopard cannot change its spots." More specifically, however, one can understand it as a commentary on migrants' inability to assimilate into their host societies, an avowal that "one cannot renounce one's origins" (Bailleul 2005:141). Natives will remain natives, and strangers will remain strangers.

This proverb, like the sentiment it articulates, turns out to be widespread in Africa. A cursory Web search reveals equivalent expressions in Wolof, Sonrai, and Pulaar. Congolese musician Casimir Zao uses a version of it to reproach his compatriots who travel to France and put on French airs after returning home. In his song "Pierre de Paris" (1982), he sings of a Congolese named Pierre who wears French clothes and only speaks French. Zao scolds him in Kikongo with the words "Ntí kà wú tìtùkáákà / Ngáándù kó mù maambbà"—"Never can a tree trunk / Be transformed into a crocodile in the water" (see Milandou 1997:120). Wherever it originated, today this expression has become something of a pan-African phenomenon.

During fieldwork on Brazzaville's West African immigrants, the log-and-crocodile proverb provided a lens through which I came to view host-stranger dynamics. The structural tensions between Malian, Guinean, and other foreign traders and their Congolese clientele, the religious chasm separating Muslim West Africans from Christian Congolese, and the widespread belief among Brazzaville-born West Africans that their futures lay elsewhere all seemed to stem from a mind-set shared by hosts and strangers that meaningful integration was virtually impossible. For all their proximity and economic interdependence, Congolese and West Africans inhabited separate worlds, and most saw no point in trying to bridge the social distance between them. Even for those born and raised in Congo and irrespective of their official nationality, a common discourse of strangerhood (see chapter 4) restricts their rights and limits their ability to participate in the affairs of the host society.

Yet, in many respects, Brazzaville's West Africans are fortunate, for other intra-African migrants have found themselves in far more precarious positions in recent years. Anti-immigrant sentiments in South Africa have led to beatings, murders, and the annual deportation of hundreds of thousands of *makwerekwere*—foreign Africans—since the end of apartheid, as well as waves of popular violence generally depicted by news media as xenophobic. In early 2006 the government of Equatorial Guinea expelled hundreds of West African traders and seized their property, with no apparent legal justification. Two years later Mozambican police arrested more than 160 West African immigrants, confiscated their documents and property, and placed them on chartered repatriation flights to their countries of origin, prompting allegations of abuse. In 2009 and 2010 the government of Libya—one of the most vocal exponents of African unity—rounded up and expelled hundreds of Malians, along with thousands of other African migrants. This action was part of a broad campaign, tacitly encouraged and partially funded by the European Union, to curb the flow of clandestine African migrants through Libya and into southern Europe. After the rebellion against Muammar al-Qaddafi began in Libya in early 2011, Malians were among the hundreds of thousands of sub-Saharan immigrants forced to flee that country, after many of them became victims of mob violence.[1]

Even immigrants linked to their hosts by bonds of common ethnicity, language, and intermarriage currently live under the threat of deportation. In late September 2009 the government of Congo-Brazzaville closed its border with the Angolan enclave of Cabinda to protest the expulsion of thousands of foreign Africans from Angolan territory; Angolan security forces were accused of robbing and raping those who were expelled and destroying valid residence permits. Yet earlier that year, in an action dubbed "Operation Sterilization," Brazzaville police rounded up nationals of the Democratic Republic of Congo who were allegedly undocumented (*en situation irrégulière*) and expelled them across the Congo River to Kinshasa after taking their money and cell phones. Several hundred people, including a citizen of Congo-Kinshasa married to a citizen of Congo-Brazzaville, were swept up in the dragnet. The Congo-Kinshasa government eventually reciprocated against immigrants from Angola and Congo-Brazzaville allegedly *en situation irrégulière* on its own territory, throwing out 30,000 Angolans through organized sweeps that degenerated into mob-driven pogroms. Migrants, as usual, were political pawns: Angola's deportation of more than 160,000 migrants to Congo-Kinshasa since 2003 has been part of a wider government campaign to gain leverage over contested offshore oil deposits.[2]

Although West Africans in the region portray the alleged antagonism of Congolese and Angolans toward outsiders as alien to their own ethos of hospitality, their home countries are not immune to spasms of hostility toward African foreigners and other strangers. In Mali, for example, outbreaks of mass hysteria over accusations of "penis-shrinking" sorcery have repeatedly targeted foreign Africans.[3] For years Bamako residents have regarded African immigrants from Anglophone countries—especially, but not exclusively, Nigeria—as bandits, prostitutes, and con artists.

Being a stranger in Africa today is fraught with peril, but contemporary threats against foreign residents in African countries have numerous precedents beginning in the colonial era.[4] The governments of Ghana and Nigeria carried out mass deportations of each other's citizens in the late 1970s and early 1980s, resulting in more than a million displaced persons. In Gabon mob violence against immigrants—tolerated and even incited by public officials—has been "a recurring ritual of civic expression that solidified a sense of Gabonese privilege and identity" since independence in the 1960s (Gray 1998:390). In 1964 Congo-Kinshasa expelled immigrants from Congo-Brazzaville, Rwanda, Burundi, and Mali. Idi Amin's 1972 deportation of Uganda's Asian community was an exception to the rule: the victims of mass expulsions have usually been fellow Africans, and anti-immigrant hostility has likewise concentrated on fellow Africans. Still today, as Kersting (2009:11) puts it, "most of the xenophobia in Africa is an Afro-phobia."[5]

What makes present-day anti-immigrant crackdowns on the continent stand apart from their predecessors is not their scale but their adverse timing. The imperative to migrate has become overpowering for an increasing number of Africans. A combination of structural, economic, and political forces has made cross-border migration an indispensable strategy, even for residents of stable, peaceful countries. Throughout West Africa, young men have come to see emigration as an inevitable stage of their lives. Cameroonian scholar Achille Mbembe (2008:108) describes among African youth today "an unprecedented revival of imaginaries of the faraway," accompanied by "an equally unprecedented increase of migratory practices and experiences of displacement."[6]

It is true that for many young Africans hope for the future rests on dreams of escape—"not progress, then, but egress," as Ferguson (2006:192) concludes. Such dreams are fueled by frustration with the seemingly intractable problems of poverty and corruption at home, and the goal is often mere survival. Yet research on transnational mobility suggests that in many African communities, especially those with long-standing patterns of return migration, progress and egress are not mutually exclusive. Migration abroad is a time-honored route to economic betterment and improved social standing at home. Young people living in such communities face strong pressure to migrate from parents and other kin, who stand to benefit from the remittances they would send.[7] Their governments have little incentive to intervene, since remittances constitute a massive source of foreign exchange and, in any case, there are not enough jobs at home.

If the people I have known in Congo and Mali are any indication, most African migrants nowadays aspire to go to wealthy countries in Europe and North America, where they believe economic opportunities and the capacity for earnings (and therefore remittances) are greatest. Yet the governments of these countries do not want them. Entry visas for countries like France, Spain, the United States, the Netherlands, or Canada have become all but impossible to obtain, and deportations of existing undocumented immigrants from those countries are now a daily occurrence. Stepped-up maritime patrols and border enforcement by North African governments under the coordination of Frontex, the European Union's border security agency, make clandestine migration routes to Europe more perilous and expensive: the cost of passage from Morocco to Spain through human smuggling operations has soared to an estimated $3,000 per head. Africans desiring to go abroad thus face a grave dilemma. In the words of Chabal (2009:145):

> Their desire for migration has increased as a result of the failure of their national economies but their ability to migrate has been reduced, rais-

ing thereby the cost of that survival option. This has been economically wasteful and has been detrimental to the development of the continent. Unfortunately, the precarious nature of everyday existence in Africa has made migration ever more desirable. It is now a vicious cycle.

With attractive destinations in the northern hemisphere placed ever further out of reach, most African migrants must continue to set their sights on other African countries. Yet these countries are witnessing flare-ups of hostile rhetoric and violence. Residents of communities such as Brazzaville, where popular anti-immigration discourse has long been absent or muted, feel they have crossed an important threshold: one Congolese official, justifying his government's mass deportation of migrants from across the river, declared that "Brazzaville has become a city where immigration has reached intolerable levels" (*Le Potentiel* 2009). Such statements mirror calls in the Congolese media for adopting more restrictive immigration policies, inspired by measures implemented in France.[8] Hostile rhetoric against foreigners in Brazzaville and other African capitals bears growing resemblance to similar discourses in North America and Europe.

Most crucially, over the long term intra-African migrants and their offspring born abroad face what Chabal (2009:57) calls "the politics of non-belonging," limiting their opportunities and restricting their liberties in African host societies. In the preceding chapters I have shown how West African migrants and their descendants in Congo cannot become full citizens but remain permanent strangers there. Their situation is hardly unusual in Africa: from Côte d'Ivoire to Kenya and from Cameroon to Zimbabwe, the problem of non-belonging is acute.[9] We thus return to the metaphor of the log floating in the water, never to become a crocodile. Like the proverb itself, resistance to immigrant assimilation appears widespread on the African continent. But what are the origins of these dynamics of exclusion? Must there be a contradiction between mobile lives and fixed identities? We can trace the answers to these questions to the cultural, historical, and political forces that have shaped contemporary constructions of belonging in postcolonial African societies.

Identity, Culture, History

The log-and-crocodile proverb with which I began this chapter brings to mind another now familiar Bamanan saying, "Tunga tè danbe dòn" ("Exile knows no dignity"). *Tunga*, the space of exile or strangerhood, is where an individual's ascribed status and dignity (*danbe*) cannot be appreciated, and where, consequently, that individual cannot expect to enjoy the same rights and recognition as at home. This mind-set discouraged many of my immigrant informants in Brazzaville from protesting violations of their rights and fostered an attitude of resignation toward abuse. The very place-bound nature of *danbe* might suggest that these West Africans voluntarily establish a close link between identity and locality, constructing social reproduction as contingent on a specific geographical context.

Such cultural logics have been identified as a key factor underlying the "politics of non-belonging." Chabal (2009) argues that the assimilation of migrants throughout the African continent is hindered by what he calls the "constraints of origin," powerful imaginaries of loyalty binding migrants to their ancestral homes. For him these constraints are absolute and inflexible: "Of the more significant markers of 'foreignness,'" he writes, "the two that are most immutable have to do with the land of the ancestors and the burial ground. These are indeed the ultimate tests of belonging. Those who have come from elsewhere have left their ancestors behind. There is nothing they can do about this" (63). Indeed, the importance of burial rituals as a supreme symbol of membership in one's local community is evident in contemporary African societies from Cameroon and Kenya to Nigeria. Many African urban dwellers see funerals "at home" in their rural community of origin as mandatory and burial elsewhere as a form of social disgrace for both the deceased and surviving kin. Some groups employ rituals symbolically connecting their members to native soil, such as (among the Ewondo of Cameroon) burying the placentas of newborns in family compounds.[10]

Chabal's "constraints of origin" might explain an entrenched pattern of restrictive approaches to citizenship in African societies, where emphasis on "ethnic citizenship" rather than "civic citizenship" complicates or altogether forecloses the possibility of immigrant integration. As Meyer Fortes (1975) has pointed out, in colonial Asante society even lifelong residence was not enough to confer citizenship upon strangers, who could only become full members by being adopted into local lineages. "A free stranger could never become a full citizen of his host community," Fortes wrote, "for one reason because he never ceased being a citizen of his natal community and no one could be a citizen in two separate communities" (244). Strangerhood, or at best some inferior form of citizenship, was often a durable condition that extended to one's offspring.

The exclusive nature of kin-based systems of belonging might account for the wide array of penalties levied upon outsiders in many African societies. During the colonial era, chiefs extracted high tributes from settler farmers, ranging in the Gold Coast from one-tenth to one-third of their cocoa harvests, and in towns such as Kumasi non-Asante residents had to pay local landlords double the rents paid by Asante residents.[11] Such rents are reminiscent of the informal "stranger penalties" levied upon West African merchants and other immigrants in Brazzaville (see chapter 4). In these settings, strangers are believed to owe their hosts a debt of gratitude for being allowed to settle on the host's ancestral territory. They must express that gratitude in part by paying various tributes or rents, and in part by respecting the terms of what I have called the "stranger's code": to keep in their host's good graces, strangers must abstain from ostentatious displays of wealth and surrender certain privileges they might enjoy at home. Above all, they must avoid the political domain—it is not seen as fitting, writes Geschiere (2009:64), "for a guest to go into politics and dominate his 'landlord' in the latter's own house."

Cultural scripts laying out the proper roles of hosts and strangers are indeed powerful forces underlying territorial identities and exclusionary social dynamics in many parts of Africa. Yet they are hardly the absolute, immutable barriers to belonging that observers like Chabal claim, nor do they apply equally to everyone. Where funeral customs are concerned, not all Africans value "home burial" so highly: Muslims, for example, often place little importance on their place of burial, as Islamic funeral rites are normally conducted within a day after death, and most West Africans in Brazzaville bury their dead in a Muslim cemetery on the outskirts of town. During my fieldwork there I never heard of a single body being "repatriated" from Congo for burial in the deceased's community of origin, nor did I hear any expressions of discontent with this arrangement from West Africans who, by Chabal's thinking, ought to see the burial of a relative on foreign soil as an affront.

More to the point, resistance to assimilation does not represent some timeless quality of African culture. On closer inspection, outsiders' potential to integrate into African populations turns out to be highly contingent on historical developments, especially those of the colonial period. During the centuries before the European colonization of southern Africa, many individual refugees and shipwreck survivors assimilated into various southern African societies in the sixteenth century, and chiefs were eager to recruit newcomers into their communities. In the pre-colonial Asante kingdom, pathways existed whereby immigrants could lose their stranger status, and it was taboo to mention someone's foreign ancestry; some strangers could even become members of the local political elite. The emphasis that many "native" populations place nowadays on their autochthonous status is itself an ironic contradiction, for their own foundational myths usually cast them as settlers from elsewhere.[12]

Considerable scholarship suggests that the African fixation with territorial belonging has rather shallow historical roots. What has distinguished most African societies until quite recently was a relative *lack* of concern for place-based forms of identification and sovereignty. For Kopytoff (1987:22), African societies were actually characterized by "indifference to rootedness in physical space" and "indifference to a permanent attachment to a particular place." Since the support of human followers was far more valuable than property, leaders accessed status and power primarily through social rather than geographic space. "Where people are wealth and power, competition takes the form of competition over people," state Kopytoff and Miers (1977:39). In other words, Africans valued "wealth in people" more highly than "wealth in things," including land—although the two were obviously interchangeable to some degree.[13] Leaders commonly practiced highly *inclusive* politics, seeking to expand their followings by attracting as many people into their groups as possible. The degree of assimilation, of course, varied between groups, and not all incorporated outsiders could attain the status of full citizens in each society. Neither, however, did they remain consistently marginalized as strangers: this seems to be a recent phenomenon in many African societies.

As for the logs-and-crocodiles doctrine of fundamental non-assimilation, few African migrants, in my experience, see identity as an intrinsic quality impervious to social context. After all, they worry that their offspring born abroad will lose their culture, language, and religious identity, and they take extraordinary pains to insulate these offspring from host-society influences. As described in chapter 4, most West African immigrant parents in Brazzaville send their Congo-born children at a young age to be raised by uncles, aunts, and grandparents in the parents' West African communities of origin, believing that children raised in Brazzaville will almost inevitably "become Congolese" despite the parents' best efforts. They do this knowing that they may not see their children for many years. That this practice is widespread on the continent suggests that many Africans regard cultural assimilation not as impossible but as all too likely a scenario to avoid. Out of the question, it seems, is that they acquire genuine *citizenship* in the host society, a guarantee of not only belonging but also basic rights.

Throughout the continent, discourses about politics and place have shifted. Studying land tenure in West Africa, Lentz (2006:2) finds that "non-territorial strategies of belonging have lost considerable ground. . . . Everybody must be able to point to a 'home land' or a 'home village,' if he or she wishes to participate fully and have a say in the local decision-making process or be heard in the national political arena." In a wide range of African communities, processes to turn migrants and strangers into natives have come under pressure.[14] With respect to political systems, where "wealth in people" once prevailed, today "zero-sum is perceived to be the name of the game, and 'the less the merrier' the watchword," as Coplan (2009:376) notes of post-apartheid South Africa. The concept of national citizenship based on shared values and equal rights has been undermined by "the concept of nations as a federation of communities defined by descent or by some form of essential 'primordial' membership" (Lentz 2006:2). Indigeneity, writes Mamdani (2001:657), is "the litmus test for rights under the postcolonial state." In short, ethnic citizenship is supplanting civic citizenship. To return to a paradox I identified in the introduction to this book, the central irony here is that, even as African lives and livelihoods become ever more mobile, *place* figures more centrally than ever before in the construction of African selves. This leads Geschiere (2009:1) to describe the upsurge in autochthony movements—in Africa and around the world—as "the flip side of globalization": from the Netherlands to Russia to Fiji to the United States, groups representing themselves as "true natives" have mobilized to exclude others perceived as aliens. The most serious consequences of this process may be in Africa, where multiple forces have combined to make the question of belonging especially charged.

The Anchoring of Identities

The language we use to describe the relationship between human beings and place is potent. Arboreal metaphors of "rootedness" encourage us to associate people with immobility and to overlook the fundamental role of migration in human history.[15] To replace such language of fixity, I propose the term "anchoring": mobility makes human beings more like nautical vessels than trees. Like vessels, we can also remain at rest in certain locations under the right conditions; all it takes is some kind of anchor. Anchoring, in this metaphor, means establishing a connection between our individual and collective identities, on the one hand, and a specific geographic location, on the other.

Several interrelated factors underlie the anchoring of African identities in recent decades. Two parallel lines of analysis trace this process to the establishment of European colonial rule on the continent. One focuses on the political sphere: policies such as British indirect rule and the French *politique des races* were designed to facilitate control of subject populations by identifying "true natives" in each locality and recognizing (or even reconstituting) native political structures through which colonial authorities could exercise power. In their bid to fix unruly and itinerant populations in place, colonizers organized their African subjects into discrete, stable political units ("tribes") based on presumed ties of autochthony and ethnicity, assigning each a territorial homeland, codifying a body of "customary laws" for its administration, and installing an authoritarian chief to rule over it.[16] This explanation casts the colonial-era reformulation of native political authority as a case of "invented tradition" granting Africa's so-called customary rulers unprecedented powers to allocate land, collect rents, and exclude strangers. Chiefs thus achieved "dominance in the name of tradition which they had not exercised in the past" (Ranger 1983:260) and used the legitimizing force of custom to favor powerful interests—rulers over their subjects, elders over youth, men over women, and "indigenous" populations over strangers and settlers. By equating African communities with tribes, European colonizers and their native representatives excluded migrants from local land tenure and political representation, forcing them into a permanent "stranger slot" where access to land was contingent upon paying tribute to native landlords.

The second line of scholarly analysis concentrates on the economic sphere, specifically the commodification of colonial African economies and the introduction of cash crops. The advent of commercialized agriculture in the colonies transformed the relationship between people and land by boosting demand for labor and farm plots. Land became a potential source of wealth both for the people cultivating it and the customary rulers with sovereignty over it. Rights to land were acquired through complex processes of negotiation between farmers (both kin and strangers), elders, and chiefs. Land commercialization gave chiefs an incentive to expand the category of "stranger," since they could extract rents from strangers but not native farmers. Among the Asante, therefore, by the early twentieth century a stranger was no longer understood as a non-Asante outsider but rather as "a native who is living or working on land belonging to a division whose Head Chief he does not serve" (Berry 2001:20). This redefinition provided early impetus to the process of exclusion, allowing chiefs to classify even co-ethnics from neighboring communities as strangers, and to tax them accordingly.

The Asante case highlights the fact that transfigured notions of belonging do not stem solely from the innovations and impositions of European colonial authorities. They have arisen, in at least equal measure, from ongoing contestations of custom among Africans themselves, set in motion by the process of colonization. "Colonial 'inventions' of African tradition served not so much to define the shape of the colonial social order," writes Berry (1992:328), "as to provoke a series of debates over the meaning and application of tradition which in turn shaped struggles over authority and access to resources." In the course of these debates, which continue today, some African actors have been able to accumulate and consolidate advantages for themselves and their constituencies to the detriment of vulnerable groups, especially migrants. The changes wrought in identity formation are consequently not the exclusive product of colonial policies. One should likewise be wary of overstating the role of structural economic transformation, for the marginalization of purported outsiders has occurred even in areas where agricultural commodification and the penetration of capitalist enterprise were limited or absent. Writing about West Africa, Berry (2006:250) encapsulates the views of a growing number of scholars for whom the impact of European colonization is only part of the equation: the contemporary importance of custom in issues of belonging, she contends, is "as much a product of post-independence struggles over the constitution of state authority and the terms of political participation, as it is an ineradicable legacy of colonial rule."[17]

The process of postcolonial African state formation also helped to harden boundaries between hosts and strangers. In many countries the inclusive era of nation building that prevailed in the 1960s and 1970s, with its emphasis on civic citizenship and universal rights, has been succeeded by an era of state decentralization and formal (if not substantive) democratization, dynamics which since the early 1990s have operated in tandem with neoliberal "free market" economic reforms. In the context of diminishing state resources and increasing competition for votes, politicians have learned to deploy discourses of indigeneity to their advantage, disqualifying rivals or their supporters from participation in the electoral process based on their allegedly exogenous origins. Belonging is, in Geschiere's words, "a choice weapon for manipulating elections" (2009:52). The inauguration of formally democratic regimes has thus accompanied the de facto and sometimes de jure exclusion of whole populations from political representation. The process of crafting modern African nations has in this manner entailed a parallel creation of strangers whose rights and whose very future in the new political dispensation are highly uncertain.

In tracing the spread of the politics of non-belonging in modern African societies, we cannot ignore the role of the economic catastrophe afflicting much of Africa since the latter half of the 1980s. As evidenced in the case of

Congo, mounting government debt coupled with a steep and protracted fall in the country's primary export dealt a major macroeconomic shock. In Congo it was oil; in many other African countries the problem involved other commodities—copper in Zambia and Congo-Kinshasa, coffee and cocoa in Côte d'Ivoire and Cameroon. The ensuing debt crisis, the imposition of structural adjustment reforms, and rising unemployment all contributed to a more volatile social and political climate, in which the issue of access to public resources and national wealth became increasingly combustible. As long as economic opportunity was expanding in Côte d'Ivoire, for example, Ivoirians could ignore the question of strangerhood. Once the country's economic "miracle" faded in the 1990s, however, defining who was "in" and who was "out" became the core problematic of national politics.

Given that Africa has the world's highest demographic growth rates and its population has tripled over the last century, population pressures have surely contributed to intensifying conflicts over land and citizenship on the continent. In areas like the forest belt of Côte d'Ivoire, zones that were new frontiers for settlement or cash crop production a generation ago have become the scenes of growing tension over access to land, and perceptions of land scarcity are widespread. Yet deepening divisions between hosts and strangers, between "first comers" and "latecomers," between *autochtones* and *allogènes* are also evident in relatively underpopulated zones, such as the rainforests of southeastern Cameroon where communities are small and land remains abundant.[18]

The lesson here is that no single variable can explain the rise of the "politics of non-belonging" in African societies; a complex range of factors has fundamentally altered the relationship between people and the places they inhabit. One symptom of this changed relationship is the rising prevalence of nativism, a rhetorical configuration centered on themes of cultural identity, custom, and autochthony. Nativist discourse on the continent sets rigid boundaries on the types of identities one can represent as authentically African. Mbembe (2002:266) describes identity production in postcolonial Africa as dominated by a "cult of locality," an obsession with territorial belonging and the supposed cultural authenticity it confers. Nativism, for him, leads the African subject into a historical dead end, where "criticisms of African imaginations of the self and the world remain trapped within a conception of identity as geography" (271).

Such a conception cannot tolerate hybrid constructions of the self. I have shown how second- and third-generation West African immigrants in Brazzaville, the so-called *tabushis*, are compelled to respect the clear cultural boundaries separating the immigrant population from its Congolese hosts (see chapter 6). In matters of religious faith, dress, food, and personal style, one has to project a cultural affiliation that is unambiguous and "pure." One must be either West African or Congolese; one cannot be "a little of both." Children of cross-border marriages are likewise discouraged from blurring the boundaries between national and cultural groups. Historian Didier Gondola, the son of one parent from Kinshasa and one from Brazzaville, describes the pressure he faced in constructing and representing his own identity: "Being Congolese and Zairean [i.e., from Congo-Kinshasa] raises doubts on both banks of the river," he writes (1996:13). "Such individuals are supposed to pick sides, in other words to deny half of themselves." Dual national heritages are shunned in the African postcolony, where the logic of autochthony makes it "inconceivable that Africans might have multiple ancestries" (Mbembe 2002:256).

Mbembe and others use broad brushstrokes in describing this phenomenon as a generic condition of the "African postcolony." The trend I have described in this chapter is by no means universal on the African continent, however. There are countries where strangerhood is not politicized, where identity construction does not increasingly center on a territorial base. The question of autochthony is less of a concern for people in, for example, Botswana or Tanzania than for those in Côte d'Ivoire or Kenya. My contention is not that the trend toward nativism and greater exclusion of so-called outsiders applies universally in Africa, nor even that it is a particularly African problem: it is, after all, the "flip side of globalization." It does seem to me, however, that this restrictive trend has been especially acute in those African societies, like Congo, where state institutions have been unable to guarantee basic rights and where the very idea of nation building has lost considerable sway in recent decades. Amid such conditions, the legacy of colonialism and the misuse of the postcolonial state have combined with global economic and political conjunctures to yield a gathering crisis of belonging.

It is in precisely these African societies that the analogy of the log and the crocodile can be useful for representing contemporary dynamics of identity production, cultural essentialism, and ethnic "boundary maintenance" (cf. Barth 1998 [1969]). Yet this analogy also obscures the historical generation of these dynamics and the ways that various actors and groups have contested them before, during, and since the period of European colonization. It further propagates the fallacy that geography is coterminous not only with identity but with destiny itself.

Cosmopolitan Futures?

In response to the surging "politics of non-belonging" on the continent, African voices have arisen to challenge the rhetoric of autochthony and nativism. Achille Mbembe has been at the forefront of this challenge, as has Ghanaian philosopher Kwame Anthony Appiah, who has articulated a different vision for societies in Africa and throughout the world. In *Cosmopolitanism: Ethics in a World of Strangers* (2006), Appiah describes the very notion of cultural purity as an oxymoron. Attempts to fix human identity in place, he argues, rest on a fundamental error: migration and cultural hybridization are not the exceptions to human history but its very essence. It is possible, even necessary, to imagine a future in which openness to outside influences and human circulation is celebrated as a virtue. Such a valuation rises above mere tokenism: "The humanist requires that we put our differences aside," writes Appiah (1997:638–639); "the cosmopolitan insists that sometimes it is the differences we bring to the table that make it rewarding to interact at all."

Realizing such a cosmopolitan future would require a fundamental reworking of the relationship between people and place. In African societies, Mamdani argues (2001:663–664), the only way out of the nativist trap is "to rethink the institutional legacy of colonialism, and thus to challenge the idea that we must define political identity, political rights, and political justice first and foremost in relation to indigeneity." Leaders must break from the pattern of governance set by their postcolonial predecessors, and citizens must stand firm against the tempting illusion that state boundaries ought to enclose a common cultural community.[19] With respect to land use and political rights in African societies, the current state of closure need not be the blueprint for the future; earlier models for the incorporation of outsiders can be adapted to the twenty-first century. Only a generation ago in Côte d'Ivoire—one of today's "hot spots" of autochthony discourse and violence—official openness to outsiders was state policy and justified in terms of basic African values of hospitality. In the past, as Bøås (2009:34) states, "compromises and the institutions to regulate them also existed. These cannot automatically be rediscovered and reformulated, but it is possible to imagine a less exclusive version."

Scholars are not the only Africans calling for a reimagining of identity and belonging in their societies. Since the late 1990s Ivoirian reggae musician Tiken Jah Fakoly has campaigned tirelessly against the ethnocentric doctrine known as *ivoirité* propagated by many of his country's leaders, which casts not only immigrants but even natives of Côte d'Ivoire's northern Muslim region as aliens. In "Nationalité," a song from his 1999 release *Cours d'histoire* ("History class"), Fakoly points out that most of the country's ethnic groups originally migrated to what is now Ivoirian territory from beyond its current borders during the pre-colonial period. He sings about a "cosmopolitan land" where these ancestors settled, implying the land could become cosmopolitan again. In other songs, even as he condemns neocolonialism and the ravages of global capitalism on African lives and livelihoods, he excoriates African politicians for fomenting discord along ethnic, regional, and religious lines to shore up their own power. "No one used to talk about Northerners nor Southerners," he sings in a composition about Côte d'Ivoire titled "Le Pays Va Mal" ("The Country's Going Wrong") (2002); "No one used to talk about Christians nor Muslims / But today they've ruined everything [*ils ont tout gâté*]." His outspoken views against the abuse of power have earned Fakoly considerable renown in West Africa and beyond but also forced him into exile following the outbreak of civil war in Côte d'Ivoire a few months after "Le Pays Va Mal" was released.

Many ordinary migrants, for their part, also long for more open societies and inclusive identities. Among my West African informants in Brazzaville, Barou, the thirty-nine-year-old auto parts dealer from Mali, was perhaps the most articulate in this regard.

> Moi, personnellement, l'homme n'a pas de chez soi. L'homme n'a pas de chez soi. Lorsque vous arrivez à vous investir quelque part, là où tu vas travailler, là où tu vas dormir, là où vous avez votre famille, c'est déjà chez vous! C'est déjà chez vous.
>
> [For] me, personally, a man has no home. A man has no home. When you manage to settle somewhere, where you can work, where you can sleep, where you have your family, that's already your home! That's already your home.

Barou's words echo those of another Malian migrant, sixty-two-year-old trader El Hajj Bassirou Diallo in Bouaké (Côte d'Ivoire), quoted by Daouda Gary-Tounkara (2008:9):

> Je pense que partout où l'on est, on est autochtone, partout où l'on est, c'est la terre des hommes, c'est la terre des hommes.
>
> I think that wherever you are, you're native. Wherever you are, it's the world of men, it's the world of men.

Such statements indicate that these migrants do not see strangerhood as a desirable or inevitable condition in their lives, that they think of themselves more like nautical vessels than trees, and that they do not necessarily accept the logic that human beings need one special place where they exclusively belong. As individuals who have experienced *tunga* (exile or life abroad), they understand both the yearning for a home left behind and the trouble with settling back in their community of origin. Having lived in cities in other parts of West Africa, the Congo Basin, or elsewhere, they know that they cannot simply resume their former lives in rural villages. They want to preserve the living standards and access to modern amenities that accompany city life, and also preserve the savings accumulated through their economic activities abroad. For them, the village of origin is a place to visit, attend family gatherings, and (perhaps) someday be buried, but it is seldom a place to live or start a business (see chapter 2). Most of the successful Malian traders I knew in Brazzaville owned or were building homes in Bamako, even though none originally hailed from there.[20]

This observation raises the question of whether diasporic existence itself is something these migrants voluntarily construct and maintain or whether it is forced upon them. As a migration researcher, I reject the notion that migrants are automatically assumed to be "homeward-looking," that they belong entirely and exclusively to their country or community of origin. Some of my informants, such as Aisha (see chapter 6), have indeed "anchored" their identities in distant ancestral homelands which they may never have experienced physically. Others, however, have settled permanently in Brazzaville, although they are more likely to represent this choice as a necessity than a virtue. Still others would surely choose to remain in Congo if not for the state of "existential insecurity" in which they live as strangers in the city (see chapter 4). Some descendants of West African migrants living in Brazzaville, such as Moussa, Mata, and Ladji (see chapter 6), had no meaningful connection to their ancestral homelands and preferred to identify as Congolese when granted the opportunity. To cast persons of West African descent in Congo uniformly as part of any internal African diaspora (e.g., a Malian diaspora, a Soninke diaspora, or a Togotalan village diaspora) would be to overlook instances of integration, whether actual or aspirational. The very act of classifying a migrant or migrant's offspring as a member of a diaspora can have powerful and unwelcome consequences for that individual. "There is a danger," Bakewell (2008:15) points out,

> that in looking for diasporas within Africa we may help to "invent" diasporas by naming them ... by describing people as a diaspora, there is an implica-

tion that they have this connection with a homeland elsewhere. . . . This helps to mark them out and secure their exclusion. Thus, there is a danger that carelessly referring to people as a diaspora may help to bring a diaspora into existence.

For some migrants, such a diasporic connection may be more imaginary than real; it can be imposed on them primarily because of their foreign-sounding names or even their choice of clothing rather than because their actual loyalties lie elsewhere. Scholars of transnational networks must therefore work to overcome notions of primordial attachments between people and place, and guard against applying the diaspora concept too broadly. Migrants throughout human history "have moved on and helped to create new identities in new places," Bakewell continues (2008:16). "Today people move and are able to take their identity and links with them. The danger is that not only are they able to do this, but they may be *expected* to do so" (emphasis added). The mere existence of Africa's internal diasporas must not blind us to cases of people like Moussa or Mata who would rather opt out of diasporic identities.[21]

Cosmopolitanism may seem a remote possibility for people in many contemporary African societies, given the appeal and seemingly self-evident nature of nativist discourses on their continent. Yet my research reveals broad resistance to these discourses that undermines conceptions of "geography as identity." There can be no "returning" to some imagined age when people remained in place and did not migrate to secure their livelihoods, when "pristine" human populations did not trade, intermingle, and intermarry. Ever since forerunners of *Homo sapiens* first left the Rift Valley more than one million years ago, migration has been at the very core of human existence. At the beginning of the twenty-first century migration remains a vital activity for millions of people, and its importance is likely only to increase. Among West African youths, Ba (2008:49) finds a growing perception of emigration "as a universal right, because the law of persons is superior to that of states and nations. . . . There is a natural right, a fundamental freedom of each individual to circulate and live without constraint in the country of his/her choice." This aspiration for transnational mobility is widely shared by young people across the globe.[22]

Such evidence foreshadows increasing tensions between youths' desire for mobile lives, on the one hand, and nativist discourses and state regimes of border control, on the other. The issue of who has access to migration and to the transnational spaces of mobility is shaping up to be one of the most contentious questions of the twenty-first century. Much as the world has been stratified by disparities of race and class, it is becoming equally stratified by disparities of mobility. Those with the means and official authorizations to cross borders enjoy far greater political and economic freedoms than those without. "Differentiated mobility" is the order of the day: some people become migrants, and others are effectively imprisoned by their immobility.[23]

If, as Ferguson (1999:248) contends, Africans are at the "end of the queue" in the new world order, they still have some capacity to engage with the global economy and carve out spaces for themselves within it. Despite over a century of colonial and neocolonial exploitation, they have not surrendered their agency. It seems unlikely that inhabitants of regions like the western Sahel will be able to sustain their families and communities without continued recourse to large-scale emigration. Their example should encourage us to consider migration, not closure, as the norm in human history. What if, in the words of Lambert (2002:xvii), "we work from the assumption that other things being equal, people do and will choose to move, that they will change their residence, that they will reach out to make the wider political and economic context part of their communities?" This question grows more critical every day.

Throughout the world, and especially in places like the Sahel, the migration imperative remains as strong as ever. As long as governments of wealthy countries remain opposed to more open immigration policies, however, most Africans who leave their countries of origin will move elsewhere in Africa. Some will become proletarian cogs in the machinery of global capitalism, and others will become entrepreneurs pursuing opportunity in areas too marginal or risky for global capital to profit from directly. They will go on seeking their fortunes, and sometimes making them, as strangers in the interstices of the global economy. The experiences of the intra-African migrants I have studied indicate that their path, despite its material necessity and economic appeal, is also marked by humiliation and exclusion, and their lives characterized by insecurity, uncertainty, and the denial of fundamental rights. Where perceived primordial ties to territory remain a key building block in the construction of human selves—where social and political forces systematically anchor or re-territorialize identities—migrants will remain exiled strangers. Only when that situation changes will they be assured of some degree of dignity in their lives, and perhaps be empowered to reap more of globalization's rewards and fewer of its risks.

EPILOGUE
DISPLACED DREAMS

In the second decade of the twenty-first century Brazzaville faces uncertain prospects. The city cannot offer the economic opportunities it once did, as Kinshasa has largely supplanted it as a regional commercial hub. In an ironic reversal of its former situation, by the time of my fieldwork Brazzaville was dependent on imports from Kinshasa, even for essential commodities like gasoline and aviation fuel. Moreover, countries such as the Central African Republic and Chad, which once exported their raw materials down the Congo River through the Congolese capital, today use alternative outlets. Deforestation and climate change have made the river un-navigable throughout much of the year, and Brazzaville's port facilities have suffered years of neglect. Even most of the timber harvested in Congo's northern forests no longer passes through the capital city on its way to the coast but transits overland via Cameroon. As regional commercial flows have progressively bypassed Brazzaville, the city has lost its primary economic raison d'être, and Congo's national economy has grown ever more reliant on exports of offshore oil, accounting for 90 percent of government revenues.[1] Congo's role in the twenty-first-century global economy is essentially what it was during the colonial era—a source of raw materials, with little value added and few jobs generated at home. Despite double-digit economic growth and an expanding state budget, most Congolese still lived in poverty in 2011, and rates of malnutrition remained high.[2] Living conditions continued to stagnate, and even in Brazzaville electricity had become a scarce commodity: "It seems like the more years go by, the more the number of Congolese with access to electricity diminishes," wrote one Congolese journalist (*La Semaine Africaine* 2010a). To underscore the country's state of abjection, in late 2010 a polio outbreak killed two hundred Congolese (IRIN 2010b). Immigrants in Congo increasingly looked elsewhere to pursue their dreams.

The day after Papa Doucouré's death in December 2005, as news of the tragedy spread throughout Brazzaville's West African population, I sat with a young Guinean *aventurier* named Samba at our customary hangout next to a neighborhood dry goods shop. Samba was convinced that the Doucouré shooting resulted from Congolese hostility toward foreigners, and he complained of constantly encountering such antipathy. As long as he remained in Congo or any other African destination, he said, he would never escape this hostility. "This is why we all want to go to the U.S.," he said.

"But these things happen in my country, too," I protested. "Haven't you heard of Amadou Diallo?" Samba knew all about his late compatriot, who was gunned down by New York City police officers in 1999 while reaching for his wallet to produce identification. Samba saw no parallel. "That was a *bavure*, a mistake," he argued, insisting that what happened in Congo was a deliberate abuse of power. At least in America, he continued, there was rule of law; there were investigations and trials when abuses occurred. (I did not point out to Samba that all four policemen involved in the Amadou Diallo shooting were acquitted.)

Samba's peers widely subscribed to this idealized view of the United States. Even older, established West Africans fantasized about living there, seeing it as a place where they could finally escape both the burdens of kin demands and the strictures of the stranger's code. Draman, the forty-seven-year-old son of a successful Malian immigrant father and a Congolese mother, ran his family's business empire (including retail shops, trucks, and rental housing) and had many dependents in Brazzaville. He struggled to meet his economic and kin obligations, and privately hoped to make a life somewhere else. In a hushed voice, Draman spoke of his dream of living in America, a country he had never visited. When I asked why he wanted to go there, his reply revealed an imagined hierarchy of global migrant destinations.

> *Americans are the most powerful on earth. Americans are evolved [évolué]. Americans have ease—for them everything's easy, in every domain. If you want to go live there peacefully, you'll be well off. If you want to go work, you'll work. If you want to get medical treatment, you get*

treatment. It's the end of the world! The end of the world. I think one must start small and grow larger. But one shouldn't.... One climbed up, one came to Congo, one goes back to Mali ... no. If we left Mali to come to Congo, we should leave Congo to go to the U.S. That's the end of the world.

For Draman, leaving Congo for his fatherland, Mali, would be moving in the wrong direction, *downward;* one must climb *up* the ladder, ideally continuing until reaching the country at the top—America, "the end of the world." In this respect Draman and many other men I have met throughout Africa share a common imaginary about the "world system" of opportunity and power, and about where their countries, not to mention my own, fit into it.

"I like Americans," Draman continued. "I like their way of living together. I don't know if I've made myself understood. If I get to America still in my fifties, strong, I'll work hard. If I get there in my sixties and can't work, I can at least live there the rest of my days," he said, adding, "with my wife and children." What, I asked, about his many brothers, sisters, nieces, and nephews? "Well," Draman said, "whoever can make it there and join me, let him come and join me. On his own, *de sa manière* [in his or her own manner]. Because I'm getting old, I'm getting tired." Like so many West Africans in the city, he wanted out.

While members of Africa's internal diasporas increasingly aspire to leave the continent altogether, many of the aventuriers I knew in 2005 have moved, for want of better options, to other African destinations—Gabon, Congo-Kinshasa, Angola, even Mozambique. A few have tried to reach Europe, although I am unaware of any who have succeeded. Nor am I aware of any aventurier who has gone back to his home country.

I know of two migrants who definitively returned "home" from Brazzaville: in 2008 Vieux Diallo and his wife, Hawa, flew to Mali after nearly five decades abroad. He phoned me shortly before making the move to ask if I could help finance their journey. By the time I got back in touch with the old man he had already relocated to Bamako. There he and his wife found that they had become a different type of stranger, adjusting to life in the homeland they had not known since the early 1960s, learning their way around a city made almost unrecognizable by years of rapid growth. In 2010 I visited them in an outlying neighborhood of Bamako. Then in his eighties, Diallo could no longer work because of failing eyesight, and Hawa was unable to find a place to sell in Bamako's saturated marketplaces. The couple relied on contributions from kin and friends to get by. When I arrived at their sparsely furnished apartment, I found them in the dark having a lengthy argument with two young neighbors over an unpaid bill for the electric meter they shared. The old man expected his neighbors to cut him a break because of his age, but they refused. I offered Diallo some money to help pay his share, and later asked him if he had regained some degree of *danbe*, dignity, by returning to Mali. "Even here we are having problems with *danbe* these days," he responded wearily.

While disheartened by my friends' plight, I was even more troubled by the fact that Bamako at that time was experiencing immigration-related tensions of its own. Given the city's relative calm, it had begun to draw refugees and other migrants from around the region. It had seen a particularly large influx of Guineans, who fled their country's political violence in 2008 and 2009 only to become scapegoats for crime, prostitution, and corruption in the Malian capital. Stories circulated of young Guinean men being beaten, even killed, by mobs after getting in motorcycle accidents. These stories were eerily reminiscent of those I had heard describing attacks against young West Africans in Congo. For Brazzaville residents, native and stranger alike, the distinction between Malians and Guineans was all but meaningless: they worked and lived alongside one another, had common ethnic identities, spoke the same languages, and worshiped in the same mosques. For Bamako residents, this same distinction could spark deadly hostility.

The difficulties and violence migrants encounter as they move from one African destination to another are striking, not merely because they give the lie to visions of globalization as a leveling force but because they challenge the very notion of a unified African homeland. The construct of a single "African Diaspora" rests largely upon such a notion, which is why this construct traditionally excluded Africans migrating within the continent. But Africa's diasporas are multiple, and Africa's migrants are no less likely to suffer harassment and discrimination in Congo, Côte d'Ivoire, or Angola than in France or the United States. Their experiences compel us to recognize the power of an idea, which I have called strangerhood, to shape and constrain human mobility across geographic space, national boundaries, and cultural divisions.

Appendix 1. Notes on Methods

If the methodological challenges facing James Ferguson (1999) in the Copperbelt seemed unusual at the close of the twentieth century, they have become more familiar today to anthropologists studying contemporary patterns of social change, cultural flux, and human mobility—commonly understood as components of globalization. Since the 1990s social scientists have sought to adapt ethnography to the study of global processes (Stoller 1997; Hannerz 1998; Burawoy et al. 2000). We have applied ethnographic approaches which, while necessarily local in their scope, illuminate macro-level social processes by examining their micro-level manifestations.

One technique for applying ethnographic methods to global processes is multi-sited fieldwork (Marcus 1998). This type of research is especially useful for studying migration flows, since, by their definition, they concern more than one geographic location. Unfortunately multi-sited fieldwork also demands more time, preparation, and money than single-sited fieldwork, and the challenges of learning about a community and gaining acceptance in it are multiplied with each additional research site. In planning my fieldwork, I chose to concentrate on Brazzaville and rely mainly on my previous experience in Mali for insights into the culture of the sending region. My fieldwork began in Bamako, Mali, where I renewed contacts from previous research and gathered information about flows of people, goods, and information between Bamako and Brazzaville. After a month in Mali, my family and I took the route most Malians use to travel to Central Africa, flying on Air Mauritania from Bamako to Brazzaville, via Abidjan and Cotonou. We returned to Bamako (again on Air Mauritania) the following year for a final stage of research lasting another month. The two Bamako legs of the fieldwork enabled me to identify and pursue transnational connections between Mali and Congo.

In Brazzaville my primary avenue of approach was participant observation—the practice of studying a community while taking part in its daily life. After a month of searching, my family and I moved into a two-room apartment on the Avenue de France, close to the Poto-Poto market. We shared a residential compound with a Congolese family as well as a group of young Togotalans forming their own household. Starting with our neighbors and the friends and kin of our contacts in Mali, we gradually built up relationships with men and women who had come to Brazzaville from throughout West Africa. I spent much of each day in the market learning about the commercial activities of these immigrants, and after sunset attended Qur'anic study classes at a neighborhood mosque. I also occasionally attended meetings of various immigrant associations. My wife, Oumou, interacted with merchants and others doing errands in the market, visited with the West African women cooking daily meals in our courtyard, and made frequent outings to meet friends around town.

Although much of what we learned about the study population came from informal conversations, we also recorded and transcribed interviews with more than 130 individuals during our year in Brazzaville. These interviews were semistructured: we asked interviewees a set of questions on topics from basic demographic information to their attitudes toward life in Congo. Owing to cultural norms that would have made it awkward for some interviewees to respond to questions from a member of the opposite sex, Oumou interviewed female informants and I interviewed males. We diverged from the standard questions whenever the situation called for additional questions. Some interviews were short and matter-of-fact, others lengthy and free-ranging. To maximize the level of candor I could expect from informants, I generally only conducted interviews with people I had met on at least one or two previous occasions and whom I had informed in advance of the nature of my research and the sorts of questions I might ask.

Informants were not randomly selected. In choosing an individual to interview, I kept several axes of diversity in mind, including gender, ethnicity, professional activity, nationality, and specific region of origin, and I made a special effort to seek out second- and third-generation immigrants born in Congo. Though I had initially hoped to conduct a scientific survey of West African immigrants in Brazzaville based on a random sample of its members, assembling a sampling frame for this population proved unworkable. A large number of West Africans in Congo reside there without Congolese government sanction or documentation. Mali's consulate in Brazzaville keeps a register of Malian citizens in the country, but because registration is voluntary, this document is far from comprehensive. With the consul's authorization, I culled six months' worth of entries from this register, some one thousand individuals in all, for analysis. I also hired a research assistant, a well-educated and respected Malian in his fifties with no apparent political liabilities, to approach and interview several dozen Malians selected randomly from this group of a thousand.

Unfortunately my assistant made little progress: after logging about twenty interviews, he reported that the people he had sought out were often reluctant to speak with him, and many were downright uncooperative. Listening to the recordings of his interviews, in which responses were brief and unhelpful, I came to appreciate the merits of getting to know one's informants before interviewing them. Surveying a random sample of individuals establishes one form of unimpeachable scientific rigor by eliminating selection bias, but it also entails speaking primarily to strangers in the conventional sense, people who may be uncomfortable with their interviewer or misunderstand the purpose of the interview, and who consequently are much more likely to withhold accurate, valuable information (see Bleek 1987; Dougnon 2007). Random sampling therefore undermines the very utility of the interview or survey being conducted. We subsequently scrapped the idea of "cold interviewing," and in the end I felt that my small research team gained a more truthful picture of people's lives through non-random methods than we could have through a sample survey. Toward the end of my Brazzaville fieldwork, I also conducted a survey of Congolese university students to assess their attitudes toward West African immigrants. I began by administering a questionnaire to a pretest group of students, and later spoke to these students about their opinions in a focus group format. Finally, I revised the questionnaire and administered it to 279 undergraduate and graduate students in various classes (see chapter 4 and Appendix II).

A final remark on ethnography and its limitations: although more than half our interviewees were women, my time as a participant observer was mostly spent in the company of men. In Mali, and throughout West Africa, there are barriers to socializing with people of the opposite sex. Unlike in some Muslim societies, gender segregation, *purdah*, or female sequestration are not widely practiced there; a Malian male may interact with females from outside his family in many situations, but he is expected not to linger in those situations. Males and females generally prefer to occupy separate spaces, and much of my participant observation had to take place in spaces dominated by West African men—market shops and mosques in particular. Readers may notice in the chapters on trade and Islam that my ethnographic data stem primarily from interactions with men. I recognize this shortcoming and the constraints it imposes, observing that other male ethnographers working in the western Sahel (e.g., Soares 2005b; Dougnon 2007) have encountered similar difficulties in portraying women's perspectives. I hope to have offset the underrepresentation of women in some chapters of this book with other chapters in which women and their points of view receive greater visibility. It remains true that the space of migration for these West Africans is highly gendered, and that the positive valuation on mobility in Mali and many other parts of West Africa rarely, if ever, extends to females (Koenig 2005), for whom autonomous movement outside certain socially approved pathways remains highly stigmatized. As migrants, women in these societies therefore must represent themselves and their mobility as dependent upon males—their husbands and fathers—and for the most part I cannot depict them otherwise here. This is a deficiency that I hope other researchers of intra-African migration will rectify.

Appendix 2. Survey Results

I. Responses to Multiple-choice Questions

In your opinion, should Islam be among the religions officially recognized by the Congolese state?

Yes	No	No opinion
146	88	41

Which nationality is most common among West Africans in Brazzaville?

Beninese	Ivoirian	Guinean	Malian	Senegalese
9	4	1	176	83

For how long has the West African community been present in Congo?

20–30 years	30–50 years	50–80 years	80 or more years
58	101	44	34

How many West African friends do you have in Brazzaville or elsewhere in Congo?

None	One or two	Three to five	Six or more
161	39	25	41

In your opinion, which would be the best state policy with respect to immigration by West Africans?

Make entry easier	Leave as is	Make entry more difficult	No opinion
44	21	182	27

In your opinion, Congo would benefit if a policy of expulsion were applied to:

No one	Undocumented immigrants only	All immigrants without distinction	Only specific nationalities	No opinion
15	153	32	16	50

II. Responses to Statements

1. Congolese, in general, are not good at commerce.

Agree strongly	Agree somewhat	No opinion/ Don't know	Disagree somewhat	Disagree strongly
158	27	11	10	65

2. Congolese, in general, prefer being civil servants to being entrepreneurs.

Agree strongly	Agree somewhat	No opinion/ Don't know	Disagree somewhat	Disagree strongly
186	13	21	5	47

3. Congolese are benevolent toward foreigners in Congo.

Agree strongly	Agree somewhat	No opinion/ Don't know	Disagree somewhat	Disagree strongly
202	14	24	0	33

4. The Congolese government respects the rights of foreigners as much or more than it respects the rights of Congolese.

Agree strongly	Agree somewhat	No opinion/ Don't know	Disagree somewhat	Disagree strongly
165	8	28	3	67

5. Islam is concordant with mores in Congo.

Agree strongly	Agree somewhat	No opinion/ Don't know	Disagree somewhat	Disagree strongly
43	6	100	2	113

6. West Africans are respectful of the law.

Agree strongly	Agree somewhat	No opinion/ Don't know	Disagree somewhat	Disagree strongly
70	13	38	14	136

7. West Africans are overly involved in Congolese internal politics.

Agree strongly	Agree somewhat	No opinion/ Don't know	Disagree somewhat	Disagree strongly
103	5	66	5	93

8. West Africans are clean and hygienic.

Agree strongly	Agree somewhat	No opinion/ Don't know	Disagree somewhat	Disagree strongly
15	13	23	8	213

9. West Africans isolate themselves too much from Congolese.

Agree strongly	Agree somewhat	No opinion/ Don't know	Disagree somewhat	Disagree strongly
128	18	47	12	68

10. West Africans are honest.

Agree strongly	Agree somewhat	No opinion/ Don't know	Disagree somewhat	Disagree strongly
42	13	32	10	170

11. West Africans are not well educated.

Agree strongly	Agree somewhat	No opinion/ Don't know	Disagree somewhat	Disagree strongly
145	19	46	9	52

12. West Africans like Congolese people.

Agree strongly	Agree somewhat	No opinion/ Don't know	Disagree somewhat	Disagree strongly
81	12	61	12	93

13. West Africans often corrupt the administration in order to do their business.

Agree strongly	Agree somewhat	No opinion/ Don't know	Disagree somewhat	Disagree strongly
222	2	17	2	23

14. West Africans fully pay their financial obligations (taxes, etc.) to the Congolese state.

Agree strongly	Agree somewhat	No opinion/ Don't know	Disagree somewhat	Disagree strongly
84	11	23	6	144

15. West Africans' current integration in Congolese society is problematic.

Agree strongly	Agree somewhat	No opinion/ Don't know	Disagree somewhat	Disagree strongly
124	13	61	5	60

16. West Africans' manufacture of medallions is responsible for the shortage of coins in Congo.

Agree strongly	Agree somewhat	No opinion/ Don't know	Disagree somewhat	Disagree strongly
169	7	53	2	33

17. West Africans' presence is a positive thing overall for Congo.

Agree strongly	Agree somewhat	No opinion/ Don't know	Disagree somewhat	Disagree strongly
83	19	49	11	100

18. West Africans are favored by the Congolese government in business compared to autochthons.

Agree strongly	Agree somewhat	No opinion/ Don't know	Disagree somewhat	Disagree strongly
221	2	23	1	21

19. West Africans are favored in judicial matters compared to autochthons.

Agree strongly	Agree somewhat	No opinion/ Don't know	Disagree somewhat	Disagree strongly
163	11	51	2	38

20. West Africans' activities constitute a brake on Congo's economic development.

Agree strongly	Agree somewhat	No opinion/ Don't know	Disagree somewhat	Disagree strongly
137	11	39	9	70

Notes

Introduction

1. In any case, as Carling (2002:8) points out, "there is no categorical analytical distinction between the 'forced' and 'voluntary' migration, since all migration involves both choices and constraints."

2. For World Bank data on net migration flows and remittances from Mali and other countries, see Ratha and Xu (2008). The figure of four million Malians living abroad is often cited by officials, scholars, and journalists, e.g., Findley (2004) and the United Nations Integrated Regional Information Networks (IRIN; 2006).

3. The literature on Soninke and other Sahelian migrants in France dates back to the 1970s; prominent examples include Kane and Lericollais (1975), Quiminal (1991), Razy (2007), Sargent and Lacharché-Kim (2006), and Timera (1996). For official estimates of the distribution of Malian migrants abroad, see Délégation Générale des Maliens de l'Extérieur (DGME; 2001); on land purchases in Bamako, see Bertrand (2009).

4. Migration within southern Africa has been studied for generations: see, among many others, Crush and McDonald (2002), Harries (1994), Murray (1981), and Schapera (1947). On rising levels of intra-African and other South-South migration, see Bakewell (2009), Pison (2010), and Ratha and Shaw (2007).

5. Recent scholarship on "new African diasporas" includes volumes by Arthur (2010), Konadu-Agyemang, Takyi, and Arthur (2006), Koser (2003), and Okpewho and Nzegwu (2009), and an article by Zeleza (2010). On the distinction between Africa's New and Old World diasporas, see Manning (2009).

6. For studies of Dominicans in the United States, see Levitt (2001); on Mexicans in the United States, see R. Smith (2006); on Caribbeans in the United Kingdom, see Olwig (1997); on Chinese in the Pacific Rim, see Ong (1999).

7. The survey published in 2003 was conducted the year before, prior to the U.S. invasion of Iraq. In later surveys by the same firm, Baghdad overtook Brazzaville as the "world's worst city." The consulting firm in question subsequently stopped disseminating its complete rankings, releasing only lists of top-ranked cities on its website.

8. The literature on strangers in Africa was most notably established by Elliot Skinner (1963). Later publications on the topic include those by Pellow (2008), Schildkrout (1970, 1978), Schler (2008), and Shack and Skinner (1979).

9. Scholars framing their work around "Soninke migration" include Kane and Lericollais (1975), Manchuelle (1997), and Quiminal (1991).

10. Bamanan is the "ethnographically correct" version of the ethnic label "Bambara" (reflecting the name these people use for their own ethnic category), and Maninka is the equivalent of "Malinke" or "Mandinka." The Halpulaaren people, renowned in West Africa for their cattle herding, are also known as Fulani or Peul; the main dialects of their language are called Pulaar and Fulfulde. The Dogon are believed to be the dominant group among Malian immigrant populations in Ghana, Cameroon, and even South Africa (Cissé 2009; Dougnon 2007).

11. Prominent studies of emigration from the Senegal River Valley include those by Bredeloup (2007), Condé et al. (1986), and Findley and Sow (1998). Manchuelle (1987) has documented the importance of the Soninke in opening up migration routes to Central Africa. For studies of specific "stranger districts" in African cities, see, e.g., A. Cohen (1969) on Ibadan's Sabo, Pellow (2008) on Accra's Sabon Zongo, or Schler (2008) on Douala's New Bell.

12. Critiques of the transnationalism concept have been levied by Castles (2007) and Waldinger and Fitzgerald (2004), among others.

13. In Mali and many of its neighboring countries, this pattern is known as *senenkunya*, though there are several minor variations in the name's orthography (see Bailleul 2000:358). Joking relationships are not unique to this particular region but are present throughout Africa and beyond (see Canut and Smith 2006).

14. Other more derogatory labels for members of this group are also in use in Brazzaville (see chapter 4).

15. All informants in this book, whether West African or Congolese, are identified with pseudonyms. For a discussion of my research methods, see Appendix 1.

16. Modibo Keita's unpopular "back to the land" policies of the early 1960s caused many Malians to leave the country; see Gary-Tounkara (2008).

17. During my fieldwork, the FBI announced plans to open up regional offices in West Africa (see Reuters 2005). As for me, my sole connection to the U.S. government was that just under 30 percent of my research funding had been awarded by the National Science Foundation.

18. Other common languages included Kikongo in the southern half of Brazzaville, Pulaar among West African Halpulaar immigrants, and classical Arabic used in mosques. The average Poto-Poto resident speaks 4.5 languages (Kubu Turé 2006).

1. The Avenue of Sergeant Malamine

1. Curtin (1975) describes the factors that made the use of native militia preferable to large European forces in the early period of European penetration of West Africa. On the origins of the tirailleurs Sénégalais, see Echenberg (1991) and Mann (2006).

2. Manchuelle (1997) discusses the elite nature of laptot recruitment. The rank and file of the tirailleurs, by contrast, was drawn heavily from slaves, although some of its commissioned and noncommissioned officers came from noble families (Echenberg 1991).

3. Brazza's first expedition (1875–1879) has been documented in print by Brunschwig (1966) and online by the French Ministry of Culture (http://www.brazza.culture.fr/en/index.html).

4. Called Stanley Pool during the colonial era, today it is known as Malebo Pool or simply the Pool.

5. The most colorful, but probably apocryphal, rendering of Stanley's confrontation with Malamine is contained in Brousseau 1925; for all its inaccuracies, this version was reproduced decades later under the title "How Brazzaville Stayed French" (Borge and Viasnoff 1995:23–27). See Chavannes (1929:171) for a less improbable account.

6. On the launching of the Mission de l'Ouest Africain, see Chavannes (1935:44–47.), Coquery-Vidrovitch (1969b), and West (1972:124–125).

7. Although Chavannes (1929:179) claimed that the flag was still being flown in M'Foa, Coquery-Vidrovitch cites evidence to the contrary, adding that Makoko Iloo had little real power in the area (1969b:115–116).

8. "The name Brazzaville has often resounded in geographers' conferences," wrote Guiral (1889:231) a few years after his mission to relieve Malamine. "I don't know what it represents today, but I must admit that in April 1882, it pains me to say, it was not much to speak of. The description of Brazzaville in 1882 could be contained in one sentence: the Brazzaville post was Malamine's hut!"

9. The French colony's official name was Moyen-Congo or "Middle Congo," but in these pages I refer to it simply as "Congo," affixing the definite article ("the Congo") only to identify the river. On Brazza's inflated estimates of the new colony's potential wealth, see Coquery-Vidrovitch (1965:80, 1969a:187).

10. Rabut (1989:95), for example, describes the Bangui station in 1890 as manned by two Europeans, one Senegalese scribe, and twelve laptots, as well as about four dozen workers recruited elsewhere in the region. For figures on French military and administrative presence in Congo, see Coquery-Vidrovitch (1969a:191, 2001:91).

11. The recruitment figures for militia and railway labor come from Gondola (1996:37). See also Cookey (1965) and Sautter (1967) on the recruitment of railroad workers in British colonies, and Hochschild (1998) on the rift between Britain and Belgium over labor abuses in the Congo colony.

12. Belgian recruitment of labor in Senegal and the Gambia is described by Manchuelle (1987:238–248).

13. For documents from this period, see Alis (1894), Chavannes (1937), and Rabut (1989). On problems with French military recruiting efforts in West Africa, see Coquery-Vidrovitch (2001:91n5).

14. On the growth of the colonial militia, see Chavannes (1937:304), Coquery-Vidrovitch (2001:92), and Wagret (1963:30).

15. The Congo colony's concessionary regime is amply documented by Coquery-Vidrovitch (1965, 1969a, 2001) and Soret (1973).

16. Fuller descriptions of these methods can be found in Coquery-Vidrovitch (2001:174–190).

17. Descriptions of West Africans in concessionary company employ can be found in Coquery-Vidrovitch (2001:293) and Martin (1995:25–26).

18. On recruitment of labor in Asia and elsewhere for Congo's railroad, see Sautter (1967). Geschiere (2009:15) describes French colonial authorities as tending "to oppose migrants' dynamics to locals' indolence and resistance to change."

19. The name "Poto-Poto" comes from the Bamanan word *pòtòpòtò* for watery mud, an apt name for this location on a low-lying plain, much of which floods during the rainy season.

20. The relocation of Brazzaville's West African neighborhood is described in Kane (n.d.) and Martin (1995:36). See also Balandier (1985) and Gondola (1996) on the early years of Poto-Poto's West African population.

21. Descriptions of the Muslim and West African populations of colonial Leopoldville are drawn from Comhaire (1948), Gondola (1996), and Manchuelle (1987).

22. See Brunschwig (1972), Guiral (1889), and Schnapper (1959) on the operations of these trading posts in the early stage of French presence in Equatorial Africa.

23. The origins of retail trade in Brazzaville are documented by Gondola (1996:37) and Martin (1995:30). Soninke oral histories were gathered by Adams (1977:88ff.).

24. On the significance and origins of sartorial distinction in Brazzaville society, see Gandoulou and Balandier (1989) and Gondola (1996:240).

25. The competition for status among Soninke migrants is described by Manchuelle (1987, 1997). Whereas Bayart (2000, 2009) defines "strategies of extraversion" as a tool of African elites, Manchuelle finds that Sahelian migration to Congo was not limited to nobles and the politically privileged.

26. On the city as a crucible of new social identities, see Gondola (1996); on the postcolonial political legacy of colonial urban formation, see Bernault (2000).

27. These high school enrollment levels were documented by Soret (1978:167). By comparison, the World Bank (1998) estimated primary school enrollment rates in Mali at only 35 percent as recently as the 1990s.

28. Early tensions between Congolese natives and West African immigrants are described by Bernault (1996:148) and Manchuelle (1987:447n). West Africans, especially Dahomeyans and Togolese, also owned many of Brazzaville's bars and nightclubs. One of the first Congolese-owned clubs established there was named Congo Zoba, an ironic appropriation of the foreigners' derogatory term intended "to show the *Béninois* [or Dahomeyans] that the Congolese, too, were capable of doing big things" (Bazenguissa-Ganga 1997:26).

29. Wagret (1963:92) describes the significance of civil servants in the electoral process during the late colonial period: more than half of the candidates for public office in the elections of June 1959 were listed as *fonctionnaires*. Bazenguissa-Ganga (1997:23–26) discusses civil service employment as a condition for membership in the postcolonial elite.

30. The Bamanan word *jatigi* designates a person who has responsibility for someone else; it encompasses various roles from landlord to artistic patron.

31. Still today, men from Congo-Kinshasa supply much of Brazzaville's domestic labor.

32. On caste and social status in Sahelian West Africa, see Conrad and Frank (1995).

33. On West Africa's early diamond rush, see van der Laan (1965). Bredeloup (1999) writes that most immigrants to these areas came from Mali, especially the zone around the western town of Nioro near the Mauritanian border.

34. On the deportation of foreigners from mining areas, see Bredeloup (1998, 2007); on the origins of Brazzaville's diamond trade and colonial authorities' response to it, see *Journal Officiel de l'AEF* (1938:968) and Radio France Internationale (2004).

35. On Brazzaville's diamond firms, see Bredeloup (1994, 2007); on the smuggling of gemstones from Congo-Kinshasa, see Lenzen (1970) and MacGaffey (1987).

36. Ian Parker (1995) describes ivory-smuggling networks operating throughout East and Southern Africa as being primarily in Malian and Senegalese hands.

37. See Hung (1987:17–34) on food production and food prices in Congo during this period.

38. By contrast, in 2010 Congo officially counted sixty thousand government employees (including ten thousand in the military), several thousand of whom were believed to exist on paper only (Agence France Presse 2010). On the growth of Congo's civil service, see Hung (1987:32) and Dorier-Apprill, Kouvouama, and Apprill (1998).

39. Economic statistics for this period were obtained from Dorier-Apprill, Kouvouama, and Apprill (1998), Hung (1987), and the International Monetary Fund (IMF) (2005).

40. Figures on the Congolese economy and debt problems are drawn from AFP (2004), Dorier-Apprill, Kouvouama, and Apprill (1998), and the International Monetary Fund (2005). Corruption and mismanagement in Congo's oil revenues have been documented by the Fédération Internationale des Droits de l'Homme (2004), Global Witness (2004, 2005), and Harel (2006).

41. On Congo's civil wars and political violence from the early 1990s, see Yengo (2006).

2. Enterprising Strangers

1. The English liner notes for Oumou Sangaré's song "Yala" (*Oumou*, on Nonesuch Records, 2004) aptly translate the term as "roaming about for no good purpose."

2. See, e.g., Devauges (1977), Dzaka and Milandou (1994, 1995), and Tsika (1995).

3. It is also worth noting that 117 of the 122 women in the sample listed their profession as *ménagère* (housewife), even though many took part in various types of economic activity.

4. Devauges (1977) describes the importance of certain foodstuffs in the Congolese economy. See Initiative for Central Africa (2004) on the cross-border origins of those foodstuffs.

5. West African commercial activity in Chinese cities has been studied by Bertoncello and Bredeloup (2007).

6. I have found no satisfactory way to differentiate between the "formal" or "informal" sectors of the Congolese economy, and the distinction I use here based on regulatory criteria is only an expedient, hence my use of quotation marks. See Portes (1994) for a thorough analysis of "informal economies."

7. Devauges (1977:35) counted just thirty-one wholesaler importers in Brazzaville in 1970, most of them foreigners.

8. President Sassou's regime, in a tacit admission of responsibility for its militiamen's rampage, did pay compensatory damages to the French supermarket chain Score and to the U.S. government, each of which had seen its Brazzaville properties looted, damaged, or destroyed during the 1997 conflict.

9. Robberies of commercial establishments committed by unnamed agents of the security forces are a perennial item in the Congolese press; see, e.g., *La Semaine Africaine* (2008, 2009b, 2010b, 2010c). No mention is made in these reports that any of the culprits were brought to justice.

10. Official statistics on the Congolese economy can be found in country reports by the International Monetary Fund (2005). In 2010 the government raised the official minimum wage to 54,000 francs per month—still only about $100.

11. (1) The *Contrat de Bail* is a tax based on the monthly rent for one's shop, payable annually to the Direction Générale des Impôts in the national treasury; (2) the *Patente*, equivalent to four times a single month's shop rent, is payable annually to the Mairie (city hall); (3) a 30,000 franc ($60) annual payment to the Caisse Nationale de Sécurité Social, the social security agency, is required, whether or not one has any employees or intends to retire in Congo; (4) the *Impôt Général Forfaitaire*, or *IGF*, a tax on business income, ranges from 80,000 francs to 700,000 francs ($160 to $1,400) for a typical shop, paid annually to the national tax office; (5) 800 francs ($1.40) is collected per week for market sweeping; (6) a 4000 franc ($8) monthly *Contrôle de Baraque* is collected by the city government, originally intended for shops in improvised settings (*baraques*) but now applied to every shop in the market; and (7) a monthly fee to a private security firm for policing the marketplace, amounting to 5,000 francs (about $12) from shopkeepers or 1,000 francs from stall merchants.

12. Selections from the literature on transnational entrepreneurial groups include, on South Asians in East Africa, Oonk (2004, 2010); on Chinese in the Pacific Rim, Dobbin (1996) and Ong (1999); and on Lebanese in West Africa, Peleikis (2000), Leichtman (2005), and Beuving (2006).

13. See also the analyses of middleman minority groups by Bonacich (1973) and Bonacich and Modell (1980).

14. On "ethnic economies," see Light and Gold (2000); on transnational entrepreneurs, see Portes and Jensen (1987), Portes, Guarnizo, and Haller . (2002), and Zhou (2004). The term "global tribes" was coined by Kotkin (1993) and "market-dominant minorities" by Chua (2003).

15. See, e.g., Calderisi (2006), Chua (2003), Harrison (1992), Harrison and Huntington (2001), and Kotkin (1993).

16. See the discussion in Kennedy (1988: chap. 7).

17. On commerce's noble associations in Mali, see Vuarin (1997); on its negative connotations in Congo, see Devauges (1977:49–52), MacGaffey and Bazenguissa-Ganga (2000:10), and Tsika (1995).

18. Food production and consumption figures on the Senegal River Valley can be found in Findley, Ouedraogo, and Ouaidou (1988:49); see also Whitehouse (in press) on the symbolic role of agricultural labor for Togotalan migrants. It is worth noting that people from nonagricultural regions of Mali, such as the desert provinces of Gao, Kidal, and Timbuktu, were virtually absent from the migrant population in Brazzaville, although this may simply reflect the small population sizes of these provinces.

19. When necessary, they may fall back on wage work, as did some of my Togotalan friends who worked as bicycle messengers in New York but were merchants prior to coming to the United States. As Hart (1970) demonstrates, wage earning and enterprise are seldom mutually exclusive activities in Africa.

20. Notable anthropological studies of this phenomenon have been written by A. Cohen (1969), Hart (1988), and MacGaffey and Bazenguissa-Ganga (2000).

21. For definitions of social capital see, e.g., Johnston and Percy-Smith (2003), Portes (1998), Robison, Schmid, and Siles (2002), and Sandefur and Laumann (1998).

22. The World Bank's celebration of social capital is exemplified by a report authored by Grootaert (1998). More critical approaches to the concept can be found in Elyachar (2002) and Fine (2001).

23. Examples include Arrow (1999), Fine (2001), Meagher (2005, 2006), Smith and Kulynych (2002), and Solow (1999). Thompson (2011) suggests that the popularity of the social capital concept in the social sciences is declining.

24. Rubio (1997) highlights what he calls "perverse social capital" in the dealings of Colombian criminal groups; Bayart, Ellis, and Hibou (1999) examine the ways that social networks have brought about the "criminalization" of African states; Browning (2009) identifies potential linkages between strong neighborhood social capital and criminality; Portes (1998) offers insight into the ways that social networks may have negative consequences outside of criminal activity; and Silvey and Elmhirst (2003) demonstrate the gendered limitations of social networks.

25. The Soninke equivalents of *danga* and *dangaden* are *langa* and *langareme*, respectively.

26. On *bunganga*, see Devauges (1977: chap. 6) and MacGaffey and Bazenguissa-Ganga (2000:126–133). *Kindoki*, the usual term for sorcery in Congo, is a different phenomenon and refers to practices knowingly employed by malevolent agents to diminish another's life force. On the prevalence of sorcery beliefs in Brazzaville, see *Jeune Afrique-L'Intelligent* (2004).

27. On the occult and Congolese politics, see Bernault (2005, 2010), Eaton (2006), and Gruénais, Mouanda Mbambi, and Tonda (1995).

28. On the entrepreneur's social dilemma in Southeast Asia, see Geertz (1963) and Foster (1974).

29. On religious conversion and enterprise, see A. Cohen (1969), Dorier-Apprill (2001), Dzaka and Milandou (1994), and Portes and Landolt (1996); on Islamic reformism and commerce in West Africa, see Amselle (1985), Kaba (1974), and Warms (1992); on secular associations and enterprise, see Meagher (2005).

30. Vuarin (1997) discusses the stresses Malians face pertaining to demands from kin. Chinese commercial success in Bamako has been documented by Bourdarias (2009) and Kernen and Vulliet (2008). As Granovetter (1995) shows, the association between commerce and out-

siders applies to many settings outside Africa as well. For instance, "the merchant is always a stranger" appears as a chapter title in Prashad's (2001) study of Afro-Asian cultural connections.

31. On Congolese entrepreneurs abroad, see MacGaffey and Bazenguissa-Ganga (2000), Douma (2003), and Dzaka (2001); on laws restricting the Congolese labor market, see Syfia Congo (2006); and on Pentecostalism in Brazzaville, see Dorier-Apprill (2001) and Missié (2007).

32. See a similar account of Ghanaian labor preferences and restrictions in G. Clark (2010:169–170).

33. Indeed, *danbe* may be equated with ascribed status (Koné 2010).

34. On French co-development programs, see Daum (2002) and Gubert (2008); on France's accord with Congo, see Nkou (2007).

35. On downward-leveling norms, see Portes (1998) and Meagher (2006:572); on social relations as a deterrent to AIDS testing, see Steinberg (2008); and on social relations as a double-edged sword, see Portes (1998) and Portes and Landolt (1996).

3. Among the Unbelievers

1. See Soares (2005b:52–54) on the development of this perception among French colonizers in West Africa, who took what they called *l'Islam noir,* or "black Islam," to be distinct from true Islam.

2. This proverb is quoted by Kepel (1987:131).

3. For an overview of Islam's history in West Africa, see Levtzion (2000).

4. The "Suwarian tradition" was first discussed by Wilks (1968). Detailed discussions of the Suwarian tradition have also been published by Launay (1990, 1992), Levtzion (2000), and Wilks (2000).

5. On the relationship between faith and politics in Muslim West Africa, see Gérard (1997), Launay (1990, 1992), and Levtzion (1978).

6. This is not to imply that interpretations of Islam across the region were uniform or even particularly stable during the pre-colonial period. Scholars trained in the Arabian Peninsula mounted a number of challenges to prevailing clerical authority, including *jihad* movements in the eighteenth and nineteenth centuries (cf. Robinson 2000). Another crucial development in the shaping of West African Islam was the spread of Sufi brotherhoods from North Africa, beginning with the Qadiriyya in the eighteenth century and assuming its fullest expression with the expansion of the Tijaniyya in the nineteenth and early twentieth centuries (cf. Cruise O'Brien and Coulon 1988).

7. On the contradictory relationship between French colonialism and Islam, see Cruise O'Brien (1967), Hiskett (1984), and Triaud (2000).

8. See Kaba (1974) and Launay (1990) on increased mobility for West African Muslims throughout the twentieth century.

9. See Amselle (1985) and Kaba (1974) on the spread of Arab-influenced Islamic reformism in the western Sahel.

10. On West Africa's "Islamic sphere," see Launay and Soares (1999) and Soares (2004, 2005b). "Arabized" Islam is a term adopted by LeBlanc (1999, 2000) based on her research in Côte d'Ivoire. A global trend toward Islamic standardization is observed by Lapidus (2001).

11. See Martin (2009) on the history of Catholicism in Congo.

12. On "Wahhabism" and Islamic fundamentalism in West Africa, see Amselle (1985), Kaba (1974), and Piga (2003). The problem with the label "Wahhabi," beyond its connotations in Western news media with violent Saudi-backed jihadists, is that the Muslims to whom it is ap-

plied usually think of themselves simply as followers of the Sunna—the example set by the Prophet Muhammad—and not of the label's namesake, the eighteenth-century Saudi-born reformist Muhammad bin 'Abd al-Wahhab (cf. Algar 2002). The term "fundamentalist," originating in American Protestantism, privileges certain scriptural interpretations as more authentic, accurate, or "fundamental" than others, thus obscuring the highly flexible, contingent, and dynamic nature of such interpretations.

13. I place this name in quotation marks throughout this text because one could interpret the word "Sunni," as reformists tend to apply it to themselves and to their mosques, to suggest that other Muslims in Brazzaville are *not* Sunni or do not follow the Sunna, an implication many of my informants would find offensive.

14. On the leadership crisis in Kinshasa's mosque, see Manchuelle (1987:452–454). Most of my historical descriptions of Brazzaville's Muslim places of worship are drawn from Kane (n.d.). The pioneering role of migrants returning from Congo in spreading Islamic reformism in the Senegal River Valley is discussed by Timera (2003).

15. For examples of heightened religiosity among Muslim migrants, see Rouch (1956) on Ghana, Kepel (1987) on France, R. Mandel (1990) on Germany, and D'Alisera (2004) on the United States.

16. In the Bamanan language, to find out whether someone is Muslim one asks not "Are you Muslim?" but rather "Do you pray?"

17. According to a hadith cited by my informants, women are discouraged from praying in mosques, although according to one Islamic legal tradition they should not be prevented from doing so (cf. Mahmood 2005:87n14). Their attendance at mosques both in Mali and in Brazzaville is therefore quite low and limited to reformist mosques.

18. See Soares (2005a) on the enduring separation of religious and political power in Mali.

19. The Tablīghī Jamāʿat is an apolitical organization founded in India in the 1920s that aims to bring about a global Islamic society through the reformation of individual conduct; see Metcalf (1993) and Janson (2005).

20. The role of religion in integrating immigrants to the United States is discussed by Herberg (1955) and Levitt (2007). Kepel (1987) examines the specific role played by Islam in integration processes in France.

4. The Stranger's Code

1. As we shall see, non-African residents of Congo, such as Europeans and Asians, are generally in a separate category of strangerhood entailing expectations and obligations quite different from those applied to foreign African residents. On the powerlessness of Pan-Africanist discourse in the face of rising xenophobia, see Kersting (2009).

2. Fassin (1994:769) discusses the way immigrants from the former Zaire have been blamed for spreading HIV in Brazzaville. See West (1972:267) on the early demonizing of *Zaïrois* by Brazzaville residents. Migrants from Congo-Kinshasa have long confronted similarly negative stereotypes in Angola, where the Portuguese word *zaïrense* became "synonymous with marginality and delinquency, non-respect for established state economic rules . . . , unlawfulness and affronts to 'good morality'" (Mabeko-Tali 2003:200).

3. Some informants claimed that the Soninke verb *wara*, meaning "to put down, leave alone," shouted by some immigrant shopkeepers urging Congolese customers not to handle their merchandise, was eventually appropriated by Congolese and applied generally to West Africans.

4. These informal rules could be described as the "politics of the belly" (Bayart 2009) or as the "instrumentalization of disorder" (Chabal and Daloz 1999).

5. On the killing of Father Angelo Radelli, see Panapress (2005).

6. The high costs of legality for migrants fuel the problem of illegality, in Congo as elsewhere (cf. de Soto 1989; MacGaffey and Bazenguissa-Ganga 2000).

7. On the victimization of African migrants within the African continent by border guards, police, and traffickers, see the British Broadcasting Corporation (BBC) (2005), IRIN (2005), *New African* (2007), and Saleh (2010).

8. The number of deportees cited in *L'Essor* (1977) included 2,737 Malians, 2,364 Senegalese, 577 Beninese, and 489 Mauritanians.

9. In Bamako, *L'Essor* (1977) opined that "the prime mover in this expulsion" had been the expansion of Congolese state control over the national economy.

10. The next largest categories of stereotypes listed by survey respondents were lawlessness/corruption, with forty-one, and *méchanceté*, or wickedness, with thirty-nine cases; other popular categories included violence and racism.

11. On Congolese state dealings with arms merchants and offshore banks, see Harel (2006); on the Sassou family's control of Congo's economy, see Dulin and Merckaert (2009:19).

12. Gary-Tounkara (2008:226–233) recounts incidents of immigrant workers being deported from Côte d'Ivoire simply for expressing political opinions or asking for better working conditions.

13. Compare to Chua (2003:282).

14. Kinshasa natives' resentment toward West Africans is documented by Bredeloup (2007:156) and Manchuelle (1987:455). See Bredeloup (1994) and Gondola (2003) on expulsions of immigrants from Congo-Kinshasa during this period.

15. Moukoko (1999:31) identifies arrogance as "one of the attributes of the Congolese political elite" (see also Bazenguissa-Ganga 1997:167); initially based on the educational distinctions of a privileged few, this prerogative soon came to be justified by purely political privileges.

16. As noted in chapters 2 and 3, these same aspects also help West Africans preserve their commercial niche in the host economy.

17. See Bonacich (1973:589–592) on the inevitability of conflict between middleman minorities and their hosts.

18. See the analysis by Douglas (1984) of "purity and danger," as well as Baumann's (1997) discussion of purity and strangers.

19. On the role of international soccer matches as an impetus to xenophobic violence in Africa, see Whitehouse (2009).

5. Transnational Kinship

1. The distinction between "transnationality" and "transnationalism" is unclear, but scholars favor the latter term and I use it exclusively here.

2. Examples of nonmigrant transnationalism are discussed in Levitt and Waters (2002).

3. Portes (2001, 2003; Portes, Guarnizo, and Haller 2002) constructs transnationalism around physical mobility, whereas Itzigsohn et al. (1999) and Jackson, Crang, and Dwyer (2004) prefer a broader approach.

4. This reckoning is frequently incorrect: with the $600 Mamadou had at the start of his trip, he could have purchased one-way airfare to Brazzaville and a Congolese entry visa.

5. I place the term "undocumented" in quotation marks, because Mamadou's example illustrates that even those who supposedly lack documents often have legitimate forms of documentation but are unable or unwilling to provide them to the political authorities of the host country.

6. See Hondagneu-Sotelo and Avila (1997) on the "mobility bias" of research on transnationalism. The "full house" concept comes from Stephen Jay Gould by way of James Ferguson (1999:42).

7. See Goldring (1999) and Levitt and de la Dehesa (2003) for examples of these and similar programs sponsored by sending-country governments in Mexico and the Caribbean.

8. From the DGME website at http://www.maliensdelexterieur.gov.ml.

9. Many Africanist scholars have challenged the validity of the "civil society" paradigm in Africa; see Chabal and Daloz (1999: chap. 2) and Ferguson (2006: chap 4).

10. Notable schisms have affected HCME chapters in New York (*L'Essor* 2005) and France (Panapress 2006); several chapters have seen the formation of rival executive councils (*L'Indépendant* 2009).

11. On rural-to-urban migration in West Africa, see Gugler (1971, 2002), Little (1957, 1965), Piot (1999), and Trager (2001).

12. For example, the official site of a Mauritanian Soninke village is http://www.diaguily.org; the Association des Travailleurs Maliens du Sambaga en France (http://www.atmsf.fr.st) represents the France-based workers of a village in western Mali. See Daum (2000) on the proliferation of Malian hometown associations; see Le Guay (2002) on sister-city relationships between Malian and French communities. On hometown associations in other settings, see Mazzucato and Kabkia (2009) and Mercer, Page, and Evans (2009).

13. See *Jeune Afrique–L'Intelligent* (2005) and Sow (2005) on Koniakary's associational ties with its migrants and their communities of residence in France.

14. The association between female mobility and prostitution is discussed in Findley (1994) and Ba (2002, 2003). When asked about their plans and how long they wished to stay, women interviewees almost invariably replied that the matter was entirely up to their husbands, or to God—although many women hastened to add that if their husbands said they were to return to West Africa, they would pack their bags and be ready to leave the next day.

15. These surveys were conducted by Condé et al. (1986) and Pollet and Winter (1971).

16. Bredeloup (1994, 1995b, 2002) observes the utility of polygamous marriage among diamond traders and the advantages afforded these traders by marrying into elite families in their host countries. I noticed during my fieldwork that West African wives outnumber non–West African wives in such households.

17. See also Fainzang and Journet (1988) and Razy (2007) on steps taken by Sahelian migrants in France to shield their children from French cultural influences.

18. Transnational motherhood has been documented in other contexts by Hondagneu-Sotelo and Avila (1997) and Silvey (2006). Bledsoe (1990), Findley and Diallo (1988), and Isiugo-Abanihe (1985) discuss the practice of child fostering in West African societies. For descriptions of Chinese "parachute" and "satellite" kids, see Waters (2005:365) and Zhou (1998). On Filipina transnational mothers, see Parreñas (2005), and on the role of extended kin in transnational parenting of Caribbean children, see Chamberlain (1999). George (2005:166–167) discusses transnational care arrangements for children of migrant nurses from Kerala, India.

19. For cases of U.S.-based immigrant parents sending children home, see Matthei and Smith (1998) on Belize, Menjivar (2002) on Guatemala, Orellana et al. (2001) on Yemen and Korea, and Viruell-Fuentes (2006) on Mexico.

20. The *madrasa* in the western Sahel is a hybrid educational institution with little resemblance to its homonym in South Asia. See Brenner (2001) on the emergence of this institution in Mali during the twentieth century.

6. Children of Exile

1. This claim was, unfortunately, all too credible; see *New York Times* (2007) on the collapse of services at this hospital because of government mismanagement and corruption.

2. Journalistic standards in every aspect of this case were low: the few local reporters and bloggers who covered Doucouré's killing at all either misreported the victim's name, age, and other crucial information (*Afriqu'Echos Magazine* 2005; Mwinda.org 2005) or omitted such details altogether (*La Semaine Africaine* 2005c). An annual U.S. government human rights report (Department of State 2007) described the anonymous victim merely as a "Malian businessman" and mistakenly put his death in September rather than December. Nobody who reported on the incident had apparently spoken to anyone who knew the victim or the precise circumstances of his death.

3. See Dantioko (2003) for a Soninke definition of *tabuusi*, and Diaby (2003) for a Bamanan definition of *tabusi*.

4. See Dougnon (2007: chap. 4) for similar views regarding Dogon migrants in Ghana.

5. Similarly Dougnon (2007:226) finds that children born to Malian immigrants in Ghana often hope to emigrate to Europe or North America, as they are unable to relate to their parents' country of origin and see limited prospects for themselves in Ghana.

6. See Bazenguissa-Ganga (1997:203) on this incident.

7. The distinction between "bright" and "blurred" cultural boundaries is discussed by Alba (2005).

8. The concept of cultural bifocality was introduced by Rouse (1991) and further explored by Levitt (2001).

9. Notable Western political scientists (e.g., Bayart 2009; Chabal and Daloz 1999) have applied this critique broadly to postcolonial African states. See Bayart (2009:138–140) and Bazenguissa-Ganga (1997) on the specific case of the Congolese state.

10. See Missié (2005) on the "dieback of the state" and the survival strategies of the growing number of Congolese excluded from their country's wealth.

11. Accounts of voting irregularities and false voting documents can be found in Mwinda.org (2009) and *La Semaine Africaine* (2009a). The problem of improperly obtained citizenship documents is widespread throughout the developing world; see Sadiq (2009).

12. See the review by Ceuppens and Geschiere (2005), as well as Geschiere (2009).

Conclusion

1. On host-immigrant tensions in South Africa, see Coplan (2009), Danso and McDonald (2001), Hassim, Kupe, and Worby (2008), Landau and Misago (2009), Morris and Bouillon (2001), and Nyamnjoh (2006). On expulsions from Equatorial Guinea, see *Les Echos* (2006); on expulsions from Mozambique, see Agence de Presse Panafricaine (2008); on Libya, see BBC (2010) and Manson (2011).

2. Reports of Angola's expulsion of Congolese were carried by AFP (2009) and *Dépêches de Brazzaville* (2009); the regional politics behind this measure was discussed in *Africa Confidential* (2009, 2010) and IRIN (2010a).

3. Most victims of these attacks have specially been Hausa from Niger and Nigeria; see J.-J. Mandel (2008).

4. Recurring waves of migrant expulsions by African governments are detailed by Brédeloup (1995a), Peil (1971), and Perouse de Montclos (2002).

5. On the case of Gabon, see also Loungou (2003) and Pambo-Loueya (2003). On the 1964 expulsion from Congo-Kinshasa, see Gondola (2003); on rising "Afro-phobia" in South Africa, see Gqola (2008).

6. See Lambert (2002) and Piot (2010) on desires for displacement among young people in Senegal and Togo, respectively.

7. See Ba (2008) and IRIN (2006) on the social pressures on West African youth to emigrate.

8. President Nicolas Sarkozy's policy of *immigration choisie*, or selective immigration, which aimed to admit skilled migrants while excluding others, sparked one Congolese commentator to advocate similar restrictions in Congo (Mwinda.org 2008).

9. On the politics of belonging in contemporary Africa, see Geschiere (2009), Lonsdale (2008), Manby (2009), and Ndlovu-Gatsheni (2009).

10. The return of a migrant's remains to their communities of origin is a theme explored in Cohen and Odhiambo (1992), Geschiere (2009: chap. 2), Piot (1999), and D. Smith (2004).

11. On chiefs, land tenure, and strangers in Kumasi, see Berry (2001).

12. The integration of strangers is a theme explored by Berry (2001), Schildkrout (1970), and Wilson (1979), and Geschiere (2009) discusses the tension between origin myths and native status.

13. See the analyses by Bledsoe (1980) and Guyer (1995) on the relationship between wealth in people and wealth in things.

14. For a regional perspective on this dynamic, see Kuba and Lentz (2006).

15. See the discussion in Malkki (1992).

16. Mamdani (1996, 2001) has provided the most thorough elaboration of this analysis.

17. See also Kuba and Lentz (2006), and Dorman, Hammett, and Nugent (2007).

18. On land conflict in Côte d'Ivoire, see Bøås (2009); on Cameroon, see Geschiere (2004, 2009).

19. Ghana has made some progress in this regard: see Kobo (2010).

20. Market women in Kumasi, Ghana, similarly construct retiring to one's village as a "powerful symbol of failure and destitution in old age" (G. Clark 2010:224).

21. See Linger (2003) on the pitfalls of the diasporic concept among Brazilian citizens of Japanese descent.

22. See Geschiere (2009) on the appeal of nativism. The aspiration for transnational mobility among Africa's youth across the globe is reflected in Piot's (2010) discussion of the overwhelming demand in Togo for U.S. entry visas. Nor is this desire particular to Africa: a survey of three thousand teenagers in ten cities throughout the world found that four out of five believed that people should be able to live in any country they choose, and two out of three personally hoped to emigrate to secure a better future. One in seven, moreover, claimed to be willing to risk his or her life in order to emigrate (BBC 2006).

23. On differentiated mobility see Massey (1993:62) and Bauman, who writes, "mobility has become the most powerful and most coveted stratifying factor; the stuff of which the new, increasingly world-wide social, political, economic and cultural hierarchies are daily built and rebuilt" (1998:9).

Epilogue

1. See *Le Monde* (2008) on the decline of Brazzaville's port, and Inter Press Service (2007) on the Congolese economy's increasing reliance on oil revenue.

2. Reports by various NGOs highlight persistent, widespread poverty and food insecurity throughout the country, raising doubts over whether "pro-poor" growth was possible in Congo (Africa Info 2011; International Food Policy Research Institute 2010; Secours Catholique 2011).

Bibliography

Adams, Adrian. 1977. *Le long voyage des gens du fleuve.* Paris: Maspero.
Africa Confidential. 2009. "Throwing Out the Neighbours." Vol. 50, no. 22 (November 6): 7–8.
———. 2010. "At Stake: Oil, Migrants and Gemstones." Vol. 51, no. 22 (November 5): 2.
Africa Info. 2011. "Congo-Brazzaville: Plus de 80% des congolais mangent une seule fois la journée." May 27. http://fr.allafrica.com/stories/201105270761.html, accessed June 3, 2011.
Afriqu'Echos Magazine. 2005. "Congo-Brazzaville: Un Malien abattu par la police: la communauté ouest-africaine profondément indignée." December 20. http://www.afriquechos.ch/article.php3?id_article=1062, accessed October 2, 2009.
Agence Congolaise d'Information (ACI). 1977. "Clôture du séminaire des gérants de boutiques à commissions." Press Release, October 13.
Agence France Presse. 2004. "Le FMI félicite le Congo pour la mise en œuvre de son programme de référence." August 23. http://www.africatime.com/congo/popup.asp?no_nouvelle=137814, accessed August 27, 2004.
———. 2009. "16.000 Congolais expulsés d'Angola depuis août." October 7. http://www.maliweb.net/category.php?NID=51368&intr, accessed October 12, 2009.
———. 2010. "Congo: 5.000 fonctionnaires 'introuvables,' la masse salariale réduite." December 30. http://www.africa1.com/spip.php?article6330, accessed December 30, 2010.
Agence de Presse Panafricaine. 2008. "85 Maliens expulsés du Mozambique endommageant l'avion qui les ramène à Bamako." January 15. http://www.apanews.net/apa.php?page=show_article&id_article=52022, accessed March 6, 2008.
Agier, Michel. 1983. *Commerce et sociabilité: les négociants soudanais du quartier zongo de Lomé (Togo).* Paris: ORSTOM.
Alba, Richard. 2005. "Bright vs. Blurred Boundaries: Second-Generation Assimilation and Exclusion in France, Germany, and the United States." *Ethnic and Racial Studies* 28, no. 1: 20–49.
Algar, Hamid. 2002. *Wahhabism: A Critical Essay.* Oneonta: Islamic Publications International.
Alis, Harry. 1894. *Nos Africains.* Paris: Hachette.
Amin, Samir. 1969. *Le monde des affaires Sénégalais.* Paris: Éditions de Minuit.
Amselle, Jean-Loup. 1985. "Le Wahabisme à Bamako (1945–1985)." *Canadian Journal of African Studies* 19, no. 2: 345–357.

Anderson, Benedict. 1983. *Imagined Communities: Reflections on the Origin and Spread of Nationalism*. London: Verso.
Appiah, Kwame Anthony. 1997. "Cosmopolitan Patriots." *Critical Inquiry* 23, no. 3: 617–639.
———. 2006. *Cosmopolitanism: Ethics in a World of Strangers*. New York: Norton.
Arrow, Kenneth J. 1999. "Observations on Social Capital." In *Social Capital: A Multifaceted Perspective*, ed. P. Dasgupta and I. Serageldin, 3–5. Washington, DC: World Bank.
Arthur, John A. 2010. *African Diaspora Identities: Negotiating Culture in Transnational Migration*. Lanham, MD: Lexington Books.
Ba, Cheikh Oumar. 1995. "Un exemple d'essoufflement de l'immigration sénégalaise: les sénégalais au Cameroun." *Mondes en développement* 23, no. 91: 31–44.
———. 2002. "Les migrantes de la moyenne vallée du fleuve Sénégal: un groupe marginalisé." In *Les migrations au féminin*, ed. M. Charef, 193–208. Agadir: Éditions Sud Contact.
———. 2003. "Les Sénégalaises en Afrique centrale: de la migration d'accompagnement à l'émergence des groupes de femmes autonomes." In *Être étranger et migrant en Afrique au XXe siècle: Enjeux identitaires et modes d'insertion*, Vol. 2, *Dynamiques migratoires, modalités d'insertion urbaine et jeux d'acteurs*, ed. C. Coquery-Vidrovitch, O. Goerg, I. Mande, and F. Rajaonah, 279–292. Paris: L'Harmattan.
———. 2008. "Les tendances migratoires clandestines en Afrique de l'Ouest: Etudes de cas du Ghana, Mali, Mauritanie et Sénégal." Report of the Open Society Initiative for West Africa (OSIWA).
Bailleul, Charles. 2000. *Dictionnaire Bambara-Français*. Bamako: Éditions Donniya.
———. 2005. *Sagesse Bambara: Proverbes et sentences*. Bamako: Éditions Donniya.
Bakewell, Oliver. 2008. "In Search of the Diasporas within Africa." *African Diaspora* 1, no. 1: 5–27.
———. 2009. "South-South Migration and Human Development: Reflections on African Experiences." United Nations Development Programme Human Development Reports, Research Paper 2009/07.
Balandier, Georges. 1966. *Ambiguous Africa*. Trans. H. Weaver. London: Chatto and Windus.
———. 1985. *Sociologie des Brazzavilles noires*. 2nd ed. Paris: Presses de la Fondation Nationale des Sciences Politiques.
Barou, Jacques. 2001. "La famille à distance: Nouvelles strategies familiales chez les immigrés d'Afrique Sahélienne." *Hommes et migrations* 1232 (July–August): 16–25.
Barten, Janneke. 2009. *Families in Movement: Transformation of the Family in Urban Mali, with a Focus on Intercontinental Mobility*. Leiden: African Studies Centre.
Barth, Frederik. 1998 [1969]. *Ethnic Groups and Boundaries: The Social Organization of Cultural Difference*. Long Grove: Waveland.
Bauman, Zygmunt. 1997. *Postmodernity and Its Discontents*. New York: New York University Press.
———. 1998. *Globalization: The Human Consequences*. Cambridge: Polity.
Bayart, Jean-François. 2000. "Africa in the World: A History of Extraversion." *African Affairs* 99:217–67.
———. 2009. *The State in Africa: The Politics of the Belly*. 2nd ed. Trans. M. Harper, C. Harrison, and E. Harrison. Malden: Polity.
Bayart, Jean-François, Stephen Ellis, and Béatrice Hibou. 1999. *The Criminalization of the State in Africa*. Bloomington: Indiana University Press.
Bazenguissa-Ganga, Rémy. 1997. *Les voies du politique au Congo: Essai de sociologie historique*. Paris: Karthala.

Belloncle, Guy. 1981. *Le caïman et le tronc d'arbre: Carnets de brousse maliens*. Paris: L'Harmattan.

Bernault, Florence. 1996. *Démocraties ambiguës en Afrique centrale, Congo-Brazzaville, Gabon: 1940–1965*. Paris: Karthala.

———. 2000. "The Political Shaping of Sacred Locality in Brazzaville, 1959–97." In *Africa's Urban Past*, ed. D. Anderson and R. Rathbone, 283–302. Portsmouth, NH: Heinemann.

———. 2005. "Magie, sorcellerie et politique au Congo-Brazzaville et au Gabon." In *Démocratie et mutations culturelles en Afrique noire*, ed. M. Mbekale, 21–43. Paris: L'Harmattan.

———. 2010. "Colonial Bones: The 2006 Burial of Savorgnan de Brazza in the Congo." *African Affairs* 109/436: 367–390.

Berry, Sara. 1992. "Hegemony on a Shoestring: Indirect Rule and Access to Agricultural Land." *Africa* 62, no. 3: 327–355.

———. 2001. *Chiefs Know Their Boundaries: Essays on Property, Power, and the Past in Asante, 1986–1996*. Portsmouth, NH: Heinemann.

———. 2006. "Privatization and the Politics of Belonging in West Africa." In *Land and the Politics of Belonging in West Africa*, ed. R. Kuba and C. Lentz, 241–263. Boston: Brill.

Bertoncello, Brigitte, and Sylvie Bredeloup. 2007. "The Emergence of New African 'Trading Posts' in Hong Kong and Guangzhou." *China Perspectives* 2007, no. 1: 94–105.

Bertrand, Monique. 2009. "Les migrants internationaux dans les villes ouest-africaines." *Politique Africaine* 114:156–170.

Beuving, J. Joost. 2006. "Lebanese Traders in Cotonou: A Socio-Cultural Analysis of Economic Mobility and Capital Accumulation." *Africa* 76, no. 3: 325–351.

Bibeau, Gilles. 1975. "La communauté musulmane de Kisangani." In *Kisangani, 1876–1976: Histoire d'une ville*, ed. B. Vergaegen, 181–238. Kinshasa: Presse Universitaire Zaïroise.

Blalock, Hubert M. 1967. *Toward a Theory of Minority-Group Relations*. New York: Wiley.

Bledsoe, Caroline. 1980. *Women and Marriage in Kpelle Society*. Stanford, CA: Stanford University Press.

———. 1990. "The Politics of Children: Fosterage and the Social Management of Fertility among the Mende of Sierra Leone." In *Births and Power: Social Change and the Politics of Reproduction*, ed. W. Handwerker, 81–100. Boulder, CO: Westview.

Bleek, Wolf. 1987. "Lying Informants: A Fieldwork Experience from Ghana." *Population and Development Review* 13, no. 2: 314–322.

Bøås, Morten. 2009. "'New' Nationalism and Autochthony—Tales of Origin as Political Cleavage." *Africa Spectrum* 2009, no. 1: 19–38.

Bonacich, Edna. 1973. "A Theory of Middleman Minorities." *American Sociological Review* 38:583–594.

Bonacich, Edna, and John Modell. 1980. *The Economic Basis of Ethnic Solidarity: Small Business in the Japanese American Community*. Berkeley: University of California Press.

Borgé, Jacques, and Nicolas Viasnoff. 1995. *Archives de l'Afrique noire*. Paris: Trinckvel.

Bourdarias, Françoise. 2009. "Mobilités chinoises et dynamiques sociales locales au Mali." *Politique Africaine* 113:28–54.

Bourdieu, Pierre. 1986. "The Forms of Capital." In *Handbook of Theory and Research for the Sociology of Education*, ed. J. Richardson, 241–258. New York: Greenwood.

Bredeloup, Sylvie. 1994. "L'aventure contemporaine des diamantaires sénégalais." *Politique Africaine* 56:77–93.

———. 1995a. "Expulsions des ressortissants ouest-africains au sein du continent africain (1954–1995)." *Mondes en développement* 23, no. 91: 117–121.

———. 1995b. "Les diamantaires de la vallée du Sénégal." In *Entreprises et entrepreneurs Africains*, ed. Y.-A. Fauré and S. Ellis, 219–227. Paris: Karthala.

———. 1998. "Le diamant, le commerçant du fleuve Sénégal et la ville." *Annales de la recherche urbaine* 78:95–102.

———. 1999. "La fièvre du diamante au temps des colonies (Afrique)." *Autrepart* 11:171–189.

———. 2002. "Femmes de diamantaires en migration: Entre isolement et aisance matérielle." In *Les migrations au féminin*, ed. M. Charef, 151–173. Agadir: Éditions Sud Contact.

———. 2007. *La Diams'pora du fleuve Sénégal: Sociologie des migrations africaines*. Paris: IRD Éditions.

Brenner, Louis. 2001. *Controlling Knowledge: Religion, Power, and Schooling in a West African Society*. Bloomington: Indiana University Press.

British Broadcasting Corporation (BBC). 2003. "Brazzaville—'World's Worst City.'" March 3. http://news.bbc.co.uk/2/hi/africa/2815105.stm, accessed January 5, 2007.

———. 2005. "Morocco Expels Migrants to Mali." October 12. http://news.bbc.co.uk/2/hi/africa/4333690.stm, accessed October 20, 2005.

———. 2006. "Youths Want No Migration Controls." December 4. http://news.bbc.co.uk/go/pr/fr/-/2/hi/in_depth/6198696.stm, accessed September 18, 2009.

———. 2010. "How Libya Became a Dead End for Migrants." June 17. http://news.bbc.co.uk/2/hi/world/africa/10338790.stm, accessed June 21, 2010.

Brousseau, Georges. 1925. *Souvenirs de la Mission Savorgnan de Brazza*. Paris: Société d'Éditions Géographiques, Maritimes et Coloniales.

Browning, Christopher R. 2009. "Illuminating the Downside of Social Capital: Negotiated Coexistence, Property Crime, and Disorder in Urban Neighborhoods." *American Behavioral Scientist* 52, no. 11: 1556–1578.

Brunschwig, Henri. 1966. *Brazza explorateur: L'ogooué, 1875–1879*. Paris: Mouton.

———. 1972. *Brazza explorateur: Les traités makoko, 1880–1882*. Paris: Mouton.

Burawoy, Michael. 2001. "Manufacturing the Global." *Ethnography* 2, no. 2: 147–159.

Burawoy, Michael, Joseph A. Blum, Sheba George, Zsuzsa Gille, Teresa Gowan, Lynne Haney, Maren Klawiter, Stephen Lopez, Sean Riain, and Millie Thayer. 2000. *Global Ethnography: Forces, Connections, and Imaginations in a Postmodern World*. Berkeley: University of California Press.

Calderisi, Robert. 2006. *The Trouble with Africa: Why Foreign Aid Isn't Working*. New York: Palgrave MacMillan.

Canut, Cécile, and Étienne Smith. 2006. "Pactes, alliances et plaisanteries: Pratiques locales, discours global." *Cahiers d'etudes africaines* 184: 687–754.

Carling, Jørgen. 2002. "Migration in the Age of Involuntary Immobility: Theoretical Reflections and Cape Verdean Experiences." *Journal of Ethnic and Migration Studies* 28, no. 1: 5–42.

Castles, Stephen. 2007. "Twenty-First-Century Migration as a Challenge to Sociology." *Journal of Ethnic and Migration Studies* 33, no. 3: 351–371.

Ceuppens, Bambi, and Peter Geschiere. 2005. "Autochthony: Local or Global? New Modes in the Struggle over Citizenship and Belonging in Africa and Europe." *Annual Review of Anthropology* 34:385–407.

Chabal, Patrick. 2009. *Africa: The Politics of Suffering and Smiling*. New York: Zed Books.

Chabal, Patrick, and Jean-Pascal Daloz. 1999. *Africa Works: Disorder as Political Instrument*. Bloomington: Indiana University Press.

Chamberlain, Mary. 1999. "The Family as Model and Metaphor in Caribbean Migration to Britain." *Journal of Ethnic and Migration Studies* 25, no. 2: 251–266.
Chamberlain, Mary, and Selma Leydesdorff. 2004. "Transnational Families: Memories and Narratives." *Global Networks* 4, no. 3: 227–241.
Chavannes, Charles de. 1929. "Le Sergent Sénégalais Malamine." *Annales de l'Académie des Sciences Coloniales* 3:159–187.
———. 1935. *Avec Brazza: Souvenirs de la Mission de l'Ouest Africaine (mars 1883–janvier 1886).* Paris: Plon.
———. 1937. *Le Congo Français: Ma collaboration avec Brazza (1886–1894). Nos relations jusqu'à sa mort (1905).* Paris: Plon.
Chua, Amy. 2003. *World on Fire: How Exporting Free Market Democracy Breeds Ethnic Hatred and Global Instability.* New York: Doubleday.
Cissé, Pierre. 2009. "Migration malienne au Cameroun: A la conquête du secteur informel." *Hommes et Migrations* 1279:38–51.
Clark, Gracia. 2010. *African Market Women: Seven Life Stories from Ghana.* Bloomington: Indiana University Press.
Clark, John F. 2005. "The Collapse of the Democratic Experiment in the Republic of Congo." In *The Fate of Africa's Democratic Experiments: Elites and Institutions,* ed. L. Villalón and P. VonDoepp, 96–125. Bloomington: Indiana University Press.
Cliggett, Lisa. 2005. *Grains from Grass: Aging, Gender, and Famine in Rural Africa.* Ithaca, NY: Cornell University Press.
Cohen, Abner. 1969. *Custom and Politics in Urban Africa.* Berkeley: University of California Press.
Cohen, David W., and E. S. Atieno Odhiambo. 1992. *Burying SM: The Politics of Knowledge and the Sociology of Power in Africa.* Portsmouth, NH: Heinemann.
Cohen, Robin. 1997. *Global Diasporas: An Introduction.* Seattle: University of Washington Press.
Coleman, James C. 1988. "Social Capital in the Creation of Human Capital," *American Journal of Sociology* 94:S95–120.
Comhaire, Jean. 1948. "Note sur les musulmans de Léopoldville." *Zaïre* 2, no. 3: 303–304.
Condé, Julien, Pap Diagne, N. G. Ouaidou, K. Boye, and A. Kader. 1986. *South-North International Migrations: A Case Study: Malian, Mauritanian, and Senegalese Migrants from Senegal River Valley to France.* Paris: Development Centre of the Organization for Economic Co-operation and Development.
Conrad, David, and Barbara Frank. 1995. *Status and Identity in West Africa: Nyamakalw of Mande.* Bloomington: Indiana University Press.
Cookey, S. J. S. 1965. "West African Immigrants in the Congo, 1885–1896." *Journal of the Historical Society of Nigeria* 3, no. 2: 261–270.
Cooper, Frederick. 2001. "What Is the Concept of Globalization Good For? An African Historian's Perspective." *African Affairs* 100:189–213.
Coplan, David B. 2009. "Innocent Violence: Social Exclusion, Identity, and the Press in an African Democracy." *Identities: Global Studies in Culture and Power* 16:367–389.
Coquery-Vidrovitch, Catherine. 1965. "Les idées économiques de Brazza et les premières tentatives de compagnies de colonisation au Congo Français, 1885–1898." *Cahiers d'etudes africaines* 17:57–82.
———. 1969a. "French Colonization in Africa to 1920: Administration and Economic Development." In *Colonialism in Africa, 1870–1960,* ed. L. Gann and P. Duignan, 1:165–198. Cambridge: Cambridge University Press.

———. 1969b. *Brazza et la Prise de Possession du Congo: La Mission de l'Ouest Africain, 1883–1885*. Paris: Mouton.

———. 2001. *Le Congo au temps des grandes compagnies concessionnaires, 1889–1930*. 2nd ed. Paris: Éditions de l'EHESS.

Cruise O'Brien, Donal B. 1967. "Towards an 'Islamic Policy' in French West Africa, 1854–1914." *Journal of African History* 8, no. 2: 303–316.

Cruise O'Brien, Donal B., and Christian Coulon. 1988. *Charisma and Brotherhood in African Islam*. Oxford: Clarendon.

Crush, Jonathan, and McDonald, David A. 2002. *Transnationalism and the New African Immigration to South Africa*. Toronto: Canadian Association of African Studies.

Curtin, Philip D. 1975. *Economic Change in Precolonial Africa: Senegambia in the Era of the Slave Trade*. Madison: University of Wisconsin Press.

D'Alisera, JoAnn. 2004. *An Imagined Geography: Sierra Leonean Muslims in America*. Philadelphia: University of Pennsylvania Press.

Danso, Ransford, and David A. McDonald. 2001. "Writing Xenophobia: Immigration and the Print Media in Post-Apartheid South Africa." *Africa Today* 48, no. 3: 115–137.

Dantioko, Oudiary Makan. 2003. *Dictionnaire Soninke—Français*. Bamako: Éditions Jamana.

Daum, Christophe. 2000. "Typologie des organisations de solidarité internationale issues de l'immigration." Paris: Groupe de recherches et d'études migrations et transformations sociales, Institut Panos, Ministère des Affaires Étrangères.

———. 2002. "Aides au 'retour volontaire' et reinsertion au Mali: un bilan critique." *Hommes et migrations* 1239:40–48.

Délégation Générale des Maliens de l'Extérieur (DGME). 2001. "Répartition des maliens de l'extérieur par juridictions (estimations 2001)." Bamako: Ministère des Affaires Etrangères et des Maliens de l'Extérieur.

Department of State. 2007. "2006 Human Rights Report: Republic of the Congo." Country Reports on Human Rights Practices. http://www.state.gov/g/drl/rls/hrrpt/2006/78729.htm, accessed December 19, 2010.

Dépêches de Brazzaville. 2007. "La société Congo-Tôle présente ses installations au ministre Emile Mabonzo." December 24. http://www.brazzaville-adiac.com/index.php?action=depeche&dep_id=19887&oldaction=liste&regpay_id=0&them_id=0&cat_id=3&ss_cat_id=0&LISTE_FROM=0&select_month=12&select_year=2007, accessed July 10, 2009.

———. 2009. "Le Congo décide de fermer sa frontière avec l'Angola." October 3. http://www.brazzaville-adiac.com/index.php?action=depeche&dep_id=33274&cat_id=2&oldaction=home&regpay_id=0, accessed October 5, 2009.

de Soto, Hernando. 1989. *The Other Path: The Invisible Revolution in the Third World*. New York: Harper and Row.

Devauges, Roland. 1977. *L'Oncle, le ndoki, et l'entrepreneur: la petite entreprise congolaise à Brazzaville*. Paris: ORSTOM.

Diaby, Moussa. 2003. *Lexique de Base Bamanankan—Français*. Bamako: Ministère de l'Education National.

Dobbin, Christine. 1996. *Asian Entrepreneurial Minorities: Conjoint Communities in the Making of the World Economy, 1570–1940*. Surrey: Curzon.

Dorier-Apprill, Elisabeth. 2001. "The New Pentecostal Networks of Brazzaville." In *Between Babel and Pentecost: Transnational Pentecostalism in Africa and Latin America*, ed. A. Corten and R. Marshall-Fratani, 293–308. Bloomington: Indiana University Press.

Dorier-Apprill, Elisabeth, Abel Kouvouama, and Christophe Apprill. 1998. *Vivre à Brazzaville: Modernité et crise au quotidien*. Paris: Karthala.
Dorman, Sara, Daniel Hammett, and Paul Nugent. 2007. *Making Nations, Creating Strangers: States and Citizenship in Africa*. Boston: Brill.
Douglas, Mary. 1984 [1966]. *Purity and Danger: An Analysis of Concepts of Pollution and Taboo*. New York: Routledge.
Dougnon, Isaie. 2007. *Travail de Blanc, travail de Noir: La migration des paysans dogon vers l'Office du Niger et au Ghana (1910–1980)*. Paris: Karthala.
———. 2009. "Migration for 'White Man's Work': An Empirical Rebuttal to Marxist Theory." *African Identities* 7, no. 3: 353–371.
Douma, Jean-Baptiste. 2003. *L'immigration congolaise en France: entre crises et recherche d'identité*. Paris: L'Harmattan.
Dulin, Antoine, and Jean Merckaert. 2009. "Biens mal acquis: A qui profite le crime?" Comité Catholique contre la Faim et pour le Développement. http://www.ccfd.asso.fr/BMA/img/PDF/BMA_totalBDcorrige.pdf, accessed July 16, 2009.
Dybowski, Jean. 1893. *La route du Tchad: Du Loango au Chari*. Paris: Firmin-Didot.
Dzaka, Théophile. 2001. "Formation à la culture entrepreneuriale et identité ethnique au Congo-Brazzaville chez les entrepreneurs bakongo: une analyse par la confiance et les réseaux sociaux." *Proceedings of the 7th Journées scientifiques du réseau thématique de la Recherche Entrepreneuriat*, 89–104, Agence Universitaire de la Francophonie, Mauritius, July 4–6, 2001.
Dzaka, Théophile, and Michel Milandou. 1994. "L'entrepreneuriat congolais à l'épreuve des pouvoirs magiques: une face cachée de la gestion culturelle du risque?" *Politique Africaine* 56:108–118.
———. 1995. "Entrepreneurs de Brazzaville: cinq réussites singulières." In *Entreprises et entrepreneurs africains*, ed. Y.-A. Fauré and S. Ellis, 89–97. Paris: Karthala.
Eaton, David. 2006. "Diagnosing the Crisis in the Republic of Congo." *Africa* 76, no. 1: 44–69.
Echenberg, Myron. 1991. *Colonial Conscripts: The Tirailleurs Sénégalais in French West Africa, 1857–1960*. Portsmouth, NH: Heinemann.
Eickelman, Dale F., and James Piscatori. 1996. *Muslim Politics*. Princeton, NJ: Princeton University Press.
Elyachar, Julia. 2002. "Empowerment Money: The World Bank, Non-Governmental Organizations, and the Value of Culture in Egypt." *Public Culture* 14, no 3: 493–513.
Englund, Harry, and Francis B. Nyamnjoh. 2004. *Rights and the Politics of Recognition in Africa*. London: Zed Books.
Fainzang, Sylvie, and Odile Journet. 1988. *La Femme de Mon Mari: étude ethnologique du mariage polygamique en Afrique et en France*. Paris: L'Harmattan.
Faist, Thomas. 2000. "Transnationalism in International Migration: Implications for the Study of Citizenship and Culture." *Ethnic and Racial Studies* 23, no. 2: 189–222.
Farmer, Paul. 1993. *AIDS and Accusation: Haiti and the Geography of Blame*. Berkeley: University of California Press.
Fassin, Didier. 1994. "Le domaine privé de la santé publique: Pouvoir, politique et sida au Congo." *Annales histoire science sociale* 4:745–775.
Fédération Internationale des Droits de l'Homme. 2004. "Rapport: Gestion de la rente pétrolière au Congo Brazzaville: mal gouvernance et violations des droits de l'homme." http://www.fidh.org/article.php3?id_article=1073, accessed July 16, 2009.
Ferguson, James. 1999. *Expectations of Modernity: Myths and Meanings of Urban Life on the Zambian Copperbelt*. Berkeley: University of California Press.

———. 2006. *Global Shadows: Africa in the Neoliberal World Order.* Durham, NC: Duke University Press.
Findley, Sally. 1994. "Does Drought Increase Migration? A Study of Migration from Rural Mali during the 1983–85 Drought." *International Migration Review* 28, no. 3: 539–553.
———. 2004. "Mali: Seeking Opportunity Abroad." Migration Policy Institute, http://www.migrationinformation.org/Profiles/display.cfm?ID=247, accessed December 16, 2009.
Findley, Sally, and Assitan Diallo. 1988. "Foster Children: Links between Urban and Rural Families?" Paper presented to the IUSSP African Population Conference, Dakar, November 7–12.
Findley, Sally, Dieudonné Ouedraogo, and Nassour Ouaidou. 1988. "From Seasonal Migration to International Migration: An Analysis of the Factors Affecting the Choices Made by Families of the Senegal River Valley." Dakar: IUSSP African Population Conference bulletin, November 1988, 4.3.39–53.
Findley, Sally, and Salif Sow. 1998. "From Season to Season: Agriculture, Poverty, and Migration in the Senegal River Valley, Mali." In *Emigration Dynamics in Developing Countries,* ed. R. Appleyard, 1:69–143. Brookfield, VT: Ashgate.
Fine, Ben. 1999. "The Developmental State Is Dead—Long Live Social Capital?" *Development and Change* 30:1–19.
———. 2001. *Social Capital versus Social Theory: Political Economy and Social Science at the Turn of the Millennium.* London: Routledge.
Fortes, Meyer. 1975. "Strangers." In *Studies in African Social Anthropology,* ed. M. Fortes and S. Patterson, 229–253. London: Academic Press.
Foster, Brian L. 1974. "Ethnicity and Commerce." *American Ethnologist* 1, no. 3: 447–448.
French, Howard. 1997. "Bamako Journal: Here, an Artist's Fame and Fortune Can Be Fatal." *New York Times,* September 11. http://www.nytimes.com/1997/09/11/world/bamako-journal-here-an-artist-s-fame-and-fortune-can-be-fatal.html, accessed July 16, 2009.
Gandoulou, Justin-Daniel, and Georges Balandier. 1989. *Dandies à Bacongo: Le culte de l'élégance dans la société congolaise contemporaine.* Paris: L'Harmattan.
Gary-Tounkara, Daouda. 2008. *Migrants soudanais/maliens et conscience ivoirienne: Les étrangers en Côte d'Ivoire (1903–1980).* Paris: L'Harmattan.
Geertz, Clifford. 1963. *Peddlers and Princes: Social Change and Economic Modernization in Two Indonesian Towns.* Chicago: University of Chicago Press.
Gellner, Ernest. 1983. *Nations and Nationalism.* Ithaca, NY: Cornell University Press.
George, Sheba Mariam. 2005. *When Women Come First: Gender and Class in Transnational Migration.* Berkeley: University of California Press.
Gérard, Étienne. 1997. "Les médersas: Un élément de mutation des sociétés ouest-africaines." *Politique Étrangère* 4 (winter): 613–627.
Geschiere, Peter. 1997. *The Modernity of Witchcraft: Politics and the Occult in Postcolonial Africa.* Charlottesville: University of Virginia Press.
———. 2004. "Ecology, Belonging, and Xenophobia: The 1994 Forest Law in Cameroon and the Issue of 'Community.'" In *Rights and the Politics of Recognition in Africa,* ed. H. Englund and F. Nyamnjoh, 237–261. New York: Zed Books.
———. 2009. *The Perils of Belonging: Autochthony, Citizenship, and Exclusion in Africa and Europe.* Chicago: University of Chicago Press.
Geschiere, Peter, and Francis B. Nyamnjoh. 2000. "Capitalism and Autochthony: The Seesaw of Mobility and Belonging." *Public Culture* 12, no. 2: 423–452.
Giddens, Anthony. 1990. *The Consequences of Modernity.* Cambridge: Polity/Blackwell.
———. 2000. *The Third Way and Its Critics.* Cambridge: Polity.

Glick Schiller, Nina, Linda Basch, and Christina Szanton Blanc. 1995. "From Immigrant to Transmigrant: Theorizing Transnational Migration." *Anthropological Quarterly* 68, no. 1: 48–63.

Glick Schiller, Nina, Ayş Çağlar, and Thaddeus C. Guldbrandsen. 2006. "Beyond the Ethnic Lens: Locality, Globality, and Born-Again Incorporation." *American Ethnologist* 33, no. 4: 612–633.

Global Witness. 2004. "Time for Transparency: Coming Clean on Oil, Mining, and Gas Revenues." http://www.globalwitness.org/reports/show.php/en.00049.html, accessed October 23, 2006.

———. 2005. "The Riddle of the Sphinx: Where Has Congo's Oil Money Gone?" http://www.globalwitness.org/reports/show.php/en.00084.html, accessed October 23, 2006.

Gluckman, Max. 1963. "Gossip and Scandal." *Current Anthropology* 4:307–316.

Goldring, Luin. 1999. "Power and Status in Transnational Social Spaces." In *Migration and Transnational Social Space*, ed. L. Pries, 162–186. Brookfield, VT: Ashgate.

Gomez, Michael. 2005. *Reversing Sail: A History of the African Diaspora*. New York: Cambridge University Press.

Gondola, Charles Didier. 1996. *Villes Miroirs: Migrations et identités urbaines à Kinshasa et Brazzaville, 1930–1970*. Paris: L'Harmattan.

———. 2003. "Bisso na Bisso: Entre Congolais à Kinshasa, ca. 1930–1964." In *Être étranger et migrant en Afrique au XXe siècle: Enjeux identitaires et modes d'insertion*, Vol. 2, *Dynamiques migratoires, modalités d'insertion urbaine et jeux d'acteurs*, ed. C. Coquery-Vidrovitch, O. Goerg, I. Mande, and F. Rajaonah, 77–96. Paris: L'Harmattan.

Gqola, Pumla Dineo. 2008. "Brutal Inheritances: Echoes, Negrophobia, and Masculinist Violence." In *Go Home or Die Here: Violence, Xenophobia, and the Reinvention of Difference in South Africa*, ed. S. Hassim, T. Kupe, and E. Worby, 209–221. Johannesburg: Wits University Press.

Grabowski, Richard. 1997. "Traders' Dilemmas and Development: A Variety of Solutions." *New Political Economy* 2, no. 3: 387–404.

Granovetter, Mark. 1995. "The Economic Sociology of Firms and Entrepreneurs." In *The Economic Sociology of Immigration*, ed. A. Portes, 128–165. New York: Russel Sage Foundation.

Gray, Christopher J. 1998. "Cultivating Citizenship through Xenophobia in Gabon, 1960–1995." *Africa Today* 45, no. 3–4: 389–410.

Grootaert, Christiaan. 1998. "Social Capital: The Missing Link?" Social Capital Initiative, Working Paper No. 3, World Bank. http://siteresources.worldbank.org/INTSOCIAL-CAPITAL/Resources/Social-Capital-Initiative-Working-Paper-Series/SCI-WPS-03.pdf, accessed July 21, 2009.

Gruénais, Marc-Eric, Florent Mouanda Mbambi, and Joseph Tonda. 1995. "Messies, fétiches et lutte de pouvoirs entre les "grands hommes" du Congo démocratique." *Cahiers d'etudes africaines* 137:163–193.

Gubert, Flore. 2008. "(In)coherence des politiques migratoires et de codéveloppement françaises." *Politique Africaine* 109:42–55.

Gugler, Josef. 1971. "Life in a Dual System: Eastern Nigerians in Town, 1961." *Cahiers d'etudes africaines* 11:400–429.

———. 2002. "The Son of the Hawk Does Not Remain Abroad: The Urban-Rural Connection in Africa." *African Studies Review* 45, no. 1: 21–41.

Gupta, Akhil, and James Ferguson. 1997. "Beyond 'Culture': Space, Identity, and the Politics of Difference." In *Culture, Power, Place: Explorations in Critical Anthropology*, ed. A. Gupta and J. Ferguson, 33–51. Durham, NC: Duke University Press.

Guyer, Jane I. 1995. "Wealth in People, Wealth in Things—Introduction." *Journal of African History* 36:83–90.

Hannerz, Ulf. 1996. *Transnational Connections: Culture, People, Places.* New York: Routledge.

———. 1998. "Transnational Research." In *The Handbook of Methods in Cultural Anthropology,* ed. R. Bernard, 235–256. Walnut Creek, CA: Altamira.

Harel, Xavier. 2006. *Afrique, pillage à huis clos: Comment une poignée d'initiés siphonne le pétrole africain.* Paris: Fayard.

Harrison, Lawrence E. 1992. *Who Prospers? How Cultural Values Shape Economic and Political Success.* New York: Basic Books.

Harrison, Lawrence E., and Samuel P. Huntington. 2001. *Culture Matters: How Values Shape Human Progress.* New York: Basic Books.

Hart, Keith. 1970. "Small-Scale Entrepreneurs in Ghana and Development Planning." *Journal of Development Studies* 6, no. 3: 104–120.

———. 1975. "Swindler or Public Benefactor? The Entrepreneur in His Community." In *Changing Social Structure in Ghana: Essays in the Comparative Sociology of a New State and an Old Tradition,* ed. J. Goody, 1–35. London: International African Institute.

———. 1988. "Kinship, Contract, and Trust: The Economic Organization of Migrants in an African City Slum." In *Trust: Making and Breaking Cooperative Relationships,* ed. D. Gambetta, 176–193. New York: Blackwell.

Hassim, Shireen, Tawana Kupe, and Eric Worby. 2008. *Go Home or Die Here: Violence, Xenophobia, and the Reinvention of Difference in South Africa.* Johannesburg: Wits University Press.

Herberg, Will. 1955. *Protestant, Catholic, Jew: An Essay in Religious Sociology.* Garden City, NY: Doubleday.

Harries, Patrick. 1994. *Work, Culture, and Identity: Migrant Laborers in Mozambique and S. Africa, 1860–1910.* Portsmouth, NH: Heinemann.

Hiskett, Mervyn. 1984. *The Development of Islam in West Africa.* New York: Longman.

Hochschild, Adam. 1998. *King Leopold's Ghost: A Story of Greed, Terror, and Heroism in Central Africa.* New York: Houghton Mifflin.

Hondagneu-Sotelo, Pierrette, and Ernestine Avila. 1997. "'I'm Here, But I'm There': The Meanings of Latina Transnational Motherhood." *Gender and Society* 11, no. 5: 548–571.

Hung, G. Nguyen Tien. 1987. *Agriculture and Rural Development in the People's Republic of the Congo.* Boulder, CO: Westview.

Inda, Jonathan Xavier, and Renato Rosaldo. 2001. "Introduction: A World in Motion." In *The Anthropology of Globalization: A Reader,* ed. J. Inda and R. Rosaldo, 1–27. Malden, MA: Blackwell.

Initiative for Central Africa. 2004. "Focus on Cross-Border Exchanges between Brazzaville/Congo and Kinshasa/DRC." http://www.inica.org/webdocuments/EN/DOC%20AND%20MEDIA%20CENTER/CROSS-BORDER%20STUDIES/brazza-kin_en.pdf, accessed April 1, 2007.

Inter Press Service (IPS). 2007. "La société civile veut veiller à la transparence pétrolière." November 6. http://fr.allafrica.com/stories/200711060650.html, accessed November 8, 2007.

International Food Policy Research Institute. 2010. "Global Hunger Index." http://www.ifpri.org/publication/2010-global-hunger-index, accessed April 4, 2011.

International Monetary Fund (IMF). 2005. "Republic of Congo: Enhanced Heavily Indebted Poor Countries (HIPC) Initiative—Preliminary Document." IMF Country Report No. 05/391. http://www.imf.org/external/pubs/cat/longres.cfm?sk=18680.0, accessed August 11, 2006.

IQRA: Bulletin Mensuel Islamique de Formation et d'Informations Générales. 2001. "Une délégation du Conseil National Islamique à la Présidence." No. 7 (October): 4. Published in Brazzaville by the Islamic Council of Congo.

Isiugo-Abanihe, Uche C. 1985. "Child Fosterage in West Africa." *Population and Development Review* 11, no. 1: 53–73.

Itzigsohn, José, Carlos Dore Cabral, Esther Hernández Medina, and Obed Vázquez. 1999. "Mapping Dominican Transnationalism: Narrow and Broad Transnational Practices." *Ethnic and Racial Studies* 22, no. 2: 316–339.

Jackson, Peter, Philip Crang, and Claire Dwyer. 2004. "Introduction: The Spaces of Transnationality." In *Transnational Spaces*, ed. P. Jackson, 1–23. New York: Routledge.

Janson, Marloes. 2005. "Roaming about for God's Sake: The Upsurge of the *Tabligh Jama'at* in the Gambia." *Journal of Religion in Africa* 35, no. 4: 450–481.

Jeune Afrique–L'Intelligent. 2004. "Forte croyance au kindoki." February 23. http://www.lintelligent.com/articleImp.asp?art_cle=LIN22024forteikodnio, accessed February 25, 2004.

———. 2005. "Du Sahel à Paris." May 29. http://www.jeuneafrique.com/jeune_afrique/article_jeune_afrique.asp?art_cle=LIN29065dusahsirap10, accessed December 11, 2006.

Johnston, Gordon, and Janie Percy-Smith. 2003. "In Search of Social Capital." *Policy & Politics* 31, no. 3: 321–334.

Jonsson, Gunvor. 2008. "Migration Aspirations and Involuntary Immobility in a Malian Soninke Village." Working Paper No. 10, International Migration Institute, University of Oxford. http://www.imi.ox.ac.uk/pdfs/working-paper-10-migration-aspirations-and-immobility, accessed July 16, 2009.

Journal Officiel de l'AEF. 1938. Brazzaville: Imprimerie Officielle.

Kaba, Lansiné. 1974. *The Wahhabiyya: Islamic Reform and Politics in French West Africa*. Evanston, IL: Northwestern University Press.

———. 2000. "Islam in West Africa: Radicalism and the New Ethic of Disagreement, 1960–1990." In *The History of Islam in Africa*, ed. N. Levtzion and R. Pouwels, 189–208. Athens: Ohio University Press.

Kane, El Hajj Alioune. N.d. "Chronologie d'un siècle d'Islam au Congo." Unpublished manuscript.

Kane, Francine, and André Lericollais. 1975. "L'Émigration en Pays Soninké." *Cahiers ORSTOM* 12, no. 2: 177–187.

Kennedy, Paul. 1988. *African Capitalism: The Struggle for Ascendancy*. New York: Cambridge University Press.

Kepel, Gilles. 1987. *Les Banlieues de l'Islam: naissance d'une religion en France*. Paris: Éditions du Seuil.

Kernen, Antoine, and Benoit Vulliet. 2008. "Les petits commerçants et entrepreneurs chinois au Mali et au Sénégal." *Afrique Contemporaine* 228:69–94.

Kersting, Norbert. 2009. "New Nationalism and Xenophobia in Africa—a New Inclination?" *Africa Spectrum* 2009, no. 1: 7–18.

Kivisto, Peter. 2001. "Theorizing Transnational Immigration: A Critical Review." *Ethnic and Racial Studies* 24, no. 4: 549–577.

Kobo, Ousman. 2010. "'We Are Citizens Too': The Politics of Citizenship in Independent Ghana." *Journal of Modern African Studies* 48, no. 1: 67–94.

Koenig, Dolores. 2005. "Multilocality and Social Stratification in Kita, Mali." In *Migration and Economy: Global and Local Dynamics*, ed. L. Trager, 78–102. Walnut Creek, CA: Altamira.

Konadu-Agyemang, Kwado, Baffour K. Takyi, and John A. Arthur. 2006. *The New African Diaspora in North America: Trends, Community Building, and Adaptation.* Lanham, MD: Rowman & Littlefield.

Koné, Kassim. 2010. "The Lyrics and the Rhythm That Determined Bamanaya." Paper presented at the Annual Meeting of the African Studies Association, San Francisco.

Kopytoff, Igor. 1987. "The Internal African Frontier: The Making of African Political Culture." In *The African Frontier: The Reproduction of Traditional African Societies,* ed. I. Kopytoff, 3–84. Bloomington: Indiana University Press.

Kopytoff, Igor, and Suzanne Miers. 1977. "African 'Slavery' as an Institution of Marginality." In *Slavery in Africa: Historical and Anthropological Perspectives,* ed. S. Miers and I. Kopytoff, 3–81. Madison: University of Wisconsin Press.

Koser, Khalid. 2005. *New African Diasporas.* New York: Routledge.

Kotkin, Joel. 1993. *Tribes: How Race, Religion, and Identity Determine Success in the New Global Economy.* New York: Random House.

Kuba, Richard, and Carola Lentz. 2006. *Land and the Politics of Belonging in West Africa.* Boston: Brill.

Kubu Turé, Matondo. 2006. "Comment refaire la société? Les sociabilités horizontales de Brazzaville." In *Brazzaville, une ville à reconstruire,* ed. R. Ziavoula, 143–155. Paris: Karthala.

Lambert, Michael C. 2002. *Longing for Exile: Migration and the Making of a Translocal Community in Senegal, West Africa.* Portsmouth, NH: Heinemann.

Landau, Loren B., and Jean Pierre Misago. 2009. "Who to Blame and What's to Gain? Reflections on Space, State, and Violence in Kenya and South Africa." *Africa Spectrum* 2009, no. 1: 99–110.

Lapidus, Ira M. 2001. "Between Universalism and Particularism: The Historical Bases of Muslim Communal, National, and Global Identities." *Global Networks* 1, no. 1: 37–55.

La Semaine Africaine. 1977. "Seuls les Congolais doivent exercer le commerce de détail." October 2, no. 1273, 9.

———. 2005a. "La Force publique est responsable du pillage à Bacongo." November 3, no. 2543, 5.

———. 2005b. "Editorial: Pourquoi mettre nos opérateurs économiques à genoux?" December 13, no. 2550, 1.

———. 2005c. "Brazza, boutiques mortes!" December 16, no. 2551, 4.

———. 2008. "Des téléphones portables emportés par des militaires vandales à Brazzaville." December 30, no. 2855, 6.

———. 2009a. "Des jeunes se vantaient, avant le vote, de posséder plusieurs cartes d'électeurs." July 21, no. 2912, 6.

———. 2009b. "Les agents de la Force publique seraient-ils mal formés?" July 28, no. 2914, 6.

———. 2010a. "Les Congolais plus que jamais déçus par les délestages intempestifs." June 15, no. 3001, 3.

———. 2010b. "Un ressortissant malien menacé et extorqué de sa marchandise!" June 18, no. 3002, 6.

———. 2010c. "Spectaculaire vol à main armé, non loin de la mosquée de Moungali." September 7, no. 3024, 6.

———. 2010d. "Alphonse Ngatsé, président du C.n.l.d: 'Il faut réviser les conditions d'accès à la nationalité congolaise.'" September 7, no. 3024, 3.

Lasswell, Harold D. 1965. *World Politics and Personal Insecurity.* New York: Free Press.

Launay, Robert. 1977. "Joking Slavery." *Africa* 47, no. 4: 413–422.

———. 1990. "Pedigrees and Paradigms: Scholarly Credentials among the Dyula of the Northern Ivory Coast." In *Muslim Travelers: Pilgrimage, Migration, and the Religious*

Imagination, ed. D. Eickelman and J. Piscatori, 175–199. Berkeley: University of California Press.

———. 1992. *Beyond the Stream: Islam and Society in a West African Town*. Berkeley: University of California Press.

Launay, Robert, and Benjamin F. Soares. 1999. "The Formation of an 'Islamic Sphere' in French Colonial West Africa." *Economy and Society* 28, no. 4: 497–519.

Le Guay, Céline. 2002. "Entre St.-Denis et le Mali, une citoyenneté sur deux continents." *Hommes et migrations* 1239:33–39.

LeBlanc, Marie Nathalie. 1999. "The Production of Islamic Identities through Knowledge Claims in Bouaké, Côte d'Ivoire." *African Affairs* 98:485–508.

———. 2000. "Versioning Womanhood and Muslimhood: 'Fashion' and the Life Course in Contemporary Bouaké, Côte d'Ivoire." *Africa* 70, no. 3: 442–481.

Leichtman, Mara. 2005. "The Legacy of Transnational Lives: Beyond the First Generation of Lebanese in Senegal." *Ethnic and Racial Studies* 28, no. 4: 663–686.

Lentz, Carola. 2006. "Land Rights and the Politics of Belonging in Africa: An Introduction." In *Land and the Politics of Belonging in West Africa*, ed. R. Kuba and C. Lentz, 1–34. Boston: Brill.

Lenzen, Godehard. 1970. *The History of Diamond Production and the Diamond Trade*. Trans. F. Bradley. New York: Praeger.

Les Echos. 2006. "La chasse aux Maliens en Guinée équatoriale." March 22. http://www.malikounda.com/nouvelle_voir.php?idNouvelle=6662, accessed September 9, 2009.

L'Essor. 1977. "Expulsés: Une indemnisation promise mais difficile à confirmer." November 1, no. 7723; 3.

———. 2005. "Maliens de New-York: la fracture." No. 15607, December 26. http://www.essor.gov.ml/cgi-bin/view_article.pl?id=11497, accessed December 10, 2006.

Levitt, Peggy. 2001. *The Transnational Villagers*. Berkeley: University of California Press.

———. 2007. *God Needs No Passport: How Migrants Are Transforming the American Religious Landscape*. New York: New Press.

Levitt, Peggy, and Rafael de la Dehesa. 2003. "Transnational Migration and the Redefinition of the State: Variations and Explanations." *Ethnic and Racial Studies* 26, no. 4: 587–611.

Levitt, Peggy, and Nina Glick Schiller. 2004. "Conceptualizing Simultaneity: A Transnational Social Field Perspective on Society." *International Migration Review* 38, no. 3: 1002–1039.

Levitt, Peggy, and Mary Waters. 2002. "Introduction." In *The Changing Face of Home: The Transnational Lives of the Second Generation*, ed. P. Levitt and M. Waters, 1–30. New York: Russell Sage Foundation.

Levtzion, Nehemia. 1978. "Islam in West African Politics: Accommodation and Tension between the *'ulamā'* and the Political Authorities." *Cahiers d'etudes africaines* 71:333–345.

———. 2000. "Islam in the Bilad al-Sudan to 1800." In *The History of Islam in Africa*, ed. N. Levtzion and R. Pouwels, 63–91. Athens: Ohio University Press.

Li, Peter S. 1993. "Chinese Investment and Business in Canada: Ethnic Entrepreneurship Reconsidered." *Pacific Affairs* 66, no. 2: 219–243.

Light, Ivan, and Steven J. Gold. 2000. *Ethnic Economies*. San Diego, CA: Academic Press.

L'Indépendant. 2009. "Le nouveau président du HCME, Habib Sylla: 'Notre combat n°1 est de faire en sorte qu'il y ait un seul Conseil par pays.'" February 1. http://www.maliweb.net/category.php?NID=40830, accessed February 20, 2009.

Linger, Daniel T. 2003. "Do Japanese Brazilians Exist?" In *Searching for Home Abroad: Japanese Brazilians and Transnationalism*, ed. J. Lesser, 201–214. Durham, NC: Duke University Press.

Little, Kenneth. 1957. "The Role of Voluntary Associations in West African Urbanization." *American Anthropologist* 59:579–596.

———. 1965. *West African Urbanization: A Study of Voluntary Associations in Social Change.* Cambridge: Cambridge University Press.

Lonsdale, John. 2008. "Soil, Work, Civilisation, and Citizenship in Kenya." *Journal of Eastern African Studies* 2, no. 2: 305–314.

Loungou, Serge. 2003. "Immigration et xénophobie au Gabon." *Géopolitique Africaine* 10:251–266.

Mabeko-Tali, Jean-Michel. 2003. "'Congolenses,' 'Congoleses,' 'Zairenses': l'immigration centre-africaine et la problématique identitaire angolaise." In *Être étranger et migrant en Afrique*, Vol. 1, *Politiques migratoires et construction des identités*, ed. C. Coquery-Vidrovitch, O. Goerg, I. Mande, and F. Rajaonah, 189–206. Paris: L'Harmattan.

MacGaffey, Janet. 1987. *Entrepreneurs and Parasites: The Struggle for Indigenous Capitalism in Zaire.* New York: Cambridge University Press

MacGaffey, Janet, and Rémy Bazenguissa-Ganga. 2000. *Congo-Paris: Transnational Traders on the Margins of the Law.* Bloomington: Indiana University Press.

Mahmood, Saba. 2005. *The Politics of Piety: The Islamic Revival and the Feminist Subject.* Princeton, NJ: Princeton University Press.

Malkki, Liisa. 1992. "National Geographic: The Rooting of Peoples and the Territorialization of National Identity among Scholars and Refugees." *Cultural Anthropology* 7, no. 1: 24–44.

Mamdani, Mahmood. 1996. *Citizen and Subject: Contemporary Africa and the Legacy of Late Colonialism.* Princeton, NJ: Princeton University Press.

———. 2001. "Beyond Settler and Native as Political Identities: Overcoming the Political Legacy of Colonialism." *Comparative Studies in Society and History* 43, no. 4: 651–664.

Mampouya, Eric. 2009. "Le Far West du GENERALOCIDAIRE Jean François NDENGUET." http://www.congoinfos.com/article-le-far-west-du-generalocidaire-jean-francois-ndenguet-40301837.html, accessed November 30, 2009.

Manby, Bronwen. 2009. *Struggles for Citizenship in Africa.* New York: Zed Books.

Manchuelle, François. 1987. "Background to Black African Emigration to France: The Labor Migrations of the Soninke, 1848–1987." Ph.D. dissertation, Department of History, University of California, Santa Barbara.

———. 1997. *Willing Migrants: Soninke Labor Diasporas, 1848–1960.* Athens: Ohio University Press.

Mandel, Jean-Jacques. 2008. "Les rétrécisseurs de sexe: Chronique d'une rumeur sorcière." *Cahiers d'etudes africaines* 189–190:185–208.

Mandel, Ruth. 1990. "Shifting Centres and Emergent Identities: Turkey and Germany in the Lives of Turkish *Gastarbeiter*." In *Muslim Travellers: Pilgrimage, Migration, and the Religious Imagination*, ed. D. Eickelman and J. Piscatori, 153–171. Berkeley: University of California Press.

Mann, Gregory. 2006. *Native Sons: West African Veterans and France in the Twentieth Century.* Durham, NC: Duke University Press.

Manning, Patrick. 2009. *The African Diaspora: A History through Culture.* New York: Columbia University Press.

Manson, Katrina. 2011. "Sub-Saharan Africans Bear Brunt of Rebels' Ire." *Financial Times*, March 30. http://www.ft.com/cms/s/0/f4fff59c-560e-11e0-8de9-00144feab49a.html#axzz1I5pg3B8q, accessed March 30, 2011.

Marchés Tropicaux et Méditerranéens. 1977. "Mise au point officielle après les expulsions." September 30, 2766.

Marcus, George. 1998. *Ethnography through Thick and Thin.* Princeton, NJ: Princeton University Press.
Martin, Phyllis M. 1995. *Leisure and Society in Colonial Brazzaville.* New York: Cambridge University Press.
———. 2009. *Catholic Women of Congo-Brazzaville: Mothers and Sisters in Troubled Times.* Bloomington: Indiana University Press.
Massey, Doreen. 1993. "Power-Geometry and a Progressive Sense of Place." In *Mapping the Future: Local Cultures, Global Change,* ed. J. Bird, B. Curtis, T. Putnam, G. Robertson, and L. Tickner, 59–69. New York: Routledge.
Matthei, Linda Miller, and David A. Smith. 1998. "Belizean 'Boyz 'n the Hood'? Garifuna Labor Migration and Transnational Identity." In *Transnationalism from Below,* ed. M. Smith and L. Guarnizo, 270–290. New Brunswick, NJ: Transaction.
Mazzucato, Valentina, and Mirjam Kabki. 2009. "Small Is Beautiful: The Micro-Politics of Transnational Relationships between Ghanaian Hometown Associations and Communities Back Home." *Global Networks* 9, no. 2: 227–251.
Mbembe, Achille. 2002. "African Modes of Self-Writing." *Public Culture* 14, no. 1: 239–273.
———. 2008. "The New Africans: Between Nativism and Cosmopolitanism." In *Readings in Modernity in Africa,* ed. P. Geschiere, B. Meyer, and P. Pels, 107–111. Bloomington: Indiana University Press.
Meagher, Kate. 2005. "Social Capital or Analytical Liability? Social Networks and African Informal Economies." *Global Networks* 5, no. 3: 217–238.
———. 2006. "Social Capital, Social Liabilities, and Political Capital: Social Networks and Informal Manufacturing in Nigeria." *African Affairs* 105/421:553–82.
Menjivar, Cecilia. 2002. "Living in Two Worlds? Guatemalan-Origin Children in the United States and Emerging Transnationalism." *Journal of Ethnic and Migration Studies* 28, no. 3: 531–552.
Mercer, Claire, Ben Page, and Martin Evans. 2009. "Unsettling Connections: Transnational Networks, Development, and African Home Associations." *Global Networks* 9, no. 2: 141–161.
Metcalf, Barbara D. 1993. "Living Hadith in the Tablighi Jama'at." *Journal of Asian Studies* 52, no. 3: 584–608.
Milandou, Augustin-Marie. 1997. "'Type connu! Qui ne le connaît pas?' Anonymat et culture populaire à Brazzaville." *L'Homme* 141:119–130.
Ministry of Culture, Republic of France. "Pierre Savorgnan de Brazza, 1852–1905." http://www.brazza.culture.fr/fr/index.html, accessed July 11–22, 2006.
Missié, Jean-Pierre. 2005. "Dépérissement de l'état de stratégies de survie en Afrique centrale: le cas des exclus sociaux au Congo-Brazzaville." In *Afrique Centrale: Crises economiques et mécanismes de survie,* ed. D. Mukawa and G. Tchouassi, 315–325. Dakar: CODESRIA.
———. 2007. "Les eglises de réveil et l'imaginaire sorcellaire au Congo." In *Les eglises et la Société Congolaise Aujourd'hui: Economie religieuse de la misère en société postcoloniale,* ed. J. Tonda and J.-P. Missié, 123–153. Paris: L'Harmattan.
Le Monde. 2008. "Ensablement et pollution étranglent le bassin du fleuve Congo." November 30. http://www.lemonde.fr/archives/article/2008/11/29/ensablement-et-pollution-etranglent-le-bassin-du-fleuve-congo_1124893_0.html, accessed December 1, 2008.
Morris, Alan, and Antoine Bouillon. 2001. *African Immigration to South Africa: Francophone Migrants of the 1990s.* Pretoria: Protea/IFAS.
Moukoko, Philippe. 1999. *Dictionnaire générale du Congo-Brazzaville.* Paris: L'Harmattan.

Murray, Colin G. 1981. *Families Divided: The Impact of Migrant Labour in Lesotho*. New York: Cambridge University Press.

Mweti. 1977. "Le Col. Joachim Yhomby-Opango a reçu deux émissaires sénégalais et mauritanien." October 8, no. 11, 1–2.

Mwinda.org. 2005. "Brèves: Banditisme." December 22. http://www.africatime.com/Congo/nouvelle.asp?no_nouvelle=230553&no_categorie=UNEhttp://www.mwinda.org/, accessed December 24, 2005.

———. 2008. "A quand le droit à l'immigration choisie pour le Congo?" December 27. http://www.mwinda.org/index.php?option=com_content&task=view&id=579&Itemid=5, accessed December 29, 2008.

———. 2009. "Vraie-fausse carte d'identité." July 2. http://www.mwinda.org/index.php?option=com_content&view=article&id=444:pseudo-presidentielle-echos-de-campagne&catid=85:journal, accessed July 5, 2009.

Ndlovu-Gatsheni, Sabelo J. 2009. "Africa for Africans or Africa for 'Natives' Only? 'New Nationalism' and Nativism in Zimbabwe and South Africa." *Africa Spectrum* 2009, no. 1: 61–78.

Neuville, Didier, Charles Bréard, and Pierre Paul François Camille Savorgnan de Brazza. 1884. *Les voyages de Savorgnan de Brazza: Ogôoué et Congo (1875–1882)*. Paris: Berger-Levrault.

New African. 2007. "West Africa: Being Fleeced at the Borders." March, 24–25.

Newell, Sasha. 2006. "Estranged Belongings: A Moral Economy of Theft in Abidjan, Côte d'Ivoire." *Anthropological Theory* 6, no. 2: 179–203.

———. 2012. *The Modernity Bluff: Crime, Consumption, and Citizenship in Côte d'Ivoire*. Chicago: University of Chicago Press.

Nkou, Jean-Claude. 2007. "Le Congo et la France signent un accord sur la gestion concertée des flux migratoires." http://www.congo-siteportail.info/Le-Congo-et-la-France-signent-un-accord-sur-la-gestion-concertee-des-flux-migratoires_a114.html, accessed July 17, 2009.

Nyamnjoh, Francis. 2006. *Insiders and Outsiders: Citizenship and Xenophobia in Contemporary South Africa*. New York: Zed Books.

Olwig, Karen Fog. 1997. "Cultural Sites: Sustaining a Home in a Deterritorialized World." In *Siting Culture: The Shifting of Anthropological Object*, ed. K. Olwig and K. Hastrup, 17–35. New York: Routledge.

Okpewho, Isidore, and Nkiru Nzegwu. 2009. *The New African Diaspora*. Bloomington: Indiana University Press.

Ong, Aihwa. 1999. *Flexible Citizenship: The Cultural Logics of Transnationality*. Durham, NC: Duke University Press.

Oonk, Gijsbert. 2004. "The Changing Culture of the Hindu Lohana Community in East Africa." *Contemporary South Asia* 13, no. 1: 7–23.

———. 2007. *Global Indian Diasporas: Exploring Trajectories of Migration and Theory*. Amsterdam: Amsterdam University Press.

Orellana, Marjorie F., Barrie Thorne, Anna Chee, and Wan Shun Eva Lam. 2001. "Transnational Childhoods: The Participation of Children in Processes of Family Migration." *Social Problems* 48, no. 4: 572–591.

Pambo-Loueya, Constant-Félix. 2003. "Les étrangers et le travail au Gabon: repatrier . . . unique solution?" In *Être étranger et migrant en Afrique au XXe siècle: enjeux identitaires et modes d'insertion*, Vol. 2, *Dynamiques migratoires, modalités d'insertion urbaine et jeux d'ascteurs*, ed. C. Coquery-Vidrovitch, O. Goerg, I. Mande, and F. Rajaonah, 333–352. Paris: L'Harmattan.

Panapress. 2005. "Un prêtre italien lynché à mort." July 29. http://www.panapress.com/pana-pagination-3-397-2-lang2-SOC-REL-index.html, accessed December 29, 2006.
———. 2006. "Crise interne au Haut conseil des Maliens de France." July 11. http://www.panapress.com/freenewspor.asp?code=fre131027&dte=11/07/2006, accessed December 10, 2006.
Parker, Ian. 1995. "Ivory and the African Entrepreneur." In *Entreprises et entrepreneurs africains*, ed. Y.-A. Faure and S. Ellis, 483–494. Paris: Karthala.
Parreñas, Rhacel Salazar. 2005. *Children of Global Migration: Transnational Families and Gendered Woes*. Stanford, CA: Stanford University Press.
Peil, Margaret. 1971. "The Expulsion of West African Aliens." *Journal of Modern African Studies* 9, no. 2: 205–229.
Peleikis, Anja. 2000. "The Emergence of a Translocal Community: The Case of a South Lebanese Village and Its Migrant Connections to Ivory Coast." *Cahiers d'études sur la Méditerranée orientale et le monde turco-iranien* 30:297–317.
Pellow, Deborah. 2008. *Landlords and Lodgers: Socio-Spatial Organization in an Accra Community*. Chicago: University of Chicago Press.
Pérouse de Montclos, Marc-Antoine. 2002. "Violences xénophobes en Afrique." *Manière de voir* 62 (March–April): 21–4.
Piga, Adriana. 2003. "L'idéologie islamique dans les villes de l'Afrique subsaharienne entre mysticisme et fondamentalisme." In *Islam et villes en Afrique au sud du Sahara: entre soufisme et fondamentalisme*, ed. A. Piga, 7–54. Paris: Karthala.
Piot, Charles. 1999. *Remotely Global: Village Modernity in West Africa*. Chicago: University of Chicago Press.
———. 2010. *Nostalgia for the Future: West Africa after the Cold War*. Chicago: University of Chicago Press.
Pison, Gilles. 2010. "Le nombre et la part des immigrés dans la population: comparaisons internationales." *Population & Société* 472. http://www.ined.fr/fichier/t_publication/1520/publi_pdf1_472.pdf, accessed November 30, 2010.
Polgreen, Lydia. 2007. "Unlikely Ally against Congo Republic Graft." *New York Times*, December 10. http://www.nytimes.com/2007/12/10/world/africa/10congo.html, accessed December 30, 2010.
Pollet, Eric, and Grace Winter. 1971. *La société Soninke: Dyahunu, Mali*. Brussels: Éditions de l'Institut de Sociologie, Université Libre de Brussels.
Portes, Alejandro. 1994. "The Informal Economy and Its Paradoxes." In *The Handbook of Economic Sociology*, ed. N. Smelser and R. Swedberg, 426–449. Princeton, NJ: Princeton University Press.
———. 1998. "Social Capital: Its Origins and Applications in Modern Sociology." *Annual Review of Sociology* 24:1–24.
———. 2001. "Introduction: The Debates and Significance of Immigrant Transnationalism." *Global Networks* 1, no. 3: 181–193.
———. 2003. "Conclusion: Theoretical Convergencies and Empirical Evidence in the Study of Immigrant Transnationalism." *International Migration Review* 37, no. 3: 874–892.
Portes, Alejandro, and Leif Jensen. 1987. "What's an Ethnic Enclave? The Case for Conceptual Clarity." *American Sociological Review* 52:768–771.
Portes, Alejandro, and Patricia Landolt. 1996. "The Downside of Social Capital." *American Prospect* 7, no. 26: 18–21.
Portes, Alejandro, and Julia Sensenbrenner. 1993. "Embeddedness and Immigration: Notes on the Social Determinants of Economic Action." *American Journal of Sociology* 98, no. 6: 1320–1350.

Portes, Alejandro, and Min Zhou. 1992. "Gaining the Upper Hand: Economic Mobility among Immigrant and Domestic Minorities." *Ethnic and Racial Studies* 15, no. 4: 491–522.
Portes, Alejandro, Luis E. Guarnizo, and William J. Haller. 2002. "Transnational Entrepreneurs: An Alternative Form of Immigrant Economic Adaptation." *American Sociological Review* 67:278–298.
Portes, Alejandro, Luis E. Guarnizo and Patricia Landolt. 1999. "The Study of Transnationalism: Pitfalls and Promise of an Emergent Research Field." *Ethnic and Racial Studies* 22, no. 2: 217–237.
Le Potentiel. 2009. "Congo-Kinshasa: Dr Galessamy Ibombot: 'Brazzaville est devenue une ville où l'immigration a atteint un niveau insupportable.'" September 1. http://fr.allafrica.com/stories/200909010259.html, accessed September 4, 2009.
Pourtier, Roland. 1998. "1997: les raisons d'une guerre 'incivile.'" *Afrique contemporaine* 186:7–32.
Prashad, Vijay. 2001. *Everybody Was Kung Fu Fighting: Afro-Asian Connections and the Myth of Cultural Purity.* Boston: Beacon.
Pringle, Robert. 2006. "Democratization in Mali: Putting History to Work." *Peaceworks* 58. Washington, DC: United States Institute of Peace. http://www.usip.org/pubs/peaceworks/pwks58.pdf, accessed December 15, 2006.
Quiminal, Catherine. 1991. *Gens d'ici, gens d'ailleurs: Migrations Soninke et transformations villageoises.* Paris: C. Bourgois.
Rabut, Elisabeth. 1989. *Brazza Commissaire Général: le Congo français 1886–1897.* Paris: Éditions de l'Ecole des Hautes Etudes en Sciences Sociales.
Radio France Internationale. 2004. "Le paradis perdu des diamants de la guerre." August 13. http://www.rfi.fr/actufr/articles/056/article_29853.asp, accessed August 8, 2006.
Radio Free Europe–Radio Liberty. 2009. "EU's 'Fortress Europe' Buckles under Immigrant Siege." September 22. http://www.rferl.org/content/EUs_Fortress_Europe_Buckles_Under_Immigrant_Siege/1828516.html, accessed October 2, 2009.
Ranger, Terence. 1983. "The Invention of Tradition in Colonial Africa." In *The Invention of Tradition,* ed. E. Hobsbawm and T. Ranger, 211–262. New York: Cambridge University Press.
Ratha, Dilip, and William Shaw. 2007. "South-South Migration and Remittances." http://siteresources.worldbank.org/INTPROSPECTS/Resources/South-Southmigration Jan192006 .pdf, accessed July 23, 2009.
Ratha, Dilip, and Zhimei Xu. 2008. *Migration and Remittances Factbook.* http://www.worldbank.org/prospects/migrationandremittances, accessed July 23, 2009.
Razy, Elodie. 2007. "Les sens contraires de la migration: La circulation des jeunes filles d'origine soninké entre la France et le Mali." *Journal des Africanistes* 77, no. 2: 19–43.
Recensement Général de la Population et l'Habitat. 1974. Ministère du Plan, Republic of Congo.
Reuters. 2005. "Drugs, Gems, and Militants Draw FBI to West Africa." July 29. http://www.utexas.edu/conferences/africa/ads/974.html, accessed December 29, 2006.
Riccio, Bruno. 2006. ""Transmigrants" mais pas "nomades": Transnationalisme mouride en Italie." *Cahiers d'études africaines* 181:94–114.
Robinson, David. 2000. "Revolutions in the Western Sudan." In *The History of Islam in Africa,* ed. N. Levtzion and R. Pouwels, 131–152. Athens: Ohio University Press.
Robison, Lindon J., A. Allan Schmid, and Marcelo E. Siles. 2002. "Is Social Capital Really Capital?" *Review of Social Economy* 40, no. 1: 2–21.
Roth, Joshua Hotaka. 2002. *Brokered Homeland: Japanese Brazilian Migrants in Japan.* Ithaca, NY: Cornell University Press.

Rouch, Jean. 1956. *Migrations au Ghana (Gold Coast)*. Paris: Société des Africanistes.
Rouse, Roger. 1991. "Mexican Migration and the Social Space of Postmodernism." *Diaspora* 1, no. 1: 8–23.
Rubio, Mauricio. 1997. "Perverse Social Capital—Some Evidence from Colombia." *Journal of Economic Issues* 31, no. 3: 805–816.
Sadiq, Kamal. 2009. *Paper Citizens: How Illegal Immigrants Acquire Citizenship in Developing Countries*. New York: Oxford University Press.
Saleh, Heba. 2010. "Plea for Egypt to Rescue Hostages." *Financial Times*, December 28. http://www.ft.com/cms/s/0/d3e8fec8-12b4-11e0-b4c8-00144feabdco.html#axzz19heqpyCq, accessed December 29, 2010.
Sandefur, Rebecca L., and Edward O. Laumann. 1998. "A Paradigm for Social Capital." *Rationality and Society* 10, no. 4: 481–501.
Sanders, Margaret. 1983. "Measurement of Levels of Living in the People's Republic of the Congo since 1950." *Journal of Economic History* 43, no. 1: 243–250.
Sanneh, Lamine. 1996. *Piety and Power: Muslims and Christians in West Africa*. Maryknoll, NY: Orbis Books.
Sargent, Carolyn F., and Stéphanie Larchanché-Kim. 2006. "Liminal Lives: Immigration Status, Gender, and the Constructions of Identities among Malian Migrants in Paris." *American Behavioral Scientist* 50, no. 1: 9–26.
Sautter, Gilles. 1967. "Notes sur la construction du chemin de fer Congo-Océan (1921–1934)." *Cahiers d'études africaines* 26:219–299.
Schapera, Isaac. 1947. *Migrant Labour and Tribal Life*. London: Oxford University Press.
Schildkrout, Enid. 1970. "Strangers and Local Government in Kumasi." *Journal of Modern African Studies* 8, no. 2: 251–269.
———. 1978. *People of the Zongo: The Transformation of Ethnic Identities in Ghana*. Cambridge: Cambridge University Press.
Schler, Lynn. 2008. *The Strangers of New Bell: Immigration, Public Space, and Community in Colonial Douala, Cameroon, 1914–1960*. Pretoria: University of South Africa Press.
Schnapper, Bernard. 1959. "La fin du régime de l'exclusif: le commerce étranger dans les possessions françaises d'Afrique tropicale (1817–1870)." *Annales Africaines* 1959:149–199.
Schulz, Dorothea E. 1999. "Pricey Publicity, Refutable Reputations: *Jeliw* and the Economics of Honour in Mali." *Paideuma* 45:275–292.
Secours Catholique. 2011. "Congo Brazzaville: Le Pétrole ne Coule Pas Pour les Pauvres." http://www.secours-catholique.org/IMG/pdf/Rapport_Pe_trole_Congo_fev_2011.pdf, accessed March 6, 2011.
Shack, William A., and Elliott P. Skinner. 1979. *Strangers in African Societies*. Berkeley: University of California Press.
Shankar, Shalini. 2008. *Desi Land: Teen Culture, Class, and Success in Silicon Valley*. Durham, NC: Duke University Press.
Silvey, Rachel. 2006. "Consuming the Transnational Family: Indonesian Migrant Domestic Workers to Saudi Arabia." *Global Networks* 6, no. 1: 23–40.
Silvey, Rachel, and Rebecca Elmhirst. 2003. "Engendering Social Capital: Women Workers and Rural-Urban Networks in Indonesia's Crisis." *World Development* 31, no. 5: 865–879.
Simmel, Georg. 1950. "The Stranger." In *The Sociology of Georg Simmel*, ed. and trans. K. Wolff, 402–408. London: Free Press.
Skinner, Elliott P. 1963. "Strangers in West African Societies." *Africa* 33, no. 4: 307–320.
Smith, Daniel Jordan. 2004. "Burials and Belonging in Nigeria: Rural-Urban Relations and Social Inequality in a Contemporary African Ritual." *American Anthropologist* 106, no. 3: 569–579.

———. 2008. "'Kano Hides a Poor Man': Rural-Urban Migration and the Burdens of Kinship." Presented at the Annual Meeting of the American Anthropological Association, San Francisco.

Smith, Robert. 1999. "Reflections on Migration, the State, and the Construction, Durability, and Newness of Transnational Life." In *Migration and Transnational Social Spaces*, ed. L. Pries, 187–219. Brookfield, VT: Ashgate.

Smith, Robert. 2006. *Mexican New York: Transnational Lives of New Immigrants*. Berkeley: University of California Press.

Smith, Stephen Samuel, and Jessica Kulynych. 2002. "It May Be Social, but Why Is It Capital? The Social Construction of Social Capital and the Politics of Language." *Politics & Society* 30, no. 1: 149–186.

Soares, Benjamin F. 1999. "Muslim Proselytization as Purification: Religious Pluralism and Conflict in Contemporary Mali." In *Proselytization and Communal Self-Determination in Africa*, ed. A. An-Na'im, 228–245. Maryknoll, NY: Orbis Books.

———. 2004. "Islam and Public Piety in Mali." In *Public Islam and the Common Good*, ed. A. Salvatore and D. Eickelman, 205–226. Boston: Brill.

———. 2005a. "Islam in Mali in the Neoliberal Era." *African Affairs* 105:77–95.

———. 2005b. *Islam and the Prayer Economy: History and Authority in a Malian Town*. Ann Arbor: University of Michigan Press.

Solow, Robert M. 1999. "Notes on Social Capital and Economic Performance." In *Social Capital: A Multifaceted Perspective*, ed. P. Dasgupta and I. Serageldin, 6–12. Washington, DC: World Bank.

Soret, Marcel. 1978. *Histoire du Congo, Capitale Brazzaville*. Paris: Berger-Levrault.

Sow, Moussa. 2005. "Coopération décentralisée: Villetaneuse au chevet de Koniakary." Maliba.com, December 19. http://www.maliba.com/modules.php?name=News&file=article&sid=3138, accessed December 11, 2006.

Stanley, Henry Morton. 1885. *The Congo and the Founding of Its Free State: A Story of Work and Exploration*. London: Sampson Low.

Steinberg, Jonny. 2008. *Sizwe's Test: A Young Man's Journey through Africa's AIDS Epidemic*. New York: Simon and Schuster.

Stoller, Paul. 1997. "Globalizing Method: The Problems of Doing Ethnography in Transnational Spaces." *Anthropology and Humanism* 22, no. 1: 8–94.

Syfia Congo. 2006. "Congo Brazzaville: travailleurs étrangers indésirables et indispensables." January 20. http://www.syfia.info/fr/article.asp?article_num=4298, accessed January 28, 2006.

Taylor, Charles. 1994. "The Politics of Recognition." In *Multiculturalism: Examining the Politics of Recognition*, ed. A. Gutmann, 25–74. Princeton, NJ: Princeton University Press.

Thompson, Denise. 2011. "Social Capital and Its Popularity." *International Journal of Social Inquiry* 4, no. 1: 3–21.

Timera, Mahamet. 1996. *Les Soninke en France: D'une histoire à l'autre*. Paris: Éditions Karthala.

———. 2002. "Righteous or Rebellious? Social Trajectory of Sahelian Youth in France." In *The Transnational Family: New European Frontiers and Global Networks*, ed. D. Bryceon and U. Vuorela, 147–154. New York: Berg.

———. 2003. "Trajectoires du fondamentalisme parmi les communautés Soninke musulmanes immigrées en France." In *Islam et villes en Afrique au sud du Sahara: Entre soufisme et fondamentalisme*, ed. A. Piga, 293–303. Paris: Karthala.

Trager, Lilian. 2001. *Yoruba Hometowns: Community, Identity, and Development in Nigeria*. Boulder, CO: Lynne Rienner.

Triaud, Jean-Louis. 2000. "Islam in Africa under French Colonial Rule." In *The History of Islam in Africa*, ed. N. Levtzion and R. Pouwels, 169–187. Athens: Ohio University Press.
Trouillot, Michel-Rolph. 2003. *Global Transformations: Anthropology and the Modern World.* New York: Palgrave Macmillan.
Tsika, Joseph. 1995. "Entre l'enclume étatique et le marteau familial: l'impossible envol des entrepreneurs au Congo." In *Entreprises et entrepreneurs africains*, ed. Y.-A. Fauré and S. Ellis, 251–265. Paris: Karthala.
Turner, Victor. 1969. *The Ritual Process: Structure and Anti-Structure*. Chicago: Aldine.
United Nations Integrated Regional Information Networks (IRIN). 2005. "West Africa: Rights Activists Urge UN to Investigate Abuse of Migrants." October 13. http://www.irinnews.org/Report.aspx?ReportId=56711, accessed October 2, 2000.
———. 2006. "Mali: Culture of Migration Faces Tough New Realities." November 6. http://www.irinnews.org/Report.aspx?ReportId=61471, accessed August 25, 2009.
———. 2010a. "Angola-DRC: Expulsions Mark Rising Tensions over Resources." October 28. http://www.irinnews.org/report.aspx?Reportid=90906, accessed November 1.
———. 2010b. "Second Phase of Immunization Under Way as Polio Outbreak Kills 200." December 10. http://allafrica.com/stories/201012100943.html, accessed December 13, 2010.
Van der Laan, H. L. 1965. *The Sierra Leone Diamonds: An Economic Study Covering the Years 1952–1961*. New York: Oxford University Press.
Vansina, Jan. 1990. *Paths in the Rainforest: Toward a History of Political Tradition in Equatorial Africa*. Madison: University of Wisconsin Press.
Vennetier, Pierre. 1963. "L'urbanisation et ses conséquences au Congo (Brazzaville)." *Les cahiers d'outre-mer: Revue de géographie* 64:263–280.
Viruell-Fuentes, Edna A. 2006. "'My Heart Is Always There': The Transnational Practices of First-Generation Mexican Immigrant and Second-Generation Mexican American Women." *Identities: Global Studies in Culture and Power* 13:335–362.
Vuarin, Robert. 1997. "Les entreprises de l'individu au Mali: Des chefs d'entreprises innovateurs dans le procès d'individualisation." In *L'Afrique des individus*, ed. A. Marie, 171–200. Paris: Karthala.
Wagret, Jean-Michel. 1963. *Histoire et sociologie politiques de la République du Congo (Brazzaville)*. Paris: Librairie Générale de Droit et de Jurisprudence.
Waldinger, Robert, and David Fitzgerald. 2004. "Transnationalism in Question." *American Journal of Sociology* 109, no. 5: 1177–1195.
Wallerstein, Immanuel. 1974. "The Rise and Future Demise of the World Capitalist System: Concepts for Comparative Analysis." *Comparatives Studies in Society and History* 16, no. 4: 387–415.
Warms, Richard L. 1992. "Merchants, Muslims, and Wahhabiyya: The Elaboration of Islamic Identity in Sikasso, Mali." *Canadian Journal of African Studies* 26, no. 3: 485–507.
Waters, Johanna L. 2005. "Transnational Family Strategies and Education in the Contemporary Chinese Diaspora." *Global Networks* 5, no. 4: 359–377.
Weber, Max. 2001. *The Protestant Ethic and the Spirit of Capitalism*. New York: Routledge.
West, Richard. 1972. *Brazza of the Congo: European Exploration and Exploitation in French Equatorial Africa*. London: Jonathan Cape.
Whitehouse, Bruce. 2009. "Migrants et insécurité existentielle: Le cas de Brazzaville." *Hommes et migrations* 1279:80–87.
———. In press. "Centripetal Forces: Reconciling Cosmopolitan Lives and Local Loyalty in a Malian Transnational Social Field." In *West African Migrations: Transnational and Global Pathways in a New Century*, ed. O. Vaughan and M. O. Okome. New York: Palgrave McMillan.

Wilks, Ivor. 1968. "The Transmission of Islamic Learning in the Western Sudan." In *Literacy in Traditional Societies,* ed. J. Goody, 162–197. Cambridge: Cambridge University Press.

———. 2000. "The Juula and the Expansion of Islam into the Forest." In *The History of Islam in Africa,* ed. N. Levtzion and R. Pouwels, 93–115. Athens: Ohio University Press.

Wilson, Monica. 1979. "Strangers in Africa: Reflections on Nyakyusa, Nguni, and Sotho Evidence." In *Strangers in African Societies,* ed. W. Shack and E. Skinner, 51–66. Berkeley: University of California Press.

Wimmer, Andreas, and Nina Glick Schiller. 2003. "Methodological Nationalism, the Social Sciences, and the Study of Migration: An Essay in Historical Epistemology." *International Migration Review* 37, no. 3: 576–610.

Wolf, Eric. 1982. *Europe and the People without History.* Berkeley: University of California Press.

World Bank. 1998. "U.S.$21.5 Million for Grassroots Development in Mali." Press Release, no. 98/1723/AFR: http://web.worldbank.org/WBSITE/EXTERNAL/NEWS/0,,contentMDK:20016875~menuPK:34466~pagePK:34370~piPK:34424~theSitePK:4607,00.html, accessed August 7, 2006.

———. 2007. "Overview: Social Capital." http://go.worldbank.org/CoQTRW4QF0, accessed July 14, 2009.

———. 2009. "Doing Business 2010." http://www.doingbusiness.org, accessed September 15, 2009.

Yengo, Patrice. 2006. *La guerre civile au Congo-Brazzaville: 1993–2002, "Chacun aura sa part."* Paris: Karthala.

Zeleza, Paul Tiyambe. 2010. "African Diasporas: Toward a Global History." *African Studies Review* 53, no. 1: 1–19.

Zhou, Min. 1998. "'Parachute Kids' in Southern California: The Educational Experience of Chinese Children in Transnational Families." *Educational Policy* 12, no. 6: 682–704.

———. 2004. "Revisiting Ethnic Entrepreneurship: Convergencies, Controversies, and Conceptual Advancements." *International Migration Review* 38, no. 3: 1040–1074.

Index

agriculture: in Congo, 34, 52; and origins of stranger status, 212–213; in West Africa, 1, 2, 26, 73, 74, 87
Angola: and diamonds, 49, 89, 153, 154; expulsion of migrants from, 48, 204–205, 224; as migrant destination, 89, 152–153
Appiah, Kwame Anthony, 190, 216
army, colonial, 18, 26, 36. *See also* security forces, Congolese; *tirailleurs sénégalais*
autochthony, 13, 209–212, 215, 216
aventuriers, 58, 73, 84–90, 126, 127, 153–155, 176, 178, 222

Bacongo (Brazzaville neighborhood), 38, 41, 55, 65, 73
Balandier, Georges, 42, 43, 45
Bamako, 2, 5, 49, 65, 68, 73, 83, 144–145, 225; anti-immigrant tensions in, 205, 224; as destination for returning migrants, 171, 186, 218, 223; real estate market in, 4
Bamanan (ethnic group), 14, 26, 46, 93; language, 16, 20, 21, 92, 110–111, 145, 171, 172, 174, 183, 185, 186, 192, 236n10
baraka (favor), 80–81
"Beach affair," 54–55, 138–139
Belgian Congo. *See* Congo-Kinshasa
Belgium, 27, 29, 33–37
Benin, 17, 37, 99, 130
Berry, Sara, 212–213
bounded solidarity, 75–77
Brazza, Pierre Savorgnan de, 27–34, 36–38
Brazzaville: economy of, 52–54, 66, 221–222; establishment of, 33, 35, 38–39, 237n8; insecurity in, 54–55, 65, 239n9; population growth of, 42–43, 45, 52; West Africans in, 38–39, 42–47; "World's Worst City," 10–11. *See also* Congo-Brazzaville
Bredeloup, Sylvie, 51, 166
bunganga (supernatural aggression), 80–81. *See also* sorcery
Burundi, 48, 49, 205

Camara, Malamine, 25–27, 28, 29–34, 39, 56
Cameroon, 36, 43, 214, 221; autochthony dynamics in, 207, 208; migrants from, 85–87, 154; migrants in, 12, 88, 127
caste, 16, 46, 63, 87, 88
Central African Republic, 37, 38, 47, 48, 237n10
Chabal, Patrick, 199, 201, 206–209
Chad, 36, 37, 38, 53, 100, 221
Chavannes, Charles de, 29, 30, 32–34
Chemin de Fer Congo-Océan. *See* railroads, establishment of
children: and cultural identity, 22–23; as dependent migrants, 11; education of, 43, 166–169, 171, 173, 175; fostering of, 163–164, 166–170, 171, 177, 179; and transnational migration, 153, 163–179. *See also* schooling
China: diaspora in the Pacific Rim, 69; as place of business for African entrepreneurs, 4, 62, 76, 152, 162; as source of entrepreneurs in Congo, 60; as source of entrepreneurs in Mali, 83

Christianity in Congo, 84, 99, 100, 118, 204
citizenship, 15, 22, 23, 182, 197–201, 210–211, 213; ethnic vs. civic, 208, 211; multiple, 152–153, 156; rights pertaining to, 124, 142, 147–148, 208. *See also* identity
civil service in Congo: development of, 44–45, 52–53; economic importance of, 53, 56–57, 238n38; West Africans in, 43
civil society, 157, 159, 200, 244n9
civil war in Congo, 11, 54–55, 60, 63, 65, 146, 152, 186
Cobra militia, 54, 65, 239n8
colonialism: in Congo Basin, 21, 25–44; relationship to nativism in Africa, 211–214
commerce: in clothing, 40–41, 63, 73; development among West Africans in Congo Basin, 39–47, 56–57, 59–60; in foodstuffs, 61–62; and Islam, 96–97, 103; in Mali, 2–3, 72, 83; and middleman minorities, 69. *See also* diamond trade; entrepreneurship
Communauté Malienne du Congo (COMACO), 158–159
concessionary companies, 37–38, 41
Congo, Democratic Republic of. *See* Congo-Kinshasa
Congo, Republic of. *See* Congo-Brazzaville
Congo Basin, 21, 27, 31, 34, 39, 41, 45, 51, 55, 56, 59, 70, 102, 103, 140, 153, 155, 218
Congo River, 27, 28–31, 33, 35, 47, 221; Pool, 27, 28, 30, 31, 32, 39, 236n4
Congo-Brazzaville: armed conflict in, 54–55, 65; colonial establishment of, 27–34; colonial rule of, 34–44, 47–48; governance and politics in, 126, 128, 138–141, 194; independence of, 51–52; as migrant destination, 4, 11, 21–22, 53; urbanization in, 52–53. *See also* Brazzaville; economy of Congo
Congo-Kinshasa: as Belgian colony, 34, 35–36, 42–43, 48; business climate in, 67; independence of, 51; migrants from, 16, 45, 53, 88, 118, 198, 205, 242n2; migrants in, 39, 40, 48–49, 51, 56, 102, 140. *See also* Kinshasa
contrôles (document verification measures), 116–117, 122–124, 126, 128

Coquery-Vidrovitch, Catherine, 34, 36, 38, 40
corruption, 198, 206, 224; in business, 60, 117, 124; in Congolese and West African perceptions of each other, 135, 137, 145; in the justice system, 68, 76, 128
cosmopolitanism, 9, 152–154, 190, 216–219
Côte d'Ivoire, 17, 27, 45, 152, 183, 199; autochthony dynamics in, 13, 144, 207, 214, 215; conceptions of labor in, 82, 86, 87; diamonds in, 47–48; Islam in, 95–96; migrants in, 4, 15, 18, 46, 49, 73, 98, 121, 217, 224, 243n12
culture: and enterprise, 60, 71–75, 84; hybridization of, 195–197, 214–215; migrants' efforts to retain, 100, 135, 149–151, 163–179, 210; migrants' performance of, 186–187, 191–192, 194–195; and place, 9–10; and strangers, 11–14; and xenophobia, 144–146. *See also* identity

Dahomey. *See* Benin
danbe (dignity), 21, 88–89, 207–208, 224, 241n33
danga (curse), 79–80
debt, 54, 67, 143, 214
democratization, 213
Diallo, Amadou, 222
diamond trade, 47–51
diaspora: African, 6–7, 13, 18, 224; auxiliary, 39, 41; internal to African continent, 7, 9, 10, 17–18, 70, 84, 134, 147; limitations of concept, 218–219, 246n21; South Asian, 184; and strangers, 11; trade, 22, 41, 70, 96
Diawara, Ange, 193–194
Direction Générale des Maliens de l'Extérieur (DGME), 156–158, 160
discrimination, 9, 17, 69–70, 76, 135, 147, 191, 200, 224; in the form of exactions, 122–125, 128, 142, 154, 180–181; in the form of harassment, 120–122, 139–140, 192; legal, 126–127; "stranger penalty," 127–129
Dogon (ethnic group), 14, 87, 88, 177, 236n10
domestic organization, 22–23, 74–75; and parenting, 163–179

Doucouré, Papa, 180–182, 200–201, 245n2
dress: Congolese, 41, 59, 64; West African, 39, 59, 93, 105, 112, 120, 181, 185, 188, 189, 192, 197
Dubai, 4, 74, 152, 165

economy of Congo, 52–54, 66, 198, 221–222; after expulsion of migrants, 133; formal vs. informal, 63–64; marketplaces, 61–65; regulation of, 67–68
education. *See* schooling
enforceable trust, 76–77, 162
entrepreneur's social dilemma, the, 79; solutions to, 81–85
entrepreneurship: challenges of, 65–68; characteristics of, 74–75; and kinship obligations, 79–81; among native Congolese, 59–60, 61, 71–72, 83–84; taxation and regulation of, 67–68, 122–124, 239n11; among West African migrants, 39–42, 45–47, 59, 61–65. *See also* commerce
Equatorial Guinea, 204
ethnicity: and bounded solidarity, 76; in Brazzaville, 20, 38, 42, 55, 78, 191, 199, 204; and citizenship, 203, 208, 211; in colonial cities, 42; and enterprise, 70, 71; and Islam in pre-colonial West Africa, 96, 98; in research design, 14–18; among West African migrants, 14–15, 45–46, 236n10
expulsion of migrants, 48; from Congo-Brazzaville, 129–134, 205, 207; from Congo-Kinshasa, 140, 205; from other African countries, 204–205; from Western countries, 206

faso (homeland), 88–89, 137, 167–168, 170–171, 172–173, 175
Ferguson, James, 20, 54, 206, 225
fieldwork, ethnographic, 10–12, 18–21, 225–228
Fortes, Meyer, 11–12, 69, 208
France: as colonial power in Africa, 21, 25–38, 39–40, 42–44, 48, 54, 56, 97; as destination for African migrants, 4, 10, 84, 90–91, 104, 115, 140–141, 152, 161, 162, 169, 174, 196, 203, 206, 224

funerals, 83, 124, 157, 182, 208, 209

Gabon: anti-immigrant tensions in, 205; French exploration of, 27, 32, 34, 36; as migrant destination, 4, 162, 223; trading posts in, 39–40
Gaulle, Charles de, 42
gems. *See* diamond trade
gender roles, 105, 107, 164–166, 190–191, 239n3, 242n17, 244n14
Geschiere, Peter, 146, 209, 211, 213, 237
Ghana: entrepreneurs in, 79, 81–82; migrants in, 104, 177, 205, 236n10, 245n5; as source of migrants, 4; strangers in, 12, 212, 246n19
globalization, 7–10, 144, 211, 215, 220
Gondola, Charles Didier, 37, 53, 215
Guinea: business climate in, 68; diamonds in, 47–48; migrants from, 15, 48, 51, 53, 61, 119, 123, 126, 152, 153–154, 181, 222

Halpulaaren (ethnic group), 14, 45–46, 96, 110, 187, 236n10
Hart, Keith, 79, 81, 240n19
HCME (*Haut Conseil des Maliens de l'Extérieur*), 157–158, 160
hometown associations, 112, 161–163, 244n12

identity, 6, 76, 170, 183, 191, 196, 210; "anchoring" of, 211–215; hybrid, 195–197, 214–215, 216; Muslim, 93–94, 96, 97, 103–108, 145; national, 16, 159–160, 191, 196; and place, 9–10, 175, 178, 208, 211, 220; urban, 42. *See also* cosmopolitanism
identity documents, 126, 130, 153–154, 156, 185–186; fraud and devaluing of, 134, 198–199, 245n11
indigeneity. *See* autochthony
integration of migrants, 13–14, 69, 91, 135, 232; difficulty of, 121, 184, 191–193, 204, 208–209; hosts' resistance to, 144–145, 207, 212–213; potential for, 189–191, 209–211, 218. *See also* Islam; strangers
Islam: and Congolese government, 100; and immigrant integration, 94, 100, 114–115; among immigrants in Congo, 93–94, 99–108; internal divisions in, 99, 101–103,

272 / Index

109–111, 114; among native Congolese, 100, 108–114; and prayer, 93, 103–108; and proselytizing, 112–114; reformist, 98, 102, 110; relationship with commerce, 96–97, 103; and Sufi brotherhoods, 97, 101–102, 110; Suwarian tradition of, 95–97, 103, 112; in West Africa, 92–93, 95–99, 241n6. *See also* mosques in Brazzaville

jatigi (hosts), 45, 46, 50, 174, 176–177, 238n30
jewelers, 63, 186
joking relations, 16–17, 236n13

Kayes (Malian region), 185
Keita, Modibo (Malian president), 18–19, 236n16
Kenya, 4, 49, 207, 208, 215
Kinshasa: colonial origins (as Leopoldville), 35, 39; migrants from, 16, 45, 53, 88, 118, 198, 205; migrants in, 39, 40, 48–49, 51, 56, 102, 140; population growth, 42–43; regional economic role of, 221; West Africans in, 39
kinship: and enterprise, 70; and social capital, 75–78; and social obligations, 78–81; and transnational migration, 163–179
Koniakary (Malian town), 161–162

labor, 9, 22, 35, 38, 43, 52, 84–89; forced, 27, 42, 43, 87
labor migration, 3, 4, 6, 9, 87, 97
land tenure, 147, 210–212
language, 12, 16, 20–21, 27, 28–29, 236n18; and colonial schools, 43; as marker of difference, 119, 145, 200; and mosques, 110–111; and social reproduction, 163, 167, 170–171, 173–174, 176, 185, 187, 188, 190–192, 210
laptots: abuses committed by, 36–37; and commerce, 40; labor conditions of, 34–35; recruitment of, 26–27, 32, 56, 236n2. See also *tirailleurs sénégalais*
Launay, Robert, 17, 96, 97
law, rule of, 117, 124, 128, 131–132, 143, 223
Lebanese, 68, 69, 72, 83, 84, 100, 181

Leopold II (King of Belgium), 27, 29, 30, 31, 35, 37
Leopoldville. *See* Kinshasa
Libya, 152, 204; Libyan entrepreneurs in Mali, 83
Lingala (language), 13, 20, 44, 110, 118, 173, 174, 176, 185, 186, 188, 190

Makoko Iloo I (Congolese king), 27–28, 32–33, 237n7
Mali, 1–6, 16–17, 68, 72, 82–83, 203; anti-immigrant tensions in, 145, 205, 224; government of, 92, 130–131, 140, 156–161, 181; Islam in, 82, 92–95, 105–106, 112, 222–224; migrants from, 18, 20, 44, 46–49, 53, 58–61, 63–65, 72–76, 86–90, 99, 116–117, 119, 120, 123–124, 130, 133, 137–139, 141–142, 149, 168, 170–179, 181–191, 198–199, 200, 204, 217–218. *See also* Bamako; Togotala (Malian town)
Mamdani, Mahmood, 211, 216, 246n16
Manchuelle, François, 3, 26, 27, 37, 39, 40, 44, 168
manufacturing, 64–65
marriage: between migrants and hosts, 39, 47, 51, 130, 144–145, 147, 149, 164, 165, 187, 188; polygamous, 165, 244n16; and transnational households, 165–166
Mauritania, 17, 36, 130
Mbembe, Achille, 206, 214, 215, 216
M'Foa (early site of present-day Brazzaville), 28–33, 236n7
middleman minorities: and culture, 71–75; defined, 69–70; and host-society politics, 137, 146; and social capital, 75–78
migration, 3–6, 15, 211, 216, 219–220, 246n23; from Africa to Europe, 5, 7, 50, 75, 91, 128, 152, 154, 169, 204, 206–207, 223; aspirations to, 85, 205–206, 219, 246n22; factors behind, 41, 57, 59, 74, 82–90, 206, 220; and information, 89–90; intra-African, 4, 5, 204, 207, 220; rewards of, 41, 91, 206; rural to urban, 42–43, 52, 82, 161, 244n11; South-South, 5, 91; transnational, 9, 16, 75, 150; types of, 3; "undocumented," 127–128, 155, 244n5. *See also* labor migration

Mission de l'Ouest Africain, 31–34
Morocco, 100, 128, 206
mosques in Brazzaville: as community focal points, 106–108; establishment of, 38–39, 64, 100, *101*, 107–108; *grande mosquée*, 46, 102, 110, 188, 189; leadership of, 46, 100, 110–111; Ouenzé (King Faisal) mosque, 110–111, 113; and prayer, 93, 104–107; Sufi, 19, 92; "Sunni," 102, 110, 111, 113, 176, 182
Mozambique, 162, 204, 223. *See also* Southern Africa
Mwinda.org, x, 128

nativism, 214–216, 219. *See also* xenophobia
neoliberalism, 2, 8, 13, 213
Ngouabi, Marien (Congolese president), 129, 194
Nigeria: expulsion of migrants by, 205; as migrant destination or transit point, 40, 73–74, 127–128, 153; migrants from, 17, 35, 45–46, 99, 130, 205; strangers in, 12, 88, 114
nongovernmental organizations (NGOs), 2, 109. *See also* hometown associations
nonmigrants, 90, 93, 151, 170, 175
North Africa, 5, 154, 206. *See also* Morocco

Office de Radiodiffusion Télévision du Mali (ORTM), 160
oil extraction in Congo, 52–54, 66; economic effects of, 55, 59, 137, 197, 214, 221

Pan-Africanism, 118, 194
patron-client networks, 51, 78, 124, 132, 138, 140–141, 193
Pointe-Noire (Congolese city), 11, 38, 45, 64, 65, 66, 107, 152, 162, 173
politics: and belonging, 207–208, 210, 213, 216; Congolese, 44, 52, 55, 80, 153, 193–194, 197–198; and Islam in West Africa, 95–97, 102; and strangers, 69, 138–141, 209
Portes, Alejandro, 72, 75, 76, 78, 91, 150, 151, 177
Poto-Poto (Brazzaville neighborhood), 11, 15, 20; colonial demarcation of, 38–39;

marketplace, 41, 59, 61, 67, 85–86, 122, 123, 146, 226; migrants in, 38–39, 45–46, 64–65, 73, 93, 102, 110, 113, 121, 129, 176, 182; origin of name, 237n19
poverty: in Congo, 53–54, 66, 221, 246n2; in West Africa, 4, 68, 154

railroads, establishment of: in Congo Basin, 35, 38, 39; in Senegal, 35
remittances, 4, 75
rights: human, 22, 180; to land, 212; migrants' voluntary surrender of, 141–144, 148, 204, 207–208; political and legal, 43, 56, 126–127, 147, 156, 211; and territory, 10, 214, 216. *See also* citizenship

Sassou-Nguesso, Denis (Congolese president), 54, 55, 66, 112, 134, 137, 181, 194
Saudi Arabia: influence on Islamic ideas and practices, 98, 102, 109, 111; pilgrimage to, 45, 95, 98, 102, 152
schooling, 2, 3, 4; in Congo, 43, 52, 53, 72, 75; *madrasas*, 173–174, 175, 244n20; in Mali, 74, 75, 142, 162, 238n27; of migrants' children, 170, 171, 173, 175, 185–188; Qur'anic, 38, 73, 188
security forces, Congolese: abuses committed by, 54–55, 65, 122–125, 128, 138–139, 180–181, 239n9; colonial-era formation of, 36–37. *See also* "Beach affair"
Senegal, 4, 17, 33–34, 36, 45, 46, 48, 88, 95, 102, 130; migrants from, 9, 15, 25, 35, 38–41, 43, 51, 53, 63, 99, 127, 152, 179, 183, 187, 192. See also *laptots*; *tirailleurs sénégalais*
Senegal River Valley, 15, 74, 102
Sierra Leone, 35, 38, 47, 48, 49, 104
Simmel, Georg, 11, 13, 69, 148
Soares, Benjamin, 96, 97, 98, 99, 101, 102
social capital, 75–78, 91; and criminality, 78
social networks, 22, 75–81, 90, 91, 176, 179, 191
Soninke (ethnic group): in Brazzaville, 14–15, 46, 72, 185–186, 198; and commerce, 2–3, 71, 84; language, 13, 16, 20, 110–111, 113, 163, 172, 174, 183, 185, 192, 240n25; and migration, 14–15, 26, 36,

39, 41, 72, 88, 93, 95, 96, 169; and polygamy, 165
sorcery, 80–81, 119, 205, 240n26
South Africa, 49, 113, 162, 204, 211
Southern Africa, 4, 209
Spain, 4, 10, 206
Stanley, Henry Morton, 29–31, 55
strangers: advantages of stranger status, 114; and colonial rule, 211–213; and electoral politics, 213; and forms of labor, 87; relations with hosts, 147; Simmel's concept of, 11–12; "stranger penalty," 127–129, 209; "stranger's code," 137–144, 147–148, 181, 194, 197, 209. *See also* integration of migrants

Tablighi Jama'at, 113–114
tabushi (West Africans raised abroad), 170–171, 176, 183–201, 215
tailors, 18, 59, 61, 63, 66
Téké (ethnic group), 27, 29
Thailand, 4, 62, 73, 152
Tiken Jah Fakoly (reggae singer), 59, 216–217
tirailleurs sénégalais, 26, 34–35, 37–38
Togotala (Malian town), 1–6, 8, 10, 71, 74, 79, 83, 86, 137, 161, 163–164, 169; migrants from, 11, 14, 88, 152–153, 162–163, 164, 172, 195, 226
Touré, Amadou Toumani (Malian president), 181
trade. *See* commerce
transnational social field, 155, 160, 169, 176, 178. *See also* transnationalism
transnationalism, 9–10, 16, 150–152, 155, 176–179, 243n3; and child rearing, 163–179, 210; and households, 163–166; and local communities, 160–163; and nation-state governments, 156–160

tunga (space of migration/exile), 88, 137, 207, 218
Turner, Victor, 106

Ubangi-Shari. *See* Central African Republic
United States: aspirations of migration to, 85, 222–224; and global war on terror, 19, 94, 111; migrants in, 4, 9, 10, 70, 104, 114, 151, 169, 174, 177, 184, 186, 196

"wealth in people" concept, 210–211
West Africans in Congo: as colonial personnel, 34–37, 43; early settlement in Congo Basin, 38–39; local designations for, 17, 99, 119, 120, 140, 192, 242n3; role in Brazzaville's retail sector, 40–42, 44, 61–65; as seen by Congolese, 135–137, 229–233, 243n10; study population defined, 14–18; tensions with Congolese, 43–44, 56, 100, 108–110, 116–148, 238n28; as "willing migrants," 27, 56. *See also* entrepreneurship; Guinea, migrants from; Mali; Senegal; strangers
Wolof (ethnic group), 14, 16, 26, 45–46
World Bank, 4, 54, 67, 77, 78

xenophobia, 118, 144–147, 204–205. *See also* nativism

Yhomby-Opango, Joachim (Congolese president), 131, 134
Youlou, Fulbert (Congolese president), 49, 140

Zambia, 20, 48, 49, 82, 141, 162, 214. *See also* Southern Africa
Zao, Casimir, 203
Zimbabwe, 207. *See also* Southern Africa

BRUCE WHITEHOUSE has lived and worked for more than five years in Africa, particularly in Mali (where he served as a Peace Corps Volunteer) and in the Republic of Congo. He is Assistant Professor of Anthropology at Lehigh University, where he teaches courses on globalization and social change, contemporary Africa, development, and medical anthropology.

www.ingramcontent.com/pod-product-compliance
Lightning Source LLC
Chambersburg PA
CBHW060113170426
43198CB00010B/871